Meeting Culture

Photo by Lizet Hoekert

Meeting Culture

Essays in honour of Arie de Ruijter

Edited by

Walter E.A. van Beek

Mario A. Fumerton

Wil G. Pansters

Printed in The Netherlands.

ISBN 90-423-0221-6-6

Shaker Publishing BV, St. Maartenslaan 26, 6221 AX Maastricht
Tel.: (043) 350 04 24, Fax: (043) 325 50 90, http:// www.shaker.nl

Graphic design
René Hendriks – UU/FSS/IDC Vormgeving

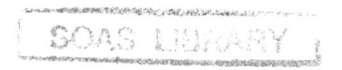

Contents

Part II   **Discourses and Arenas of Identity**

Part III   **Organizational Arenas**

Meeting Culture
An Introduction

Mario A. Fumerton, Walter E.A. van Beek and Wil G. Pansters

This volume of essays was specially written for Arie de Ruijter by his former pupils and colleagues at Utrecht University. It pays tribute to him on the occasion of his leaving the Department of Cultural Anthropology of our university. Arie de Ruijter played a crucial role in the department as an inspiring scholar, a creative organizer, and a visionary manager.

More than three decades ago, Arie de Ruijter was one of the most promising young graduates from Utrecht's anthropology programme. His mentor, Jan van Baal, meant for him to carry out doctoral research in Indonesia, but for health reasons that was not to happen. One wonders what Arie's career would have become had he indeed done fieldwork in Indonesia, and joined the ranks of those anthropologists who owe much of their professional identity to their identification with a specific region. Perhaps not very different, since, as he recently declared, his "Neolithic" mind would probably have pushed him away from regional studies after a few years. As it was, the absence of such an identity generator meant that he had his hands free; he could roam beyond the borders of the discipline and develop a perspective on the whole of the social sciences, and on the political and organisational embeddedness of academic work in the Netherlands.

His first anthropological habitat thus became theoretical reflection, with Lévi-Strauss as the object of analysis. He did not become a devout structuralist but rather moved towards a broad programme of a theory of science. From structuralism he shifted to the study of symbolic and cognitive anthropology. His main and uninterrupted interest ever since has been the fundamental debate about the concept of culture.

It was during this period that Arie de Ruijter's first major organisational challenge surfaced: he came to play a leading role in the restructuring of the anthropology departments in the Netherlands. This major operation not only succeeded against all expectations; it has also furnished the ground plan for Dutch anthropology in the decades to come and has served anthropology extremely well in the major budget cutting operations of the 1980s. There can be no doubt that de Ruijter's organisational and networking skills have shaped the way he performed anthropology. His administrative involvement first widened his view of anthropology, and increasingly de Ruijter became a general social scientist, while maintaining his roots in anthropology. The combination of a broad academic orientation with managerial and administrative engagement would, during the late 1980s, develop into his decisive support for the advancement of organisational anthropology in the Netherlands.

Throughout, ethical considerations were never far from Arie's mind. He always acted on the basis of a long Calvinistic heritage, trying to combine a clear sense of duty with deep personal loyalties. He was and is a builder, not a caretaker; he is someone who takes decisions, someone who would rather bet on an uncertain future than simply wait for it to happen. But Goethe's famous dictum *"Der Handlende ist immer gewissenlos"* describes a fundamental dilemma, which in the case of Arie was one that pitted institutional demands against the exigencies of personal loyalties.

Perhaps his major organisational achievement has been the establishment of the research school CERES, which integrated all development-related social science research in the Netherlands. Through the utter force of his (strategic) convictions—the institutional vulnerability of the disciplines which were dear to him—and his characteristic sense of responsibility, de Ruijter built one of the largest and most successful research schools in Dutch academia. After CERES had become firmly established, Arie de Ruijter started to concentrate on what was to become the object of his major intellectual and organisational efforts in recent years: *multiculturalism*. Not surprisingly, the study of multiculturalism enabled him to keep alive his original interest in the conceptual and methodological questions surrounding a general theory of culture.

The irony of Arie's institution building is that he is a less-than-moderate believer in planning, particularly in academia. What he saw was a field that was not self-organising, and so he took it upon himself to unite, to bridge, and to integrate, often against all odds. In essence, Arie loves a struggle, a real debate, and often is spoiling for a fight. Just running the shop is unappealing, he likes opposition and admires the street fighter: the "arena" concept is written all over his personality.

It should therefore come as no surprise that the first part of this volume addresses problems related to the key issue of the multicultural arena. In the second and third parts of this book, the concept of the arena is connected to discourses of identity and the field of organisations and organising. It is our belief that these three thematic fields constitute the heart of his intellectual outlook and organisational behaviour. In the end, all three thematic fields coalesce around anthropology's conceptual meeting point: culture.

Arie de Ruijter's idea of the multicultural arena emerges from his specific notion of society. "Society," he boldly declares, "is not primarily a market in which free and equal participants exchange ideas, goods and services, *but first of all a battleground, an arena*" (2000:11. Our emphasis). Elaborating further this particular understanding of society as an arena or battleground, he states: "Society is a mechanism, a vehicle for the creation or construction and legitimisation of inequality. Society is in no way a mechanism for equality" (van Rinsum and Pansters 2002:18). It is on the basis of his distinctive conceptualisation of society as an arena of contention and of strategic cooperation "in order to get access to resources" (ibid.), that leads him to approach the question of the multicultural society not as an issue of minority problems, but in terms of resource competition and its important underlying mechanisms of inclusion and exclusion (ibid.:12).

The essays contained in the first part of this volume implicitly or explicitly address, take issue with, or offer apt illustrations of Arie de Ruijter's notion of the multicultural arena. The first two essays are complementary in subject and scope. Emanuel de Kadt begins with a study of singular importance, in a world profoundly changed by the events of September 11, which puts forward the compelling argument that fundamentalism, whose influence – especially among young, embittered immigrant Muslims living in western countries who harbour deep feelings of socio-economic "exclusion" – has been increasing over recent decades, is the very antithesis of, and so poses the most serious challenge to, multiculturalism. Lieteke van Vucht Tijssen takes up the topic of cultural diversity and religious fundamentalism by putting to de Ruijter the question of whether the management of diversity in a multicultural society should be limited to organisational aspects while excluding the search for common values as an effective means of holding a society together. Taking the case study of South Africa, Henk van Rinsum follows with a critical essay that delves deeper into the puzzle of multiculturalism, wherein he contends that a major problem with de Ruijter's published works in regard to his model of the coordination of cultural diversity is that they downplay, at least implicitly, the intricate relationship between power and inequality. Next, Gert Oostindie sagaciously observes and eloquently argues that debates on immigration and in-house diversity demand a critical engagement with one's own history, for it is indeed a fact that the rise of the very concept of multiculturalism in Dutch society is a legacy of its colonial past. Ton Robben follows with an analysis of the apparent multicultural tangle contained within the persona of a retired Argentine rear admiral in an attempt to take the concept of multiculturalism to a more fundamental level, by examining how it exists within individuals and by demonstrating that ethnic identity is but one, and even then by no means the primary, exponent of that complex collection of group identifications he defines as multiculturalism. In a jointly written paper, Bas de Gaay Fortman and Mohamed Salih analyse the common discourse shared by the world's great religions and human rights in spite of the existence of major cultural differences between the practitioners of different religious traditions: namely, the primacy of human dignity. Dirk Kruijt's study of the long-term effects of migration and informality in Latin America, with particular focus on the case of Peru, aptly illustrates what de Ruijter would describe as the underlying mechanisms of socioeconomic exclusion. Yet the essay also makes the astute and important observation that despite the general disintegration of living standards and the increasingly precarious nature of civil citizenship in Latin America, shared mass poverty and the rapid expansion of the informal economy are, ironically enough, also serving to integrate what hitherto had been extremely segmented societies. Diederick Raven ends this part of the volume with an epistemological essay in which he puts forth the thesis that Christianity, with its theoretical way of learning – modelled after the sermon as the Western paradigm of transferring conceptual knowledge – is not only of fundamental importance for the "invention" of science, but essential to it as well. In effect, the essay also takes us back to de Ruijter's early interest in interconnecting the philosophy of science and methodology with substantive anthropological topics, among which the quest for a general theory of culture has long been at the fore.

The ten chapters that comprise the second part of the book address the general themes of discourses and arenas of identity, which were another two of de Ruijter's interests. The first three essays take Mexican identity as their point of departure, and as such are complementary and indeed melt into one another. Wil Pansters analyses the emergence and nature of the authenticity discourse on "Mexico" and "the Mexican" in the first half of the twentieth century, showing that a new and authentic Mexican national identity was constructed (mainly by the intelligentsia) by means of a racial, cultural, and psychological hybridization project that has come to be known as *mestizaje*. From there the baton is passed to Gerdien Steenbeek, who proceeds to demonstrate how a gender-specific rite of passage, called the *quinceañera*, which marks a fifteen-year-old's transition from the status of girl to that of a young woman, has come to be used by Mexican (and other Hispanic) immigrants living in the United States as a crucial component in defining their ethnic identity. Cultural identity construction, as Steenbeek cogently points out, can also be a gendered process. Identities, however, are not only self-imputed and self-constructed, but also ascribed; and Menno Vellinga's account of the relationship between cultural identity and the role of regional psychosocial traits and behavioral patterns in the case of Northern Mexico offers a clear illustration of this. Next, Fabiola Jara demonstrates that the label "Spanish Arawak" in the northwest district of Guyana refers not so much to an actual ethnic group as it does to a speech form or living narrative that, through the mouths of contemporary Morucan musicians, maintains the memory of the shared experiences of bygone times. Then, writing on a topic that is sure to be close to Arie de Ruijter's heart – soccer – Kees Koonings argues that a Levi-Straussian structuralist analysis of sport in Brazil, especially of widely popular ones like soccer and Formula 1 racing, reveals not only the ways in which people give meaning to and come to terms with social exclusion, but also the metaphors, ritual representations, or re-enactments which they use to mitigate or transcend it. Moving on from football to cuisine, Geert Mommersteeg's anthropological study of food in the context of a home for the Indo-Dutch elderly in the Netherlands shows how for these individuals to talk about their unique cuisine is concomitantly to talk about a collective non-Dutch past that defines the core of their distinct identity in the Netherlands. In the essay which follows, Wim Hoogbergen writes about the Maroons of Suriname, focusing on the issue – also one of de Ruijter's earlier interests – of the methodological complexity of combining evidence from oral history with archival material dating back to colonial times. Homing in on one of Arie de Ruijter's lesser-noted interests, Jan de Wolf presents a previously unpublished narrative of a Bukusu mytheme, which he had recorded in 1969 while doing fieldwork in West Kenya. In the next chapter, Jeroen Vermeulen provides a semiotic analysis of the formation of identity at a Christian school for higher vocational education in the Netherlands using actor-network theory. Completing this part of the volume is Frank Bovenkerk's thought-provoking essay on the relationship between the emancipation of women and their place in organised crime.

The third and final part of this volume deals with the theme of organisational arenas. For those who know him, Arie de Ruijter's organisational accomplishments and reflexive managerial talents are what perhaps constitute the most lasting impression of the man. This is not surprising given that he himself admits that "I always try to find a place for my intellectual interests in concrete forms of organisation" (van Rinsum and Pansters 2002:12). Indeed, one might even say that de Ruijter is the very embodiment of the intertwining of praxis and conceptual reflection into one dynamic and dialectic whole. His concept of the arena, for example, assumed concrete substance when, as a builder of academic organisations, networks, and research programmes, he came to experience and understand the logic of enabling constraints, the limits of strategic actions, the importance of institutional power, and the significance of language. This conceptual idea pervades Arie de Ruijter's thinking right down to the level of personal introspection. Reflecting on his role of the academic administrator he once wrote, "I cherish the illusion of being the spider in the web of my life. The counter-image of the fly trapped in the web scares and disgusts me" (1997: 119). Even so, this sense of freedom of action is inevitably an illusion, for one is always "...embedded – and thereby subjected to the workings of – an immense web of interdependencies, meanings and interactions" (ibid.). Consequently, he came to develop a managerial style that brought to boardroom meetings a grounded realisation of the inevitability of systemic developments combined with an unrelenting drive to develop an agenda for strategic action. It was therefore quite foreseeable, if not inevitable, that Arie de Ruijter should be one of the midwives in the birth of organisational anthropology at Utrecht University, and has ever since been involved in its development and application.

Walter van Beek begins this section with an essay in which he, as president of an international sport organisation, finds himself the target of an attempted coup initiated by Russian colleagues to oust him from his position. He subsequently analyses this personal experience in terms of Russian culture and its confrontation with Western notions of sports management and politics. Following with another study of Russian culture, Rieke Leenders analyses the Russian notion of reciprocity known as *blat* in order to shed light on the question of why Russian immigrants in the Netherlands so often find it difficult to forge friendships based on trust with Dutch people. Next, Jan Boessenkool sketches the history of the emerging sub-discipline of organisational anthropology, and expounds his preference for the arena metaphor in that it helps to break the illusion that organisational practice is focused on consensus and harmony. The relevance of an anthropological perspective on professional communities and divisions within complex organisations is further elaborated by Wim Koot. Then Paul Verweel and Peter Leisink present an essay in which they make a plea for the recognition of the rationality of community relations alongside mechanical task-centered rationality in organisations. The next two essays are complementary, and have as their common subject matter asylum seekers in the Netherlands. First, Marja Gastelaars examines the impact that the local networking efforts of the institution responsible for providing residences to asylum seekers in the Netherlands is having on the space needed by these individuals in order to achieve "self-reliance" in their everyday lives. The second study by Karin Geui-jen describes the significance that accommodations at asylum centres have for individual asylum seekers, as well as for the staff and the management of these centres. Lastly, Jan Ooijens reports on the achievements of, and continuing challenges to, educational curriculum adaptation in Honduras.

This brief summary of the main themes of the essays collected here gives at least some idea of their variety and range. The diversity of these studies is not only testimony of the breadth of de Ruijter's own interests and inspirational contributions to anthropology in the Netherlands. In fact, they may also be seen to reflect the very realities of the world we live in, where complexity, resource competition, globalisation and multiculturalism are the norms. While some may choose to paint the meeting of cultures within the arena of multiculturalism as a rosy picture of "rainbow" encounters, Arie de Ruijter has always attempted, in characteristic fashion, to uncover premises and presuppositions behind discourse and presentation. He has always sought to discover the underlying mechanisms of inclusion and exclusion, and to meet undaunted and head-on such ugly and unpleasant issues as inequality and increasing xenophobic feelings towards the "Other." It is to Arie de Ruijter's lasting credit that, as a scholar and an academic administrator, he has not sought comfortable refuge in status and core positions earned in the past, or in merely accepting the supposition of coexisting cultural diversity, but has made it a personal goal to establish linkages between diverse disciplines and concepts, and to build bridges between cultures over which others may pass.

Bibliography

de Ruijter, A. 1997. De ladder op omlaag? Een postmodern ego-document. In A. van Dijk and P. Verweel, eds., *De ladder op omlaag? Een psychologie van besturen,* pp.119-126. Assen: Van Gorcum.

de Ruijter, A. 2000. *De multiculturele arena*. Tilburg: Katholieke Universiteit Brabant. (Inaugural address.)

van Rinsum, Henk J., and Wil Pansters. 2002. The Interview: 'I have a 'Neolithic' mind.' *CERES magazine*. Autumn. (Interview with Arie de Ruijter, 31 October 2002.)

Part I

Multicultural Arenas

1

The Fundamentalist Threat to Multi-culturalism, with Special Reference to Islam

Emanuel de Kadt

During the last year that Arie spent at Utrecht, the events and repercussions of 'September 11' have dominated not only the news, but also the perceptions of many people of what was happening in their societies. We have seen a massive show of force on the part of the USA in its 'war on terrorism', with President Bush-supported by the vast majority of Americans- assuring the world that America will eventually catch up with these criminals and eliminate them. Europeans are on the whole rather more circumspect, and also rather less united in their views. Yes, the condemnation of terrorist acts against civilians, and of course especially the barbarity of September 11 and more recently that of Bali and Mombassa, is virtually unanimous. But European explanations of what may have contributed to the situation in which some Islamic fundamentalists can become indiscriminate homicidal maniacs, only concerned with 'teaching America a lesson', are rather more varied.

I became interested in fundamentalism in the early 1990s, some time before it became a household word. It had to remain on the back burner because 'fundamentalism and development' was not regarded as a core issue at my then base, the Institute of Development Studies at the University of Sussex. Over the past year I have returned to the theme.[1] In this piece I argue that fundamentalism and its manifestations are directly relevant to the issue of multiculturalism, so close to Arie's heart, and it is the link between these two phenomena that I want to explore. I contend that fundamentalism, whose influence – certainly among Muslims – has been increasing over recent decades, is the very antithesis of multiculturalism.

Fundamentalism explained

Much has been written on fundamentalism over the last twenty years or so, most visibly through the five massive volumes of the "Fundamentalism Project" of the American Academy of Arts and Sciences published in the first half of the 1990s (e.g., Marty and Appleby 1991 and 1995). The output continued in the latter part of the 1990s at a slightly less frantic pace, only to pick up again recently.

The term "fundamentalism" has its origin in a series of pamphlets published in the US between 1910 and 1915, entitled "The Fundamentals: A Testimony to the Truth". In 1920, a journalist and Baptist layman named Curtis Lee Laws appropriated the term "fundamentalist" as a designation for those who were ready "to do battle royal for the Fundamentals." There are many overlapping definitions. A serviceable one given on the

Internet², in an excellent "Profile Report" that is a good starting point for newcomers, is that of Bruce Lawrence (1989), who published an important comparative study around the same time that the Fundamentalism Project started. It runs as follows. Fundamentalism is "... the affirmation of religious authority as holistic and absolute, admitting of neither criticism nor reduction; it is expressed through the collective demand that specific ... dictates derived from scripture be publicly recognized and legally enforced. ... The most consistent denominator is opposition to Enlightenment values."

All fundamentalisms legitimate their existence by reference to a body of sacred writings. The belief in the fundamental and unalterable truth of those writings constitutes a prime test of faith for fundamentalists. The texts are beyond critical comment, and the social or historical context at the time of their origin is regarded as irrelevant: they are "valid for all time." When fundamentalists study those texts they tend to see themselves as uncovering truths that have been hidden by people's inability to comprehend or see³; and such incomprehension is often regarded as the consequence of "betrayals" of earlier generations. In fact, history may be regarded by fundamentalists as dominated by such betrayals, in a process of decline from an original ideal state (Caplan, 1987a).

The non-fundamentalist Islamic scholar Mohammed Arkoun (cited in Watt 1988:1) contends that for fundamentalists many things are not only unthinkable *(impensable)*, but are in fact "unthought" *(impensé)*. Fundamentalists hold a world-view centred on the idea that, possibly even at one particular moment in time, God revealed the "correct" way to act in the world. The content of this revelation retains its validity throughout the ages – indeed, forever. This "timelessness" of the fundamentalists' views contrasts with the approach of non-fundamentalists. Non-fundamentalists do, to a greater or lesser degree, locate texts in history, and interpret doctrines or laws as responses to conditions in their time. For them "... the very idea of truth is seen to be the outcome of social and cultural conditions, and thus to be understood historically and contextually" (Caplan 1987a:21).

It is that certainty of the correctness of their own views that makes fundamentalists unreceptive to the tenets of multiculturalism – in fact, antagonistic to it. This is the central fact that needs to be seriously considered in any discussion of multiculturalism and its future in contemporary Europe, and it figures prominently in Thomas Meyer's recent short book, *Identity Mania* (Meyer 2001). He argues in one of the most politically charged views of fundamentalism that, notwithstanding their differences, all fundamentalisms are linked by a common element: "... a style marked by an antagonistic approach to cultural differences, a strategy – oriented to gain supremacy – of politicizing their own culture against the culture of the others, both within their own societies and outside" (Meyer 2001:8).

In his Inaugural address at Tilburg University, Arie referred to a similar issue: namely, the situation where "... one group is able constantly and consistently to thrust its own definition of reality on the other groups, or even to prescribe it" (de Ruijter 2000:8. My translation). Yet he did so merely in passing and without reference to fundamentalism, thereby seeming to suggest that this could be dismissed as exceptional. For Arie multiculturalism is the norm, as it is "of all times and places." That may be true, but so is the fact that the opponents of multiculturalism are "of all times and places." The critical issue is which of the two statements has greater social or political relevance in a particular place and at a particular time. In the today's world I am far from sure.

Modernity as the fundamentalists' *'bête noire'*

Today's multicultural societies owe much to the changes set in train by the Enlightenment, which eventually produced what we now call "modernity." We use that concept to contrast our kind of world with the world where tradition is paramount. Modern society is *human-centred;* human autonomy is the ultimate end (Sivan 1995). In the modern world, people are oriented primarily to the future rather than to the past or even the present. They are concerned above all with increasing their opportunities for choice, with widening their range of options, with seeing things as they *could* be rather than as they are. That said, modernity also leads to doubts and uncertainties. It produces a state of mind that no longer easily accepts the traditional religious interpretations, which explain evil and suffering in daily life and help one to cope with them (Webber 1987). In a modern society everything "religious" is up for grabs, so to speak.

Another aspect of modernity is that its culture deals, above all, with differences. Meyer concludes from this that the essence of modernity is pluralism – the capacity to create room for cultures to evolve alongside each other. "The culture of the modern age provides a framework for different ways of life and world-views without itself constituting a particular way of life" (Meyer 2001:6). Modernity is therefore not the same as the "culture of the West," which is a term better used for the historical, pre-modern culture of Western Europe that also dealt in absolute certainties (remember the Inquisition).

Modernity has created problems for Western societies. The constant questioning leaves people disoriented. James Hunter argues that the condition of modernity creates a crisis of meaning for individuals, which in turn leads to anomie, other – directedness, spiritual homelessness. Somewhat apocalyptically he contends that it results in a "permanent identity crisis," and engenders "...conditions that are anthropologically intolerable" (1981:7).[4] It is, of course, precisely the aim of fundamentalism to respond to this process and to attempt to reverse it, through a denial of openness, ambiguity, uncertainty, and also of multiculturalism as we understand it today. By promoting a closed system of faith and order, fundamentalisms pick out *one* alternative as the only acceptable one. Arie refers to the same problematic in his discussion of the strategies that people develop in reaction to the perceived threats of globalisation (arguably modernity's most recent manifestation). People may try to cope with those changes through a hybrid response, selectively incorporating some of the new cultural elements while rejecting others. Alternatively they may choose the fundamentalist route, and emphasise the retention and strengthening of traditional elements. The term "fundamentalist" is here given a wider sense than its original religious meaning (de Ruijter 2000).

If modernity has created problems for the West, how much more so for societies elsewhere. In the West, and notably in Europe, modernisation and secularisation were carried by the educated classes. With the spread of public education, these came to embrace the vast majority of the population. In most non-Western societies, by contrast, the people educated in the "European" mould have remained a minority. Yet it was this minority who came to hold the reins of government: they were the modernisers, they made the laws and changed the workings of the state. Thus, they directly affected the lives of the majority. This majority, both uneducated in Western knowledge and usually poor, remained at the margins of the institutions which embodied those Enlightenment views. They continued to live by traditional norms, handed down from generation to generation within the family and the local – perhaps religious – community. Nevertheless, they had to deal with "modern" public institutions that implicitly assumed that they, too, had changed. The result was an even greater disorientation and perplexity than in 'the West,' where modernity had emerged. People somehow came to feel that they didn't belong in the world around them. Ultimately it led to problems of identity. (See below.) People were left to wonder who they really were, and no longer knew what was expected of them (Watt 1988).

In this kind of situation people look for support, for a way out of the uncertainty or anomie. In Western societies those affected often sought their salvation in new religious movements – tightly organised, "communitarian," demanding and closed. In non-Western societies, by contrast, people tended to seek solace and support from *traditional* religious organisations, whose leadership promises moral certainty and anchorage. So it is in this reaction to the travails of modernity that we find one cause of the "return to fundamentals," of fundamentalism.

This reaction to modernity was a factor of particular importance in the Islamic world, also because some of the basic moral mechanisms there differ substantially from those prevalent in the West. Arab-Islamic culture emphasises external rather than internal moral controls, with ethics being public rather than private, collective rather than individual, shame-related rather than guilt-related. Westernisation brings a shift to the latter concepts. Yet these are inadequately internalised by individuals, and, in Ayubi's view, this has been one of the main causes of psychological and social problems (and corruption) in many contemporary Arab societies (Ayubi 1991). He argues that there is "...a high degree of dissonance, and conflict, between the 'traditional' values to which the individual has been socialised ... and the 'modern' values by which economic, administrative and legal organisations are supposed to be governed, especially in the urban, semi-industrialised and rather impersonal environment of the city" (ibid:44).

A somewhat different perspective is offered by Gellner (1995), who emphasises that Islam has for centuries had a High variant and a Low variant. The High variant is rule-oriented, individualistic and scripturalist, and congenial to the urban bourgeoisie and urban scholars. The Low variant addresses itself to the less sophisticated rural dwellers. The High version has at various times tried to convert the Low version with an attempted reformation (internal Jihads, he calls these). This was successfully achieved only once the colonial and post-colonial state had become strong enough to impose itself upon "...those rural, self-administering units (generally known as tribes) which had been the social basis for the [Low] version of Islam" (ibid:284). The con-comitant centralization of society favoured a centralized variant of religion, which leads Gellner to argue that, for the first time in history, the High variant of Islam actually man-aged, over the last hundred years, to carry out a successful Reformation. Not everyone would agree that those changes can be called a Reformation, and I, too, have doubts in this respect. In fact, I argue in the final section of this paper that Islam now requires an aggressive Reformation from within, if "moderate" Islam is to emancipate itself from the exclusivist and "triumphalist" approach which it still largely shares with the funda-mentalists. Gellner also makes the point that the dominant High variant – particularly its fundamentalist variety, I would argue – presented Islamic societies with a ready-made alternative to modernity, once this came to be rejected in the reaction to West-ern domination.

Perplexed individuals or malfunctioning societies?

So the advent of modernity and its non-traditional values can create problems for indi-viduals trying to adjust to their environment. But, as Arie's work testifies, a significant characteristic of modern societies is that they are increasingly multicultural, that they contain within them groups that draw their values from different backgrounds, from dif-ferent "civilizations." Thus Western Europe has seen the number of immigrants from other cultures grow over the past decades. In the Netherlands they have mainly been Islamic, above all from Turkey and Morocco. In fact, by the turn of the century Mus-lims made up around 4.5% of the population in the Netherlands.[5] Such immigrants often hail from precisely the "disorienting" contexts just described. Looking at the issue from a more general perspective, Samuel Huntington (1998) argues that the West has not dealt well with this changing reality.

Huntington's approach is by no means simplistic, and he deals with political (strategic) questions, as well as with broader issues of values. Across civilizations he sees incompatible convictions, based on values, in a wide range of areas: state and cit-izen, woman and man, religion and the relation with God, rights and duties, the indi-vidual and society. Those differing values are central to his argument, for he believes that these value incompatibilities have often led to conflicts.

Huntington also argues that the West has attempted to teach the world to see humanity's history from a Western perspective, projecting the view that the world should strive for a *universal* – yet Wester-based – civilisation through a process of mod-ernisation. However, the five-century-long dominance of Western civilization, which has led to Western arrogance – precisely the accusation levelled at the West by many fundamentalist Muslims – is coming to an end. This lesson has not yet been learned, and Huntington believes that the West is unwisely trying to swim against the tide of his-tory. The West should now abandon its project to make typically Western constructs universal (human rights, for example, or the justification for humanitarian interventions), as this is likely to generate dangerous coalitions against it of other civilisations, possibly leading to truly unmanageable conflicts.[6] Yet he also stresses the other side to the coin: he believes that the complement to this "withdrawal" from its universalistic pretensions must be for the West to stand fast and to strengthen its core, historical Western culture. He prefers to assimilate migrants into Western culture rather than promote multi-culturalism, and prefers to hold on to the centrality of the individual rather than to switch to group rights. Stated dramatically, he wants to draw up the bridges and keep the other cultures out, or at least prevent them from changing the nature of Western civilization.

There has been considerable criticism of Huntington's views, much of it politically inspired. With some of that criticism I agree, notably that he is mistaken in making civilization or culture the *one* issue to consider in present-day reality. Reality is multi-dimensional and cannot be reduced to one factor alone.[7] Moreover, conflicts have a multiplicity of causes (Verstraete 1998). If, indeed, any *one* type of cause predominates, I would argue that it is socio-economic rather than value-driven. That is to say, conflicts continue to ensue to a significant degree when people are disgruntled about the economic situation, about *exclusion*, about their position in an increasingly unequal society. This is also a significant factor in driving people to fundamentalism as an alternative, as I shall argue below.

Even so, Huntington deserves recognition for his insight that, firstly, culture has become a much more visible issue in current discussions, and secondly, that it must also be considered a key factor in relation to future developments. Thus, after a period in which political, economic and social rights were in the forefront of attention, more recently *cultural rights* have moved centre stage, with various "cultural minorities" (including refugees, indigenous peoples, gays and feminists) clamouring for their recognition (Dueñas 1998; also Donders 2002). Following Huntington's approach, there are also indications that the world is in the throes of a shift of one civilizational model (i.e. "Western dominance"), to another – "pluriformity."

In spite of Huntington's prescriptions to the contrary, within many societies that pluriformity is expressing itself as multi-culturalism. In a considerable number of Western democracies multi-culturalism is being pursued from the centre of the political spectrum. It remains in vogue as an objective for many politicians and is also in favour with significant sections of the public and with analysts. Thomas Meyer (2001), who is representative of the analysts who take this "multi-cultural" perspective, makes three basic points.

First, there are great similarities in the basic values between different civilizations. Most people are likely to agree with this first point, yet it is worth pointing out that different aspects of those basic values get stressed in different cultures at different times, making them in fact rather less alike. Second, Meyer insists that there are no fundamentalist, traditional, or modern cultures (or civilizations), but that fundamentalism, traditionalism, and modernism are three different ways of understanding each major culture and of giving it practical expression. He calls these "styles of civilization" – styles which lead to different approaches in handling one's own culture. Meyer argues that the main confrontations and conflicts are not *between* civilizations, but *within* them, as these three styles are present in virtually all. And he points out that the three styles show similarities among themselves. Such similarities exist, for example, between modern Islam and modern Christianity, and these are greater than, say, those between fundamentalist and modern (or even traditional) Christianity. All traditionalists tend to defend the patriarchal system, hierarchy, and the extended family. For them, religion is central in the lives of individuals and communities. All fundamentalists oppose both modernism and traditionalism within their own religion or culture; they all want to achieve lasting supremacy and make religion the very core of identity. Meyer's third basic point is his repeatedly expressed view that when conflicts arise around cultural issues, these are almost necessarily politically "engineered" by small strategic groups. I have little sympathy for such a conspiracy theory of history, though he would probably have been less wide of the mark had he used the term "exploited" instead of "engineered." I would argue that factors other than deliberate political action or conspiracy are more significant in accounting for the success or otherwise of fundamentalist movements. Two examples of other such factors are (a) the failure to achieve significant economic improvements for the poorer sections of a population, while inequalities grow, and (b) the disjunction which young people from rural or small town environments encounter between what they learned at home and the approach of modern science. People are above all pushed towards fundamentalism by failure, uncertainty, economic trauma, and so on. One may add that the failure of Communism, already alluded to above, is also significant in this respect, as it has made fundamentalism into "... one of the few remaining political options ... as a protest against secularization and consumerism. ... Islamic fundamentalism challenges the universalistic claims of western natural and social sciences, and offers an alternative model of understanding and significance" (Turner 2002:28).

Paradoxically, Meyer reaches a conclusion that has echoes of Huntington when he sees a "global cultural fault line" not between civilizations, but within them, because of this politicisation of cultural differences by the fundamentalists. Conflict is likely because it is inherent in fundamentalism to want to gain supremacy, and then to keep it. In that sense it is thoroughly anti-democratic. Like that of the Marxist-Leninists in their time, the fundamentalists' political ambition to stay in power, and impose their world-view on all citizens, provides a one-way street in politics – *once in, never out*.

Yet a couple of important nuances need to be attached to this conclusion. In the first place, such an outcome obviously depends on fundamentalism being able to take the first step on the road to becoming dominant. The chance that that will happen differs considerably from one context to another. So far, it has been quite low in advanced Western societies. It is probably moderate in those African countries with "mixed" populations, ethnically and religiously speaking. But it is likely to be substantial in countries where Islam is dominant. And if, indeed, Islam is becoming more prominent in Western societies, then there are danger signs for these societies, too.

In the second place, there are doubts about the capacity of fundamentalists, once in power, to "deliver" on what their citizens ultimately expect from them – good government in some sense, and a modicum of economic well-being. With their simple and pure call they may provide political hope and contribute to political emancipation. Yet they have neither been particularly successful in the creation of an effective social and economic order, nor, on the whole, in pointing the way to lasting social reform (Lubeck 1988; Meyer 2001). Except in relation to the private sphere of life, fundamentalists usually avoid spelling out in detail how they might reform the system they so abhor.[8] When they come to power their policies towards the public sphere are often little different from those of their predecessors. Meyer calls fundamentalism a "false enticement," as "... none of the known fundamentalisms of this world has come up with a convincing and achievable socio-economic programme which might have some chance of resolving the crises that fundamentalist leaders have tirelessly exploited for their own gain."[9]

Identity and its manipulation

I shall now make a brief digression to consider the relevance of identity and identity formation to these processes. When societies were much less complicated than the one in which we now live, say until the Renaissance, it would not take much thought for a person to answer the question, "who are you?" You were a man or a woman, an adult or a child. Apart from that, what mattered was your place in society: peasant or squire, soldier or merchant. In Europe, before the Reformation, you wouldn't have had to think about your religion. Virtually everybody was a Christian. There was little chance that your self-perception would be "out of kilter" with the way others thought of you – unless, of course, you had what we nowadays call mental illness.

Today, in Western societies, identity and identity formation are a great deal more complex than they were in those less complicated societies. Because we "play so many roles," and those roles are not activated at the same time, our individual identity emerges from a negotiation between our self-image and the image of ourselves held by the people with whom we interact. Identity is hence not something we possess once and for all: it emerges out of a social process that tries to achieve an equilibrium between conflicting expectations. Given that different people have different images as well as different expectations of us, we have to be able to endure ambiguity and ambivalence. Usually we have a dominant identity, one that gets activated most of the time and which we would spontaneously name if asked – our profession, for example. Subsidiary parts of our identity, the images of ourselves held by *some* others, are kept in the back of our mind; we have to be able to maintain a distance from the role that we adopt in each case.

It is precisely fundamentalism's aim to overcome these tensions and reinstate an unambiguous sense of identity. Heilman notes that neither Jewish nor Muslim fundamentalists accept a division between their social and religious selves: they reject multiple identities, or *personas*, and want to overcome the "frustrating compartmentalization" of the life of those who seek to live in the secular and religious worlds. "For haredi [ultra-Orthodox] Jews this means a rejection of the acculturative model of the Jewish enlightenment or *haskalah* that urged people to be 'a man in the street and a Jew in the home'.... The same might be said about those who have revived their attachment to Islam. They seek to be *kamal*, complete, and reject the idea of having several faces." (1995:87)

Take a step back from fundamentalism and recall what happened in Africa when the colonies became independent.[10] People, there, had to be made to think of themselves as Ghanaians, Tanzanians or Nigerians, rather than as villagers who belonged to a lineage or to a tribe. In the years after independence, African rulers tried hard to forge such national identities, and they had a measure of success in getting people to think of themselves in such national terms – especially where an active struggle for independence had preceded the hand-over of power.

Nevertheless, people in Africa remained above all rooted in their primordial small-scale communities, based on kinship, lineage and locality – particularly in the rural areas. While identities were multiple, those primordial ones remained strongest. However, there was one significant twist to this tale. In Africa, an intermediate identity level between the primordial groups and the nation-state has taken on increased prominence, partly naturally, and partly as a result of deliberate manipulation by people seeking power – *the ethnic group*. Ake (1994) has even argued that ethnic groups have become the primary repository of loyalty.

Of course, ethnicity is neither simply constructed, nor simply given. It is well captured in Ake's expression as a "dialectic of imagination and reality...constituted by the choices and actions of real people in the struggles of social existence....Whether it is real or imagined, ethnicity is for its adherents a total experience, the epicentre of their very being" (1994:52). And Ake sees political ethnicity as "...an unequivocal commitment to the defense of a way of life, all that is meaningful and valuable, materially, culturally and spiritually" (ibid.). While Ake leans towards the "given" or "natural" conception of ethnicity as identity, others emphasise that ethnicity is often pushed for political reasons. In those circumstances ethnicity changes from being mainly a *cultural* characteristic of people, linked to one of a number of "identities," to being a *politically* defined label.[11]

And so we return to our central theme. We have only to substitute religion for ethnicity to see that the above discussion is relevant to fundamentalism and multiculturalism. Fundamentalism tries to reduce the modern person's complex identity to only *one* aspect, the religious one. Where fundamentalism seeks to impose its certainties on society as a whole, thereby negating the very essence of multiculturalism, religion becomes a politically defined label, just as happened with ethnicity in Africa. Moreover, it becomes the only politically relevant one. Thomas Meyer describes this exclusive focus on one aspect of identity as "identity mania": "Identity mania seeks nothing but identity, the very same in all life contexts and for all the others at that" (2001:17). For him, fundamentalism is the modern-day identity mania.

Where does this leave us with multiculturalism?

David Ingleby (2000) used his inaugural lecture as Professor of Intercultural Psychology at Utrecht University to consider some of the burning issues around multiculturalism in the Netherlands. His is, on the whole, a balanced view, though one that pulls
no punches in criticizing Dutch society and its academic establishment for not taking
multiculturalism seriously. For some 20 years now, Netherlands policy towards immigrants has been based on the principle of "integration with maintenance of one's own
culture." Nevertheless, as he points out, various surveys have demonstrated that a substantial part of Dutch society believes that immigrants should adjust themselves "completely" to Dutch culture and customs. He shows that immigrants from other cultures
now merely fill a place in society that in earlier times – in fact, until the 1950s – was
occupied by autochthonous Dutch people. Class divisions in society (and the existence
of cultural differences between the classes) are nothing new. But recently they have
taken on more pronounced "inter"-cultural characteristics[12], resembling in some ways
the vertical pluralism *(verzuiling)* that for decades existed in the Netherlands between
the three great "pillars" of society – the Catholics, the Protestants, and the Secularists
(included in this category are the Humanists).[13] During the long years that *verzuiling*
was dominant in the Netherlands – roughly speaking, until the 1970s – people lived out
their entire life within institutional structures that kept them shielded from the ideas
prevalent in the other "pillars," as well as from intimate social contact with members of
other pillars (Lijphart 1968). Every school, hospital, voluntary association, even trade
union was characterised either as Catholic, Protestant (various varieties), or secularist,
and the social interaction of each and every person was basically with "their own kind."
But the significant difference with an equivalent in today's multicultural social structure
would be that those pillars were thoroughly embedded in Dutch society, while its members shared the basic non-religious values of all Dutchmen and women. The "social
ghettos" were *part* of the Netherlands; cultural differences between them were relatively minor. Yet today, those cultural differences are the defining characteristic.

Ingleby highlights the dilemma of people in all societies with multiple value systems: "How can I respect the norms and values of others without disavowing my own
norms and values?" (2000:10). He also points to the pitfalls of focusing attention above
all on what distinguishes, differentiates, immigrant groups from the "host" society, for
in many respects the similarities are just as striking. Yet in his critique of Dutch social
services, for example, he hammers on the need to develop new instruments and procedures that are better attuned to the (different) psychological needs of people who
have grown up in a different culture, and whose expectations and experiences of interpersonal relations are not at all the same as those of their Dutch neighbours.

Well, yes – and no. Yes, in that there are indeed too few channels of communication between the different immigrant communities and the Dutch to make the
achievement of a more than "passive" multicultural society a reality. People do live side
by side, but nevertheless with pretty impermeable walls between them – and not much
is being done institutionally in Dutch society to open up those walls. There is little

knowledge of the other, little dialogue, in fact little interest. "Let them become like us" appears to remain a widespread feeling.

But no, because it takes two to tango. I do not want to fall into the trap of blaming the victim – there are, after all, many from the "immigrant" communities who in some sense genuinely want to become part of the host society. Also, those immigrant communities hail from different backgrounds. In the case of the Netherlands, for example, the Netherlands Antilles and Surinam are significant "sender" societies. Yet as I have already mentioned, in the Netherlands, like in a number of other European countries, a significant proportion of immigrants now come from societies where Islam is the predominant culture and religion – in the Dutch case, notably from Morocco and Turkey.

Non-Islamic fundamentalism

Before I deal with Islam and multicultural societies, and also in order not to lose a sense of perspective, I briefly want to discuss the situation prevalent among Christians, as well as in Israel.[14] The greatest stronghold of Christian fundamentalism is the United States. Yet successive Supreme Court judgments have upheld the view that religion should not influence institutions in the public sector. Fundamentalists from the 'Bible Belt' in the South and Southwest have not taken kindly to those judgments, which clearly implied that all religions are equally worthy of protection. They held that only their religion was the true one, and they wanted their long-held beliefs to be reflected in public life, and certainly to be taught to their own children in school. Nevertheless, their pleas did not have the desired effect: so far, the outcome has been to confirm that there should be no teaching of religion in schools in the public sector. The separation of state and religion remains intact (Bruce 1990).

Christianity – like Islam – has an urge to convert, and this gets stronger as one moves towards Christian fundamentalism. Yet the separation of church and state is by now so well established in "Western," majoritarian Christian societies that any tendencies in the opposite direction are kept reasonably well in check. The acceptance of other religions on an equal footing is usually explicitly mentioned in their Constitutions and is also deeply embedded in their political culture. In that minimal sense, at least, multiculturalism is not challenged.

That is harder to argue in the case of Judaism: fundamentalists and those close to them have managed to exercise real political power in the state of Israel. The ultra-orthodox want the consequences of their particular view of Judaism to be accepted by the rest of the community, or even to be imposed on it (Heilman and Friedman 1991). Largely as a result of the system of pure proportional representation, in which the (extreme) Right can be very tough in the bargaining that precedes the formation of a coalition government, many concessions have been wrested from the state, including the exemption from military service for the large number of students at traditional schools of religion (*yeshivot*). Aspects of Sabbath laws have been incorporated into secular legislation, and the Orthodox religious establishment totally controls matters of personal status in relation to Jews (marriage, divorce, definition of who is a Jew). Even so, these matters continue to generate intense political disagreements, and the long-term outcome is by no means clear.

Islam and the multicultural society
Let me return, then, to the position on these issues of Islam, the culture of by far the greatest number of non-autochthonous Dutch people. Many commentators have point-ed out that in its heyday, when the rule of Islam extended from the Eastern Mediter-ranean to the Iberian peninsula (al-Andalus), when it was self-confident and powerful, Islam was tolerant and respectful of other religions, particularly of the Abrahamic. Yet the Western "folk memories" of the conflicts between Christians and Muslims mostly revolve around "Muslim invaders" – Moors in Spain, Turks threatening Vienna – not around the (later) invasions by Europeans of virtually the whole of the Islamic world (Mortimer 1991). It is also conveniently forgotten that that tolerant Islam of the Golden Age was displaced by a militant and grossly intolerant Christianity. Centuries later, those Islamic rulers were subjected and humiliated by the colonial powers, even if subse-quently they were "culturally" tolerated (more by the British than by the culturally assertive French). It is this waning of its influence, and the increasing feeling of rela-tive powerlessness, that is said to have made Islam closed-minded and repressive, sus-picious of outside ideas and influences (Modood 2002).

It is important to keep this historical reality in mind, so we can better understand the complex causes of present-day obstacles to multiculturalism. It is the outcome of those historical processes with which we are faced today. Yet history has taken anoth-er twist. In the here and now of Western European multicultural societies, we have to deal with a culture and religion of growing importance that is fundamentally convinced of its own "correctness." That was brought home in 1989 with the Rushdie affair in Britain; in the same year there was a major controversy in France about girls wearing headscarves to school. Earlier, the issue of multiculturalism – and particularly the issue of why in Western Europe people from Islamic societies were so much *more* different than other non-autochthonous groups – had not figured prominently on the political agenda (Mortimer 1991).

Of course, the views propounded in the Qur'an provide useful authoritative quotes for quite a range of different perspectives and situations, and do not all point in the same direction and. Such different perspectives have emerged in the course of the last hundred years or so – including a "modernist" Islam, which has attempted to reconcile Islam with modernity through a more "scientific" approach to its teachings. The Muslim concept of *ijtihad*, or independent reasoning, helped in this task: it made possible the bypassing of the establishment clergy, "... much in the way the Protestant reformation challenged the Catholic Church" (Schulze 2002:10).

Modernist Muslims are obviously not fundamentalists, and there are many Islam-ic organisations in Europe that testify to that.[15] Their wish to be able to live their lives according to their religious precepts is entirely reasonable and, in a sense as a matter of principle, they should be able to expect support for this from Western "pluralists." Nevertheless, even their approach seems in tension with that secularism which it took Western societies so long to establish. As Mortimer argues, in the 1990s Islam came to be seen by many as "... a religion so firmly implanted in the political and social sphere, so inimical to any distinction between those things which are God's and those which are Caesar's, that it would never allow its adherents to become reliably law-abiding citizens of a secular and tolerant society" (1991:12). That sounds, and is, surely an exaggeration, yet from an Islamic perspective a not too dissimilar assessment is made by Sardar, who shows approvingly how Islamic scholars have come to reject the whole apparatus of concepts and approaches of "development studies" because these are materialistic and deny the fact that "... to be a complete human being, an individual must direct all his or her activities towards the service of God" (1996:47). Ba-Yunus goes even further: "In Islam personal worship and obedience to the rules of other institutions are the two sides of the same coin. One cannot exist without the other.... Above all, it means that for a Muslim to be pious, altruistic and peaceful within and without, not only is a personal devotion to God a requirement, but also an Islamic institutional environment in which to live as a Muslim" (2002:107). Is it then unreasonable to draw the conclusion from this that Islamic piety, in and by itself, gravitates towards one of the central characteristics of Islamic fundamentalism, the transformation of the surrounding society into one that is "Islamic"?

Add to this the earlier mentioned socio-economic factors that make fundamentalism an attractive option for "excluded" Muslims, and we should not be surprised to see in Europe an increasing influence of fundamentalist viewpoints among non-autochthonous communities from Islamic countries. That is worrying, because those viewpoints are essentially dismissive of some of the central values of the host society. When people hold that their beliefs are unquestionably true, there can be no genuine respect for the positions of others. And then the basis for a multicultural society is undermined.[16]

The position of moderate Islam in this respect is really not so very different – even though it lacks the fundamentalist militancy. As Islam is being seen as governing all aspects of life, and having answers to all of them, the Islamic "column" (in the sense of *verzuiling*) tends towards keeping itself hermetic and impermeable, shielded from outside influences, and self-reinforcing. The words of the Prophet continue to be quoted in all schools of Islam as though they were indeed divinely given, true for all times *and for all people*. Islam is presented – and not only by the fundamentalists, as is the case among Christians and Jews – as the final and perfected religion that should be embraced by all humanity. That is no basis for genuine respect, in spite of the earlier mentioned acceptance of the special relationships with Judaism and Christianity, the other Abrahamic religions. Jews and Christians, too, should be brought to accept the truth of Islam, they too should be converted if at all possible – because Islam *knows* it is right, and has no truck with the idea that others may be right too. Of course, as I have indicated, this also holds for certain currents in Judaism and Christianity (the fundamentalists among them), but assertive self-confidence seems more centrally embedded in Islamic culture, shared as it is by *all* varieties of Islam. It finds its ultimate expression in the call for *jihad*, or holy struggle.

The mention of *jihad* can easily lead to misunderstandings, however. Fundamentalism may be an extreme form of religiosity, and also imply an aggressive rejection of what we now call multiculturalism. But that does not make *all* fundamentalists into violent political extremists, ready to die – let alone kill – for their beliefs. Yes, there *are* extremist fundamentalists. However, in a general sense, fundamentalists, including Muslim fundamentalists, should *not* be equated with extremists.

There have been suggestions recently that such an identification has been systematically promoted both in the media and in academic writing, notably by the so-called Orientalist or neo-Orientalist school associated with Bernard Lewis and his followers, including Daniel Pipes (1990). Thus Donnan and Stokes, in the Introduction to the book Donnan edited, write that Islamic fundamentalism came to be associated "in the popular western imagination" with "...bearded, kalashnikov-carrying clerics, urban carnage and scimitars dripping with blood" (2002:8). Of course such an association is nonsense, and as Milton-Edwards in an otherwise alarmingly biased and one-sided article rightly argues in the same book, "...in reality the Islamic terrorists and radical Islam remain an exceedingly small cohort of disparate groupings and movements that have emerged out of a variety of political contexts. Their power and impact have been exaggerated; [yet] they have become the name of Islam" (2002: 42).

Indeed, from the time the perceived threat of Communism disappeared with the collapse of that system and its protagonist, the Soviet Union, Islam has to an extent taken over the role of the threatening "Other" to the West – and increasingly so also internally, within in Europe (Donnan and Stokes 2002). Even so, I doubt whether something approaching the distorted image of Islam painted by Donnan, Stokes and Milton-Edwards actually exists in the "popular imagination," with the possible exception of some otherwise also "extremist" (right wing) circles in the USA.

Nevertheless, leaving aside the confusion between fundamentalism and extremism, unresolved problems remain in Western societies in relation to most, if not all, varieties of Islam. With the very real chance of continuing indiscriminate attacks by Muslims on non-Muslims, a much more robust renunciation on the part of the non-violent Muslim majority is called for of some of the ideas that can underpin violence, notably the very concept of *jihad* and all it stands for – without "ifs" and "buts" and circumlocutions. Such a renunciation would also be the first step towards an even more important goal: reconsidering those teachings of Islam that stand in the way of a wholehearted acceptance of multicultural societies, which is to say societies where no particular group can or does lay claim to superiority. At present, significant sections of the Islamic community deny the importance of multiculturalism to democratic societies. This could seriously impair the social and political workings of those societies over the longer term.

If multiculturalism in western Europe is to have a real chance of success, that great majority of non-violent Muslims must face up to a stark and for them no doubt difficult fact: their Holy Book continues to provide not only the justification for terrorism for those who wish to read it in a certain way, it also lays large obstacles in the way of those who favour a multicultural society. That can only be reversed by a widespread, focused, organised and determined insider Muslim effort. As I have already stated, it seems to me that Islam now requires an aggressive Reformation – because without that, "moderate" Islam will not free itself from the "triumphalist" approach which it largely continues to share with the fundamentalists. Devotees of multiculturalism, like Arie, and other outsiders, can do no more than bring this forcefully to the attention of their Islamic friends and interlocutors.[17] What they *can* do, however, is ensure that the link between fundamentalism and "exclusion" is brought frequently into the public arena – and keep forcefully pleading that advanced Western societies use a greater portion of their considerable resources to improve the life chances of people from originally immigrant, non-Western and above all Muslim families, and especially of young people. In this sense, too, it takes two to tango.

Notes

1   So far this has yielded a Memorial Lecture for my ex-Sussex colleague and friend Bill Epstein, then an article for The Jewish Quarterly (de Kadt 2002). Parts of the present paper draw heavily on the latter, notably in sections 1, 2. and 4. I am grateful to friends and colleagues for critical comments on (earlier versions of) this paper – in particular to Louk de la Rive Box, Donal Cruise O'Brien, Jenny Goldschmidt, and Dirk Kruijt. Of course the responsibility for the views expressed remains entirely my own.
2   HTTP://CTI.ITC.VIRGINIA.EDU/~JKH8X/SOC257/NRMS/FUND.HTML
3   Even so, such a return to the 'original' text never has a determined outcome as it always involves reformulation and selection. Not everything is 'rediscovered': the texts are diverse enough to underpin many different views. But what the fundamentalists reassemble involves one particular set of 'readings' of those texts – those that are 'sterner' and more militant. It results in different fundamentalist groups from within the same tradition having different teachings. Nevertheless, each group sees its own teaching as the only 'correct' one (Caplan 1987a; Ayubi 1991).
4   He builds on the ground-breaking work of Peter Berger (1967; 1977).
5   Calculated on the basis of data given in NRC Profiel 17 december 1998, on NRC website: HTTP://WWW.NRC.NL/W2/LAB/PROFIEL/ISLAM/
6   Pinxten (1998) notes that he has three quite sensible central pieces of advice for Western policy-makers: (1) abstain from intervening in conflicts in other civilisations; (2) extend representation in the UN Security Council, especially to Islamic countries; (3) follow the rule to strengthen and extend what is *common* to all civilisations.
7   Dueñas (1998:110) aptly summarises the criticisms of Huntington as follows: (1) defining civilisations through their religions is confusing and incorrect; moreover, civilisations are much less homogeneous than Huntington suggests, and internal conflicts exist also over political, social and economic issues; (2) not all conflicts lead to violence/war: conflicts are often negotiable; (3) reality cannot be explained in purely cultural terms: other factors (economic, social) are also important; (4) Huntington's main objective is not analytical, but strategic: influencing U.S. foreign policy.
8   In some cases they have contented themselves with retreating from society. The ultra-orthodox Jews are a typical example. They do not offer alternatives to the established structures of state or economy, but retreat from "the world" into small communities. These survive by carv-

ing out a niche for themselves *in* that world (e.g. New York electronics business), or by being maintained through the support of people *from* that world.

9   Both Afghanistan under the Taliban and Iran under the current mixed regime, in which the mullahs continue to have great (veto) power, are convincing examples. One might even make a similar case for the New Christian Right in the USA. Their leaders were "co-opted" by the Republican Party, and they gave substantial electoral support to Ronald Reagan, and later to George W. Bush. They used their power where it existed – locally, in the "Bible-belt" – to promote the *religious* causes close to their heart. In national politics they basically promoted the interests of their main supporters in socio-economic terms, and had no views of their own. The other side of the coin is that whatever their rhetoric, neither Reagan nor Bush Jr. effectively implemented any of the fundamentalists' core demands (Bruce 1990).

10 The following four paragraphs draw substantially on my Inaugural Lecture at Utrecht University (de Kadt 1999)

11 Recall the genocidal horrors perpetrated in 1994 on the Tutsis by the Hutu militias in Rwanda: these followed years of increasingly antagonistic labelling of people in these ethnic terms. Since the genocide such labelling has not ceased: the post-genocide government has used the label *génocidaire* in ways quite similar to the previously used ethnic designations, implicitly justifying abuses and demonising large numbers of people. The official message became that for every (Tutsi) victim there was a (Hutu) killer – that meant that there must have been around a million *génocidaires*. (Wagner 1998)

12 As Dirk Kruijt pointed out to me, being (seen to be) part of a culturally "alien" underclass is particularly problematic for the second generation within immigrant communities, a problem made worse by the fact that their position is inherently ambiguous. Conversely, one could argue that it is precisely this ambiguity which makes it possible culturally to "move out," thereby grasping such opportunities as exist in the host society (Donal Cruise O'Brien - personal communication)

13 One might add that multiculturalism is, in fact, at times explicitly interpreted by persons from those "other" cultures, notably by Muslims, in terms of *verzuiling*. Sometimes this is even mentioned explicitly, as in an interview for the "profile" published in the NRC on 17 December 1998, in which Üzeyir Kabaktepe, a leader of the Turkish Islamic organisation Milli Gorus, ends his poignant account of how his small son is subjected to ridicule in school for following his Islamic beliefs, as follows: "Don't get me wrong: I don't complain about the Netherlands. If I compare how Muslims fare here and in Turkey, they're much better off here. But multiculturalism has to go together with *verzuiling*" (my translation) HTTP://WWW.NRC.NL/W2/LAB/PROFIEL/ISLAM.

14 For more detail, see de Kadt (2002)

15 A good example in the Netherlands would be the organisation Islam en Burgerschap (Islam and Citizenship), but there are many more. See, for example, on the Islam and Citizenship website, the condemnation of the threats by Muslims to a prominent Dutch (ex-)Islamic politician who changed her political allegiance *and* signified her intent to leave Islam, signed by almost 20 Islamic organisations in the Netherlands: HTTP://WWW.ISLAMENBURGERSCHAP.NL

16 I believe it was a similar perception by substantial numbers of Dutch voters which explains the origin of the 'phenomenon Pim Fortuyn'.

17 This point has also been made by Schulze (2002).

Bibliography

Ake, Claude, 1994, "A world of political ethnicity", in: BERG, Rob, van den, and Ulbe BOSMA, eds. *The Historical Dimension of Development, change and conflict in the South,* Min of Foreign Affairs, DVL/OS, Series Poverty and Development, Vol 9, The Hague.

Ayubi, Nazih N., 1991, *Political Islam. Religion and Politics in the Arab World,* London and New

York, Routledge.

Ba-Yunus, Ilyas, 2002, "Ideological dimensions of Islam. A critical paradigm", in: Donnan (ed) 2002

Berger, Peter, 1967, *The Sacred Canopy,* New York, Doubleday.

Berger, Peter, 1977, *Facing up to modernity: excursions in society, politics and religion,* Harmondsworth, Penguin.

Bruce, Steve, 1990, The Rise and Fall of the New Chistian Right. Conservative Protestant Politics in America 1978-1988, Oxford, Clarendon Press.

Caplan, Lionel, 1987a, 'Introduction', in: CAPLAN ed. 1987.

Caplan, Lionel ed. 1987, *Studies in Religious Fundamentalism,* Houndmills and London, Macmillan.

de Kadt, Emanuel, 1999, *'Back to Society and Culture: On aid donors' overblown concern with "governance" and "democratisation",* Inaugural lecture, University of Utrecht, Dept of Cultural Anthropology

de Kadt, Emanuel, 2002, "Fundamentalism, Religion, Identity", *The Jewish Quarterly,* Vol 49, No 3, Autumn, pp 51-57

de Ruijter, Arie, 2000, *De multiculturele Arena,* Tilburg, Katholieke Universiteit Brabant.

Donders, Yvonne M., 2002, *Towards a right to cultural identity?,* Antwerp (etc.), Intersentia.

Donnan, Hastings ed. 2002, *Interpreting Islam,* London, SAGE Publications.

Donnan, Hastings and Martin Stokes, 2002, "Interpreting Interpretations of Islam", in: Donnan ed. 2002.

Dueñas, Marc, 1998, "Over de botsing der beschavingen: Oorsprong, polemiek, balans", *Noord-Zuid Cahier,* Vol 23 Nr 1, pp 103-116

Gellner, Ernest, 1995, "Fundamentalism as a Comprehensive System: Soviet Marxism and Islamic Fundamentalism Compared", in: Marty and Appleby eds. 1995.

Heilman, Samuel C., 1995, "The Vision from the Madrasa and Bes Midrash: Some Parallels between Islam and Judaism", in: Marty and Appleby eds. 1995.

Heilman, Samuel C. and Menachem Friedman, 1991, "Religious Fundamentalism and Religious Jews: the Case of the Haredim", in Marty and Appleby eds. 1991.

Huntington, Samuel P., 1998, *The Clash of Civilizations and the Remaking of World Order,* Touchstone Books, London.

Hunter, James Davison, 1981, 'The New Religions: Demodernization and the Protest Against Modernity', in WILSON ed. 1981

Ingleby, David, 2000, *Psychologie en de multiculturele samenleving: Een gemiste aansluiting?,* Inaugural lecure Universiteit Utrecht, CERES, Utrecht.

Lawrence, Bruce B., 1989, *Defenders of God: The Fundamentalist Revolt against the Modern Age,* San Francisco, Harper and Row.

Lijphart, Arend, 1968, *The politics of accommodation; pluralism and democracy in the Netherlands,* Berkeley, University of California Press.

Marty, Martin E. and R. Scott Appleby eds. 1991, *Fundamentalisms Observed,* University of Chicago Press, Chicago and London.

Marty, Martin E. and R. Scott Appleby eds. 1995, *Fundamentalisms Comprehended,* Chicago and London, Univ of Chicago Press

Meyer, Thomas, 2001, *Identity Mania. Fundamentalism and the Politicization of Cultural Differences,* tr by Madhulika Reddy and Lew Hinchman, London and New York, Zed Books.

Milton-Edwards, Beverley, 2002, "Researching the radical. The quest for a new perspective", in: Donnan ed. 2002.

Modood, Tariq, 2002, "Muslims and the West. A Positive Asset for the West", *BSA Network,* British Sociological Association, January.

Mortimer, Edward, 1991, "Christianity and Islam", *International Affairs,* Vol 67, No 1, January, pp 7-13.

Pinxten, Rik, 1998, "Ontwikkeling en cultuurschok. Huntington over de botsing tussen beschavingen", *Noord-Zuid Cahier,* Vol 23, No 1, pp 9-20.

Pipes, Daniel, 1983, *In the Path of God. Islam and Political Power,* New York, Basic Books

Sardar, Ziauddin, 1996, "Beyond Development: An Islamic Perspective", *European Journal of Development Research,* Vol 8 No 2, December, pp 36-55.

Schulze, Kirsten E., "Militants and Moderates", *The World Today,* January, pp 10-13.

Sivan, Emmanuel, 1995, 'The Enclave Culture', in: Marty and Appleby eds. 1995.

Turner, Bryan S., 2002, "Orientalism, or the Politics of the Text", in: Donnan ed. 2002.

Verstraete, Ghislain, 1998, "Cultuur en conflict: een doos van Pandorra?", *Noord-Zuid Cahier,* Vol 23 Nr 1, pp 35-52

Webber, Jonathan, 1987, 'Rethinking Fundamentalism: the Readjustment of Jewish Society in the Modern World', in: Caplan, ed. 1987.

Wagner, Michele D., 1998, "All the Bourgmestre's Men: Making Sense of Genocide in Rwanda", in: Bernault, Florence and Thomas Spear, Guest Editors, Crisis in Central Africa: The History of Politics and the Politics of History, *Africa Today,* Vol 45 No 1.

Watt, William Montgomery, 1988, *Islamic Fundamentalism and Modernity,* London and NY, Routledge.

2

Sword or Plough, Arena or Field?
About the Management of Cultural Diversity

Lieteke van Vucht Tijssen

Introduction

Arie de Ruijter already thought of the title "Ideology as a Weapon" in the 1980s, when the social sciences were still fostering the romantic image of exotic people and cultures as a counterweight against what Max Weber called the *"kälte hände rationeller ordnungen"* ("cold hands of rational order"), of our own minority cultures as Archimedean points for the critics of the modern abstract society, and of culture as the exalted good that raises the individual above the daily bustle. He has never been able to depart from that theme ever since. Society is an arena in which culture is a strategic weapon, he still argued in 2000, in his inaugural lecture entitled *The Multicultural Arena,* at the University of Tilburg. And recently, at a UNESCO round table discussion on the common values between cultures, he remarked that he likes the search for it, but that he feels that in the end everything is about interests.

The article with the proposed title "Ideology as a Weapon," which we were going to write together, was never finished. But I would nevertheless like to take the opportunity once again to debate with him the meaning of "culture." My main question for him is whether the management of diversity in a multicultural society should indeed be limited to organisational aspects while excluding the search for common values as an effective means of holding a society together.

In the first section of this essay I will, with the help of lesser-known works of Max Weber, further radicalise the basic assumption of de Ruijter. In the second section I delve deeper into the organizing function of culture. In the third section I will discuss ideology as a weapon in (post)modern society. In the fourth and last section, I will make connections to the notion of management of diversity.

Divine allies and heavenly interests

Since Marx, innumerable analyses and comments have been devoted to the relationship between economic interests and culture, in which the legitimising and emancipating positions of culture are considered. Even Max Weber's cultural sociology can be largely read as a dialogue with Marx. Like Marx, Weber makes a distinction between "ideologies" and "cultures" that confirm the existing relations, and cultures that express the interest of a specific social class in the transformation of it. He also emphasizes that religions, ideologies, and cultures can have their roots in class interests. Unlike Marx, he argues that religions, ideologies, and cultures also have their own dynamics by

which they can release themselves from the interests of the class from which they originated.[1]

Weber's own theory assumes a "chemical marriage" *(Wahlverwandtschaft)*
between coinciding social developments, each of which have different roots that can
slow down or strengthen each other (van Vucht Tijssen 1985:85- 91). The best-known
and debated effect of this is shown in Weber's analysis of the relationship between the
Protestant ethics and the spirit of capitalism (Weber 1920:3-30). In the usual interpretations of Weber's work there is so much emphasis on that relationship that other aspects,
in the present context just as relevant for the analysis of the nature and the meaning of
cultures, have been pushed into the background.

With respect to earthly interests, besides the economical interests, power relations
play an important role in his work. Of course, in actual practice they are closely connected. For a good understanding of the development and the use of cultures, however, it is worthwhile to separate the various aspects in the course of analysis. In his sociological analysis of the origin of Judaism and Christianity, Weber makes a great
distinction between economical interests/relations and power relations. Weber believes
that the origin of Judaism can mainly be attributed to a power struggle, although the
struggle for life also played a part in that genesis.[2] In this article I would like to concentrate on the power aspect.

In his lesser-known (and in the world of religious sociologists very controversial)
study entitled *Der Wirtschaftsethik der Weltreligionen. Das antike Judentum (Economical Ethics of World Religions. Ancient Judaism),* Weber does not treat the Bible as simply a source of religious stories, religious enlightenment, and commandments, but as
an anthropological account of the congenial, economic, and political relations in
ancient Israel, in connection with the developing system of values and standards that
would eventually become Judaism. At the time of the rise of Judaism, Israel was a
hybrid of an urban, agricultural, and nomadic society. The numerous cities in the area
were surrounded by farms, and part-Bedouins, and semi-nomads who travelled from
place to place to graze their cattle. The power struggle between these tribes crystallized
when, during the dynasty of King Omri, these three sections of society become unified
under the rule of a central capital (Weber 1976:65). A crucial element in that struggle
and in the preceding struggle between the different groupings was the *berith:* the
covenant that symbolized the oath that the different tribes made with each other. The
legitimacy of this *berith*, however, rested on a greater covenant that superseded earthly interests: the covenant between the tribes of Israel and God (Yahweh). In this
alliance with a divine power lies the original essence of Judaism.

At the time that the covenant with Yahweh was made, Israel was still a polytheist
society. Yahweh was but one of the many gods that were worshipped by the ancient
Israelites. That they choose him, above all others, as their heavenly ally, was because
he was seen as a strong war god, with the power to bring them victory in their earthly wars. In exchange for his support in wars against their many enemies, the Israelites
promised not only to make offerings to Yahweh, but also to act according to what Yah-

weh deemed "good behaviour." Every victory was thus considered a reward for their good behaviour, yet at the same time every loss was considered the consequence of unfaithfulness to their covenant with Yahweh (Weber 1976:90-100).

Initially, these commandments and interdictions related particularly to food and sexuality. They applied particularly to the warriors preparing for war. But as the urban society in Israel began to dominate, and the Israelites exchanged their rustic weaponry of farm implements for more sophisticated arms like swords, spears, and chariots, the commandments and interdictions were generalized to all the people of Israel. The two tablets containing the Ten Commandments, which Moses brought down from Mount Sinai, exemplifies this generalization of God's commandments to all Israelites.

God's rewards for "good" behaviour came not only in the form of victory in battle, but also by way of other supernal rewards. Weber calls these *"Heilsgüter"* [goods of salvation] (Weber 1920:149,150), and were the good things that one could expect to receive in heaven, if he died having lived a virtuous and devout life.[3]

On the other hand, defeat in battle but also such adversities as natural disasters were regarded as punishments from Yahweh for disobedience to the holy commandments.[4] In short, Judaism and Christianity originated from the need to obtain power over one's enemies through a covenant with a powerful war god. In this sense, ideology and culture are literally transformed into a weapon against the enemy.

A second factor that plays an important role in Weber's analysis of the origin of Judaism, which is mentioned in his other works, was the need for charismatic leaders. By this Weber refers to ambitious people, often not members of the ruling elite, who with their ideology are able to mobilize downtrodden sections of the population against the ruling powers. Thus, Judaism developed in the context of tension between hereditary, urban rulers and ambitious individual from outside the city, who try to gain the powerful backing of the common people through the use of ideology[5] (Weber 1976:52-54, 88-89). In these circumstances, the dominant rulers are often depicted as corrupt or sinful (e.g. King Saul), while the charismatic challenger (e.g. David) is not only righteous but also blessed by God. As such, the covenant between God and the Faithful becomes a weapon in the hands of those who rebel against earthly, hereditary rule; and the charismatic leader appoints himself to lead those of the Faithful who are seeking to advance socially.[6]

Ideology and social order

The power of a chemical marriage between an ideology and a political and/or economically powerful social stratum lies in the symbolic legitimisation of the social order in which this power is embedded. As a consequence it seems to get a quasi-universal legitimacy. Ideologies confer a certain legitimacy, which the bearers of the ideology can always use.

In their book *De la Justification (The Justification)*, the French sociologists Boltanski and Thévenot analyse these kinds of ideologies and their components, concentrating on (Western) political ideologies. According to the authors, the foundation of these ideologies is the idea of "the society." They specify it with the word *"cité"*, which cannot be translated (Boltanski and Thévenot 1991:96). I will use the word "community," and besides the physical entity I will also mean "imagined communities" in the sense used of the cultural/ideological community, as used by Anderson (1983).

The common principle of the communities analysed by Boltanski and Thévenot is the idea that the community *(communauté humanitaire)* essentially includes all people. Furthermore, every system differentiates between two possible conditions for the members of the community: a higher and a lower condition. This difference is accompanied by a hierarchy of values and a formula for the investments (sacrifices) needed in order to reach "the rewards and the happiness" *(biens et bonheurs)* that belong to the highest condition. After all, every (cultural) community has an order of merit (grandeur) linked to the idea of a common interest *(le bien commun)*, and a "paradisiacal" condition *(l'éden)*. The thought of the common interest/good stands in contrast with egoistical pleasure. To reach the highest stage of merit and the paradisiacal condition, the individual has to sacrifice this pleasure for the sake of the welfare of the community (ibid.:96-101.) On the basis of these characteristics they make an ideal distinction between five *communities:* (1) the *inspired community,* (2) the *domestic community,* (3) the *civil community,* (4) the *community of public opinion,* and (5) the *industrial community*[7] (ibid.:106-157). In the scope of this article I will focus my examination particularly on the inspired, the industrial, and the civil communities.

The "inspired community" *(cité inspirée)* includes earthly existence and a supernal atmosphere. The differentiating principle is the idea of the supernal existence as the higher, and the earthly existence as the lower levels. The egoistical interests that have to be sacrificed in order to attain the highest form of happiness and the highest things for the community and for the individual are pre-eminently the worldly things. What Weber calls as *"heilsgüter"* ("goods of salvation") are, in this *"cité,"* pre-eminently the highest goods. The highest personality ideal is the saint, or the ascetic, who abandons these earthly goods and pleasures. Self-selected poverty is the highest merit (ibid.:106-116).

Directly opposite is the industrial community. It is pre-eminently of this world, and the contrast between a higher and a lower condition runs along the lines of poor and rich. The highest merit in this community is to generate income and welfare for the community as a whole. The most meritorious personalities are those who possess the ideas and the organizational skills necessary to reach this highest goal. The "little man with the little ideas" represents the lower condition. The personal investment someone has to make in order to reach the highest state of merit consists primarily of intellect, time, and money. The accompanying personality ideal is the wealthy, successful entrepreneur[8] (ibid.:150-157).

The third ideal type is that of the civil community. The distinguishing feature here is the feasibility of utilizing free will. Independence is therefore the highest stage, and subordination the lower. This applies both to the individual and to the community. The charismatic leader who gives voice to the struggle for independence, and who can connect that with an outlook on the nature and direction of a *"volonté general",* a kind of a public will, is the highest personality ideal in this community[9] (Boltanski and Thévenot 1991:137-150) The highest merits are for the people that do not abandon their individual will, but connect it authentically, of their own free will, to the *"volonté general."*

The range of these "ideological regulation systems" reaches beyond the human community. They affect the meaning given to living and to inanimate nature. In the world of the inspired community, nature is inhabited by mysterious supernatural powers, like good and bad spirits, demons etc., while that same reality in the industrial community consists primarily of natural resources, energy sources, and other means of production (think of horsepower). In the domestic community, which we have not discussed here, animals, for example, can become pets, and as such, true members of community. In this *"cité"* children and seniors are given a place too, which is not the case in other community models[10] (Boltanski and Thévenot 1991:116-126).

Boltanski and Thévenot show that the "parameters" of different communities are constantly utilized when events are legitimised and made acceptable by them, in particular the case of when it is a matter of the disruption of what is considered "normal" in the prevailing community ideal (ibid.:48-53).

It is tempting to see the ideal types of Boltanski and Thévenot especially as historical types that succeeded each other in time, even if it were only because the idea of the inspired community was, in time, defeated by the industrial community as the dominant ideology.[11] In the Netherlands, just like in many other parts of the world, we now have to deal with the dominance of the community of public opinion. Actually, the different community cultures and the inherent ideals are still present in western society. The inspired community is still the dominant ideal for many religious people. But also artists, who understand beauty as a higher principle, scientists, who assume that truth is the highest good, or people who are looking for new spirituality, strive for this kind of community ideal – implicitly or explicitly.

Ideology as a weapon in (post) modern society

Our modern society is characterized by a plurality of community ideals, with basic principles, highest goals, and personality ideals that often are at odds with each other. This differentiation and this plurality of worldviews, especially, can drive groups or categories to start a battle using their own ideology as a weapon for elevating or imposing their worldview as the dominant one. That is the cradle of many fundamentalist movements, not only within Islam but also within Christianity.

In the tradition of Weber, three contemporary sociologists, Lechner, Arjomand and Kupferschmidt, have done some research into the nature and origins of religious fundamentalism in western society. Each of them connects the rise of fundamentalist movements in the twentieth century with the modernization and differentiation of culture, not only the Euro-American society, but also in Arabic society. Lechner defines fundamentalism as a form of "undifferentiated values pointed toward the reconstruction of society" (Lechner1995b:95-96). According to him, the quest of fundamentalists is to restore certain principles that are considered fundamental and sacred in society as a whole.

Processes of modernization put into perspective the religious and ideological cosmologies from which many people derive their feelings of identity, meaning, fellowship and security. Instead of that, they give people a combination of abstract and relative non-committal values and standards. (Zijderveld, 1970) The accompanying identity gravitates towards subjectivity and is therefore extra vulnerable. The search for fundamental values can be considered as a reaction and a counterbalance to the harmful effects of existing values and standards, and for some people the "unbearable lightness of being" that modern society has replaced it with. An example of this is the so-called "Moral Majority" in the United States. (Lechner 1995b)

Arjomand is preoccupied with the phenomenon of the multicultural society and its connection with expanding Muslim fundamentalism, particularly in the wake of September 11. As one of the main causes for the rise of these fundamentalist movements, Arjomand considers a process that he calls the *disruption of moral standards*. In contrast to anomy, which Durkheim defines as a complete lack of moral standards, the disruption of moral standards is a matter of an existing set of identity and morality standards and values being threatened by a new set. Normative disruption results from the tensions created by an antagonistic placement of these contending complexes of values and standards next to each another (ibid.) In other words, it is a matter of struggle for dominance between two cultures. This struggle occurs in the western and the Arabic countries that modernized rapidly since the 1950s. When the bearers of this process, the local elite, implicitly or explicitly raise for discussion the plausibility and effectiveness of the established religious convictions, and if the "common" man and woman cannot keep up with the pace and consider the process strange and external, a feeling of disruption of moral standards is quickly created (ibid.:31).

Fundamentalist movements do not spring up everywhere that a confrontation occurs between modernization processes and traditional patterns. In the Islamic world the reactions vary from adjusted Islamic modernism via an orthodox and politicised fundamentalism, to a rigid traditionalism that rejects all modernization (ibid.). But where fundamentalist movements do rise, the orthodox interpretations of the Islam are almost always used as a weapon in the hands of the rising elite looking for power and a constituency.

What do these potential charismatic leaders look like, according to Arjomand? In the last decades of the twentieth century, the ever-broadening accessibility of higher education in Arabic countries drew new generations of youth from the smaller cities and the countryside to the urban universities. And just like in Europe in the 1960s and the 1970s, the public space that grew around the universities was strongly politicised by these new intelligentsia. In Islamic countries, that politicisation process was essentially channelled into an Islamic activism led by young intellectuals (ibid.:31, 32).

Who are those intellectuals? Where do they come from, and what drives them on? Their origin is rather hybrid. On the one hand they are recruited from the new categories of youth who are the first in their families to go to university. On the other hand, they come from groups and social sections of society that feel threatened by the industrialization and modernization of their country. Their choice for Islamic activism is inspired by a search for that which the abstract values and standards of modern society do not offer – "authenticity." This they try to find in the written fundamentals of Islam.[12] As Arjomand observes, "here the search for authenticity takes the form of the search for the fundamentals of Islam and all later and foreign accretions are seen as corrupting" (ibid.33).

In his essay entitled "The Muslim Brotherhood and its Ramifications," Kupferschmidt adds another dimension to Arjomand's observations. He shows that the most fundamentalist intellectuals have studied modern subjects like science, medicine, or engineering, and not the "classical" subjects like arts or law. He concludes that they have strong ambitions to get ahead in society, and at the same time to signify the promise of a modern future for Arabic countries. A political activist movement of fundamentalist persuasion, which at the same time is a choice against modern political movements like liberalism and socialism (and Arjomand also mentions nationalism), exemplified by the *Muslim Brotherhood* in Egypt, gives them pre-eminently the platform for that, especially when other paths to power are blocked (Kupferschmidt 1995:57). Therefore, we are talking here about a paradoxical movement. Although fundamentalist movements manifest themselves as "de-modernisation movements," the *social and cultural factors* that have contributed to their rise are intrinsic to the same modernization processes to which they resist. Urbanization is one such factor. Islamic fundamentalism is not a rural movement, but pre-eminently an urban phenomenon. The cities, with their mosques, Koran schools, and other centres for religious education become important centres for religious vitality movements, particularly in times of rapid urban growth; religious activity also increases. Simultaneously, a rapid social and economical expansion in those cities usually leads to forms of normative disturbance that can become a breeding ground for fundamentalist disturbance.

In other words, contemporary Islamic fundamentalist movements have been established by a "chemical marriage" between young ambitious Muslim intellectuals and a social class that turns against the dominant powers and their culture, which is similar to the one between the charismatic leaders that were at the root of Judaism and their constituency. In both cases, strong ideology seems to be a powerful weapon.[13]

The search for common values and the management of diversity

The favourite metaphor of de Ruijter is society as an arena in which the contending parties each battle for honour and victory. An ideology as a weapon can be very useful in such an arena. Against the background of Weber's analysis of the origins of Judaism, the arena is a moderate metaphor. In an arena a life-and-death battle can be fought, but an arena also presupposes a physical boundary of the battle, a limited number of participants and an element of sports and games. In addition, the warring parties do not strive primarily for the grace of a strong god, but for that of the crowd. If we interpret ideology and culture as that which legitimises the behaviour of people, as Boltanski and Thévenot do, then we must ask what makes ideology a sharper weapon: the grace of and the covenant with a strong god, or the assent of the public.[14]

In our society, the industrial and civil communities have become superseded, as the carriers of standards and values, the religious institutes that support it. Nevertheless, or perhaps just because of it, the approval and the grace of a divine power, and the heavenly rewards it promises to bestow to the faithful, still play an important role for many people. The inspired "cité" is for them as alive as for the people at the beginning of Judaism.

The contrasts between the different parameters that are the foundation of the different world views in modern society, added to the rise of fundamentalist movements with Christian and Islamic origin, seem to confirm the position of de Ruijter that social cohesion cannot be established by the means of culture, and that integration is not the way to do it (de Ruijter 2000:32). In his inaugural lecture in Tilburg, de Ruijter uses the following argument to elucidate this thesis:

> This point of view starts with the recognition that we are all submitted to many continuously changing cultural spheres and orientations. Between them there is no longer a systematic and consistent relation, there is no unequivocal relation. More than ever it is evident that not a single cultural situation is homogeneous…. As a consequence, culture is more than ever in motion; a culture is partly inconsistent and incoherent, it is unequally divided over differently positioned persons, and culture does not succeed in providing uniform recipes for action (ibid.:31-32).

He concludes therefore that a multicultural and multi-ethnic society has to limit itself to the organisation of diversity by means of concrete interactions, and that we should entertain illusions about common values as bridges between cultures. In this "coordination vision," it is all about reconcilability of notions and practices (ibid.:31).

For de Ruijter, the way to control the battle between cultures in which ideology is indeed the main weapon – as Huntington forecasts in his book *The Clash of Civilisations* – is bringing it within the walls of the multicultural arena, where it can coordinate the actions of people without attempting to find common denominators for them. At first sight, a good example of a successful strategy is the system of religious and socio-political "pillars," that was characteristic of Dutch society until the beginning of the 1960s. What de Ruijter proposes, seems indeed to be a typical Dutch solution.

At present, the question of how to deal with religious and cultural diversity is once again high on the agenda of Dutch society and politics. It refers in particular to ways of dealing with the Islamic communities in our country. Without a doubt, with many first generation Muslim immigrants, there has been a disruption of moral standards à la Arjomand. Having mainly come from a traditional, religious, rural society, many of these people could not feel at home and could not develop their own identity in the modern, urban society of the Netherlands. It is not surprising that they sought footing and communality in a strict preservation of their original worldview.[15] Apart from that, the Dutch government's policy on culture assumed that these first generation immigrants would return to their lands of origin, and has therefore concentrated for years on preserving the original culture of these people. Also reinforcing this process of "un-integration" was the romantic movement in sociology and anthropology that wanted to leave intact the original culture of immigrant groups and societies.

But the segregation of these categories, and the enforced preservation of their cultures, is not an answer. For many, returning to the country of origin was not an option. Furthermore, the process of family reunification that permitted second and third generation immigrants to bring over their partners from their countries of origin, the urgent question that arises is how are we going to deal with this in the Netherlands. This problem is exacerbated by the globalisation of fundamentalist Islam.

Is de Ruijter's answer to these developments adequate? Is integration out of the question? Is it indeed not worthwhile to look for common values? And is coordination as a form of pacification the only option? Without a doubt, de Ruijter earns praise for his attempt to emphasize the difficulties that the idea of the search for common values and the quest for integration can bring.

As I have shown earlier in this article, Lechner and Arjomand point out that many people (and in particular those who have moved from a rural to an urban environment) experience the abstract and differentiated character of our society as a normative disorder. The result has been an antagonistic juxtaposition of rival or competing complexes of values and norms, and all the tension that this brings. As already argued, many individuals in this position react with a quest for the "de-differentiation" of our modern culture. As such, differences between various cultures will widen as new and ascendant social categories, in search of power, enter the chemical marriage.

The analytical tools of Boltanski and Thévenot can help us see what may happen. When the ideology of the inspired community is used as a weapon, and a power struggle arises around the question of what the highest ideals are, and who has the right to (supernal) rewards, and when that power struggle by charismatic personalities is utilized to mobilize and empower a group that feels discriminated against (see Weber), the differences will be heavily emphasized and exploited.

Boltanski and Thévenot also show that personal identities are firmly anchored in the hierarchy of the values of a community, and the accompanying personality ideals. De Ruijter also rightly emphasizes the relationship between the identity of people, and the society and culture they come from (de Ruijter 2000:18-20). Identities are socially and culturally anchored, and are at the same time deeply rooted in the individual; we cannot change them with the snap of our fingers. To de Ruijter this again is a strong basis on which to plead for the management of diversity without striving for common values. And this is exactly what is happening with the Islamic fundamentalist movements. Another good example of such an approach, which leads to an expansion instead of a reduction of the gap between Islam and the autochthonous culture, in which cultural instead of religious radicalism plays an important role, is the Flemish-Moroccan leader Jallah and his Arab-Euro Liga. When these kinds of movements emerge, the search for bridging principles is in vain. De Ruijter's coordination approach then seems to be the most sensible solution.

Nevertheless, that does not mean that I fully support the conclusions of de Ruijter. That his theory seems to apply in this kind of polarised situations does not mean that it also is the best way of proceeding for society as a whole. Besides, as the analytical approaches of Boltanski and Thévenot and Max Weber show, more can be said of culture as such, and of the relation between culture and interests, than de Ruijter does.

Let us now discuss these theoretical aspects. De Ruijter characterizes culture as "a complex of vague multi-interpretable and interrelated complexes of notions and practices that people have in common" (2000:31). He thus ignores the meaning of culture, and the regulating principles that we find in each culture, in the everyday lives of people. Besides, all cultures are rooted in the everyday thinking and actions of people. Cultures, rules, and principles make these actions predictable and controllable. Culture thus provides the means for people to coordinate their actions. But that is not all; in everyday life the common ways of doing and thinking also are maintained, transferred, and legitimated. In is precisely in that process that the parameters identified by Boltanski and Thévenot play an important role. From this point of view, the cultural complexity that de Ruijter identifies in modern society is not so much a colourful kaleidoscope of arbitrary elements derived from different contexts, but a complex of juxtaposed, intertwined "imagined communities," which often hold opposing ideas about the nature of the community, and the highest goods and awards to be achieved for the communities as well as for their members, the ideal personality, and the hierarchy of values.

Apart from this, de Ruijter (together with many sociologists and anthropologists) seems to make a rather radical distinction between cultures and interests, and as a consequence also between cultures and structures. Max Weber, on the other hand, shows how the interests of a community can give rise to and promote the development of values and norms, which in turn give shape to the actions of people, and in time can also come to exist separately from the context in which they developed.

I will illustrate the usefulness of the tools of Boltanski and Thévenot also with the help of a more recent empirical example. The application of the analytical types of Boltanski and Thévenot to the Dutch system of religious and socio-political pillars makes it clear that the Dutch system was not only based on the organisation of disparate pillars, it was also held together through coordination between the leaders of the separate pillars. In fact, there also existed a number of bridges between the various communities in the form of common values. (See the essay of Henk van Rinsum in this volume – editors' note.) Only, these originated not from the inspired communities as such, but from another type of community: namely, the civil one and its parameters.

The parameters of this worldly community were, as it were, used to protect the values of the inspired ones, and thus to prevent them from clashing in the worldly life.[16] "Sovereignty in the proper community " is the Protestant version of this, and the "principle of subsidiarity" (meaning that the upper government only has to do what the lower government cannot take care of) is the Catholic version. These principles are very similar. Both guarantee a spiritual and – if it is not in conflict with the values of the civil community – a worldly autonomy for the different religious and socio-political groups. At the same time, both principles prevent an ideological battle between different religious groups about the question of what is the highest good and the most paradisiacal condition in a worldly context. They regulate, as it were, only the earthly matters, without interfering with possible higher spheres of thought, and any goods of salvation that can be obtained therefrom. According to the parameters of the civil community, the leaders of the different religious and socio-political groups can be mutually accepted as the most creditable on earth, and as such also as the most authoritative. The fundamentals of the civil community will knock off the rough edges of the various worldviews, thus preventing them from being used as a weapon in a political arena, or even on a genuine battlefield; that is to say, from becoming real theocracies.

That the parameters of the civil community can bridge the two versions of the inspired community has not only to do with the nature of these parameters, in which the free will of every person plays an important role. It is also about the important role played by the nature of the parameters of the inspired community itself. Indeed, the spiritual values form the highest stage of the hierarchy, and the ascetic saint is the highest ideal of personality. Yet caring for the earth and every living thing on it also belongs to the domain of the common good. That is expressed in the principle of stewardship. Supposedly, in that principle lies the anchor, or to put it in modern terms, the *interface* between the inspired community and the civil community, whereby the latter can fulfil a bridging function.

It is not the first time in history that a successful entwining of "imagined communities" has occurred that prevents an irreconcilable battle between different communities. As Weber has shown, Protestant ethics have been able to reconcile the principles of the inspired community with those of the capitalistic economy. The cause was the idea of an "Innerweltliche Askese" [an inner worldly ascesis] that entailed a democratisation of "sacredness" as a personality ideal. It was not the people who turned their backs on the world, but the people that made an effort in daily life and produced results with their work that comply with the standards, and will eventually be chosen. Contrary to the arguments of de Ruijter, it indeed seems possible to bridge gaps between cultures and their supporting communities by means of mutually supporting (or even common) values, so long as there is a third one involved that can help link them together.

It is worth the effort to see whether this also would be possible in our present society. As a consequence of our earlier arguments, it would not make much sense to look for bridges at the level of the core values and goods of the different "imagined communities." Following Max Weber, it would instead be more interesting and fruitful to look for bridges at the level of the everyday interests of people. It would be more interesting to look for the possibility to develop common day-to-day values among people of different cultural backgrounds, starting from those interests. Again, the values of civil community can play an important role in that process.

Authoritative Dutch-Moroccan and Dutch-Turkish worldly leaders, like Ahmed Aboutaleb, Mohammed Sini, or Zeki Arslan appeal to these types of values when they plead for an active participation of their people in the surrounding worldly community. We indeed have good examples of how an appeal to daily interests can help us find common values that can help to bridge the imminent gap between the various sections of Dutch society.

The government also can play a role in marking and maintaining the central values of civil society, in a legal and a moral sense. Individual freedom, combined with responsibility for the society, are crucial elements in that. In addition to the initiatives of these civilians, the government can also contribute to the reinforcement of values and standards that bridge cultural differences. An important element in civil society, in addition to individual freedom, is the responsibility that every citizen has for the own society and its accompanying public spaces. In the last decades, that principle has been bogged down in the Netherlands, and should once again receive attention through politics and education. At a local level, this can be worked for through broadly based society schools, with the participation of the parents. Finally, the Dutch religious and socio-political pillars can serve as a handle to provide our multicultural society with bridgeheads – but not as Zijderveld proposed, by organizing an Islamic religious and socio-political pillar. Elsewhere I have shown that "pillarization" does not work in our society anymore, where religious and socio-political barriers have largely been removed (van Vucht Tijssen 2002).

What can help is the restriction of the different "imagined communities" and the accompanying values to the sphere of personal privacy, where they belong. Thanks to the religious and socio-political pillars, the inspired religious community in the Netherlands has become largely something private, and has a limited position as a public issue. Just think of the debate about the prayer at the end of the speech from the throne. The public space and the public atmosphere are regulated by the values of the civil society. That means, for example, that only modest religious symbols, like headscarves or chains with a cross, can be worn in public spaces. Chadors and other conspicuous signs of religion do not belong there.

In his analysis, de Ruijter emphasizes the importance of the coordination of practices in an arena in which people fight for their own interests. In a period which until recently was dominated by a quite rosy view on cultural diversity, his is a refreshing perspective. Besides, it shows an adequate way in which to deal which religious radicalism in modern society. Nevertheless, it is a pity that he develops this idea mainly on the basis of a limited conception of culture and its meaning. Furthermore, he does not elaborate very much on the idea of the organisation and coordination in a multicultural and multi-ethnic society as such.

In contrast to the argument of de Ruijter, it can be held that social cohesion not only results from the coordination of practices, but also comes about because people are part of various communities, each with shared interests and shared parameters about what is important and what is not. In order to keep religious fundamentalism within limits, and to support the integration of less extreme believers in society, we need, apart from a good organization and coordination, a strong and shared civil society.

De Ruijter is right, of course, when he shows that we live in a globalising world. Therefore, it is important to disengage the idea of a civil society from that of the nation-state, and instead develop a vision based on citizenship and the civic community in a global world. As a member of the Dutch National Commission to UNESCO, chairperson of the working group for the Sciences, and a member of the Scientific Steering Committee of UNESCO programme for the Social Sciences MOST, de Ruijter is in a perfect position to influence these necessary changes.

I think that the challenging ideas of de Ruijter will still gain in depth and theoretical sharpness if he would also take into account the analytical and empirical approaches both of Max Weber and of Boltanski and Thévenot. Then he would probably agree with me that the sword of ideology as a weapon in the arena of society, can also become a plough that helps to cultivate the land in order to stimulate a peaceful coexistence between different *"cités"* or "imagined communities".

Notes

1 A nice illustration of Weber's position is the popularity of socialism in the Netherlands since World War II, while the classic working class (that should function as its bearers), and the accompanying class differences almost completely disappear in the case of the Netherlands.

2 Both can be in line, but as the modern power struggles show, they can also originate from the pursuit of safety and/or dominance.

3 Just like Judaism and Christianity, Islam also promises goods of salvation. According to radical interpretations of Islam, access to paradise for all family members is the reward for suicide bombers and those who fall in jihad.

4 It is a fascinating question why Judaism did not developing as a religion in which the deity was not simply satisfied with sacrifices, but also demanded prescribed forms of behaviour. According to Weber, the cause of that lies in the secular character of the monarchy in ancient Israel. It is also important to note that divine punishments after death can also take on a supernal character, as in eternal condemnation to hell.

5 According to Weber, there is only one other religion that finds its roots in a covenant with an omnipotent God, which inspires the emergence of charismatic persons – Islam. (Weber 1976:88)

6 Weber's analysis of the political and economical roots of Judaism and Christianity was received with criticism by his contemporaries. But despite the criticisms, it is obvious that Weber's description of the social-political situation during the development of Judaism strongly resembles the political situation of Germany during Weber's lifetime. In the second half of the nine-

teenth century, the political power in Germany and Austria was still in the hands of the aristocracy and a business class that quickly lost its economic power, while the rising economical class of new industrialists was excluded from powerful positions in the machinery of government. In his famous novel *Buddenbrooks*, Thomas Mann describes these relations tersely.

7   In another book, *"Le Nouvel Esprit du Capitalisme"* [The New Spirit of Capitalism], Boltanski and Chapello argue that a new community ideal is developing, based on the idea that the community is a network and that the process manager is the highest personality ideal.

8   Community of Science

9   Boltanski and Thévenot take the idea from Rousseau that the free will consists of three conditions: the individual free will, the *volonté general* (that which the community wants), and an administrative will.

10 Although they hardly refer to Max Weber, their ideas are in line with Weber's analysis of the development of Judaism and Christianity and the processes that play a role with that. With their model they also supply an armamentarium to profoundly analyze these kinds of processes.

11 Weber's contemporary Max Scheler spoke in this context about an "Umsturz der Werte" [Upset of Values].

12 There is for that matter an interesting parallel with the search by some of the European intelligentsia. Also, the Sartrian existentialism of the fifties meets the need for authenticity, just like the psychoanalytical movement that was inspired by psychiatrists like Fromm.

13 In a recent article in *The New Yorker,* which was reproduced with the title *Ayman Al-Zawahiri, le stratège d'Al Qaida* in the French publication *Le Courier International,* the journalist Lawrence Wright shows that the leaders of Al Qaida perfectly fit the image that was outlined by Arjomand *(Le Courier International,* dec. 2003 p. 30-37.)

14 Contrary to Weber, Durkheim gives the community a crucial role as the origin and bearer of religion.

15 Sociologically speaking, this is not a new phenomenon. It was also detected in the Protestant enclaves of Catholic Brabant, or in the Catholic enclaves of Groningen.

16 Socialism also is a form of inspired community.

Bibliography

Anderson, B. 1983. *Imagined Communities, Reflections on the origin and spread of Nationalism.* London: Verso.

Arjomand, S. A. 1995. The Search for Fundamentals and Islamic Fundamentalism. In B.E. van Vucht Tijssen, F. Lechner and J. Berting, eds., *The Search for Fundmentals, The Process of Modernisation and the Quest for Meaning,* pp.27-41. Deventer: Kluwer.

Boltanski, L., and L.Thévenot. 1991. *De la Justification. Les économies de la grandeur.* Parijs: Gallimard.

de Ruijter, A. 2000. *De Multiculturele Arena.* Oratie Faculteit Sociale Wetenschappen. Tilburg: Katholieke Universiteit Brabant.

Huntington, S.P. 1998. *The Clash of Civilisations and the Remaking of the World Order.* New York: Simon and Schuster.

Kupferschmidt, U. 1995. Modernisation and Islamic Fundamentalism: The Muslim Brotherhood and its Ramifications. In B.E. van Vucht Tijssen, F. Lechner and J. Berting, eds., *The Search for Fundmentals, The Process of Modernisation and the Quest for Meaning,* pp.41- 62. Deventer: Kluwer.

Lechner, F. 1995a. Introduction Part II. Religion and the Search for Fundamentals. In B.E. van Vucht Tijssen, F. Lechner and J. Berting, eds., *The Search for Fundmentals, The Process of Modernisation and the Quest for Meaning,* pp.25-27. Deventer: Kluwer.

Lechner, F. 1995b. Fundamentalism: Origins and Influence. In B.E. van Vucht Tijssen, F. Lechner and J. Berting, eds., *The Search for Fundmentals, The Process of Modernisation and the Quest for Meaning*, pp.95-113. Deventer: Kluwer.

Scheler, Max. 1915. *Vom Umsturz der Werte*. Ges Werke Bd. 3,hrsg. Maria Scheler.Bern/München: Francke Verlag.

van de Braak, Hans, and Ton Bevers, eds. 2002. *De waarde van instituties, Essays voor Anton Zijderveld*, pp.256-282. Amsterdam:Amsterdam University Press.

van Vucht Tijssen, B.E. 1985. *Uit de ban van de rede, Een confrontatie tussen de cultuur-en kennissociologische visies van Max Scheler en Max Weber*. Utrecht: ICAU mededelingen no. 22. Duitse editie: *Auf dem Weg sur Relativierung der Vernunft. Eine vergleichenden Rekonstruktion der kultur-und wissensoziologischen Auffassungen Max Schelers und Max Webers*. Berlijn: Duncker and Humblot 1989. Vert: Sibylle Sänger.

van Vucht Tijssen, B.E., F. Lechner, and J. Berting, eds. 1995. *The Search for Fundmentals, The Process of Modernisation and the Quest for Meaning*. Deventer: Kluwer.

Vermeulen, H., and R. Penninx, eds. 2000. *Immigrant Integration, The Dutch case*. Amsterdam: Het Spinhuis.

— 2002. Institutionalisering, modernisering en het zoeken naar laatste waarden. In Hans van de Braak and Ton Bevers, eds., *De waarde van instituties, Essays voor Anton Zijderveld*, pp.256-282. Amsterdam:Amsterdam University Press.

Weber, M. 1920. *Die protestantische Ethik und der Geist des Kapitalismus. In Gesammelte Aufsätze zur Religionssoziologie dl I*, pp.17-206. Tübingen: Mohr.

Weber, M. 1920b. *Die Wirtschaftsethik der Weltreligionen. in:Gesammelte Aufsätze zur Religionssoziologie dl I*, pp.237-275. Tübingen: Mohr.

Weber, M. 1920c. *Zwischenbetrachtung, Theorie der Stufen und Richtungen Religiöser Weltablehnung. In Gesammelte Aufsätze zur Religionssoziologie*, pp.536-573. Tübingen: Mohr.

Weber, M. 1976. *Gesammelte Aufsätze zur Religionssoziologie dl III Das antike Judentum*. Tübingen: Mohr, 1920.

Zijderveld, A.C. 1966. *Institutionalisering. Een studie over het methodologisch dilemma der sociale wetenschappen*. Hilversum/Antwerpen: Paul Brand.

Zijderveld, A.C. 1970. *De abstracte samenleving. Een cultuurkritische studie van onze tijd*. Meppel:Boom.

3

Co-ordination of Diversity,
Politics of Accommodation in a New Guise?[1]

Henk J. van Rinsum

In 1997 I worked at the International Office of Utrecht University. In that year the so-called SANPAD-programme was launched. This programme tries to facilitate collaboration between South African and Dutch institutions of higher education. Utrecht University wanted to inform her partners in South Africa to the best of its abilities of the potential of this programme. I then thought that this would offer an excellent opportunity to invite Arie de Ruijter, my academic mentor for many years, on a trip to our main partner at that time, the University of the Western Cape. The Director of the Centre for Southern African Studies of that university, Professor Peter Vale, invited Arie to give a public lecture on *Multiculturalism* at his institute – a subject that was heatedly debated in South African society, long before it became a topic in Dutch politics.

At first, the inner circle of Arie's colleagues was sceptical about the chance that Arie would accept this invitation, as Arie was not known to be a frequent traveller. But he did. For me personally (and I think also for Arie), this trip was a memorable one. During this visit we made a trip to some of the large townships surrounding Cape Town, including Cross Roads en Kayelitsha. Arie was deeply moved and upset by the poverty and distress that he saw with his own eyes. When we returned to our hotel, he told me that this trip was an overwhelming, almost existential, experience that he would not easily forget.

Arie did give his public lecture. The Centre for Southern African Studies published the text of this lecture under the telling title *Multiculturalism, still muddling through?* And indeed, "mud" we saw.

Introduction

In this article I intend to formulate, in very preliminary terms, a critique of a concept that lies at the heart of Arie de Ruijter's theoretical thinking on modern European[2] (i.e. the multicultural) society: the concept of coordination of diversity. My critique of this model essentially relates to the fact that, in my opinion, power, inequality (and the intricate relationship between these two dimensions) seem to be downplayed, at least implicitly. My aim is to articulate this critique by taking the reader, via the Dutch society of the fifties and sixties, to contemporary South Africa, as I took Arie de Ruijter to South Africa.

After presenting a summary of Arie de Ruijter's publications on coordination of diversity, I will elaborate on the politics of accommodation as formulated first and foremost by Arend Lijphart. In a way, this model of accommodation seems to equal the coordination-of-diversity model. Lijphart will then take us to South Africa. But despite Lijphart's efforts and wishful thinking, it is precisely South Africa that offers a case where the politics of accommodation did not and could not work. In turn, this brings me back to my critique of the coordination model of Arie de Ruijter.

Coordination of diversity

In de Ruijter's recent publications[3] the concepts of "co-ordination" (of diversity in society) and of "arena" (being the metaphor of our society) take a prominent position. These concepts are part of his lifelong academic search for a theory of culture.

De Ruijter admits that the two concepts are ambiguously positioned against each other. According to de Ruijter, society is not so much a marketplace as an arena where actors and institutions cooperate *and* simultaneously compete in changing coalitions in order to satisfy their needs. The arena oscillates between antagonism and cooperation. There is, of course, not just one arena: reality is constructed at many levels and according to many interconnected arenas (de Ruijter 2001:13). The growth of the modern multicultural society in Europe can be seen as local arenas, which are increasingly being inserted in, and influenced by, global arena's.

One way of dealing with multiculturalisation (not as a result but as a continuous process) is the concept of "integration." De Ruijter points at the deficit of the integration-model – a model that was seen (and still is) in Dutch politics by the government and political parties as the suitable model for serving as a necessary ideological-moral base for a modern European multicultural society.[4] The integration-model assumes that a plural society can only function if there is a certain consensus, a certain level of shared norms and values, which unites people from different cultural backgrounds.[5] De Ruijter claims that this integration-model does not work because of an increasing cultural pluralism and individualisation. De Ruijter even goes one step further and argues that integration is not even needed to tie a society together. Cognitive and normative diversity is, and has been, more the rule than the exception, even in the so-called "primitive" societies. This brings him to a definition of culture as an instrument to organise diversity: *culture* being an information-processing mechanism that functions in and through practices; culture as the framework for managing diversity. In this respect a "multicultural" society is not a recently developing phenomenon. However, what is recent is the problematisation of the growth of a multicultural society in the Western hemisphere.

People, also in plural societies, only need to interact in practices *("handelings-praktijken")*. The rules underlying these practices are not fixed, but instead are constantly developing at different levels. In their interactions, people are constantly creating new rules, and changing or adapting existing ones. The practices are, of course, embedded in social relationships that are constituents of the identity of people. Not a fixed identity, but rather a composite of fragmented and sometimes conflicting cultural orientations. People construct their own identities, and those of others. This construction of identity always develops in a context of power. Arie de Ruijter explicitly refers in this respect to Foucault and Bourdieu (de Ruijter 2001: 9). The power of definition, resulting in division and in processes of inclusion and exclusion, is essential (see, for example, van Rinsum 2001). This power is multi-faceted and operates at different levels. De Ruijter stresses that power is almost never hegemonic (de Ruijter 1994: 33). Indeed, the marginalized do have instruments of opposition, or in James Scott's words, there also exist "weapons of the poor."

These theoretical reflections bring de Ruijter to what he calls the "coordination-model" as an alternative to the integration concept. *"Er is slechts verenigbaarheid nodig, niet gemeenschappelijkheid van culturen en leefstijlen. Deze verenigbaarheid is niet vooraf gegeven, die moet ontstaan uit handelingspraktijken"* (de Ruijter 1994)[6]. In this respect he refers to *Culture and Personality* of Anthony F.C. Wallace, who had already written as early as 1961 about the *organization of diversity* as opposed to what he labelled *the replication of uniformity.*

The integration-model and the coordination-model do have, according to de Ruijter, one thing in common. That is, if principles, norms, values etc. are *incompatible*, then a system of groups of people and organizations will fail to materialise or to endure.

Incompatibility is of course not the same as inequality. De Ruijter does mention the dimension of inequality when he talks about the *"materiële ongelijkheid, een indringende dagelijks ervaren werkelijkheid voor verschillende geledingen en etnische groepen in onze samenleving...."* (de Ruijter 1994).[7] In another work (de Ruijter 2001), he points at the development of a societal dichotomy that results in the concentration of larger groups of materially deprived people in the major cities in the Netherlands. According to de Ruijter a certain level of economic participation of the members of the plural society is essential in order to enable them to enter the necessary practices. He does stress the element of inequality in his contribution to the book *Globalization and Development Studies,* but one wonders whether this emphasis was "induced" by the development discourse that features prominently in that book. What is telling is that de Ruijter ends the inaugural address he delivered at Tilburg University in 2000 – which can be seen as the synopsis of his publications – with a strong plea for the coordination-concept. In this view, culture is then the instrument to organise diversity. And this coordination of diversity is materialised through practices.

The consociational model of Lijphart

I argue that the management of diversity model found a rather idiosyncratic representation in so-called "verzuilde samenleving" (pillarised society), which characterized Dutch society until the end of the 1960s. Dutch society was divided into culturally different segments, i.e. the catholic, protestant, social democratic, and liberal pillar. The main vertical lines of segregation between the pillars were drawn by the dominant worldview held by the members of each pillar. The Dutch political scientist Arend Lijphart wrote his famous book about this phenomenon of "pillarization," *The Politics of Accommodation: Pluralism and Democracy in the Netherlands* (1968). He noted that

Dutch society was also characterised by horizontal social-economic dividing lines, crosscutting the pillars. Each pillar consisted a relatively homogeneous segment of the Dutch population.

Through this structure the elites of the "pillars," while safeguarding the identity of their particular pillar, nevertheless shared overall political power, thus enabling them to manage the country (through political practices) by power-sharing in an otherwise non-sharing society. In the words of Lijphart, "accommodation" meant the "settlement of divisive issues and conflicts where only a minimal consensus exists (Lijphart 1968:103). These pillars were the organisational format of the management of diversity in the Dutch society, and the members of these pillars only interacted in practice.

Lijphart's *Politics of Accommodation* proved to be seminal for his later publications in which he further developed the concept of "consociational democracy." As an early scholar on the subject, Lijphart formulated four essential characteristics of consociational democracy: (1) executive power-sharing among the representatives of all significant groups (the grand coalition), (2) a high degree of internal autonomy for groups that wish to have it (segmental autonomy), (3) proportional representation and proportional allocation of civil service positions and public funds (proportionality), and (4) a minority veto on the most vital issues (mutual veto).

If one compares the coordination of the diversity model with the consociational model, there are undeniably many differences. It was the political scientist Lijphart who focused mainly on politics in defining the consociational model. In contrast, de Ruijter's coordination of diversity model is seen as part of an encompassing theory of culture. The Dutch pillar-society is, of course, bounded in terms of periodisation. However, an essential element shared by both models is the *non-sharing* dimension in relations between each social segment or pillar. Different – that is, *culturally different* – segments of a society are relatively autonomous. In the Dutch society of the 1950s and the 1960s, there was indeed compatibility, but not communality of cultures and lifestyles. At the same time, the existence of those pillars did not fundamentally jeopardise society because the elites of these pillars found each other in the practices of the management of the country.

Lijphart did not only analyse the Dutch system, he also advocated and prescribed this consociational model as a panacea for deeply (e.g. ethnically) divided societies. Therefore it is not surprising that Lijphart also wrote about the future of South African society. When the first cracks in the apartheid system became manifest, Lijphart also advocated this pillar-system with the hope of avoiding a possibly violent future for South African society.

Lijphart and South Africa

Under Lijphart's inspiration and with his direct involvement,[8] the pillar-model was presented in the early 1980s as an alternative to what was a deeply dividing system in apartheid-era South Africa. In his *Power-sharing in South Africa,* published in 1985,[9] he emphasised the benefits of his power-sharing theory – the consocialisational model –

in ending apartheid and avoiding bloodshed.

Lijphart ranked the consociational model among the most suitable solutions. The other solutions, according to him, were the "majoritarian model," which he regarded as "unfair and unworkable in a society that is as deeply divided as South Africa's" (Lijphart 1985:5), or the "non-democratic solution" by which suffrage of the black population would continue to be limited. Lijphart realised that this solution was not acceptable to South Africa's black population, or to the world community.[10] And lastly, there was the "partitionist solution" by which South Africa would be divided into two or more separate states. According to Lijphart, however, this solution was not realistic and "can only be thought of as a solution of the very last resort" (ibid.:6).

Lijphart noted that the majoritarian model had been given strong support by the black population in South Africa, for obvious reasons. "Few people feel much concern that after so many years of white minority domination, the roles of oppressor and oppressed might be reversed under majority rule" (ibid.:17). Even so, Lijphart argued, "majoritarianism is as inappropriate and as dangerous for South Africa's black citizens as it is for South Africa as a whole (ibid.:20). Referring to developments in Zimbabwe where Prime Minister Robert Mugabe was campaigning against the Nbele minority at that time, Lijphart contended that there was "the tendency of majority rule to become majority dictatorship in plural societies (ibid.: 21). Therefore, "majoritarian democracy would serve nobody's true interest in South Africa" (ibid.). According to Lijphart the consociational model is the only model

> ...on which the major antagonists in South Africa are likely to agree. The first choice of most whites may be the continuation of white predominance, and most blacks may prefer unconditional majority rule, but since these preferences are incompatible [sic], power-sharing is their obvious second-best solution (ibid.:10).

Lijphart participated in the so-called Buthulezi Commission that published a report in 1982, entitled *The Requirements for Stability and Development in Kwazulu and Natal.* Probably due to the participation of Lijphart himself, he noted that the "Buthulezi Commission's political and constitutional recommendations are unexceptionally consociational" (ibid.: 80). According to Lijphart it could easily serve "as a model for state government in a consociational-federal South Africa....(ibid.).

In chapter 5 of his book *Power-sharing*, Lijphart elaborates on the favourable and unfavourable conditions for the development of a consociational democracy, as applied to the South African case. The factors that he reviews are the following: (1) no majority segment, (2) segments of equal size, (3) small number of segments, (4) small populations size, (5) external threats, (6) overarching loyalties, (7) socio-economic equality, (8) geographical concentration of segments, (9) traditions of accommodation.

When assessing these factors, it is interesting (and although not surprising, nevertheless highly relevant to my argument) to note that, according to Lijphart, South Africa gives a "very unfavourable" score on one factor (the only which South Africa scored as "very unfavourable"): *socio-economic equality*. Indeed, "if there are large socio-economic differences among the segments, the poorer segments will likely feel discriminated against and the more prosperous ones may feel threatened" (Lijphart 1985: 124). Still, Lijphart optimistically added that this factor is not an "insuperable obstacle to consociationalism." And he predicted that if South Africa should regain its place in the world community (after having introduced consociational democracy, that is), new investments would stimulate "economic growth that will facilitate substantial redistribution" (ibid.: 125).

Secondly, Lijphart argued that there is no majority segment in South Africa. This is striking, but understandable, because of the method of defining the segments that Lijphart uses. "[M]y score for South Africa is based on the assumption that the South African segments must be defined in ethnic terms" (Lijphart 1985: 121). That means that the alleged black majority segment falls apart into a Zulu-segment, a Xhosa-segment, a Coloureds segment, an Indian segment etc. Also the white segment needs to be differentiated between English and Afrikaner.

Thirdly, Lijphart noted that there are long and strong traditions of consensual decision-making in the African community. Nevertheless, he concluded that "these encouraging elements are counterbalanced by a long history of white domination and black exclusion." The overall score of favourable and unfavourable factors, according to Lijphart, necessarily leads to the conclusion that South Africa's chances for creating a power-sharing system were promising.

From power-sharing to majority

Lijphart's book on South Africa was published in 1985, right in the middle of what Allister Sparks calls the era of "neo-apartheid adaptation" (Sparks 1990). This era ended with the transfer of power from President Botha to President de Klerk. Many conceived of Lijphart's ideas as yet another approach to legitimatise the system of apartheid in a modern guise – apartheid as modern racial consociationalism (see, for example, Shaw and Nhema 2001). Fifteen years later, we can evaluate his ideas and projections in retrospect.

The concept of consociationalism, including the grand coalition, did indeed work, but only in the relatively short transitional period in which CODESA (Convention for a Democratic South Africa) was set up to pave the way for a transition from apartheid to a majoritarian system. The "charter" of CODESA more or less represented the concept of power sharing as contained in the Declaration of Intent, which was signed by a large number of parties, local governments, and organisations. The South African government eventually formally endorsed this Declaration of Intent.[11] In it the undersigned parties to the declaration solemnly expressed their commitment "to bring about an undivided South Africa with one nation sharing a common citizenship, patriotism and loyalty, pursuing amidst our diversity, freedom, equality and security for all irrespective of race, colour, sex or creed; a country free from apartheid or any other form of discrimination or domination."

The ANC, a political party and liberation movement representing the overwhelming black majority, formulated its position in the negotiations as follows:

> The ANC entered negotiations with the aim of attaining its strategic objective of a united, non-racial, non-sexist and democratic South Africa....with the fundamental understanding that negotiations were not about a compromise between democracy and apartheid, but about the process towards attaining universally accepted principles of justice and human rights. (ANC documents, Strategy and Tactics, 1997)

CODESA started in December 1991 and was followed by a 'Negotiating Multiparty Process,' which began in April 1993. This multiparty Negotiation Process resulted in drafting an interim-constitution that came into effect in 1994. After elections a Constitutional Assembly was elected. They prepared and adopted by a two-thirds majority a final Constitution in 1996. A majoritarian system took over the power-sharing process in which the ANC became the dominant power through its position as the ruling political party. The leadership of the ANC was transferred from its charismatic leader and first black South African President, Nelson Mandela, to his chosen crown prince, Thabo Mbeki in 1999.

Discussion

What I have done up till now is, first, to highlight some dimensions of de Ruijter's theory of culture. Then I rounded up the discussion with Lijphart, a Dutch political scientist who had worked for many years in the United States, and his political theory in respect to South Africa's recent political history.

What lessons can we draw from the fact that the model of consocialisation (power-sharing) apparently did not work, despite Lijphart's hope and prediction, in South Africa, a society that was and still is so deeply divided, not only along ethnic lines, but also along the lines of the inequality of access to resources? Power sharing was not acceptable for the black majority, imprisoned as they had been in the apartheid-system for many years. Taking the non-sharing dimension of both the coordination of diversity model and the consociational model, it would not be far out of line to suggest that the model of coordination of diversity would also probably fail in the present South Africa.

At the same time we saw that the coordination model did work in the Dutch *'zuilen*-society', comprising culturally different and deeply divided pillars or segments. This brings us to the fundamental – in terms of both its academic and societal value – question, which is whether it might be possible to assess under what circumstances the model of coordination of diversity could or could not work.

Could one perhaps say that management or co-ordination of cultural diversity (which are in my view a new guise of politics of consociational democracy) can only work if two conditions are met? What might these two conditions be? First of all there needs to be sufficient capital (in the broad sense of the word) in the multicultural arena to facilitate indifference or positively formulated tolerance. Secondly, there need to be more of less equal "pillars" of cultural different groups; and "equal" must definitely be defined both in terms of quantity and quality. There also needs to be relatively equal access to the resources available (material, political, ideological etc.). This element relates more or less to the third criteria of Lijphart's model: proportionality. Moreover, Lijphart himself already defined the socio-economic inequality in South Africa as being the most "unfavourable" factor that hinders the fostering of consociational democracy.

If one takes these two conditions – (access to) sufficient capital, and relative equivalence of the different segments – to South Africa, it is obvious that the inequality (whatever parameters one may use to define inequality) in South Africa was (and still is) too radical to allow for a "coordination-of-diversity" way of life.

Lijphart obviously ignored the cultural boundaries of the majority segment of the black population. Notwithstanding dividing lines within the black population, it was the apartheid system itself that organised its own majority segment by the brutal consequences of an oppressive apartheid-system. In general, one may argue that Lijphart offered a Eurocentric model of the nation-state in a context where this concept was imported as an integral part of colonialism.

This brings me to the preliminary conclusion that the term *diversity* necessarily needs to be contextualised. Diversity seems to be a neutral term. Without any contextualisation its explanatory capacity is minimal. But when "diversity" is transformed into "difference," its neutrality suddenly disappears. *Difference* is by no means neutral.[12] Difference is to some extent a construction that is connected with different and differing dividing lines in society; dividing lines that include and exclude; dividing lines that dichotomise. Homi Bhabha, one of the "gurus" of cultural studies, once said:

> ...cultural difference is a process of signification through which statements of culture or on culture differentiate, discriminate, and authorize the production of fields of force, reference, applicability, and capacity (1995: 206).

Let us view society as an arena (as we saw a recurrent metaphor in many of de Ruijter's publications) in which the need for and the access to capital of different kinds is at stake. If there is enough capital available, cultural difference will probably not be a major obstacle to governing society. One can allow for tolerance, or even indifference. The extent to which the management or co-ordination of difference succeeds or fails is closely connected to the level of experienced cultural difference. Let me give the reader an example from my own experience. I live in a semi-detached house in a fairly well to do neighbourhood in rural Zeist. My neighbours, until recently, came from the right wing of the protestant church (the Gereformeerde Bond) in the Netherlands. We clearly sensed a cultural difference between us – in the clothing we wore, in the way we interacted with our neighbourhood, in the choices of schools for our children, in the way we spent our leisure time etc. But although we experienced this sense of cultural difference we could easily manage or co-ordinate this difference, as pillarized Dutch society did in the 1950s and 1960s.

But what if cultural difference is experienced in a much deeper sense, especially in a situation where inequality is acute and pervasive. This will negatively affect the potential of the co-ordination of diversity. If dividing lines run along "haves" versus the "have nots," and these dividing lines also represent asymmetrical relations of power, then a constructed and imposed cultural difference can easily develop into an instrument for trying to keep the "cultural different Other" out of our own backyard.

Dividing lines in South Africa are predominantly the lines that divide the rich and the poor, and definitely the very rich from the very poor. To a large extent, these diving lines follow the colour code of whites versus blacks. And South Africa is precisely the kind of society where the rich try to keep the poor from their backyard in an extremely literal sense of the word. In South African society difference is not managed, but fenced off!

Do we then conclude that the coordination-model is likely to fail in a society like South Africa? Not necessarily. The majority party may mitigate its dominant majoritarian position, if they think that this would, for instance, prevent society from totally falling apart – the consequence of which might even endanger the privileges of the rich and powerful. Part of this strategy may be to construct a "common denominator" within a divided society. In this respect South Africa is an interesting case because one can discern a gradual changeover from one "denominator" to a new one, which coincides with different agendas. In the middle of the '90s, the common denominator was the concept of the "rainbow nation"; South Africa was to develop into a modern society comprising different colours of one rainbow. Archbishop Desmond Tutu is thought to have coined this term from biblical sources, and adopted it to the process of reconciliation in South Africa.

But more recently, the ANC under the leadership of Thabo Mbeki is defining the overarching concept of the "African Renaissance" that is supposed to unite all groups of the supposed rainbow nation. Yet, here is a slight but critical change in terminology. The nucleus of this concept is "African." The word "Renaissance" indicates a delving back into African history to pre-colonial times. Again, the ANC-document *Strategy and Tactics* reveals the transition from the many colours of the rainbow to the prominence of one colour.

> The ANC recognises that individuals within such a nation will have multiple identities, on the basis of their physiological make-up, cultural life and social upbringing....But it is critical that the over-arching identity of being South African is promoted among all those who are indeed South African, as part of the process of building an African nation on the southern tip of the continent. The affirmation of our Africanness as a nation has nothing to do with the domination of one culture or language by another – it is the recognition of a geographic reality and the awakening of a consciousness which colonialism suppressed.

In many publications, Thabo Mbeki has depicted the concept of the "African Renaissance" in remarkably colourful terms. But at the same time this concept has also been criticised as a clear example of a hegemonic, and thus totalising, instrument that serves only to per-petuate the power of the president and his political party (see, for example, Marais 2001).

Donald Horowitz offers another strategy[13]. He raises the model of "integrative majoritarianism," which implies that elites be given incentives to search outside of their primary and narrowly defined ethnic constituencies for another model of a majoritari-an system in order to prevent schism in society. That means that, ultimately, there appears to be a way out for the coordination model.

Perhaps coordination or management of diversity, while acknowledging the dom-inant-power dimension, is merely a kind of "reciprocal altruism" (Trivers 1971; 35-67) on the part of the powerful in order to prevent society from falling apart (which would ultimately be severely detrimental to those in power). Others say that reciprocal altru-ism is merely enlightened self-interest. In his article *"Invoegen en uitsluiten: de samen-leving als arena"* de Ruijter (1998) himself seems to be following this path in his reflec-tions on the "interactiemodel" when he refers to *"welbegrepen eigenbelang"* (well-understood self-interest) as a regulating mechanism within the interaction-model. De Ruijter offers this interaction-model as a model for managing the multi-faceted arena in which many actors cooperate and antagonise.

Unfortunately, Africa does have a record of disintegrated societies where power-elites proved unable to act "altruistically," with the obvious results being collapsing societies, or to be more precise, collapsing nation-states. One should bear in mind, of course, that the nation-state is a concept that originated in Europe, and was exported and prescribed to other parts of the world. In this sense, collapsing nation-states in Africa can also be interpreted as failed attempts to establish Eurocentric models. One could identify other paradigms to analyse political developments in Africa, such as the notion of "disorder as political instrument," developed by Chabal and Daloz. Interest-ingly, they stress the importance of reciprocity in African politics: "any political action is couched in an environment of reciprocity, which dictates its symbolic and instru-mental value" (Chabal and Daloz 1958).

Coda

In this article I criticised the "coordination of diversity" model, outlined in a number of de Ruijter's thought-provoking publications, for downplaying the power and inequality dimension. I readily admit that it will be extremely difficult – if at all possible – to indi-cate and "predict" under what conditions such a model might work or fail. Societies nowadays are very complex, and are in constant flux.

Let me wind up with another vista originating from the concept of diversity that seems to be missing in de Ruijter's publications. He traces his concept of organisation of diversity back to Wallace, who in 1961 published *Culture and Personality*. Wallace defined two concepts of the nature of the relation between cultural and personality systems: (1) the replication of uniformity, and (2) the organization of diversity. However, Wallace also reflected on the ultimate moral consequences of both worldviews. According to him, the replication of uniformity inherently bears the painful fate of dealing with contradictions and conflict. On the other hand,

> From this organisation-of-diversity viewpoint grows a different sense of tragedy [sic]. The unwanted inevitability is not sin, nor conflict, but loneliness: the only partly bridgeable chasms of mutual ignorance between whole peoples and the failures of understanding between individuals (Wallace 1970: 24).

It would appear that Wallace has some guiding influence on de Ruijter in regard to his theoretical exploration of the coordination of diversity.

In this article I focussed on the dimensions of power and inequality as jeopardizing forces within de Ruijter's model. What I did not do (and neither did de Ruijter, for that matter) was to elaborate on the moral consequences of the organisation-of-diversity worldview, as Wallace did. But if Wallace is right and "loneliness," "mutual ignorance," and "failures of understanding" are indeed the "unwanted inevitabilities" of coordination of diversity, then the future of the multicultural society looks rather bleak. Are we then compelled to conclude that the tragedy of apartheid was the immoral consequence *in extremis* of the organisation of diversity?

Notes

1   I thank Peter Vale for his critical remarks on earlier versions of this text.
2   I explicitly use the adjective 'European' here. This does not mean of course that only Europe faces the development of multicultural societies. On the contrary, the concept of a multicultural society as a society comprising different groups is probably older than 'Europe'.
3   The 'South African' text is in line with other writings of Arie de Ruijter on multiculturalism, culminating in his inaugural address in Tilburg in 2000. See e.g. de Ruijter 1994, 1995, 1997, 2000 (a) and 2000 (b).
4   In a recent interview, de Ruijter distinguishes between multiculturalism, being an ideology, and multiculturalisation, being the actual process of growth of a multicultural society (van Rinsum and Pansters 2002).
5   In the present political situation in the Netherlands it seems as if consensus is thought to be only compliance with dominant, i.e. alleged 'traditional Dutch' values and norms.
6   English translation HvR: What is needed, is compatibility, not communality of cultures and lifestyles. This compatibility is not an a priori, but it develops from practices. See also de Ruijter 2000 (a): 29-30.
7   English translation HvR: 'the material inequality, a thorough, daily experienced reality for different layers and ethnic groups in our society'.
8   Lijphart mentions in his acknowledgements to *Power-sharing in South Africa* that this book is a culmination of his 'research on and thinking about the South African problem' since his first visit to 'this beautiful and troubled country' in 1971.
9   For the Dutch audience, with a special interest in the development in South Africa, a Dutch translation was published in 1987.

10 However, Lijphart does concede "the only way in which limited but expanding voting rights could possibly be acceptable to South Africa's blacks and to the world community would be if the temporary denial of these rights were of extremely short duration" (Lijphart 1985: 5).

11 See http://www.anc.org.za/ancdocs/history/transition/codesa/declaration.html.

12 See, for example, Jan Nederveen Pieterse when he says: "arguably, in itself cultural difference does not invite judgements, unless it is articulated with class, mobilisation and conflict, or confronted with rigid group boundaries" (Nederveen Pieterse 2001: 394). He adds that cultural difference can also be an inspiration.

13 Cited in Reynolds (1999).

Bibliography

ANC, 1997, *Strategy and Tactics, as amended at the 50th National Conference,* December 1997 (downloaded text).

Anonymous, 2002, *More on Most: Proceedings of an Expert Meeting. With a short introduction by Henk J. van Rinsum and Arie de Ruijter.* The Hague: UNESCO Commission.

Baines, G., 1998 'The Rainbow Nation? Identity and nation building in post-apartheid South-Africa.' *Mots Pluriel* 7: 1-7 (downloaded text).

Bhabha, H.K., 1995, 'Cultural diversity and cultural differences' in Ashcroft, B., Griffiths, G. and Tiffin, H. (eds) *The Post-colonial Studies Reader.* London: Routledge, pp. 206-9.

Brown, D. (2001). 'National Belonging and Cultural Difference: South Africa and the Global Imaginary.' *Journal of Southern African Studies* 27(4): 757-769.

Chabal, Patrick and Jean-Pascal Daloz, 1999, *Africa works: Disorder as Political Instrument.* Oxford etc.: James Currey.

de Ruijter, A, 1994, Culturele Diversiteit. In: R. Pinxten (Ed.) *Cultuurstudies* 1: 28-44.

de Ruijter, A., 1995, Cultural Pluralism and Citizenship. *Cultural Dynamics,* 7(2): 215-231

de Ruijter, A., 1997, *Multiculturalism: Still Muddling Through?* Cape Town, Centre for Southern African Studies.

de Ruijter, A, 1997. De ladder op omlaag?; Een Postmodern ego-document. In: Auke van Dijk and Paul Verweel, *De Ladder Omlaag; Een psychologie van Besturen.* Van Gorcum.

de Ruijter, A., 1998, Invoegen en Uitsluiten; de samenleving als Arena. In: *Multiculturalisme.* C. H. M. Geuijen (ed.). Utrecht, Lemma BV: 27-38.

de Ruijter, A., 2000 (a), *De Multiculturele Arena.* Tilburg, Katholieke Universiteit Brabant.

de Ruijter, A., 2000 (b), Globalization: a Challenge to the Social Sciences. In: Schuurman, Frans J. ed. *Globalization and Development Studies: Challenges for the 21st Century.* Amsterdam: Thela Thesis.

Lijphart, Arend, 1968, *The Politics of Accommodation: Pluralism and Democracy in the Netherlands.* Berkely and Los Angeles: University of California Press.

Lijphart, Arend, 1985, *Power-Sharing in South Africa.* Policy Papers in International affairs, number 24. Berkeley: Institute of International Studies, University of California. (Nederlandse vertaling door A.P. Daalder-Neukircher, 1987, *Machtsdeling: de oplossing voor Zuid-Afrika?.* Haarlem: H.J.W. Becht.

Marais, Hein, 2001, *South Africa, Limits to Change: The Political Economy of Transition.* London and New York: Zed books Ltd2.

Nederveen Pieterse, J., 2001, The case of Multiculturalism: Kaleidoscopic and Long-term Views. In: *Social Identities,* 7 (3): 393-407.

Reynolds, Andrew, 1999, *Majoritarian or Power-Sharing Government.* Unpublished Paper.

Shaw, Timothy M. and Alfred Nhema, 1995, Directions and Debates in South Africa's First Post-Apartheid Decade. *Mershon International Studies Review* (39): 97-110

Sparks, Allister, 1990, *The Mind of South Africa: The Story of the Rise and Fall of apartheid.* London: Mandarin.

van Rinsum, Henk J., 2001, *Slaves of Definition; In Quest of the Unbeliever and the Ignoramus.* Maastricht: Shaker Publisher.

van Rinsum, Henk J., and Wil Pansters, 2002, The interview: "I have a 'Neolithic' mind". *CERES Magazine,* pp. 10-19. Autumn. (Interview with Arie de Ruijter, 31 October 2002)

Wallace, Anthony F.C., 1970, *Culture and Personality* (2e edition), New York: Random House (1st Edition was published in 1961).

4

When Colonial History Comes Home

Gert Oostindie

Dutch anthropology was born out of scholarly research in the country's own colonies, mainly the Netherlands East Indies. The tradition goes back well into the nineteenth century and includes the early foundation of such respectable institutions as 'Koninklijk Instituut voor Taal-, Land- en Volkenkunde' (1851), 'Indisch Genootschap' (1854), 'Koninklijk Nederlandsch Aardrijkskundig Genootschap' (1873), and 'Nederlandsche Antropologische Vereeniging' (1898).[1] At the time, anthropology certainly played an instrumental – even if not necessarily uncritical – role to the enactment of colonial rule. Since Indonesia's independence and the growth of Dutch involvement in global development aid in the 1960s, the regional focus of anthropology widened considerably to include the entire "South." Recent pessimistic reappraisals of the net effect of development aid may, however, result in a closing down of career opportunities for anthropologists abroad, thus imposing a narrowing of the field of study, this time to the domestic cultures of the former metropolis.

In an exit interview saluting his departure from the CERES Research School and Utrecht University, Professor Arie de Ruijter somewhat wearily and overly modestly claims to be a "Neolithic" mind, always excited to find something new, yet not too interested in delving really deeply (CERES Magazine 2002:10). He also talks about his growing fascination with the problems and challenges of multiculturalism. While making all kinds of relativistic remarks about his own scholarly work – always "looking for toys" – he barely mentions the obvious fact that the rise of the very concept of multiculturalism in countries such as the Netherlands is, in itself, only a reflection of the fundamental changes brought on all of Western Europe by the relatively massive post-World War II waves of migration. The erstwhile exotic subjects of anthropological research now inhabit the metropolitan centres of the continent. Anthropology has had a hard time redefining itself in the face of this, and was quickly overtaken by the more mundane social sciences – and today by politicians mainly interested in the overnight socialisation of "non-Western" cultures in whatever they still feel to be the mainstream culture.

The object of study has moved, and with it has the discipline of anthropology. One of Arie de Ruijter's immediate predecessors at Utrecht University, Professor Jan van Baal, brought to his chair his expertise as a governor to Nieuw Guinea, the last outpost of Dutch colonialism in Asia. In the end, Arie simply saw the traditional targets of anthropological study coming his way. Thus the object of study was broadened to include the study of the once exotic Others in their new Western environment. Slowly however it began to dawn upon serious scholars that the discipline of anthropology needed to redefine itself further in order to come to terms with their own changing societies. The logical next step was the decision to think of the study of the "natives" at home and their reactions to immigrants as a serious part of anthropological study as well. And here we are.

Serious anthropology probes distance and methods to study its own societies and its own native ways of dealing with immigrant minorities and their cultures. In this context I offer here a twin case study that at first sight may appear to fall within the field of history, but on further reflection calls for a questioning which should be of some interest to anthropologists as well. The case study is about the contemporary Dutch commemoration of colonialism and its relation with present debates about multiculturalism.

From colonialism to post-colonial migrations and claims

After the Indonesian independence proclaimed in 1945 – but only acknowledged after bitter fighting and negotiations in 1949 – and the transfer of sovereignty to Suriname in 1975, only the Netherlands Antilles continued to opt for remaining part of the Kingdom, tiny remnants of a once impressive empire. While anthropological interest in these former colonies has not disappeared, it is in the field of politics and economics that bilateral relations have been most intense over the past decades. Differences in scale and potential power left The Hague often little choice but to let Jakarta set the bilateral agenda, while in its dealings with the powerless former Caribbean colonies the reverse obtained. Meanwhile significant postcolonial migrant communities began to form in the Netherlands, relatively successful in socio-economic terms and increasingly outspoken in their efforts to influence Dutch policies towards their countries of origins as well as the domestic minorities debate.

"History," and particularly Dutch collective guilt handed down through the generations, became a major argument for these postcolonial migrant communities in their multiple efforts to influence Dutch policy. The fact that Dutch-Indonesian relations have remained tenuous through more than half a century partly reflects The Hague's continuous attempt not to add to the frustrations of the over 300,000 European and Eurasian immigrants who resentfully evacuated Indonesia in the aftermath of independence. Befriending the first president Sukarno – not popular with the Dutch politicians he ousted in the first place – thus was anathema. Speaking out unequivocally (if only in retrospect) against colonialism and particularly the last colonial war of 1945-1949 apparently still remains a bridge too far. Moluccan Dutch in turn continue, if not very successfully, to urge The Hague to keep a protective eye on the relatives they left behind in Indonesia. As for the West Indies, frequent Surinamese and Antillean reminders to The Hague of a shameful colonial past and consequent contemporary responsibility go a long way in explaining the relatively massive Dutch development aid to the former Caribbean colonies.[2]

Within the Netherlands, there have been some tangible symbolic results of a postcolonial lobby over the years. Following militant actions in the 1970s, the Dutch government sought to pacify Moluccan political radicalism by acknowledging responsibility for both the invitation to this community to move "temporarily" to the Netherlands in the 1950s, and subsequently the supposed failure to offer this group either a realistic chance for return or a successful integration into Dutch society. In this context, a government-sponsored "Moluks Historisch Museum" was founded in Utrecht as a place for remembrance and education. (Presently, the museum is hosting among other activities a government-financed project to write the history of Moluccans in the Netherlands, today numbering probably some 50,000.) Other communities followed suit. The community of post-war European and Eurasian "repatriates" from Indonesia, disgruntled at the perceived metropolitan failure to protect their interests in the colony and at the subsequent cold-shouldered reception in the Netherlands, finally got its long-awaited monument, an historical community centre ("Het Indisch Huis") and some individual financial compensation by the turn of the century. In the same vein, at the urge of vociferous Caribbean organisations in the metropolis, the Dutch government decided to establish a monument in commemoration of the transatlantic slave trade and Dutch Caribbean slavery. The Hague's willingness in this respect is obviously related to the fact that by now the Netherlands is home to a community of Caribbean backgrounds numbering some 400,000 individuals, over half of which are of African Caribbean roots.

In all of this, we witness subsequent governments acknowledging responsibility for morally dubious or – from a contemporary perspective – outright wrong state actions going back decades and even centuries. In apparently seeking some kind of moral redemption for the sins of past governments, the state answers to the urges of its postcolonial citizenry. Yet as two phenomena of the past year illustrate, the return to history does not necessarily lead to consistent policy, or to an immediately obvious positive contribution to the debates on multiculturalism.

Celebrating the VOC[3]

On 20 March 2002, the Netherlands "celebrated" the establishment, exactly four centuries earlier, of the Dutch East Indies Company *(Vereenigde Oost-Indische Compagnie,* VOC). By pure coincidence, on the first of July of that same year a national monument in commemoration of the Atlantic slave trade and Dutch Caribbean slavery – in which the Dutch West Indies Company *(West-Indische Compagnie,* WIC) was a key player – was inaugurated in Amsterdam. In both the celebration of the Dutch East Indies Company and the act of repentance regarding its West Indies counterpart, Queen Beatrix and Dutch Prime Minister Wim Kok were conspicuously present in the front row.

Let us first address the festivities around the VOC. Alongside official celebrations, schools were being provided educational materials fully in tune with the celebratory intention, even if some attention was paid to the links between the early VOC exploits, violence, and colonialism. Major museums as well as tiny ones all over the country mounted a vast array of exhibitions on the VOC, its exploits, and the implications of Dutch-Asian trade for the metropolis. Stacks of books were being reprinted and published emphasizing anew the glory of an epoch that forever changed the face not only of the Netherlands, but of all countries involved.

Somewhat in the margins of these celebratory exercises, there were occasional debates – in which participating historians and other intellectuals usually tended to criticize the concept of *celebration* – and even demonstrations, mainly organised and supported by Dutchmen of Moluccan backgrounds. The media lent a sympathetic ear to the objections, and in fact many a newspaper devoted articles to the protests and commented against the celebratory mood of the whole endeavour. Yet what in the end prevailed was not the bitter (mainly to Others) but rather the sweet (mainly to the Dutch nation).

Much of the celebrations of 400 years VOC reflected pride in the roots of nation, particularly the seventeenth century in which the emerging Dutch Republic shortly was the world's first world hegemonic power. This 'Golden' epoch was to remain a touchstone in the national memory, and the colonial ventures in Asia figured prominently in that reckoning. As Johan Fabricius had it in his *Scheepsjongens van Bontekoe*, a 1923-adventure story on the early Dutch pursuits in Indonesia and still a classic boys' book today, the adventures of these 'first courageous "Masters next to God" who with their valiant crew installed our authority in the [East] Indies' was definitely an example to emulate (Fabricius 1997:7).

Both in Dutch historiography and in public awareness, colonial history was long virtually equated with the exploits in Asia, and particularly in Indonesia. Here a Eurocentric perspective was unchallenged. *"Daar wèrd wat grootsch verrich,"* roughly, "Something monumental was achieved there," reigned supreme and was easily taken to the present form all the way from Jan Pietersz. Coen's 17th-century claim that something magnificent was being achieved in the Indies under his reign. It remains fascinating how even during the 1940-1945 Nazi occupation of the Netherlands, and indeed in the years of warfare over Indonesian independence immediately after, leading Dutch politicians and civil servants continued to lull one another's concerns with incongruent assurances that they were not seen as oppressors, that their mission in the colony was far from over, and that they sincerely thought most reasonable Indonesians were ready to admit this.

Looking back on the festivities relating to the VOC which spanned over half a year, one may conclude that in spite of politely voiced objections against the whole idea of a "celebration," the festive mood aimed for was indeed maintained up to the end, in the Netherlands that is. Even if the concept of *"Daar wèrd wat grootsch verricht"* has become both obsolete and politically incorrect, it seems to have been making something of a comeback, and the VOC evidently does provide food for such pride. The Netherlands, a rather small country with limited natural resources, *did* have an impact in Asia, *did* play a vanguard role with their multinational VOC in a sense out of proportion with its own modest scale. This statement lends itself to scholarly corroboration detached of moral and political observations, and deep down the unrealistic longing to convince others of the desirability to separate the two is at the heart of the celebration project. Naive as the hopes may have been to convince Asians of this, much of the festivities may indeed have helped to convince Dutch audiences of the accomplishments of *their* VOC, which once aptly carried the epitaph "the praiseworthy company."

In contrast, official reactions in Indonesia, once the prime operating area of the VOC, were dismissive, as were those in South Africa. The response in other states once touched by the company ranged from indifferent or at best lukewarm (India, China, Sri Lanka) to moderately interested (Taiwan, Japan). The whole project of a commemoration, let alone celebration, clearly remained a unilateral Dutch pursuit, confrontational to some key foreign countries involved and at odds with any attempt to find a broader and less exclusive definition of national history and identity.

One cannot escape the conclusion that the very Dutch effort to celebrate the VOC as a precursor of innovative entrepreneurship was bound to clash not only with critical groups in the Netherlands itself, but particularly with the Asian and African countries involved. These clashes were never violent, particularly because of the reticence among the contesters. Yet the apparent insufficient anticipation of the ill feelings encountered testifies to a mixture of naiveté, perhaps fuelled by Eurocentric arrogance, and most certainly to a lack of diplomatic tact. This comes the more as a surprise bearing in mind that the concept of celebrating was partly inspired by the longing to engage in public relations in favour of the contemporary Dutch heirs to "the world's first ever multinational company." It is ironic that while the official emphasis was on early Dutch internationalism, the actual "celebrations" instead reflected contemporary parochialism.

Commemorating West Indian slavery

What about the awareness of Dutch colonialism in the West Indies? It would seem that a long history of glossing over these chapters has recently come to an end. Mirroring their minor significance to the metropolis, for centuries the Caribbean colonies were virtually non-existent in Dutch historiography and public awareness. This only started to change in the last couple of decades, the major reason being the mass migration from Suriname, and next also the Antilles, to the Netherlands. The exodus not only alerted the Dutch public to the existence of these Dutch creations in the Caribbean, but gradually also produced an outspoken Caribbean interest group perfectly capable of bringing its own versions of history to the spotlight. Hence within the last five years, the transatlantic slave trade and slavery – neglected in history textbooks, silenced in public awareness – were transformed from a Caribbean *j'accuse* to a Dutch *mea culpa*, and in the process became canonized as the single defining phenomenon in the contemporary interpretation of Dutch West Indian history. This rare *mea culpa* version of history was literally given shape with the inauguration of the monument in commemoration of slavery – almost 140 years after the official abolition of slavery in the Dutch West Indies on 1 July 1863. A worthy symbolic gesture indeed. One hopes it will not serve to mainly nourish Dutch pride in being an exemplary self-critical nation.

Thus, the history of the Dutch West Indies Company is now being canonized

under the header "something *gruesome* was achieved there." This is an astonishing contrast to the traditional Dutch interpretation of the East Indies Company. To some extent
this only reflects the fact that Dutch colonialism in Asia and its legacies were far more
important to the metropolis than its exploits in the Americas. In a sense, there is not
much to lose for the Dutch in acknowledging the inescapable fact that Dutch Atlantic
history was dominated by crass exploitation through the slave trade, slavery, and next,
Asian indentured labour. Few ever thought of the Caribbean as a veritable *lieu de
mémoire* for Dutch history; there was mainly silence in our historical representation.
Now that the silence has been shattered, not that much is lost in speaking of "deep
remorse." One feels no real objections to speak out against these long-past crimes
against humanity committed by ancestors long since passed away and forgotten in
places few in the metropolis were aware of in the first place. A cynic might conclude
that paying for a monument in commemoration of slavery even serves as a form of
moral absolution for the Dutch and damage control towards angry descendants of
African slaves.

It is all too obvious that the accommodation of its Caribbean community was a
major objective of the Dutch government, and here again there is an interesting contrast. The political clout of the Caribbean community in the Netherlands has increased
considerably in the past decades, and Dutch politics has learned to take this seriously.
This includes the recognition that colonialism was a stain on Dutch national history.
Conversely, the political leverage of the community of Indonesian backgrounds is
divided and less concerned with the distant past, but rather with the repercussions of
the Japanese occupation and the 1945-1949 warfare both for individuals and families
who eventually decided to settle in the Netherlands, and for the military who fought in
vain to break Indonesian nationalism. Heated debates on these issues, spurred by militant Moluccans and Dutch veterans, have been going on for decades and actually
resulted in official Dutch regrets to those involved who are living in the Netherlands –
again monuments and commemorating institutions, and financial compensation. Ironically, in a sense much of the criticism the Dutch government encountered during these
debates referred not so much to its colonialism, but rather to its perceived subsequent
"failure" to protect the interests of the interested parties vis-à-vis the Indonesian Republic. This context, in understatement, is not precisely conducive to a critical reappraisal
of Dutch colonialism.

The Dutch mea culpa for the slave trade and slavery fitted in with a wider Western reappraisal of colonialism. In a *fin-de-siècle* mood – perhaps heightened by the
realisation that an entire millennium was coming to an end – various Western European
countries and the United States were weighing up their own pasts at the closing of the
twentieth century. It was as if the centres of power had suddenly grown a special ear
for listening to the deafening silences of the past. In Africa, President Clinton expressed
his regret about America's role in the Atlantic slave trade, and the French and Dutch
governments openly repented for slavery in their former colonies 150 years post hoc.

Why was it the slave trade and slavery that acquired the status of acknowledged subjects for the West's justifiable self-criticism? The horror of this past is indisputable, as is the West's guilt, and hence the unmistakable hypocrisy of this stage in the history of the Western Christian project. But if horror and hypocrisy alone had been the only criterion, other episodes in national pasts would also have been in line for such public gestures. It undoubtedly helped that the Atlantic slave trade and slavery are completely over, and that they were abolished long ago. Yet just as in the Netherlands, of far more direct relevance was the appeal from the descendants of Africans who were once taken to the New World as slaves. Their anger about the past now threatened contemporary society; to continue to gloss over this past would have dangerously fuelled this anger. And so there came gestures of recognition and reconciliation, gestures that in the first instance were aimed at the current situation of the descendants of slaves who now live in the old "mother countries." The proposed message is clear, one both of redemption to the descendants of the guilty for past sins, and equally of inclusion to the descendants of past victims in metropolitan society.

Interestingly, one observes congruence not only in governmental positions, but also in the argumentation among the descendants of once enslaved Africans now living in these metropolises. Virtually all protagonists in this debate belong to the Western cultural sphere and borrow their arguments from Western ideas on freedom and history. "The slave trade and slavery contravene human freedom, which is every person's right." Ergo, these are – in the words of the French parliament – crimes against humanity. And whether in Liverpool, Bordeaux, New York or Rotterdam, there is always a string of connections and claims which link this past to the present: colour discrimination, traumatisation, social exclusion, underdevelopment. Here, too, we find a "Black Atlantic" at work.

What is next? This is currently being hotly debated. The claims of the descendants range from simple recognition to monuments, from new school books, museums and research centres to the call for restitution for the descendants of slaves, and the next step, already taken by many: the demand for large compensation payments to be made to the African countries from where those condemned to the middle passage and slavery were once abducted. And even the illusory hope that the age-old ideas on racial superiority and inferiority that developed through slavery, and the perfidious aesthetic appraisals that accompany them, will be suppressed or reversed as if by an act of God, is an illusion. For as Bob Marley sang ages ago, emancipation from mental slavery has to be fought for: it cannot be given.

What one person experiences as absurdly exaggerated expectations, may be experienced by another as the logical conclusion to those first hesitating steps. It is an illusion to expect that a consensus will grow on this subject. In the Netherlands, too, the debate itself is already a small monument to a history that was previously pushed as far back as possible into some remote corner of memory. One does observe, however, how difficult it is to engage in open debates about the interpretation of the past and the conclusions that may be drawn from it, and therefore also the question of what form a commemoration of slavery could or should take.

These debates once again confirm that every past, and certainly such a painful past, is open to interpretation, and that it is not unusual for someone's claim on the truth to be linked to their own origins. It would have been naive to think otherwise. There is a tendency among some descendants to capitalise on the victimisation of their ancestors, to draw spurious parallels with other dramas from history – primarily the persecution of the Jews by Nazi Germany – and the demand for the right to the first and last word on their own (and in this context suddenly superior) once-African origins. Such reactions, at times aggrieved by or intolerant to argument, deserve more than simply jeers, silent dismissal, or uncritical acceptance. Now that the memory of slavery is finally on the political agenda it deserves serious attention, even where it is a thorny subject. This calls for a critical revaluation of all chauvinisms, including an "African" perspective that should not get away with the pretension of superior "knowledge of experience." A Pandora's Box, but not a cause to worry too much; neither commemoration nor inclusion implies harmony.

The present in the way of the past

Returning to the VOC, it is all too evident that the choice for celebration was unfortunate and even inappropriate. Commemoration would have been a better – even if a rather oblique – motto, and at least more of an open invitation for debate. Yet this is not simply about words. This is, or should be, about the question of whether Dutch and Indonesians can see eye to eye in discussing the distant past. Most certainly the answer to that question is affirmative. Yet is seems a more recent past has stood in the way – the past, that is of decolonisation.

It is indeed striking that the Dutch government in the same year, 2002, found no objections whatsoever in letting the Crown Prince express deep remorse in Ghana over the Dutch involvement in the Atlantic slave trade, even if the host government had not really expressed any desire to discuss this at all, while at the same time The Hague still seems unable to find the right words regarding the Indonesian independence, which most certainly would be appreciated in Jakarta and beyond. Will we need another two or three centuries again? This is all about priorities, wrongly set in this case. It seems that as long as there are all too understandable Indonesian misgivings about the way the Dutch handle not only "1602" but particularly "1945," the searching for common ground regarding the VOC will continue to suffer.

That is all there is to it. Political correctness may have gone out of fashion again in the Netherlands, yet this is not about oblique self-criticism. Rather, it is about the willingness to discuss a shared past in such a way that no partner is excluded from the start. Once that common ground has been entered, debates about morality can give way to other – perhaps more pressing – discussions as well.

One need, incidentally, not surmise that this was a peculiar Dutch error of judgement. It seems very hard for whatever nation to commemorate, let alone celebrate its past without offending others. "Celebrations," writes the Haitian-American scholar Michel-Rolph Trouillot, "straddle the two sides of historicity. They impose a silence upon the events they ignore, and they fill that silence with narratives of power about the events they celebrate" (1995:118). It is a statement hard to ignore. Certainly, there is the commendable German *Vergangenheitsbewältigung*, in sharp contrast to the Japanese refusal to engage in such openness. Certainly, there has recently been a rather sudden commitment in many European countries as well as the U.S. to officially regret the transatlantic slave trade. Yet these all reflect episodes with could hardly elicit anything but shame and regret, once put in proper perspective.

Turning to historically and morally more complex episodes, it apparently becomes far more difficult not to fall back into chauvinism. This is exactly what was at the heart of the heated debates regarding the celebrations of the 1492 descubrimiento of the Americas. Though the events were eventually re-baptized into the more neutral and even cosy encuentro, and in fact one observer thought "the most striking feature of the quincentennial was the loudness of dissenting voices world-wide," in Spain the celebratory overtones remained sound and clear (Trouillot 1995:138). Do nations learn from one another's mistakes? One often finds reasons to doubt. Thus, according to the Indian historian of the VOC Sanjay Subrahmanyam, the Portuguese practically "ruined their relations" with the Asian countries involved by trying to impose a celebratory tone to *their* jubilee – five centuries after Vasco da Gama's indeed spectacular maritime exploits – of Portuguese-Asian relations.[4] Former colonizers simply have a hard time keeping a sound distance. The Dutch have proven not to be an exception to this rule.

Politicians and anthropologists

This paper paces back and forth between regions, periods, and perspectives. I have contrasted two commemorations and wondered what these contrasts tell us about the Dutch. Yet what does "the Dutch" mean in this context? In the case of the VOC celebrations, much of what I had to comment upon had to do with government behaviour and international relations. I particularly dealt with a Dutch failure to anticipate that capitalising on this past with whatever intentions was bound to be conflictive and therefore not particularly wise from a foreign relations perspective. Indirectly, such collisions should interest anthropologists too. After all, all of this is less about history as a series of past events than about cultural sensitivity – and the lack of such – about contemporary perspectives on a somehow shared past.

In the case of the commemoration of the WIC and particularly the Dutch Atlantic slave past, there are far lesser interests in the field of international relations at stake, yet higher ones in Dutch society. Here anthropological expertise might help politicians to some sensitivity. After all, emotions around the past and particularly its contemporary legacies run much higher here, if only while in the East the Dutch were, after all, only passers-by ousted before their chosen time, they virtually created the contemporary West Indies, to a large degree through slavery.[5] This is not to say anthropologists should simply tell politicians facing the challenge of managing increasingly multicultural societies to *listen* better. It is more about helping to create scenery congenial to open debates and to questioning perceived wisdoms on all sides. From personal experience,

I can only confirm that in this heavily charged field, the historical "facts" are far more vehemently debated than in most other areas of historical debate – whether these facts are the volume of the slave trade, the occurrence of slave revolts, the backgrounds to abolition, or such enormously more complicated issues as contemporary underdevelopment in Africa or individual and collective "traumatisation" during and after the experience of slavery.

Virtually all Dutch politicians who have spoken out about colonialism and its legacies have politely side-stepped such highly volatile issues – with the significant exception of the late Pim Fortuyn, who squarely advised any descendant of slaves with a professed trauma connected to the slavery past to consult a psychiatrist rather than lobby with the Dutch government (Fortuyn 2002:158). Of course, it was precisely Fortuyn who put the square refutation of multiculturalism in the centre of the political debate. We need not follow this erratic rebel to conclude that no debate on either shared past or present society can prosper without the willingness to review facts and feelings openly. Perhaps anthropology can make a contribution here at facilitating such debates. But indeed, as Arie de Ruijter puts it, a non-committal and uncritical praise of multiculturalism will not do (CERES Magazine 2002:17), neither in the debate on slavery and its legacies, nor in the wider debate on how a once relatively homogeneous society can absorb a wide variety of migrant communities without losing its own identity or denying cultural specificity to its new citizens.

Notes

1   See J.J. de Wolf, *Eigenheid en samenwerking. 100 jaar antropologisch verenigingsleven in Nederland*. Leiden: KITLV Uitgeverij 1998. Maarten Kuitenbrouwer, *Tussen oriëntalisme en wetenschap. Het Koninklijk Instituut voor Taal-, Land- en Volkenkunde in historisch verband, 1851-2001*. Leiden: KITLV Uitgeverij 2001.

2   So does the fact that development aid to Suriname was temporarily suspended after the December 1982 murder by the then military leadership of sixteen political opponents, while The Hague never took such actions towards many other countries with abysmal human rights records.

3   For a more extensive analysis of the VOC celebrations, see my 'Squaring the Circle? Commemorating the VOC after 400 Years.' *Bijdragen tot de Taal-, Land- en Volkenkunde* (forthcoming). For the Dutch slavery monument, see my 'Stony Regrets and Pledges for the Future', in Gert Oostindie ed. *Facing Up to the Past. Perspectives on the Commemoration of Slavery from Africa, the Americas and Europe*. Kingston: Ian Randle/The Hague: Prince Claus Fund 1999, pp. 9-18. I have borrowed here much from these two essays.

4   Sanjay Subrahmanyam in a debate on the VOC at Amsterdam University, 24 June 2002.

5   So there is room for a lighter touch in Indonesia. A bar and restaurant called the 'VOC/Vereenigde Oost-Indische Compagnie' was established in Jakarta some years ago without any protest, while the project to establish a restaurant called the 'WIC/West-Indische Compagnie' in Curaçao was cancelled because of fierce local protest. The restaurant is there to be sure, but the name was changed in order not to give offence.

Bibliography

de Wolf, J.J. 1998. *Eigenheid en samenwerking. 100 jaar antropologisch verenigingsleven in Nederland*. Leiden: KITLV Uitgeverij.

Fabricius, Johan. 1997. *De scheepsjongens van Bontekoe*. Amsterdam: Leopold, (originally published in 1923).

Fortuyn, Pim. 2002. *De puinhopen van tien jaar paars*. Rotterdam: Karakter Uitgevers/Speakers Academy Uitgeverij.

Kuitenbrouwer, Maarten. 2001. *Tussen oriëntalisme en wetenschap. Het Koninklijk Instituut voor Taal-, Land- en Volkenkunde in historisch verband, 1851-2001*. Leiden: KITLV Uitgeverij.

Oostindie, Gert, ed., 1999. *Facing Up to the Past. Perspectives on the Commemoration of Slavery from Africa, the Americas and Europe*. Kingston: Ian Randle/The Hague: Prince Claus Fund.

Trouillot, Michel-Rolph. 1995. *Silencing the Past. Power and the Production of History*. Boston: Beacon Press.

van Rinsum, Henk J., and Wil Pansters, 2002, The interview: "I have a 'Neolithic' mind". *CERES Magazine*, pp. 10-19. Autumn. (Interview with Arie de Ruijter, 31 October 2002)

5

The Multicultural Self
Meeting Culture inside Argentina's
Heart of Darkness

Ton Robben

In the back of a large house in the posh Belgrano neighborhood of Buenos Aires, Argentina, there was a day care center. The children played their time away in a spacious room with tiny wooden chairs, a few small tables, and colorful prints on the walls, or ran back and forth to the back garden. This would have been just an ordinary day care center in Buenos Aires, of which there were hundreds in the large Argentine metropolis, were it not that it belonged to retired Rear-Admiral Horacio Mayorga, a man with a very long trajectory in Argentina's terror and repression. The day care center was run by his daughter. One Wednesday afternoon, the 3rd of October 1990 to be exact, I spent several hours in the Admiral's home. He was a man of strong convictions and strong answers. The Admiral's hard-nosed statements, the sober design and furnishings of the living room where we spoke, the voices of the children in the background, and the episodes of violence surrounding this house, conjured up images of a multicultural tangle whose separate strands seemed hard to reconcile into one man.

In this article, I will use the persona of Rear-Admiral Mayorga to address the subject of multiculturalism that has fascinated Arie de Ruijter for more than a decade. I interpret multiculturalism here as a complex collection of group identifications, of which ethnic identity is only one exponent. Ethnicity has today been reified in the Western world as the key characteristic of multiculturality, yet as anthropologists we know that societies may also privilege other social categories such as class, gender, generation, age-set, clan, or caste. The social phenomenon of a multiplicity of cultures within one society does not stand or fall with the presence of ethnic groups, and the social principles and processes of an ethnic-cultural society are not fundamentally different from, say, a class society or a caste society. Does it not therefore make sense to broaden our investigation of multiculturalism to include how people succeed in holding on to several very different cultural frames at the same time without the ethnic component? And can we then not extrapolate these findings to multicultural arrangements that include ethnic culture as one of them? Hence, my main question is: How does multiculturalism exist within us? Or in other words, what is the multicultural self?

Self and culture: two conflicting notions

Culture is one of those essentially contested concepts in anthropology – along with power, violence, sociality, and the state – which continues to guide the discipline in untrodden directions with every new research interest. The definitions of culture abound, but Geertz' notion has had the most enduring influence on Arie de Ruijter. I will therefore use this particular concept of culture to interpret the multicultural self. According to Geertz, culture is a multi-layered web of meanings. We are born into this web, spin some threads of our own, and become entangled in the traps spun by others. In my opinion, these three formative dimensions coalesce inside the multicultural self. How do individuals live with their different group identifications, and how can they continue to participate in several very distinct cultures? Two diametrically opposed theories are relevant for this discussion: cognitive dissonance theory and shifting self theory. Both theories resonate with radically different anthropological notions of culture and self.

Cognitive dissonance theory was developed by Leon Festinger (1957), and its principal idea is that people try to bring their various cognitions into harmony with one another. A discrepancy between conflicting cognitions produces an amount of stress which the individual wishes to reduce. The greater the dissonance, the greater the desire to diminish it. As Aronson (1992:305) has stated, people attempt to "preserve a consistent, stable, predictable… morally good sense of self." We find a comparable idea about culture among cognitive anthropologists such as Roy D'Andrade and Claudia Strauss (1992), Brad Shore (1996), and Alexander Hinton (1996). They point at cognitive schemata and cultural models that are shared by the members of a society and internalized into the self. Extrapolating from these notions of self and culture to the idea of the multicultural self leads to the hypothesis that people seek to accommodate their various cultural identifications within a relatively stable and coherent self complex. The multicultural self is a cohesive whole which rejects identifications with political parties, ethnic groups, regional cultures, and the like, which lead to a cognitive dissonance with the most valued cognitions and self-representations.

The shifting self theory rejects this hypothesis about the internal consistency of the self, and states that "in all cultures people can be observed to project multiple, inconsistent self-representations that are context-dependent and may shift rapidly....The inconsistencies in these projected selves may often be associated with inconsistencies within the cultural system itself, inconsistencies that may be most clearly observed during negotiation and argument among situationally located actors" (Ewing 1990:251-252; see also Battaglia 1995; Mageo 1995). These ideas about the self show a remarkable similarity, albeit on a different level of social complexity, with a conceptualization of culture influenced by globalization theory. Culture is no longer regarded as either a blueprint for behavior or a unified whole of meanings, but rather as an ever-changing, contingent, inchoate and fragmented hybrid of meanings and practices. People draw upon a diversity of cultural scapes, such as domestic life, neighborhoods, professions, companies, political parties, ideologies, sports, religions, moralities, and ideals. The composition of cultural scapes can be the same for two individuals, but the weight attributed to each of them in a particular context varies from setting to setting. Furthermore, different identities come to the fore in different contexts which lead to situated reconfigurations of the self. As a result, the multicultural self is not a single well-integrated whole but a fluid, fragmented collection of multiple social and personal identities which are subject to ongoing self-evaluations in dialogue with a continuously transforming context.

I will take the unlikely figure of Rear-Admiral Mayorga to illustrate both notions of the multicultural self. I say "unlikely" because Mayorga was a violent person, but also a cultured person. He was a person who carried the contradictions of Argentine multiculturality within himself. It has been the merit of Clifford Geertz to draw general lessons about culture from extraordinary events, such as theater play and cockfights in Bali. In this same heuristic vein, I will take one unusual person as a means to understanding the multicultural self.

The Rear-Admiral's multicultural self

Which identity turned Rear-Admiral Mayorga into a public persona and weighed most heavily on his multicultural self? Above all, Mayorga saw himself as a navy man, albeit of a particular breed. He belonged to the naval aviation, a select group of pilots that landed on aircraft carriers, supported infantry marines storming hostile shores, and undertook daring missions across Patagonia – the same boundless expanse where Antoine de Saint Exupéry had his most harrowing experience before World War Two. Soon after taking off from the airstrip at the town of Trelew, De Saint Exupéry experienced a sense of absolute powerlessness over the machine in his hands, two wings tossing and turning in a cyclone. He relates that he moved forward less than one hundred meters in twenty minutes, utterly surrendered to the whims of nature. De Saint Exupéry found himself unable to express his helplessness: "The reason why writers fail when they attempt to evoke horror is that horror is something invented after the fact, when one is re-creating the experience over again in the memory. Horror does not manifest itself in the world of reality" (De Saint Exupéry 1967:54).

Now, Rear-Admiral Mayorga had had his own brush with horror. In fact, he inflicted, saw, and experienced horror himself. Thus, De Saint Exupéry was right only in respect to the case of victims of violence who evoke horror *after the fact;* but some perpetrators plan that same horror in advance. Mayorga was involved in many episodes of horror in Argentine post-World War Two history, at the Plaza de Mayo in Buenos Aires, at the Trelew airport forty years after De Saint Exupéry had nearly met his end, and at his own home. Was it the powerlessness experienced in Patagonia's open skies which turned Mayorga into a political hawk? Or was it the naval culture, that had hardened him so? Through what kinds of cultures did Mayorga move in his life? If culture is that layered web of meaning, in which meanings was he enwrapped?

As a cadet at the Naval Academy, Mayorga had served on board the *Libertad*, the majestic three-master whose voyage ended with the first commission of every junior naval lieutenant. This initiation ritual served to bond the young officers into a tight cohort with a strong "we"-feeling shaped in opposition to an ever-changing outer world, as one harbor made way for another, and culture after culture passed before their eyes. The octogenarian Admiral Isaac Rojas told me all about these annual voyages, which circled the globe: "The girls, aah, the girls in Tahiti." Like a twentieth-century Captain Bligh, he reveled in the exotic, the distant islands, far, so far away from Buenos Aires, with its cobble stones, patrician houses, and long avenues. I wonder what Mayorga thought of it all. How did he see Tahiti, Hong Kong, India, Cape Town, and all those other strange harbors? How much did it influence the constitution of his multicultural self? Did those foreign exotic peoples have culture, or did he and his peers regard themselves as the only cultured – and therefore the only civilized – inhabitants on this world? The voyage of the *Libertad* was, in my eyes, one long exercise in "othering" which further enhanced the "we-versus-them" attitude of the cadets, which had been formed during their years spent at the Naval Academy.

Upon his return to Buenos Aires, Mayorga must have been swept up in the political events in Argentina during the early-1950s. Around that time, the populist leader Juan Domingo Perón managed to become president of Argentina by riding on a working class ticket. The Navy, always ideologically on the right, was his staunchest opponent within the armed forces. The Navy was an elite institution with both a strict hierarchy and a strong camaraderie shaped by the close quarters at sea, and by an unpredictable natural environment in which one man had to rely completely on his mate. Strong sentiments against Perón fermented within the Navy, and Mayorga was in the middle of it all. In 1951 and 1952, military rebellions against Perón all failed, but the forces of opposition had become stronger by the mid-1955.

On Thursday morning, June 16, 1955, Perón was warned of a possible naval insurrection. An air strike on the Casa Rosada presidential palace with the intent of killing Perón had been planned for June 16, at 10 o'clock in the morning. The discovery of the plot demanded swift action from the naval rebels. The strike force included a young navy pilot by the name of Horacio Mayorga. The attack planes tried to take advantage of a fly-over in tribute to the Argentine flag to drop their deadly load of bombs (Comisión de Afirmación 1985:46). Dense fog prevented the planes from taking off on time, but when they finally did and released their fragmentation bombs at 0:40 P.M., the devastation it caused among the people who had assembled at the Plaza de Mayo to watch the aerial salute, was horrendous. The first civilians were killed by shattering glass. Many more civilian casualties were caused when a bomb hit a crowded trolley. One bomber made a direct hit on the Casa Rosada, but Perón was unhurt. He had taken refuge in the War Ministry that morning after hearing of the rebellion (Page 1983:307-309; Potash 1980:181-188).

A second bombardment was carried out at 1:10 P.M, which again caused many deaths. Meanwhile, groups of Peronists began to arrive at the Plaza de Mayo. Shouting "Perón, Perón," they formed a crowd in front of the Casa Rosada. The streets were by now filled with vehicles carrying workers coming to Perón's rescue. A number of workers were killed by machine-gun fire as they arrived at the Casa Rosada. The last assault took place around 3:30 P.M. when a squadron dropped their bombs and killed many soldiers and civilians in the zone of action before fleeing to Uruguay. Army troops loyal to Perón succeeded in retaking the Plaza de Mayo. The toll of the four-hour insurrection was 355 dead and more than 600 wounded (Page 1983:310).

The June rebellion failed, but a new conspiracy was planned for September. The Liberating Revolution *(Revolución Libertadora)* was launched on 16 September 1955 when General Lonardi rose in rebellion in Córdoba, together with all other major naval bases. Perón declared a state of siege but did not advance with his loyal troops on the rebels. On 18 September, Rear-Admiral Rojas broke the standoff by threatening to bomb the oil depots in Buenos Aires harbor and the oil refinery in La Plata. The next morning, naval salvos destroyed the oil depots in Mar del Plata. Perón feared a further escalation, delegated his army command, and took refuge in the Paraguayan Embassy on 20 September. He moved to a Paraguayan gunboat anchored in the harbor of Buenos Aires, and finally left Argentina on 3 October by twin-engine flying boat, destined for Asunción (Page 1983:325, 332; Potash 1980:200-202).

Nearly twenty years of political disenfranchisement were imposed on the Peronist movement. Cold War rhetoric and a growing fear of a Cuban-inspired insurgency war took hold of the Argentine military in the 1960s. A few attempts to start a guerrilla movement in Argentina during the 1960s failed. But growing worker unrest with the military dictatorship, the intolerable proscription of Peronism, and a revolutionary enthusiasm among the younger generation all helped to fuel a vigorous outburst of guerrilla insurgency in 1970. It would not be until 1972 before the exiled Perón could set foot once again on Argentine soil, subsequently winning the presidential elections of 1973. Meanwhile, Horacio Mayorga made his way up in the ranks of the Navy. He was a staunch anti-Peronist and a staunch anti-Communist. He favored crushing the Peronist and Marxist guerrilla organizations, and supported the counterinsurgency measures taken by the Argentine military government.

The counterinsurgency operations of Lieutenant-General Lanusse's military government proved highly successful. The principal leaders of most of the guerrilla organizations, Peronist as well as Marxist, were in prison by mid-1972. The authorities hoped to prevent guerrillas from freeing imprisoned comrades, as had happened on two occasions in 1971, in addition to impeding guerrilla commanders from planning operations from their prison cells. Many guerrilla leaders were therefore sent to Rawson, the small capital of the province of Chubut, about fifteen hundred kilometers south of Buenos Aires. Far from any major urban center and hemmed in by the icy South Atlantic on one side, and the wind-swept plains of Patagonia on the other, the maximum security prison of Rawson seemed escape-proof. By mid-1972, it held around two hundred political prisoners (Urondo 1988:32-33).

The Trelew Tragedy: the admiral and the guerrilla

The guerrilla insurgency had come to a virtual standstill by 1972 because of an effective counterinsurgency campaign. The imprisoned guerrilla commanders felt that the political process needed a spectacular action to jump-start the armed resistance, in addition to freeing valuable comrades and demonstrating that they were far from defeated. They decided to try to escape from Rawson prison. The operation was under the command of Mario Roberto Santucho, the undisputed leader of the Marxist ERP, the People's Revolutionary Army. The ERP military committee still at large had initially rejected Santucho's plan to take the prison from the inside. They had regarded this unlikely plan as the fantasy of a person who, because of his lengthy incarceration, had lost touch with reality. Instead, the ERP commanders proposed to take the prison through an attack from the outside. However, Santucho pulled rank to ensure that his audacious plan prevailed.

On 15 August 1972, at about 6:30 P.M., one of the incarcerated guerrillas, feinting a complaint, called the attention of a prison guard. The guard approached the cell and was immediately subdued. By taking hostages, a group of over one hundred guerrillas began to take over the prison: guard by guard, room by room, and pavilion by pavilion. To facilitate their escape, the guerrillas dress themselves in the uniforms of their hostages. By the time all eight pavilions had been occupied by the prisoners, around seventy guards had been subdued. The maximum-security prison was now almost completely taken, except for the front gate. The guard at the gate, Juan Gregorio Valenzuela, did not recognize the guerrilla who approached him disguised as a prison guard. Valenzuela orders the other guards to arrest the man. Gunfire erupts. Valenzuela is killed and a second guard is wounded. The mood of the prisoners turns exuberant. Once in control of the prison, the guerrillas opened the gate and began to wait for two trucks (a pickup truck and a passenger car) to come and take them to the Rawson airport. However, only the passenger car arrived. Already doubtful about the feasibility of Santucho's plan, his comrades outside the prison assumed that the operation had failed when they heard the gunshots that killed the guard. They immediately decided to flee with the three trucks. To make things worse, the guerrilla commander in charge of leading the operation from outside the prisoner got into a car accident, and was detained by the police (Mattini 1990:161-163; Tapia 1972:4-6).

Nevertheless, Santucho decided to proceed as planned to the Rawson airport, situated at about twenty-five kilometers from the prison. The six highest ranking guerrillas, among who were Fernando Vaca Narvaja and, of course, Mario Roberto Santucho, got in the car and left. In the meantime, the others called four taxis, just in case the trucks did not arrive. The car containing the six guerrilla leaders continued to the airport where a passenger plane was to due to make a scheduled stop on its flight from Comodoro Rivadavia to Buenos Aires. Four guerrillas were on board, ready to hijack the plane once it landed at Rawson airport. At the airport, the group of six escapees watched – astounded – as the plane taxied to the end of the runway for take-off. Apparently, the hijackers assumed that the prison break had failed. However, the plane's flight was prevented when one of the escaped guerrillas took charge of the control tower by posing as a first lieutenant, ordering the plane to stop under the pretense of a bomb scare. Precious minutes tick by as they wait for the second group to arrive. By 7:20 P.M., Santucho decided that they could wait no longer wait, and the plane leaves for Chile. Left behind to their tragic fate were nineteen men and five women, including Santucho's wife, who was eight-months pregnant, and Vaca Narvaja's companion (Urondo 1988:53-60).

Once the taxis had reached Rawson prison, the nineteen escapees left immediately for the airport. They arrived at 7:45 P.M., and took control of the terminal. Aware of the security risks involved, they immediately demanded the presence of a judge. After four hours of negotiations, pressured by the army's declaration of a state of emergency, and surrounded by a marine infantry unit poised for assault, the group finally surrendered. The commanding officer, Navy Captain Sosa, must have felt humiliated by the guarantees that the guerrillas managed to extract from him, for even the conscripts under his command snickered behind his back. One navy officer expressed his frustration to a journalist: "I'm disappointed. We came to liquidate them all and they're alive. If they would have fired one single shot, then we wouldn't have left one alive...." (Tapia 1972:2). The guerrillas received guarantees that they would not be harmed, and subsequently gave a press conference to explain their political ideas. They demanded to be taken to Rawson, but this prison was still in the hands of their remaining comrades. Instead, they were taken to the nearby Almirante Zar naval airbase, in Trelew.

At Trelew, the nineteen guerrillas were kept in eight cells located on both sides of a narrow passageway. They were heavily guarded, interrogated, and mistreated, but not tortured. On 22 August, at 3:30 A.M., the prisoners were awakened to hear Navy Captain Sosa saying, "They will see what it means to pick a fight with the navy." A few minutes later they heard Navy Lieutenant Bravo saying, "Now they will see what antiguerrilla terror means" (Urondo 1988:108). The guerrillas were forced to leave their cells. They were ordered to form two lines and to stand with their heads bowed. As the last inmate stepped into the passageway, two machine guns suddenly opened fire, spraying them with long bursts. Several of the prisoners threw themselves into the cells in an attempt to escape. Alberto Camps, one of the three survivors, later recalled what happened after the firing stopped: "When they stopped, one then heard the moans, the death rattles of the comrades, even curses. And then isolated shots began to sound. I realized that they were finishing them off, someone even said: 'This one is still alive,' and immediately after one heard a shot" (Urondo 1988:111). Camps was shot in the stomach by Lieutenant Bravo, immediately causing him to begin vomiting blood. Next, René Haidar was shot in the chest by another Navy officer, while María Antonia Berger was hit in the jaw after being shot in the face. Berger recalled, "I was amazed at myself that I was calm. Very, very angry at the inability to be able to make even the smallest reaction. I realized that any reaction would be wrong, because I was totally in their power, that they were killing us. That was what I most felt" (Urondo 1988:121).

These three survivors, along with three other mortally wounded comrades, played dead until help arrived. The heavy gunfire had apparently startled other guards who were not aware that a massacre was planned. It would still take at least half an hour before the paramedics arrived on the scene to take the wounded to the sick bay. The three grievously wounded guerrillas died for lack of attention. The three survivors were flown the next day to Bahía Blanca for further treatment, and would eventually be taken to the Villa Devoto prison near Buenos Aires. Outraged by this brutal turn of events, President Allende refused to extradite the six escaped guerrilla commanders and their four accomplices to Argentina, allowing them to continue to Cuba on 23 August. Allende would be overthrown two weeks later by a military coup.

This account of the Trelew killings is largely based on the testimony of the three survivors. Their suffering did not end here. They had survived the massacre at Trelew, but did would not survive the dirty war. Humiliated by the events, the Navy pursued the three with unrelenting tenacity. Camps disappeared in 1977, Berger in 1979, and Haidar in 1982.

I was told two different versions of the events by two key players in the tragedy, namely retired Rear-Admiral Mayorga, and former Montonero guerrilla commander Fernando Vaca Narvaja, who had escaped with Santucho to Chile. Rear-Admiral Horacio Mayorga, who in 1972 a navy captain, was at the time the commander of the naval air-force base Almirante Zar, which was under construction at Trelew. Mayorga gives a version of the Rawson escape that differs from the one recounted by the three survivors. He states that the guerrillas had threatened to harm the wives of some prison guards, saying, "Today your wife is visiting such a person in such a place. If you don't open the cell, we'll kill her." The cell doors were opened, but the prison guard Valenzuela, at the front gate, sensed that something is wrong. "Valenzuela went and set off the buzzers that sound in the naval base, which gave the alarm that something was happening in the prison. Santucho's wife killed him. She pumped him with fourteen shots; with this I saw everything about the delicateness of the female guerrillas."

After the six guerrillas escaped to Chile, so explains Mayorga, and the nineteen remaining comrades were taken to Trelew, he expressly ordered that if any hostages were taken that the guards should open fire at both the hostages and the guerrillas. He knew that Trelew was a security risk because the cells at the navy base were mere calabooses built for disciplining soldiers, not for holding guerrillas. According to Mayorga, when the navy guards suspected that the guerrillas had arms hidden in their cells they order them out into the passageway. "They begin to revise everything, searching for weapons, but they don't find any because [the imprisoned guerrillas] didn't have weapons. More military arrived at this moment, didn't they? They asked, 'What's happening?' And in the middle of the shouting and everything, someone said 'I was looking for weapons,' which the others heard as 'He has weapons.' The result was that they planted themselves in front of those [prisoners] who were arranged into two lines. The fire fight took place when Pujadas and the entire group rushed forward, he [Pujadas] took the pistol from the commanding officer and shot at the guards."

Mayorga arrived two and a half hours after the shooting. "My shoes were sticking to the blood in the passageway. The people were still in a cataleptic state; there was a smell of gun powder over everything." He concluded that if the Navy had really wanted to kill the guerrillas, then they would have done a better job by taking them outside to simulate an attempted escape, instead of shooting them in a narrow two-meter-wide passageway, and afterwards saving the lives of three of them.

In my interviews with him on 1 October and 13 December 1990, Fernando Vaca Narvaja, who had escaped safely from the Rawson prison with the other five guerrilla commanders, vehemently refutes Mayorga's version of the killings at Trelew:

> First, none of us is suicidal. It is known that the possibilities of, for example, an escape are studied and analyzed. In the second place....trying to escape from a military base at which they arrived at night, without knowing the watch, the building, the features, is madness. We never committed those kinds of follies. That is to say, rationally, there is nothing that supports this. In the third place, the comrades surrendered themselves openly, filmed by television, with lawyers and judges present.

Why would the guerrillas risk their lives in a unprepared escape from an unknown prison when only days before the navy commander went to lengths to guarantee their safety? And why would the Navy tirelessly hunt the survivors of Trelew for an entire decade? Simply, so Vaca Narvaja contends, because they were the only surviving witnesses of the infamous massacre. And why did the Navy not orchestrate a more credible escape by taking the prisoners outside and shooting them there? Because, says Vaca Narvaja, there were hundreds of conscripts at the naval base who would have been unwilling witnesses to the mock flight. And why, finally, were the guerrillas killed at Trelew? Vaca Narvaja offers two reasons: firstly, revenge for the daring Rawson prison escape, and secondly, recalling the words of a military officer, killing these experienced guerrillas was "a strategic investment" in counterinsurgency warfare.

After weighing the two versions, by reading the conflicting testimonies and examining the forensic autopsy reports, and by comparing the intentions of the principal actors, I am just as convinced as were Argentine human rights organizations, lawyer associations, professional associations, and the international press at the time that the Trelew killings were deliberate executions. However, the importance of Trelew does not simply stop upon ascertaining the true course of events. Each version has an internal coherence that makes it convincing when placed in a compatible cultural context that corresponds to a benign political discourse. The supporters of one version or the other do not only judge them from their professional identity, either as a naval officer or a guerrilla commander, either as right or left, Catholic, communist, or Peronist, but from an interplay with other identities. In these matters of life and death, the whole multicultural self becomes involved.

Mayorga's version of the Trelew tragedy was entirely convincing to the members of the armed forces and their political allies because it fitted in perfectly with their perception of the guerrilla's military culture, political practice, and personal character. Their own account emphasized the treachery of the guerrillas (e.g. registering a complaint under false pretense), their disregard for the lives of innocent civilians (intimidating prison guards by threatening their wives), and their blind ferocity (Santucho's pregnant wife killing the prison guard Valenzuela). Furthermore, the flights to Allende's Chile and to Castro's Cuba demonstrated that Argentina's guerrilla insurgency was not just a domestic political affair, but part of a global revolutionary strategy.

As far as the military themselves were concerned, they emphasized various aspects of their conduct: their commitment to maintaining law and order in Argentina, their correct treatment of the prisoners, their altruistic donation of blood to save lives, the due process given to the guerrillas by holding an official investigation, permitting a federal court to conduct the trial, and allowing lawyers to defend the suspects. This discourse served to legitimize the position of the military in Argentine society, convinced them of the value of their own sacrifices, and entrenched them further within an irreconcilable position. The contextual coherence of the multicultural self, summoned to interpret the killings, was thus confirmed. It all made sense, even emotionally.

Likewise, the rendition of the revolutionary left served to bolster their perception of themselves as individuals who were sacrificing their lives for the future of Argentina. It showed their dedication to the struggle (e.g. Santucho and Vaca Narvaja leaving their wives behind); their brilliance and creativity in devising the escape plan (takeover from within instead of an assault from the outside); their daring (ordering taxis to the prison); the camaraderie in prison (cooperation of Marxist and Peronist guerrillas); their professionalism, discipline, and compassion (refusing to use the civilians at the airport as hostages). They paint the military as incompetent (the easy takeover of the Rawson prison and Captain Sosa's inability to impose his conditions), ruthless (planning to attack the airport despite the presence of civilians), cruel (tormenting the prisoners), cowardly (giving the coups de grace to several mortally wounded prisoners), and without military honor (delaying the medical assistance to the wounded). This political discourse was just as convincing to the revolutionary left as the official version was to the military.

In these two renditions of the Trelew tragedy, we notice a great discrepancy between different conceptions of self and other. The guerrilla commander Vaca Narvaja sees himself (and by extension all guerrillas) as a courageous freedom fighter who is compassionate towards his fellow citizens and willing to sacrifice his life for a better society. Rear-Admiral Horacio Mayorga regards himself, and the military as a whole, as a tireless defender of the Argentine people and its institutions, concerned for the well-being of his fellow citizens, and convinced of the importance of due process. Each self-ascribed quality constitutes one component of a composite self that refers to different cultural scapes, to different webs of meaning. In the case of Mayorga, his self-perceived compassion relates to Christianity; his defense of the Argentine state relates to national history and political sovereignty; his altruism pertains to the social contract of civil society; his protection of the Argentine people pertains to his sense of family and community; and his belief in due process, to justice. This complex cultural inventory of Mayorga's multicultural self came together at Trelew, replete with its obvious contradictions. Still, his coherent multicultural self would soon come apart as the political violence in Argentina escalated after 1974, and end up being rearranged into a new composite.

The aftermath of Trelew

Tainted by his role at the Trelew navy base, Mayorga resigned his commission when Perón reassumed the presidency in 1973. His personal convictions simply would not permit him to serve under a Peronist government. Besides, he also feared revenge from the Peronist and Marxist guerrilla organizations, which had not yet demobilized. Old and new accounts were bound to be settled. According to the leftist press, Mayorga was not only one of the Navy pilots who had bombed the civilians at the Plaza de Mayo in June 1955, but had also been involved in the Trelew massacre (Cheren 1997:166).

Today, Rear-Admiral Mayorga is still haunted by the chant, "Soon you will see, soon you will see, when we avenge the Trelew dead," a chant that obsessed all the military because the chance of a revenge killing was very real. "You are talking to an ordinary admiral," Rear-Admiral Mayorga told me in 1990.

> They tried to kidnap my daughter, they came looking for her at her high
> school. They shot my guard here at the watch, and they let me know
> from Puerto Belgrano that an ERP [People's Revolutionary Army] guerril-
> la had picked up my maid at a catechism class in the church next door
> so that she would place a bomb [under my bed]....The navy made me
> change destinations every fifteen days when I retired, from Puerto Bel-
> grano I went to Salta, to Ushuaia, to Rio Gallegos and so on. And this
> may seem all very amusing, but there comes a moment that it uproots
> you from everything, and it makes you afraid, it makes you afraid. This
> is what happens.

Perón failed to control the revolutionary organizations in Argentina after returning from exile, and his death in July 1974 led to a process of political disintegration owing to resurgent violence, and to the incompetent leadership of Perón's widow and successor as president of Argentina, Isabel Martínez de Perón. The Argentine armed forces decid-ed to step in on 24 March 1976, to stamp out the guerrilla insurgency and the leftist political opposition once and for all. They disappeared tens of thousands of citizens for shorter or longer periods into secret detention centers, and assassinated around ten thousand of them.

Rear-Admiral Mayorga continued in retirement but maintained his contacts within the Navy. I asked him about the disappearances during the military dictatorship. He responded that he had always openly approved the death sentence for the guerrillas, but he disapproved of the disappearances. As he said five years earlier: "As far as I'm concerned, they should have executed them at the River Plate [soccer stadium] with free Coca-Cola and broadcast on television. But one thing yes: with a signed order" (*El Porteño* 1985 4:24). Here, the multicultural self of Trelew came apart and was rearranged in a different way. He no longer talked about due process for the con-demned guerrillas, but emphasized the importance of maintaining military honor in times of war. He believed that commanders should be responsible for their orders because orders given without written authorization undermined the honor of officers and troops, and thus the legitimacy of the armed forces.

Once more during the interview, Rear-Admiral Mayorga revealed how his multicultural self had changed in the nearly two decades since Trelew. He seemed to have forgotten his emphasis on due process and related to me on that Wednesday afternoon in October 1990 the procedure adopted by the Navy to dispose of the disappeared.

> You would take a guerrilla, obtain the information, and decide in a small committee without a trial or signature whatever fate he was going to run. It is a lie that there were no verdicts. There were verdicts. But it is true that nobody ever signed the verdict. The death of any guerrilla was always decided by at least five persons. But one thing yes, five persons who like you and me, sitting like this, said, 'That one can't go on living.' What did they do? I tell you what happened in the Navy, without any false sentiments. You will say, 'but did they....?' No, no, if not, I won't tell you anything and that's the end of it, isn't it? Very well, they injected them and threw them in the sea. They didn't....He didn't even know that he was going to die, I can assure you.

Did Mayorga intend to say with his last sentence that he had personally witnessed the body drops? Had he been on board a Fokker cargo plane that threw thirty, forty people into the ocean? Other high-ranking Navy officers have been spotted on these death flights to increase the morale of the troops. Was Mayorga also present, and how did he reconcile these merciless assassinations with his Christian self?

Final comments

What I have been trying to demonstrate with my exposé of Rear-Admiral Mayorga is that multiculturalism does not only exist among ethnic groups within the confines of the state, but also within the self; for culture is a multi-layered web of meanings, a composite of cultural domains, scapes, and identities that rearrange continuously under changing contextual circumstances. In fact, I want to argue that we experience multiculturalism first of all within ourselves as we participate in one cultural scape after another, accumulating cultural identification upon cultural identification. People, like Rear-Admiral Mayorga, strive after a cohesive, internally consistent self, and will discard cognitions and cultural identifications that rub the wrong way, while seeking out others that are more in tune with their desired self-representation. This notion of a cohesive self is not in contradiction with the multicultural self, a self which readjusts itself continuously to the changing political circumstances, as happened with Rear-Admiral Mayorga before, during, and after the dirty war. This succession of multicultural selves is not disjointed or discontinuous because many people cling throughout their adult lives to some core self-representation which towers above all others acquired along the way. In the case of Mayorga, this core self-representation was his staunch anti-Peronism and anti-communism.

Core self-representations constitute the personal foundation on which our multicultural selves are erected, through which we participate in the different cultural realities around us, and engage with political or religious ideologies to become multicultural complexes. These core selves are conceived within the home, and then branch out into society. The day care center is today often the first cultural scape outside the home, an intimate cultural environment that in one particular instance is run from a house in the heart of Buenos Aires that is saturated with the remnants of a dark past whose shadows reach back into the hearts of many tormented multicultural selves.

Bibliography

Aronson, Elliot. 1992. The Return of the Repressed: Dissonance Theory Makes a Comeback. *Psychological Inquiry* 3:303-352.

Battaglia, Deborah, ed. 1995. *Rhetorics of Self-Making*. Berkeley: University of California Press.

Cheren, Liliana. 1997. *La Masacre de Trelew 22 de Agosto de 1972: Institucionalización del Terrorismo de Estado*. Buenos Aires: Corregidor.

Comisión de Afirmación de la Revolución Libertadora. 1985. *A 30 años de la Revolución Libertadora*. Buenos Aires: Edición de la Comisión.

D'Andrade Roy, and Claudia Strauss, eds. 1992. *Human Motives and Cultural Models*. New York: Cambridge University Press.

De Saint Exupéry, A. 1967. *Wind, Sand and Stars*. New York: Harcourt, Brace.

Ewing, Katherine P. 1990. The Illusion of Wholeness: Culture, Self, and the Experience of Inconsistency. *Ethos* 18(3):251-278.

Festinger, Leon. 1957. *A Theory of Cognitive Dissonance*. Evanston, IL: Row.

Hinton, Alexander Laban. 1996. Agents of Death: Explaining the Cambodian Genocide in Terms of Psychosocial Dissonance. *American Anthropologist* 98(4):818-831.

Mageo, Janet M. 1995. The Reconfiguring Self. *American Anthropologist* 97(2):282-296.

Mattini, Luis. 1990. *Hombres y Mujeres del PRT-ERP*. Buenos Aires: Editorial Contrapunto.

Page, Joseph A. 1983. *Perón: A Biography*. New York: Random House.

Potash, Robert A. 1980. *The Army and Politics in Argentina, 1945-1962: Perón to Frondizi*. London: The Athlone Press.

Shore, Brad. 1996. *Culture in Mind: Cognition, Culture, and the Problem of Meaning*. New York: Oxford University Press.

Tapia, José Carrasco. 1972. La fuga que conmovió al continente. *Punto Final* 166:1-15.

Urondo, Francisco. 1988. *Trelew: La patria fusilada*. Buenos Aires: Editorial Contrapunto. (Originally published in 1973.)

6

The Life and Times of Religion and Human Rights

Bas de Gaay Fortman and Mohamed Salih

> "There are great cultural differences but there are also great universals."
>
> The Economist, January 9th 1993

Seen from a human perspective and as communal protection of human dignity, human rights are universal challenges to which all major traditions of the human family have subscribed. However, the many ways and means to realise this universal human ideal have been subject to controversy because of differences in the life and times in which human rights conceptions were conceived, and the life and times during which they are profiled. Another issue relates to how compliance to human rights may be reinforced by such things as reference to the life and times during which the major religious and philosophical traditions of the human family were conceived, or the life and times experienced by humans over the centuries.

In this paper we argue that human rights and religion are mutually reinforcing insofar as human rights are related to spiritual roots – and hence not conceived as "a secular religion" – and provided that religion is seen within the full dynamic context of the life and times of its adherence. However, like other ethics (religious or secular) human rights ethics are about rights and wrongs, rights and duties, norms and expectations, and not just instruments for compliance devoid of peoples' reality. In short, we contend that in the field of human rights, religion should be conceived as a mirror of the life and times during which it is practised. Concomitantly, it should be supplicated as the cultural context in which the struggle for the protection of basic human dignity has to find its spiritual roots, rather than the life and times within which it became part of the human tradition.

The life of religion

One of the main questions often encountered by the student of religion and human rights is, why have world religions that assume a sense of universality (transcending nation, state, kinship, culture and language) come to pose such serious challenges to human rights' enduring claims of counter-universality? At face value, no world religion is devoid of a modicum of advocacy and inspiration for the respect and observance of human rights. Paradoxically, the universality of human rights, and that too of religion, have at many times come been on a collision course, with each presenting a challenge to specific points of divergence. The points of divergence are, in our view, driven from the historical specificity of the early life and times of religion, which have changed tremendously throughout the centuries. The divergence as well as convergence of religion and human rights does not emanate from the general premise of the indivisibility of human rights. In retrospect, there is more in common between religion and human rights than the challenges posed by each as historical realities, or as encounters amongst civilizations.

In the Judo-Christian tradition, four of the Ten Commandments instruct us that (1) you shall not murder, (2) you shall not steal, (3) do not give false testimony against your neighbor and (4) you shall not covet your fellow's possessions. A more recent re-reading of these commandments was echoed in article 4 of the *Montreal Declaration on Judaism and Human Rights* (April 23, 1974), which reads:

> We call on Jewish communities to preserve and sharpen the traditional
> sensitivity of the Jewish conscience to the plight of the downtrodden,
> whoever and wherever they may be. We reaffirm our faith in study,
> teaching and education as means to advance human rights throughout
> the world. More than that, we pledge to be advocates and activists for
> human rights.

The life and times of Moses and the Ten Commandments and the practices of a reconstituted Jewish State are a world apart, but the essence of the message now and is the same as it was then: "Human rights are an integral part of the faith and tradition of Judaism. The beliefs that man was created in the divine image, that the human family is one, and that every person is obliged to deal justly with every other person are basic sources of the Jewish commitment to human rights (Article I of the Montreal Declaration) (Konvitz e.a., 2001).

In Christianity, the message does not differ. In the Sermon on the Mount (Matthew 5:43-48), Christians were told to defy the truism, "Love your friend, and hate your enemy". Instead, Jesus pronounced,

> But what I tell you is this: Love your enemies and pray for your perse-
> cutors; only so can you be children of your heavenly Father, who makes
> his sun shine on good and bad alike, and sends the rain on the honest
> and the dishonest. If you love only those who love you, what reward
> can you expect? Surely the tax-gatherers do as much as that. And if you
> greet only your brothers, what is there extraordinary about that? Even the
> heathen do as much. There must be no limit to your goodness, as your
> heavenly Father's goodness knows no bounds.

Human rights is portrayed as a call for respecting the dignity even of those who intend to humiliate you, thus ushering in compassion as the essence of tolerance, by which the views of others are accommodated even when these views are confrontational.

True, Islam also advocates human rights. The conception of human rights in Islam is outlined by Allamah Abu a-Ala Mawdudi (1996) as follows: Every human being has (1) the right to life, (2) the right to the safety of life, (3) respect for the chastity of women, (4) the right to a basic standard of life, (5) individual's right to freedom, (6) the right to justice, (7) equality of human beings and (8) the right to co-operate and not to co-operate with rules. Yet it is doubtful whether non-Muslims or secularists would disagree with such a notion of human rights. Moreover, the democratic credentials of the rulers of the states that proclaimed themselves to be Islamic are generally questionable, for it is obvious that they abuse human rights under the name of Islam. The reality is even worse with militant Muslims, despite the militants' insistence on the divinity of some historical cultural practices vis-à-vis controversial sharia issues, such as individual freedoms, the position of women in Islamic public law (inheritance, stoning to death for adultery), flogging and amputation of limps in cases of theft. Mawdudi hastens to lament that:

> Thus all those temporal authorities who claim to be Muslims and yet violate the rights sanctioned by God belong to one of these two categories, either they are the disbelievers or are the wrongdoers and mischief-makers. The rights which have been sanctioned by God are permanent, perpetual and eternal. They are not subject to any alterations or modifications, and there is no scope for any change or abrogation (1996: 3).

From the perspective of a larger synthesis, we may ask the following questions: Who are those Muslim, Christian and Jewish leaders who abuse human rights and still claim to be doing that in order to protect or comply with the teachings of their faith? Is the discrepancy between believe and practice a religious necessity or part of political expediency or both? This question was addressed in terms of dichotomies. Kelsay and Twiss (1994: 72-73) put it in terms of significant distinctions in the relation between religion and advocacy for human rights. The distinctions are premised in respect to: 1) appearance versus reality, 2) duties versus rights, 3) theory and practice 4) law versus morality and 5) whole versus part.

At a crude level of generalization, it is obvious that the life of a religion changes with its times, in accordance with changes in the socio-economic and political context within which the religious meaning and message are perceived and acted upon. A glimpse at the life of religion would instruct us that all world religions have emerged to redress one form or another of human right crisis. Christianity as a world religion evolved as a reaction to the disintegration of the Roman Empire and the declining morality of its city-states. This crisis ushered an age of tyranny in which civilization became synonymous with the brutality of rulers and the arrogance of aristocracy. The situation was not different for Islam, which emerged in Mecca – a city described as one immersed in vices and oppression. It was a polytheist society that had turned its back to Christianity and Judaism, instead worshipping idols and man-made Gods. The aristocracy of Mecca accumulated large amounts of wealth through extortion, exploitation, and oppression. In what was known as *Jahiliya* (the age of ignorance, an equivalent to Europe's "dark ages") in which infanticide or the killing of girls was commonplace and sanctioned by tradition (Adler, 1996).

World religions, therefore, came about as alternative civilizing missions to civilizations in crisis. Historically, one of the consequences of civilization crises was disrespect for human dignity, which the world religions strived to restore. As sources of alternative value systems and as a response to lives filled with darkness, world religions maintained a confrontation posture to injustice and the abuse of human rights, so much so that some these religions (particularly their militant versions) considered all that is not in conformity as a challenge to their authority.

However, let us not lose sight of the fact that Christianity, Judaism, and Islam are a world apart in their conception of what really constitutes what is behind the facade of the respect of human dignity. To be more precise, the difference is on whether religious and cultural differences impact on the quality of human relations and the relativity of dignity – even the receptivity of culture. The conflict between worldly politics and heavenly claims are not new in Jewish, Christian, and Islamic thought (Gustafson e.a., 1999). However, unlike Judaism and Islam, the Christian world has adopted Roman (i.e. man-made) rather than divine law. In a recent study Kraynak (2000) argues that, "Christian divine law cannot be codified directly into civil law or translated into a specific political order." In Jesus' words, it implies a distinction between duties to God and duties to the ruler (Caesar), requiring some detachment from government, and therefore presents itself as eschewing any apparent intimacy between church and state. The fear here is that a church close to government might fail in its responsibility to protect the rights of those aggrieved by government's actions (e.g as has often been vividly illustrated in the history of many Latin American countries – editor's note).

To be sure, despite each one's claim of universality, the contention between religion and the modern conception of human rights constitute a domain of competing, and at times contrasting, views vis-à-vis the debate on universality versus relativism. In other words, relativism invokes either bygone historical realities or realities reminiscent of the early life of religion; but relativism is projected by some religious establishments as at odds with the times of human rights. Orentlicher summarizes the relativists' position as follows: "Moral claims derive their meaning and legitimacy from the (particular) cultural tradition in which they are embedded." (2001: 141). In the relativists' view, "What we call universal human rights are, in fact, an expression above all of Western values derived from the Enlightenment." Understood in this light, the human rights idea is at best misguided in its core claim that it embodies universal values – and at worst a blend of moral hubris and cultural imperialism". In our view, the counter-critique of relativism centers on two points.

Firstly, cultural and religious relativists deny the relativism, and this is more so in the case of religion. In other words, with all their claims of universality, religions have constantly adapted the messages of the society of their times either to the changing global reality, or to the realities of the societies and new geographical areas to which they have expanded. In a sense the debates and competing claims within religion are as diverse and complex as their claims with other religions and secularists. While the message and meaning of the religious verse (as we have seen earlier) constitute an embodiment of human dignity, "dignity," which Ingatieff describes as "agency," "expresses itself in political and civil freedom, in the exercise of human choice and collective deliberation." Ignatieff continues,

> In effect, international human rights covenants and declarations seek to re-create for the international society of states the norms that govern the relation between citizen and state in a democratic polity, to make all human beings citizens rather than subjects of the states they give obedience to (2001: 165).

Secondly, an allied conception of the debate on Universalism versus Cultural Relativism is the problem of socio-cultural receptivity and the extent to which "difference" should be allowed to stifle the implementation of human right out of respect for distinct cultural values. Or, to frame the question more positively, to what extent should we allow negative values and traditions to frame the debate over more enduring global ethics and norms that secure dignity as agency, and agency as freedom. The assumption that cultural and value specificity is always a hindrance to human rights is not in par with the reality that some positive and enriching values can be an aid rather than an obstacle to human rights.

In essence, then, religion is the powerhouse of cultural relativism. Evidently, its impact on socio-cultural receptivity is both enduring and absorbing. Since culture is concerned with the particular and context bound norms, ethics and morality, it appears to be difficult for some religious elements to cope with the legally undisputed universality of human rights, as they are expressed in the Universal Declaration of Human Rights, as well as in various covenants, protocols, and conventions of the United Nations.

Notably, that universality does automatically guarantee universal implementation. While from a legal perspective states, nation-states are, regardless of their religious claims, under a general obligation to respect and promote human rights – particularly with respect to certain core rights, whose implementation is regarded as *obligationes erga omnes*[1] – procedures to enforce their realization by unwilling governments are of a political rather than of a judicial nature. The conclusion that Zoller reaches in his review of the UN Commission's session in 2002 is "Composed of Member States, the Commission on Human Rights has become a House of Impunity." (Zoller, 2002: 1)

Paradoxically, however, religion will not find it a comforting fact that adopting the required resolutions is realistically not possible, let alone bridging the gap between words and deeds. For obvious reasons, world religions remain divided within and without. Conversely, human rights as a "secular religion" faces a spiritual crisis in so far as the realization of its values and norms needs continuous spiritual nurturing. Indeed, in responding to political opportunism, the rhetorical strength of the human rights discourse does not, in itself, suffice. Human rights implementation will also depend on the moral strength within a particular society of the human rights idea, and the capacity of that society to see universality as a source of enrichment, rather than as a conscious conspiracy to thwart its message. Thus, the question of receptivity to human rights confronts us with the moral foundations of the human rights idea in regard to political and cultural differences. This is a rather complicated matter in which we shall delve a little deeper later on.

Naturally, problems of cultural receptivity and human rights are not confined to non-Western peoples. Apart from their implementation in Western societies themselves,[2] the very idea of universality also signifies Western responsibility for the realization of human rights for people in other parts of the world. Rapidly increasing global inequality illustrates, however, the lack of global mechanisms to correct injustices. The phrase "everywhere in the world" as used by President Franklin D. Roosevelt in his *Four Freedoms Address,* and which was subsequently endorsed in the Universal Declaration of Human Rights, now primarily requires implementation instead of standard-setting. Whichever view one takes on the question of universality of human rights norms, there is definitely a universal problem of receptivity.

It should also be realized that cultural receptivity is not a one-way process from existing and unchanging human rights norms to specific cultures. Ever since the introduction of the Universal Declaration of Human Rights, there has been a growing influence from non-Western cultures in respect of the formulation of new charters and covenants. This has meant a shift in emphasis towards duties (also in regard to communities), towards positive freedom rights (economic, social and cultural rights), and towards collective rights. In further attempts to render human rights more objective, non-Western views on justice may play an increasing role. Indeed, although an individual-centered and rights-oriented view lies at the roots of the historical process of formulating international human rights standards, a growing moral universality will require receptivity to alternative approaches to justice. In regard to economic and social rights, a predominance of non-Western (communitarian) thinking is already noticeable. As Virginia Leary concluded:

> Despite its contemporary Western origin dating to post Second World War, the antecedence informed by the earlier life of World religions and moral philosophies, the concept of human rights must now be recognized as a universal term accepted throughout the world. But the concept is a dynamic and evolutionary one that has recently been extended to cover many aspects of human dignity not contemplated under the traditional Western rubric of human rights. Western influence, dominant in the origin of the development of international human rights norms, is now only one of a number of cultural influences on the development of international human rights standards. Its contribution to the development

of human rights has been great, but it has not been unique, and other cultures have made and are making significant contributions to our collective conception of human dignity (1990: 29-30).

Not surprisingly, then, cultural justifications for continuing violations of human rights in the name of religion become untenable because they tended to come from politicians, rather than from the moderate religious establishment, be it Judo-Christian or Muslim. Religion, we note, is subject to rather strong political manipulation.

It is also noteworthy that while in their Western historical context, human rights developed as a protective concept – that is to say, to defend the autonomy of individual citizens against threats coming particularly from sovereigns (states) that would try to extend their power into the citizen's realm – in the cultural context of Africa, Asia and South- and Central America the human rights idea is of a much more *emancipatory* character: a struggle for rights of the have-nots. While our analysis has already revealed that human rights are highly *action-oriented*, this is especially so in developing countries. "Human rights," Surendra has noted, "have often been functioning as the rights of the privileged both at the world level and also in national and local societies. But the dispossessed, the underprivileged, and that is the majority of the world, they regard human rights as instruments of liberation and emancipation". In such a context human rights are used as a legal resource for social change, while also playing a significant part especially in the struggles of social movements. Essential in such struggles for social change is the "conscientization" (to borrow a term from Paulo Freire (1972) – editor's note) of those who have to fight for their own rights so that apathy and resignation to the status quo may be overcome. Hence the challenge of cultural receptivity is to get the human rights idea integrated into their hearts.

The real issue, in other words, is not the universality of the human rights idea itself, but *a universal reception of that idea*. No single "culture" (defined as a way of life transferred from one generation to the next) is fully receptive to the notion of universal human dignity and equality. It is an illusion to think that this idea might be simply disseminated by means of readable material. Indeed, the human rights project cannot escape confronting deeper questions, such as "Who is the human being?" and "What is freedom?"(Mufazzar 1994).

Clearly, then, the acceptance of responsibility for the protection of other people's dignity requires more than just a legal basis, no matter how universal that foundation may be. Indeed, the ratification of treaties, the establishment of courts of human rights, and the development of human rights jurisprudence are not enough. The moral grounds upon which responsible behavior rests have to be constantly nurtured on the basis of a worldview. Insofar as the notion of human rights finds its origin in individualism, it is *responsible* individualism that prevails. This is evidently not the same as *possessive* individualism.[3] Yet the former may easily degenerate into the latter.

It is precisely in those cultures in which possessive individualism has strong roots that great difficulties with economic and social rights are evident, already at the stage of standard-setting. While individualism may offer a sufficient moral foundation for respecting everyone's fundamental freedoms, it is inadequate as a basis for accepting other people's needs as grounds for justified claims. Economic, social, and cultural rights presuppose not just free individuals, but also a community that accepts responsibility for the fulfillment of everybody's basic needs. This, then, points once again to a crucial role of religion in efforts to overcome constraints in cultural receptivity. But before going a little more deeply into this matter, we will first turn to the issue of the times of human rights.

The times of human rights

The life of religion must have taught us that the times of human rights do not just date back to the founding of the United Nations in 1945. In fact, the drive to protect human dignity against abuse of power is as old as human history. A classic example of the supremacy of human dignity is the appeal to the higher laws of heaven by Antigone, when, as Sophocles tells us, she defied King Creon's laws by burying her brother Polynices within the walls of the city. This element of resistance in human rights is also expressed in the Dutch national anthem, in which William of Orange, in his struggle to overcome tyranny, refers to justice as a primary duty towards God, transcending any duty towards an earthly sovereign. Such instances of dignity transcending mere power may be found in all sorts of cultural and religious settings.

With regard to its *times*, then, there are two dimensions to human rights: (1) the human rights idea through the ages, and (2) the post World War II period of protection of human dignity through international law. That the human dignity of every human being ought to be respected and protected may be seen as part of the spiritual heritage of humankind. The relevant adjective here is, indeed, *spiritual*, rather than cultural. Culture, as Arie de Ruijter has taught us, is a continuous process of construing, upholding and challenging differences among people, of inclusion and exclusion, of drawing lines between "us" and "them" (de Ruijter, 2000; van London e.a., 2003). Human rights, conversely, is a *moral universal* based on a belief in the inherent dignity of the human being, a simple consequence of being born in this world, a reference to each and all.

Naturally, the contrast here is a little construed. Moral views, convictions and commitments are always imbedded in cultural settings; hence, by postulating human rights above culture, the debate between universalism and cultural relativism cannot be simply determined. Indeed, neither legal universalism nor cultural relativism settles the issue once and for all. Nor is it resolved as either supra-cultural or sub-cultural; rather, the point is that the debate between universalism and cultural relativism is *inter-cultural*. Through ages of globalization, a *global spirituality* has emerged too; and part of that is a global ethos sustaining the human rights idea. In addition to the evidence already cited above, attention may be drawn to the "Declaration towards a Global Ethic," prepared by Hans Küng and adopted by a Jewish-Christian-Muslim "Parliament of the World's Religions," in Chicago in 1993 De Gaay Fortman e.a., 1998). By checking this worldview with more than five hundred students at the Institute of Social Studies in The Hague, by coming from all different angles of our world, we found, indeed, a 100% confirmation of the human rights idea. Notably, that idea is not confined to the belief in inherent dignity, but also stipulates the existence of a communal responsibility for its protection.

The belief that basic human dignity ought to be protected follows, as was already noted, from a long history of abuse of power. Remarkably, power, as humankind has come to realize, will not automatically be exercised in accordance with values and norms tuned to respect the dignity of those affected by its use. History has taught us that perceived self- or group-interest is a driving force of formidable dimensions, which is not necessarily in line with public justice. However, while protection is evidently necessary, opinions may still differ on how to organize and implement it. One way would be to delegate that responsibility to the sovereign; another way would be to see the protection of people's dignity against abuse of power as a responsibility of the entire community.

The snag with traditional arrangements for the protection of human dignity has been well summarized in Seneca's plaintive question *"Quis custodiet ipsos custodes?"* (Who guards the guardians?).[4] Notably, this applies to modern ways of rights-based protection, too. Thus, in the international venture for human rights that started with the founding of the United Nations in 1945, states play a dual role: that of protectors as well as violators of basic human dignity. To understand this paradox let us take a closer look at what may be called "the human rights deficit."

Notably, the new global endeavor for the realization of human rights suffers from a huge *deficit* that is all too often submerged in the general plethora of human rights declarations, conferences, committee meetings, and workshops. It manifests itself in four domains: (1) impunity of state-related perpetrators of violations of civil and political rights, (2) the apparent lack of protection offered to minorities, (3) the continued barrier of the public-private divide and its paralyzing effects on the struggle against domestic violence, and (4) the violation of economic, social, and cultural rights (ESCR) in a world in which so many people's basic needs remain denied. This fundamental weakness in human rights concerns their relation to social reality. They are all too often *declared* rights, involving long and enduring struggles for implementation, rather than *acquired* rights in the sense of formal legal protection of freedoms and titles that have already acquired societal recognition as sources of *entitlements*.

The purpose of *rights* – regarded as "interests" protected by law – is to put conflicts of interests in a normative setting, and thus to prevent their manifestation as pure power struggles. Society is expected to function in such a way that rights are respected, while claims based on entitlements connected to those rights are honored. Dispute settlement should be confined to cases in which there are conflicting claims protected by different rights (between landlord and tenant, for example). Yet although rights are abstract acknowledgements of claims in the sense of a public-political commitment to offer legal protection for their realization, the world is full of denials of claims founded upon people's fundamental freedoms and basic entitlements. Actually, while the whole idea of rights is based upon the expectation that obvious violations would lead to contentious action resulting in redress, human rights often remain without effective remedies. Adequate embodiment in positive law is all too often lacking, while these rights are violated from and within centers of power. This is due to two crucial deficiencies: firstly, the often prevailing inadequacy of law as a check on power, and secondly, the lack of reception of these rights in many cultural and politico-economic contexts. An additional snag lies in the limits of human rights as a modern discourse on justice. It is in addressing these three predicaments that religion may have a crucial part to play. The problem of cultural receptivity was already discussed above. Let us therefore now look a little more closely at the times of human rights in relation to these two other contemporary snags: namely the role and rule of law, and the limits of human rights as a modern justice discourse.

The role and rule of law
Law implies order in the public-political community, and hence protection of people (personal security), their property (stability of possessions), and their contracts *(pacta sunt servanda)*. Its essence is that it binds power to certain norms, implying at the least normative processes of settling disputes. Generally, however, law is expected to attain more than just order. A deeper layer of normativity lies in the concept of public justice, stipulating what is generally considered to be right from the perspective of the community as a whole, and hence ought to be enforced. This goes beyond mere formal equality – i.e. equal treatment of equal cases; it also implies the recognition of fundamental freedoms and basic needs (social justice), too. The notion of order, in other words, has to be supplemented with justice and the *rule of Law.*

Thus, legal norms are meant not only to *regulate* in the sense of securing order, but also to reflect what is generally seen as *right* and hence ought to be enforced. Consequently, law implies a mission of a high noble character as exemplified in the inscription shown in the reading room of the Harvard Law School's library: OF LAW NO LESSE CAN BE ACKNOWLEDGED THAN THAT HER SEAT IS THE BOSOM OF GOD (De Gaay Fortman, W.F., 1962: 16). The reference to the Upright One implies a fundamental allegiance of Religion to Justice. Law, in other words, is meant to bind power to a morality that is seen as essential to the integrity of the community.[5]

However, while law is meant to ensure an orderly protection of interests, and an orderly settlement of disputes by regulating and delimiting power, it naturally reflects existing power relations at the same time. Consequently, every community and society manifests an inescapable dialectic of law and power De Gaay Fortman, B., 1990). The position of a certain country on a hypothetical scale from 100% power and 0% law, to its opposite of 100% law with 0% power, depends on factors such as the democratic character of its institutions and historically grown cultures of personal leadership[6]. Thus, there are countries in which implementation of human rights still primarily requires a struggle for law and access to justice. Notably, when it comes to implementation of the rights of the poor, the legal system as such appears to be a major constraint. One thing the World Bank's *Voices of the Poor* studies has made abundantly clear is that poor people live in adverse environments in which neither the economy nor state and law function in any way that is conducive to the realization of human rights (Narayan e.a., 2000). In such a context, the structural struggle is for the role and rule of law as such, and for access to justice as a first implication of a human-rights-based approach to poverty and underdevelopment (Molina Berrizbeita, 2002). Particularly problematic in this connection is the lack of enforcement potential at the global level. Indeed, contemporary international human rights law excels in standard setting, yet its record is mediocre with regard to monitoring and observance, and manifestly weak in enforcement and implementation (Alson, 1992).

It should be noted here that law is not to be identified with a set of rules (Dworkin, 1968). Law is a continuous process of finding and deciding in an orderly manner on what is right. The institutions upon which it is based consist, indeed, of substantive and procedural rules, but also of a personnel organization and resources to meet the demands upon it. In this respect, the newly established International Criminal Court (ICC) may be seen as a big step forward in the fight against impunity.

However, even in a well-functioning legal order, rights will not automatically be realized. The primary responsibility for implementation of subjective rights rests with the legal subjects. Indeed, it is these rights-holders themselves who would first have to initiate action. This applies to human rights too, including the rights to decent livelihoods. Thus, a self-confident and assertive attitude is an evident component of a rights approach to injustice. Here lies an obvious connection with culture and religion as possible constraints as well as potential sources of motivation and inspiration.

The liberal-democratic idea – Fukuyama (1992) views it as the end of the history of ideas – fails here. "The strong," as the Greek historian Thucydides has put it in his account of the Peloponnesian war, "do what is in their power and the weak accept their fate." In a free market economy the weak find no structural protection against unemployment, disease, disability, and old age. Dependence on the charity of the strong did not work and was considered unsatisfactory, too. In many industrialized countries measures such as workers' protection, compulsory education, professional training, and health protection constituted a structural attempt towards the realization of economic and social rights. The social struggle that led to such achievements was nurtured by religion in the sense of a set of ideas transcending individual existence. (In this sense socialism, too, may be regarded as a religion.)

Friedrich Hayek, the godfather of neo-liberalism, once wrote a book under the title *The Mirage of Social Justice*. He feels that it is only a "negative" notion of freedom (keep your hands off other people's property, allow everyone her liberty) that can be more than a mirage. Hence, for a vision of social justice we have to look elsewhere. One academic attempt lies in "non-ideal" philosophy.

The philosopher John Rawls (1972) has attempted to construct political principles of justice applicable to any society that tackles the problem of inequalities between people. His theory is based on a hypothetical social contract between citizens who, behind a "veil of ignorance" as regards their relative success or failure in acquiring entitlement positions, decide what is socially "fair." This is not the place to review his theory in critical detail, but what is noteworthy is that Rawls's rational-liberal theory of justice failed him when he tried to construct a political "law of peoples" that would legitimate human rights on the basis only of reason (Rawls, 1999; 1993). For one thing, he feels compelled to abandon the three egalitarian features of his theory of justice, which are the fair value of political liberties, fair equality of opportunity, and the difference principle.[7] Thus, his human rights concept deals only with civil rights and excludes political and socio-economic rights. His argument then implies that even representatives of hierarchical societies, committed in a rather absolute sense to certain ideologies and religions and placed behind a veil of ignorance, would accept the same "law of peoples" – including basic civil rights – as democratic societies do. But why would they? As Stanley Hoffmann has put it:

> Are societies whose governments are dogmatically committed to ideology or religion likely to respect basic human rights at all? Since there are no free elections, how would we know that their "system of law" meets "the essentials of legitimacy in the eyes of [their] own people"? Whatever the answer, what is clear is that Rawls's law of peoples has been shaped so as to appeal to a purely hypothetical group of peoples.
>
> The fallacy here is in the parallel Rawls seems to draw between an "overlapping consensus" of comprehensive doctrines that endorse a single conception of justice within a democratic political culture...,and an "overlapping consensus" of societies based on very different political conceptions of justice. Such different societies could only endorse a very weak "law of peoples." (1995: 54)

Hence, for a stronger "law of peoples," we have to look beyond "non-ideal theory" (Rawls). Indeed, we cannot escape the search for the conceptual roots of human rights within the various religions themselves. Research points to a preliminary conclusion that the idea of one person's responsibility to satisfy another person's needs is common to all world religions (Wronka, 1992). One example is the Old Testament term *Tsedâqâh*, which acknowledges the claims of the poor purely on the basis of their need. Thus, the connection with religion may provide a highly necessary cultural basis for the human rights struggle. Apart from all sorts of political and economic constraints to the implementation of human rights, there also exists a major obstacle in the cultural resistance to norms and values that imply that people are responsible for the well-being of their fellow human beings. Indeed, a *culture of contentment* predominates in the post-Cold War era, paralyzing the global "haves." Christopher Lasch (1994) spoke of a rebellion of the elites and the betrayal of democracy. With so many people excluded from a decent existence, the human rights project suffers from structural day-to-day violation.

Apparently, to find its roots in the hearts of people the human rights idea primarily requires support rather than obstruction by existing cultural identities. Here again we touch upon the role of religion. One relevant factor is, for example, the way people look at the course of events, whether as "the will of God" or as the result of human action. Another aspect concerns people's approach to power, in full submission or critically demanding accountability. One might also mention attitudes towards plurality, religious zeal based on fundamentalism – *compelle intrare* – as against tolerance and acceptance of other people's fundamental freedoms. These are just some of the elements to be taken up in our concluding observations.

The limits of human rights

Actually, human rights have assumed the role of the modern global justice discourse. Justice, as was already explained, is the set of values and norms generally considered to be essential from the perspective of the community as a whole, and whose enforcement, therefore, must be seen as a communal responsibility. Now, the point is that the international assumption of a global universal responsibility for justice took shape after World War II, and took as its starting point individual subjective rights. To understand the implications, let us take a closer look at the human rights approach to poverty and development as propagated by international agencies such as the United Nations Development Program (UNDP), in the light of Kofi Annan's appeal for "a mainstreaming of human rights." The new "approach" – "conviction" or "commitment" seem to be more appropriate terms – got a real impetus from the Human Development Report 2000, which was specifically devoted to human rights and development.

The core of UNDP's Human Development Report 2000 is chapter 4: *Rights empowering people in the fight against poverty*. Here the entire "approach" has to be made concrete. Not surprisingly, this appears to be far from easy. Basic economic rights, such as the right to a decent standard of living (article 25, Universal Declaration of Human Rights [UDHR], already quoted above), "are not just development goals". Yet, such "rights do not mean an entitlement to a handout" (UNDP, 2000: 73). Thus, a person without work cannot simply go to court and claim employment. The problem lies in the meaning and implications of human rights as "real" rights in the sense of rights with effective remedies. In his earlier publication on *Human Rights and Economic Achievement,* Amartya Sen, the auctor intellectualis of the HDR, referred to Jeremy Bentham's disqualification of "natural and imprescriptible rights" as "nonsense on stilts" ((UNDP, 2000: 94). In other words, is it really possible to protect general interests of human beings by law, or, in other terms, to abstractly acknowledge claims based on certain essential human interests? The report evidently wrestles with this problem. Resolution of the problem is sought in Dworkin's (1977) distinction between "abstract rights" and "concrete rights." "In this conception a person has concrete rights to the appropriate policies – not to food, housing and the like, which are abstract rights" (Dworkin, 1977: 77). The point is, however, that rights are abstract while claims are concrete. To have a right does not automatically imply that all claims based on titles protected by it will be honored. This depends not only on the strength of the right in question, as reflected in the values behind it and the kind of protection it offers, but also on the fulfillment of possible conditions that would have to be obtained in order to activate the right in question, as well as on competing claims by others and the relative strength of the rights held by them. This is a matter of the actual availability of the freedoms and entitlements the rights in question intend to cover. The right to health, by way of example, remains rather dormant in a juridical sense, as long as the rights-holders lack daily access to clean water and sanitary provisions.

With regard to economic, social, and cultural rights the strong language of the Universal Declaration of Human Rights was specified (and at the same time weakened) in subsequent covenants. This manifests itself particularly in the notion of *progressive realization,* a terminology also adopted in the Human Development Report 2000. That clause refers to the notion that non-implementation may be rooted in a lack of available resources. Yet, the realization of economic, social, and cultural rights is also a highly confrontational matter since efforts towards their implementation challenge existing power structures. While the Report follows earlier UNDP language as concerns the need for promoting "a rights-enabling economic environment," in reality many people live in adverse or *disabling* conditions when it comes to implementation of their basic human rights (UNDP, 2000: 118-119). The entitlement failure that lies at the root of the denial of their basic needs is the consequence of gross injustices flowing from the (unequal) distribution and use of economic and political power. Hence, rather than a mere moral discourse, human rights is also a field of struggle. Addressing the injustices behind entitlement failure is confrontational and dangerous. Observe, for example, the frightful repercussions Dalits in India are faced with when, by invoking their right to food, land, and a decent life, they stop performing humiliating services for the upper-castes.

The chapter on poverty of the HDR 2000 reveals an evident deficit in current instruments to realize the rights of the poor. Not surprisingly, the chapter is followed by one concerning indicators. It is noted here that "indicators are needed that can create a culture of accountability" (UNDP, 2000: 19). Such indicators should show the impact that a specified actor has on the (non-)implementation of a certain right. With due acknowledgement of all that is proposed here for further elaboration, we miss a focus on the link between indicators, instruments, and action. The issue is that indicators remain rather meaningless if not connected to instruments that may be employed for concrete action in the implementation of rights.

Coming back now to the reality of adverse environments in which poor people tend to live, human rights appear to be not entirely meaningless. While in such contexts judicial action is not likely to have much effect, collective action may still be based upon human rights as a forceful moral rhetoric. The point is that behind these rights are principles of justice; hence, while stating the fundamental freedoms and basic entitlements of *everyone*, they may also be seen as statements of *what is right*, or *standards of legitimacy*. In this connection, universality means that there is no legitimate use of power unless in conformity with human rights standards. In this respect human rights serve as *political instruments* (Klein Goldewijk e.a., 1999). This affects not just the power of the state, but also that of all actors, including corporations, as the UNDP Report duly notes. *Actors become duty-bearers:* there lies the crux of human rights based approaches.

So far, we have discussed the limits of human rights as a vehicle of justice. Another constraint concerns its content. Behind the various rights formulated in declarations of the UN's General Assembly, and in the various covenants and conventions, are fundamental values that constitute the core of our civilization. Indeed, concretely formulated human rights norms embody principles of justice, such as life as a value per se, liberty, equality, due process, decency *(honeste vivere)*, stability of possessions, and the quality of life.

A particularly problematic principle in this summary is equality. It is striking to note that in the fifty-five years since the adoption of the Universal Declaration of Human Rights (UDHR), income inequality, for one thing, has increased tremendously. Thus, whereas in 1960 the ratio between the upper and lower quintiles in global income distribution was 30:1, in 1990 it had doubled to 60:1, and by 2000 was 72:1. Global justice requires a primary investigation of the global structures that result in such obvious socio-economic inequality (Sen, 1999: 116ff).

One reason why apparently human rights have not served as an egalitarian discourse might well be that they have been defined in a rather absolute manner: nobody can be tortured; everyone has the right to education etc. Equality, however, has to do with the relations among people. In so far as there exists a qualification of the rights in question, what we find is the adjective "adequate" (e.g. a standard of living *adequate* to the health of everyone). While the term "adequate" could also be interpreted in a relative sense, among jurists the tendency has been to work on absolute standards, elaborated into specifications of what precise entitlements might be derived from the "core" of the right in question. There exists, however, one obvious reference to substantial equality, in article 1 (1) of the Universal Declaration of Human Rights: "All human beings are born free and *equal* in dignity and rights." However, this clause could well be seen as a specimen of *ius divinum* in the newly emerged secular religion of human rights; in other words, a confession rather than a concrete way of protecting people by law. This interpretation gains force by what follows in article 1 (2): "They are endowed with reason and conscience and should act towards one another in a spirit of brotherhood." If only that were true.

It is generally accepted, however, that the first part of article 1 of the UDHR implies formal equality or, in legal terms, equal treatment of equal cases. Not without reason is it followed by article 2, which stipulates the non-discrimination principle. Article 7 explicitly states that "All are equal before the law and are entitled without any discrimination to equal protection of the law." In article 10 we find the term "full equality" linked to a fair and public hearing by an independent and impartial tribunal.

Hence, the question remains whether article 1 has a substantial significance that would entail a lever on unequal outcomes. As equality here relates to human dignity, we argue that it does. No human being's life may be regarded as less or more valuable than that of any other creature. This ought to be reflected not merely in institutions and their accessibility to each and everyone, nor just in principles of due process, but also in *outcomes*. Indeed, there are situations in life that manifest such degrees of substantial inequality that they may be seen as evident violations of article 1. First and foremost among these is global socio-economic inequality.

Now, it could obviously be argued that this falls beyond the scope of any reasonable system of positive law. Wouldn't it be unthinkable that an individual or group would go to court to claim substantial equality? In response we should first like to note that substantial equality does not entirely fall outside the realm of private law. Notions like "undue influence," "abuse of law," and "unjust enrichment," for example, address the relations among people in processes of acquirement. In public administrative law we find such principles as putting the heaviest burdens on those with the strongest shoulders to carry it. Hence substantial equality as a reflection of *equal birth* does appear to have an impact in "the law of civilized nations."

Consequently, then, we would have to see the poor as primary actors in processes towards more substantial equality. While ascribing a primary responsibility for implementation to the rights-holders themselves is naturally in line with the subjective nature of rights in a universalistic legal system, two comments must be made here in this regard. Firstly, the international venture for the realization of human rights has attained a rather top-down character in the sense that in human rights discourse, a "deductive" perspective is usually taken. Thus it appears to be possible, for example, to distill a number of concretely specified economic, social, and cultural rights from the International Bill of Rights while going into the juridical intricacies of legal definition. What is more in line with the emphasis on individual responsibility, however, is an *"inductive"* way of conceptualizing human rights. The question here is, what are poor people's own perceptions of what is owed to them in terms of fundamental freedoms and basic entitlements? Once again, it is here that religion comes in as a primary force in relating poverty to its reverse side – wealth. Doubtless, then, an inductive approach based on religious interpretations of what is right in the eyes of God is bound to confront those in power with relative poverty. Secondly, when rights-holders are confronted with non-surmountable obstacles, the responsibilities of other actors involved in these constraints, are activated. Indeed, actors become duty-bearers. Here lies the crux of any human rights-based approach to development and poverty. To actually activate duties based on a universal responsibility for the protection of human dignity within a concrete context requires some confrontation with the powers that be. With regard to the normative character of such struggles, religion may once again play a crucial part, be it positive or negative.

Concluding observations

A discourse on the life and times of religion and human rights is important because it sheds lights on two presumably competing spheres: one concerned with the divinity of the religious script and its everlasting relevance, the other with everlasting legal instruments designed especially to cope with complex forms of human rights abuse. However, beyond this dichotomy there lies two major commonalities. First, both religion and the legal instruments developed to defend human rights privilege themselves with being the protectors of human dignity. Second, if humans are created in the image of God, how could religion use the scriptures of God in any manner other than as an agency bearing the burdensome task of protecting God's image. If this is the case, then it is not difficult to relegate the presumed differences between religion and the legal instruments to the domain of politics, where the boundaries between the duties to God and the duties to Caesar are muddled beyond recognition.

In this respect, Religion becomes Culture, and as such susceptible to cultural reciprocity, and vice versa when it assumes certain peculiaries that could be deliberately employed to stifle human dignity and its very universality. To that extent, it is a difficult logic to grasp if cultural relativism is allowed to project Religion as "Culture" rather than as "cultures," and therefore subservient to the dignity of those created in the image of God. It is therefore not at all surprising that the universality of human rights is often negated by the very politico-religious establishement that abuses human rights.

Human rights and religion cannot be avoided merely by separating the two into distinct realms of moral and legal authority, as if they had no commonalities, or by attempting to reconcile human rights with any type of religious discourse. More substantially, the common discourse of religion and human rights is found in their mutual respect for human dignity. It is only by recognizing dignity as agency, as we have alluded to earlier, that one can avoid recent attempts geared towards promoting the human rights project as though it were civil religion. This orientation is dangerous because it implies a conscious attempt to develop a counter-religion created by "man," which leads to unresolved questions about the legitimacy and desirability of adhering to man-made religions. The moral foundations of human rights as civil religion remain questionable, and its tenets untenable.

In conclusion, let us remind ourselves that when seen from the viewpoint of religion, the human rights discourse is not without limitations, for as An Na'im puts it:

> The international human rights movement is facing growing problems of irrelevance to people's daily concerns, marginalization in local and global politics, and cooptation by ruling elites, privileged classes and global economic forces in local as well as global politics. In order to resolve these problems, the movement needs to critically re-examine some of its assumptions and policies in order to recapture its original mandate, revise its concepts and methods(1998: 3).

Concomitantly, the capacity of human rights alone to foster substantial equality remains rather complicated in regard to direct judicial remedies. Yet we should like to point to the meaning of human rights as not just legal resources, but also as political *instru-*

ments. The Human Rights approach is a commitment to engage in processes of transformation, with those suffering from material injustices as the primary actors. Obviously, we are referring here not just to economic and social rights, but also to political and civil rights. In the context of the struggles that poor people are engaged in, these are also *empowerment rights.* Indeed, without guaranteed freedoms, collective empowerment will be seriously impeded. Conversely, in a complementary role with regard to civil and political rights, economic, social, and cultural rights may be seen as *sustainability rights,* for without the means of living a decent life there is no space to enjoy fundamental freedoms. In international human rights language this is expressed as the *indivisibility* and *interdependence* of human rights.

Within the perspectives on the life and times of religion and human rights, we have attempted to explore: 1) the question of legal and political sovereignty in regard to the protection of human dignity, and 2) the problem of hermeneutics in regard to both religious and human rights discourses. We used a range of examples from various religious traditions to answer the question of why such huge differences still persist amongst believers from different religious traditions, as with interpretations of human rights vis-à-vis the universality of human rights. It is our contention that both religion and human rights could benefit a great deal from an interface that is dynamic and alive, provided they both premise their engagement on the primacy of human dignity.

Notes

1   See Case of the International Court of Justice Concerning the *Barcelona Traction, Light and Power Company Limited (New Application: 1962) (Second Phase) Belgium v. Spain,* ICJ 1970, Rep. 3
2   Implementation is not unproblematic. Take, for example, the resistance against economic, social and cultural rights in the USA.
3   Possessive Individualism is the driving force of what Tawney called "the acquisitive society": "Such societies may be called Acquisitive Societies because their whole tendency and interest and preoccupation is to promote the acquisition of wealth. The appeal of this conception must be powerful, for it has laid the whole modern world under its spell. ... It is an invitation to men to use the power with which they have been endowed by nature or by society, by skill or energy or relentless egotism or mere good fortune, without inquiring whether there is any principle by which their exercise should be limited. ... It assures men that there are no ends other than their ends, no law other than their desires, no limit than that which they think advisable." (R,H. Tawney, *The Acquisitive Society,* 1920 (1948)).
4   The question was asked at the end of a dialogue in which Seneca was informed that someone had appointed a few friends to guard his wife while he was on foreign mission.
5   The term *integrity* in regard to law was coined by Dworkin. See Ronald Dworkin (1986: 404).
6   With regard to the Netherlands, for example, one may refer to Act of Desertion (Placcaet van Verlaetinghe) of 1581 in which it is stipulated that God did not create the subjects for the Sovereign's pleasure but, on the contrary, the Sovereign for the benefit of the subjects – in order to rule them with law and reason. Naturally, in the real world, law and power cannot be simply separated; as Hedley Bull once observed, "the world is very much more complicated than the arguments" (Hedley Bull, *The Control of the Arms Race,* 1962). The world is certainly more complex than reflected in Karl Marx's phrase "Right can never be higher than the economic

structure of society and the cultural development conditioned by it" (*Critique of the Gotha Programme*, 19: 21)

7   This "difference principle" stipulates that inequalities can be tolerated only if "they are to be to the greatest benefit of the least advantaged members of society."

Bibliography

Abu al-A la Mawdudi, Allamah. 1996. Human Rights in Islam. *Al Tawhid Journal* 4(3): 1-29.

Adler, P. J. 1996. *World Civilizations*. Minneapolis: West Publishing Company.

Alson, Philip. 1992. *The United Nations and Human Rights. A critical appraisal*, Oxford: Clarendon.

An Na'him, Abdullahi A. 1998. Human Rights and the Culture of Relevance: The Case of Collective Rights. In M. Castermans-Holleman, F. van Hoof, and J. Smith, eds., *The Role of the Nation-State in the 21st Century: Human Rights, International Organization and Foreign Policy*, pp. 3-16. The Hague: Kluwer International.

Bull, Hedley. 1962. *The Control of the Arms Race*, London: Weidenfeld and Nicholson.

de Gaay Fortman, Bas, and Berma Klein Goldewijk. 1998. *God and the Goods. Global Economy in a Civilizational Perspective*. Geneva: WCC.

de Gaay Fortman, Bas. 1990. The Dialectics of Western Law in a Non-Western World. In H. Burgers and J. Berting, eds., *Human rights in a Pluralist World: Individuals and Collectivities*, pp.237-251. RSC/Meckler: New York.

de Gaay Fortman, W.F. 1972. Het geheim van het recht. In W.F. de Gaay Fortman, *Recht doen*, p.16. Samson: Alphen aan den Rijn (Dies Natalis address, Free University, Amsterdam, 22 October 1962).

Dworkin, Ronald M. 1986. *Law's Empire*. London: Fontana.

Dworkin, Ronald M. 1977. *Taking Rights Seriously*, London: Duckworth and Company.

Dworkin, Ronald M. 1968. Is Law a System of Rules? In Robert S. Summers, ed., *Essays in Legal Philosophy*, pp. 25-60. Oxford: Basil Blackwell.

Freire, Paulo. 1972. *Pedagogy of the Oppressed*. London: Penguin Books.

Fukuyama, Francis. 1992. *The End of History and the Last Man*, London: Hamilton.

Gustafson, C., and Peter Juviler, eds. 1999. *Religion and Human Rights: Competing Claims*. New York: M.E. Sharppe.

Hoffmann, Stanley. 1995 "Dreams of a Just World." In *The New York Review of Books* (2 November), p. 54

Ignatieff, M. 2001. Dignity and Agency. in M. Ignatieff, ed., *Human Rights as Politics and Idolatry*, pp. 161-175. Princeton and Oxford: Princeton University Press.

Kelsay, J., and Summer B. Twiss, eds. 1994. *Religion and Human Rights*. New York: The project on Human Rights.

Klein Goldewijk, Berma, and Bas de Gaay Fortman. 1999. *Where Needs Meet Rights. Economic, Social and Cultural Rights in a New Perspective*, Geneva: WCC Publications.

Konvitz, Milton Ridvas, ed. 2001. *Judaism and Human Rights*. Somerset, NY: Transaction Publishers.

Kraynak, Robert P. 2000. *Christian Faith and Modern Democracy: God and Politics in the Fallen World*. Notre Dame: University of Notre Dame.

Lasch, Christopher. 1994. *The Revolt of the Elites and the Betrayal of Democracy*, New York: Norton.

Leary, Virginia A. 1990. The Effect of Western Perspectives on International Human Rights. In A.A. An-Na'im and F.M. Deng, eds., *Human Rights in Africa; Cross-Cultural Perspectives*, PAGES?. Washington D.C.: The Brookings Institution.

Marx, Karl. 1891. Critique of the Gotha Programme. *Neue Zeit*.

Molina Berrizbeita, Juan Pablo. 2002. *A Case for the Human Right of Access to Justice*. Coventry: University of Warwick (mimeograph).

Mufazzar., Chandra. 1994. "From Human Rights to Human Dignity." Unpublished paper presented at the International Conference "Rethinking Human Rights." Kuala Lumpur, 6-7 December.

Narayan, Deepa et al. 2000. *Voices of the Poor I: Can Anyone Hear Us?*, Oxford: Oxford University Press.

Orentlicher, D. F. 2001. Relativism and Religion. In M. Ignatieff, ed., *Human Rights as Politics and Idolatry*, pp. 141-158. Princeton and Oxford: Princeton University Press.

Rawls, John. 1999. *The Law of Peoples*, Cambridge Mass: Harvard University Press.

Rawls, John. 1993. The Law of Peoples. In Stephen Shute and Susan Hurley, eds., *On Human Rights: The Oxford Amnesty Lectures*, pp.41-82. New York: Basic Books.

Rawls, John. 1972. *A Theory of Justice*. Oxford: Oxford University Press.

Sen, Amartya. 1999. Global Justice: Beyond International Equity. In Inge Kaul et al., *Global Public Goods. International Cooperation in the 21st Century*, Oxford: Oxford University Press.

Tawney, R.H., 1948 [1920], *The Acquisitive Society*, London: Bell and Sons.

van Londen, Selma, and Arie de Ruijter. 2003. Legality, Justice and the Indigenous Cultural Dimension: The Case of the Inuit. In Karin Arts and Paschal Mihyo, eds., *Responding to the Human Rights Deficit. Essays in Honour of Bas de Gaay Fortman*, pp.133-147. The Hague/London/Boston: Kluwer International.

Watt, M. 1953. *Muhammad at Mecca*. London: Clarendon Press.

Wronka, Joseph. 1992. *Human Rights and Social Policy in the 21st Century*. New York: Lanham.

Zoller, Adrien-Claude. 2002. No one is above the law. *Human Rights Monitor* 57-58:1.

7

Integration in Poverty
The Long Term Effects of Migration and
Informality in Latin America in General and
in Peru in Particular

Dirk Kruijt[1]

Mass poverty and globalization

Mass poverty is not an exclusively Latin American phenomenon: it is growing in Asia, expanding severely in Africa, and not even the developed countries of Europe or the United States have been able to eradicate it. It is in this sense that for Latin America – as for most countries in Asia, Eastern Europe and Africa – one has to consider the consequences of the economic crisis and the foreign debt of the 1980s, and the period of economic adjustment that followed afterwards. The so-called "lost decade" of the 1980s, together with the first years of the 1990s, has witnessed the liquidation of the frontiers that hindered or prevented the free development of capitalism and the anticipated adaptation – generally carried out with much love and enthusiasm by the freely elected national governments – to the new economic regime. The globalization of prosperity arrived hand in hand with its silent companion: the globalization of poverty (Chossudovsky 1997).

As a strong medicine, and one with universal validity for the passage from a state-run development model to one based on private enterprise and the competitive market, a package composed of structural adjustment measures was developed and implemented during Latin America's globalization period. Short-term stabilization programs impelled the devaluation of national currencies, freeing of prices, and austerity in the national budget. These were generally followed by more radical programs of a structural nature in the second stage, which prescribed trade liberalization, deregulation of the financial system, privatization of state-owned industries, privatization of agricultural lands and tax reforms. This package was normally followed up with considerable reforms of the public sector, particularly the financial and social institutions within the state and municipal administrative apparatus.

These adjustment measures[2] have had their most severe effects on the condition of the urban poor. Urban prices, especially food prices, rose in the 1990s. At the level of domestic and dwelling units, survival strategies had to try to accommodate more family members and to exercise greater ingenuity in the acquisition of goods and services. Within family units, women and younger children were the ones who most rapidly felt the consequences. As a response to the changes in labor markets (both formal and informal, legal and semi-clandestine) the size of households has increased, as too did their dependence on new sources of income – principally, on family members who were able to bring home cash. This income was earned less and less in the form of regular wages, and more often than not consisted of remittances from abroad, generally sent home by men and women who have had to leave their families and homes in search of subsistence-level work elsewhere. Meanwhile, the standard of services have generally deteriorated as ever-greater emphasis was placed on private services, which for the most part were provided by the informal sector.

As a result, changes have taken place both in the characteristics of poverty and in the nature of the compensation programs that were introduced in tandem with the adjustment programs. In comparison with twenty years earlier, the profile of poverty has been considerably modified, and suggests the following general patterns:

(1) Poverty is becoming ever more an *urban phenomenon;*

(2) The *quality of life* of the poor *is improving* in terms of macro-indicators, such as life expectancy, literacy, education and access to services such as drinking water, drainage and electricity;

(3) Poverty is becoming more and more *heterogeneous*. That is to say, there is greater variety in both benefits and exclusion from services provided by the state, like social security, dwellings, education, health, etc. There is also greater variety in terms of employment, unemployment, and underemployment. During the crisis of the 1980s, and the advent of the adjustment programs, it was the urban informal sector that, above all, was seen to change. The chronically poor are now joined by the new poor, arriving from the strata of the middle and industrial working classes, and by those whose living conditions hover around the poverty line and are afflicted by informality and social exclusion;

(4) The size and composition of poor family units has changed. Furthermore, there has been a trend towards the increasing instability in the role of men as heads of families, and the over-representation of women as heads of household. In general one sees a *feminisation of poverty;*

(5) Meanwhile, the social groups that have always been associated with poverty – *ethnic groups* and *indigenous peoples* – have retained and consolidated that traditional profile.

Poverty, informality, and social exclusion

Poverty, informality, and social exclusion are not synonyms. As Cartaya (1994: 223-224) and Pérez Saínz (1996) rightly observed, the academic debate on the three concepts has cast a shadow over conceptual analysis. *Poverty* is commonly identifiable at the level of domestic units, families or dwellings. *Informality* refers primarily to an individual's position in the labor market, which basically is segmented. *Social exclusion* is a phenomenon that applies directly to the political and cultural sphere, and is associated with basic human rights and a clearly defined notion of citizenship. However, in early twenty-first century Latin America, this underlining of the theoretical differentiation between poverty, informality, and exclusion raises two objections on the academic-political level.

The first concerns the overemphasis, in general, on definitions and problems of definition, in addition to the complex procedures of methodological "operationalization," that result in a considerable proportion of the research carried being devoted to the objective mapping of poverty and social exclusion. From the studies carried out by the academic centers, the universities, the central and municipal government think-tanks, the social investment funds and the NGOs, to the diagnoses commissioned by the World Bank and the IADB, the reports are overburdened with the methodology of measurement, the indexing and quantification of the panorama of poverty, while paying scant attention to analyzing its broader social consequences. Specifically, there is a shortage of studies on the segmentation of poverty, with reference to the heterogeneity within the poor and excluded population, and the variety of vulnerable groups that have found it necessary to seek a place for survival in the urban informal sector.

The second objection concerns the implicit *underestimation* of the volume – that is, the *critical mass* – of poverty, exclusion and informality, and the mutual relations among them. This fact ought to underscore the urgent need, which up till now has too often been neglected, to analyze the similarities – rather than simply the differences – that exist between causes and consequences. The reduction of poverty; the re-incorporation of "informalized" segments of the population into the national legal order, with access to basic social security; the need to establish greater control over the exclusionary tendencies that are gradually creating second-class citizens, with more or less a permanent and hereditary base – all these fundamental problems require serious and concerted political responses in countries throughout the Latin American region.

In the remainder of this essay, I will deliberately simplify the problem by assuming a general equivalence of poverty, informality, and social exclusion in respect to their characteristics, accompanying qualities, and everyday consequences. In many countries of Latin America, the great majority of the population is poor, informal, and excluded, all at the same time. No country in the region can assume having won the struggle against poverty, or of having reincorporated the mass of the population that has disappeared into the oblivion of informality, or of having integrated the vulnerable categories – including the indigenous, *mestizo*, creole and black populations – that for generations have suffered the stigma of second class citizenship.

As far as methodology and measurement techniques are concerned, at the moment it is primarily the "poverty line" that is used as the generally accepted gauge in the quantitative studies generated by the World Bank, and the extended family of UN agencies, among which the UNDP, the ILO and UNICEF and, regionally, ECLAC, stand out.[3] Also, at the national level, the public sector and the related research institutes both adopt the same quantifying approach to poverty. However, the line of informality requires more theoretical sophistication and is not easy to construct. In an exemplary study, the ILO has tried to clarify problems of measurement with regard to the underground economy by suggesting a dividing line based on legality, registration in public registers, and payment of taxes (see Tokman 1992). From an equally quantitative approach (but also taking into account many other criteria of division), FLACSO[4], a Latin American social sciences research institute, has contributed substantially to the clarification of the relationship between poverty and informality in Central America. Finally, with regard to the issue of social exclusion, the ILO has published some trend-setting studies.[5] It is only recently that efforts have been made to try to measure "exclusion." The conceptualization of the problem of exclusion, however, can be traced back to the classic work by the political scientist Marshall (1950, 1992), and is dealt with in some recent works on the "new social question" published by the European Union (Rosanvallon 1995). With regard to Central America, a group of researchers associated with the UNDP, the ILO and PRODERE (Feliciani et al., 1995) have provided a measurement system by indices of exclusion based on multidimensional indicators.

Vulnerable groups in Latin America

Urban informality is being consolidated in metropolitan and other major cities of the Third World. As for the situation in Latin America and the Caribbean, the whole region extending from Monterrey in northern Mexico to Puerto Montt in the south of Chile seems to be invaded by informality and self-employment. Visible signs of this are informal trading on street corners and sidewalks and in the slums that gradually eat up a greater proportion of the urban area. Informality also manifests itself in the parallel labor markets, which reaches into every home where the head of the family is a woman accompanied by small children.

In Latin America, a key problem is the notion of structural heterogeneity and the difficulty of finding its location within a structure of classes. Portes (1985) described the micro-entrepreneurs and their occasional or casual workers in terms of an informal petty bourgeoisie and an informal proletariat. He viewed the informal proletariat as made up of both urban and rural workers. One outcome of this conceptual operation is that informality is inevitably seen as located within a one-dimensional system of classes.

In contrast to Portes' image, however, the idea of partially parallel economies and societies is probably more fruitful. From this point of view, the segments of society that have been forced into the informal economy find themselves excluded from the benefits of such things as stable formal employment, a regular income, trade unions, existing labor legislation, and access to the social institutions that provide basic necessities such as dwellings, health care, and education. This built-in tendency towards a dual society and, consequently, a dual economy manifests itself in the dichotomy between, on the one hand, the protected world of affluence and opportunity, and on the other the jungle of poverty and survival, whose features have become patent since the 1980s.

Viewing the matter from an external perspective, the spread and development of

Latin American informality has been astounding. It is the absolute challenge to every national government, whatever the ideology of its president, or the composition of its cabinet. The informal sector is composed not only of owners of micro-enterprises and their employees. The greater part of it is, in fact, formed by the masses of the *self-employed*, whose economic activity almost never affords them a minimal accumulation of capital, but rather is simply the vehicle for their day-to-day survival. Informal societies and informal economies throughout the region present certain common features. That is to say, at the individual level, what "informals" (i.e. those engaged in the informal economy) of whatever Latin American nationality have in common are their poverty, and their low levels of education and vocational training.

Viewing the matter from within, Latin American informality often also has an ethnic face. One might even say that the informal economy has more to do with black people than with the black market. In the Andean countries and in Central America and Mexico, features of Quechua or Maya culture mix with elements of informal society. In fact they are the same features one finds in the "economy of affection" of rural Africa (Hydén,1983) that persist as mechanisms for survival: ties of ethnicity, religion, real or symbolic family relationships, closeness to the place of birth, local neighborhood relations. Even so, in this context ethnicity also presents itself as a stratifying factor, and one should note that the rationale of the informal economy is also based on a unique and dialectical interplay of mechanisms of exploitation and solidarity. The latter is expressed in spontaneous relations of mutual support between members of the extended family; between persons with religious or racial connections; between inhabitants of slums in the same neighborhood, of adjacent blocks in the same miserable slum. A young woman obtains a poorly remunerated job from her uncle, and in a situation of emergency her children are looked after by neighbors. Indigenous immigrants recently arrived from their home villages find lodging in the house of a earlier migrants from the same community, who is now a successful trader in one of the poor districts of the capital. Solidarity is also related to the ambiguous and diffuse dynamics and relations of dependency expressed in the relationship between *padre* and *padron* – the all-powerful entrepreneur of poverty, who lays down the rules of obligation and behavior. The ambitious informal micro-entrepreneur is the *paterfamilias*, both during and after working hours. The boss provides his employees with work – work, whose conditions regarding wages, hours of labor, the few rights and the many obligations of the worker, are defined unilaterally by the boss (Alba Vega 1987).

Rather than the outcome of haphazard chance, the establishment of structures and relations of exploitation in fact follow a general pattern. The benevolent micro-entrepreneur bestows on his workers and their families a certain degree of dignity (e.g. a source of livelihood); but even as he is doing so, he is also exploiting them (e.g. low pay). In affective and symbolic terms, the firmness of the boss's embrace masks this exploitation, and in the minds of his "clients" it is legitimized and made more palatable by their need to survive, to carry on working and making a living. The bitter reality of the informal economy, however, is that it is based on the law of the social jungle. "Popular economies" are the economies of poverty in two senses: (1) the micro-enterprise generates employment – at times even mass employment – at a low cost, but (2) it is also based on the exploitation of cheap labor: women, single mothers, widows, children (even very small children), victims of war, refugees, displaced people, handicapped people, and those belonging to indigenous groups, or the descendants of the black slaves.

In any case, only a minute fraction of "informals" are involved in entrepreneurial activities. The majority is merely struggling at subsistence level to eke out a living as self-employed workers. In the literature on the financial system that underpins the micro-enterprise, some authors have applauded the presence of an enormous entrepreneurial potential among the members of informal society. Successful intervention institutions in Brazil, the Domonican Republic, Peru, and Mexico have celebrated the emergence of a new middle class from among the ranks of the poor. Nevertheless, this should not blind us to the fact that the vast majority of informal entrepreneurs and almost all the self-employed have a hard time surviving, and systematically define themselves as poor members of the working class (Goldenberg and Acuña, 1994, and Menjívar and Pérez Sáinz, 1993).

Integration in poverty: the case of Peru

The panorama of economic and social change in Peru is probably the most dramatic example to be found of present-day transformations in Latin America. Between 1960 and 1995 – in other words, over a period of 25 years – the national percentage of indigenous peasants in Peru fell from 50 to less than 25 percent (Cotler 1995). The process of mass migration from rural areas led to an expansion of towns and cities. Lima, once an elegant city of 500,000 inhabitants at the end of the 1940s, is now a depressing metropolis of eight million.[6] As can be expected, the Peruvian class structure has been affected by these demographic and urban changes. The national élite of 1960 consisted of several hundred families, whose aristocratic lifestyle was supported by their large landholdings, and by their participation in and control of the financial and banking sectors. The urban middle classes, made up of public and private sector professionals, accounted for 5 percent of the economically active population. Between 25 and 30 percent of this population was employed in local government or in the private sector. The sweeping land reform carried out by the military government during the Velasco years (1968-1975) put an end to the rural latifundista class. It also caused a profound change in land-tenancy arrangements, which exacerbated the process of migration (in massive numbers) from the countryside to the cities.

At the same time, economic forces caused the size of the middle classes – principally the white-collar and blue-collar workers – of the cities to contract considerably. Until the early 1980s, 65 percent of the economically active urban population received a formal wage or salary. However, Table 1 shows a dramatic reduction in numbers of this category, which can be explained by the rapid increase in the informal urban economy.

Table 1: Economically Active Population (EAP) in Peru (1995)

%	Persons			Persons	%
29	2,550,000	receiving wages or salary	private sector	1,560,000	18
			public sector	790,000	9
			cooperative sector	200,000	2
61	5,226,000	not receiving wages	urban independents	2,516,000	30
			peasants	1,200,000	14
			family workers	700,000	8
			informal workers	550,000	6
			domestic workers	260,000	3
10	864,000	unemployed		864,000	10
100	8,640,000			8,640,000	100

Source: Kruijt, Sojo and Grynspan (2002: 21) based upon ILO data

By synthesizing the conclusions drawn by various sources (Kruijt, 1996: 41-43), one may arrive at the following conclusions:

(1) At the beginning of the 1980s, 65 percent of the EAP was receiving a regular wage or salary. In 1995 one notes a drastic reduction in this category in the EAP. This fact is interpreted as another indicator of the growth in the Peruvian informal economy;
(2) Over the last fifteen years, four out of every five new jobs have been created in the informal sector. In the formal economy, it would seem that the capacity to generate new jobs in the urban manufacturing sector has stagnated;
(3) Comparing national census figures for 1971, 1981, and 1993, one can observe a marked increase in female employment – from 34 percent in 1971, to 50 percent in 1993. This phenomenon can be interpreted as an overall indicator of the feminization of poverty within the informal economy;
(4) The rise of underemployment in the Peruvian economy is enormous: from 26 percent in 1980 to 77 percent by 1995;
(5) Perhaps the most dramatic feature of the Peruvian economy has been the fall in real income. The average income for the male population in 1993 (in nuevos soles at 1994 values) was equivalent to 33 percent of the average income in 1980. In the case of the female population, it was 30 percent. The minimum wage paid in the private sector in 1990 was 41 percent of its real value in 1980.
(6) By comparing the data from 1990 and 2000, one can argue that the formal/informal labor market and the employment structure have been consolidated during the 1990s.

These conclusions are corroborated by the data in table 2, the evolution and stabilization of Peru's poverty:

Table 2: Peru's poverty estimates

Year	Total population (1,000x)	Total poor (1,000x)	Percentage of poor in Perú
1985 – 86	19,490	8,400	43
1991	22,000	12,145	55
1994	23,130	12,350	53
1997	24,370	12,355	51
2000	25,660	13,890	54

Source: Mauro Machuca (2002: 23)

Table 3: Urban employment structure in Peru and in Latin America (percentages)

(1) Year 1990 (Peru)			
Formal	47	public sector	35
		private sector	12
Informal	53	self employed	33
		micro-enterprises	15
		household service	5
(2) Year 1999 (Peru)			
Formal	46	public sector	7
		private sector	39
Informal	54	self employed	30
		micro-enterprises	18
		household service	6
(3) Year 1990 (Latin America)			
Formal	57	public sector	16
		private sector	41
Informal	53	self employed	22
		micro-enterprises	15
		household service	6
(4) Year 1999 (Latin America)			
Formal	53	public sector	13
		private sector	40
Informal	47	self employed	24
		micro-enterprises	16
		household service	7

Source: Webb and Fernández Baca (2001: 104) based upon ILO data.

During the 1990s – the decade of the Fujimori regime, with its strict neo-liberal policy even anchored in the Constitution of 1993 – Peru's poverty figures jumped from around 45 percent to 55 percent. As tables 3 and 4 show, Peru's informality (table 3) and poverty (table 4) during the 1990s was extreme, even in comparison with the general Latin American statistics:

Table 4: Evolution of wages in Perú (1980 = 100)

(1) real industrial salary index

Year	1992	1993	1994	1995	1996	1997	1998	1999
Lat. Am.	89	94	94	93	94	100	102	105
Peru	39	38	45	44	42	42	43	42

(2) real minimum urban salary index

Year	1992	1993	1994	1995	1996	1997	1998	1999
Lat. Am.	68	68	68	71	70	70	72	73
Peru	16	12	14	15	15	27	30	29

Source: Webb and Fernández Baca (2001: 105 – 106) based upon ILO data.

Until the last quarter of the twentieth century, Peru was geographically – as well as ethnically – divided. The population of larger urban and metropolitan areas mainly found along the coast was predominantly mestizo, while the highland region, with its the rural and indigenous communities, was inhabited by a largely monolingual Quechua-speaking Indian population. Nevertheless, starting in the mid-1960s, a spectacular process of migration, from the Indian departments to the coastal urban centers (especially Metropolitan Lima) picked up momentum. As the data in table 5 suggests, the population drain from the highland communities was the principal source of an explosive expansion of slums in and around Lima. The urban middle districts, like Miraflores (a *barrio* of the 1950s and 1960s) and San Isidro (an urbanized ex-*latifundium* since the 1930s), attracted the well-to-do families and reached saturation point by the 1970s. In contrast, new slums (such as San Juan de Lurigancho and San Martin de Porras) and invasion *barrios* dating from the early 1960s and early 1970s (Comas, Villa María del Triunfo, Villa El Salvador, and Los Olivos) have had to absorb the overwhelming flood of migrants (and later war refugees) from the 1970s onwards.

The consequence of this unprecedented, massive migration process, then, was that the *shared poverty* that it engendered served, ironically enough, to integrate what hitherto had been a segmented Peruvian society. Indeed, most slum pobladores retain family and community links in the Quechua region. Indian migrants to Lima and to other urban centers use the self-made dwellings and invaded plots of their metropolitan family and community members as a bridgehead for their own urban adventure.

Table 5: Growth of the population of Metropolitan Lima (1961 – 1993), according to selected districts

	1961	1972	1981	1993	*2001
Metropolitan Lima area	1,836,000	3,295,000	4,608,000	6,346,000	7,695,000
Miraflores (upper middle class)	8,000	100,000	103,000	87,000	88,000
San Isidro (upper middle class)	38,000	63,000	71,000	63,000	60,000
Ate (slum)	79,000	61,000	146,000	266,000	411,000
Comas (slum)		173,000	283,000	404,000	470,000
Los Olivos (slum)				288,000	344,000
S.J.Lurigancho (slum)	33,000	86,000	259,000	583,000	751,000
S.M.de Porres (slum)	97,000	231,000	405,000	380,000	448,000
Villa El Salv. (slum)				255,000	364,000
Villa Mar.Tr. (slum)		181,000	314,000	264,000	342,000

* = estimated
Source: Webb y Fernández Baca (2001: 229) based upon census data and INEI statistics

This peculiar process of "integration-through-poverty" can be illustrated by comparing census data between 1972 and 1993[7]:

(1) The Economically Active Population doubled between 1972 (3,786,200) and 1993 (7,121,400).
(2) The long-term migration pattern (10 percent in 1940, 23 percent in 1961, 26 percent in 1972, 22 percent in 1981, and 22 percent in 1993) appears to have acquired a stabilizing equilibrium of between a fifth and a quarter of the national population.
(3) The urban population grew from 59 percent in 1972 to 70 percent in 1993. The most important migration flows were traditionally directed towards Metropolitan Lima, followed by other coastal urban areas. From the 1990s onwards, intermediary urban centers in the highland and lowland regions became equally popular.
(4) The number of female-headed households in 1993 was roughly 25 percent of the national total of 4 million; 13 percent of adolescent girls is a mother (1993).
(5) The Ministry of Justice estimates that 17 percent of the young Peruvians is not documented or registered in any civil or municipal archive (1999).
(6) By 1999, an estimated 1,170,000 Peruvian children were informally employed; 150,000 of them work in mines, waste collection, menial street-based labor (e.g. vending goods or services) etc.

New social actors and new popular cultures in Latin America

These and other economic and social consequences, in Peru as well as in other Latin American countries, have entailed processes that were scarcely perceived at the time, which nevertheless have resulted in a decomposition of established class formations, and its restructuring into a new social edifice. The parallel institutions, parallel hierarchies and parallel sectors that have emerged in tandem with poverty, informality, and social exclusion are contributing to the formation of a new, more heterogeneous, economic, social, political, and cultural order. Formal and informal institutions regulate themselves with their own types of logic, morality and sanctions: the civil order of the formal economy and society, and the hidden anarchy of poverty, informality and social exclusion. Economy and society are thus intertwined in a durable symbiotic relationship.

This structural duality also has long-term consequences for the emergence of a new civil society, whose features have been influenced in significant ways and degrees by poverty, informality, and social exclusion. In the early 1980s, Matos Mar (1984) wrote a prophetic essay in which he predicted the decline of the institutional pillars of traditional Peruvian society. He also predicted the timid birth of a diversity of organizations representing micro-entrepreneurs and the informal sector in general, such as local and regional chambers of craftsmen, *comedores populares* (the community-run canteens offering cheap meals in the slums of Lima). What all of these have in common is an ambivalent relationship of dependency on professional development organizations, like religious or ecclesiastical foundations, NGOs, donor agencies, banks, and municipal and central government institutions working in the social field.[8] Nevertheless, in most of the Andean and Central American countries, the chambers of industry and commerce, the lawyers', doctors and engineers' professional associations, and the once all-powerful trade-union confederations, have experienced serious decline and weakening in the course of the 1980s. In Argentina, Brazil and Mexico the same tendencies were evident, although perhaps less dramatically. The decline in recent years of the organizational strength of national élites, of the entrepreneurial class, of the urban middle classes, of the industrial trade unions and the small rural landowners, has been parallel by the creation of social associations and movements associated with informal and excluded society. Consequently, new organizational structures of poverty, informality, and social exclusion are being born. Moreover, new social actors have gained a presence on the economic, social, and political stage, and are now seeking space of their own.

One can now recognize in these changes what amounts to an implicit alteration of the structuring of the organization of classes. There is, for example, the case of the new manufacturing and commercial establishments of the micro-entrepreneurs. One must remember that these businessmen and businesswomen constitute an elite among the poor. Yet in spite of the extent of organization attained by the informal entrepreneurs, their achievements are still only relative. For even in the case of organized micro-entrepreneurs, one must bear in mind that their progress along the organizational road has gone only as far as certain limits, and not beyond. It is worth noting that these small businessmen and women are often concurrently the full-time workers of their own businesses.

What is even more significant in Andean and Central American countries is the relative absence of any kind of union activity in the informal sector (Koonings, 2001). In this process, the dependence of the workers on the firm that employs them is reproduced, which explains the prevalence of clientelism and patronage, and the control exercised by bosses over workers. When it happens at all, the organizational activism of the small businessmen is more often than not initiated, promoted, and guided from outside, by the NGOs, the churches, or even the financial institutions that offer small-scale credit to the micro-enterprise. Most of the small proprietors' organizations are, at best, semi-autonomous.

Perhaps the most interesting manifestation of poverty, informality and exclusion in Latin America is the appearance of new actors on the national stage of civil society. This is often manifest in micro-entrepreneurs who present themselves as the new organized poor, who resemble more closely their own employees (who often are family members or relatives), rather than their counterparts in the formal economy. There is at least an apparent similarity between these and the formal organizations of the workers' movement. Both are movements of self-defense, dedicated to the improvement of the economic and working conditions of their members.

However, drawing from the example that Hobsbawm (1994) describes in reference to the insignificance and lack of maturity of the organizations defending the poor during the first generations of the industrial revolution, one may emphasize the differences between these and the guilds of the micro-entrepreneurs. Industrial trade unionism is the formal and legitimate representative of the national work force: legally protected, organized organically and hierarchically in trade unions, federations, and confederations. Union members are the industrial and managerial workers of the medium-sized and large companies of the public and private sectors. They regulate their working conditions via collective agreements, which are negotiated thanks to the pressure exercised by the mass of affiliated members.

In contrast, the trade unions, associations, or chambers of the informal sector, such as those of the micro-entrepreneurs or of a particular branch of craftsmen or self-employed workers are, at best, incipient organizations with a precarious degree of "institutionality." They are generally created *ad hoc*, to attain short-term, pragmatic objectives; for instance, a line of credit, a place to set up a market stall, spontaneous publicity, or the solution to a specific problem related to the local authorities. The same can be said of the variety of non-economic organizations, such as mothers' self-help clubs, the glass-of-milk committees, and the popular canteens. Their *raison d'être* is based on *ad hoc* but essential needs – food, security, lodging, health care, a source of income. In most cases, their creation has been induced from outside, for instance, by a private development organization, a church committee, a local financial agent, an enterprising politician, or sometimes an array of international donors. It is here that one perceives the difference between these relatively weak and dependent organizations, on the one hand, and the strong and autonomous labor movement, on the other. The spontaneous or induced affiliation of the poor depends almost by necessity on the charity of others, and is in search of a precarious stability at a more basic – and certainly more fragmented – level than that which is fought for by the existing institutions of the formal order.

Formal and informal representation

Nevertheless, a comparison between the relative loss of strength of the organized labor movement and the slow but continuous emergence of the micro-entrepreneurs and (although in lesser degree) the organized self-employed in Colombia and Peru, will help to clarify the points made above. In both countries the scaling down of the labor movement since the beginning of the 1980s has been quite extraordinary.[9] In 1991, only 7 percent of the EAP in Colombia was organized in trade unions; in Peru, only 5 percent. Data for Colombia provided by the Planning and Statistics Departments[10] show that, between 1975 and 1995, the percentage of urban employment that can be attributed to the informal economy grew from 25 to 53 percent. The importance of informality in the urban context shows itself to be evenly spread: 80 percent of statistically registered informal employment is concentrated in the four metropolitan areas of Bogota, Medellín, Cali, and Barranquilla. It is interesting to see how the official statistics for 1994 reflect the evolution of informal employment. In decreasing order, the most important categories are (1) "self-employed industrial and service workers", (2) "micro-enterprise businessmen," and (3) "family employees."[11] With regard to policies in the war on poverty – be they programs of government intervention, of donors, or of the private sector – all are characterized by an implicit strategy of "élitization within poverty." As is the case in all Latin American countries, most official and unofficial aid programs are oriented towards the upper segments – viz those relatively better off and educated – of the informal economy. In individual terms, these, of course, tend to be the micro-entrepreneurs, above all in the urban context. The general strategy often consists of a combined aid package comprising training, technical assistance and credit, offered to individual micro-entrepreneurs.

The Colombian Government and UNICEF took the initiative in 1985 to organize the First Convention of Micro-Entrepreneur Associations. Nearly a hundred chambers and other associations took part. In 1986, 120 micro-entrepreneur associations met in Medellín and set up CONAMIC, the National Micro-Entrepreneurs Confederation of Colombia. The number of affiliated associations now stands at around 140 organizations. The General Secretary of the CONAMIC, a former labour leader and now a micro-entrepreneur with three non-unionized workers, described the economic, social, and political position of the associations as "belonging neither to the ANDI (National Industrial Chamber of Commerce) nor to the organized labor movement."[12] Originally, the CONAMIC was promoted within the public sector. Nowadays, however, the organization acts as an independent institution representing the short-term and long-term interests of its affiliated associations. Most of the 140 associations have local bases at municipal level, and 5 per-cent have sectoral significance. At the national level, CONAMIC's concerns are in regard to special laws on the position and promotion of small firms and microenterprise, the fiscal régime affecting them, and interest rates on the special lines of credit.

Since the 1980s many of those affiliated to the Colombian labor unions disap-peared into the oblivion of informality and now struggle to survive as new micro-entre-preneurs, or seek a niche among the informally self-employed. The tragedy is that no trade-union leader, whether at local, regional, departmental or national level, has emerged to offer any alternative. Most of the labor leaders do not know how to respond to this increasing disaffiliation. The disappearance of old members into infor-mality sometimes causes discouragement, and at other times, panic. But on both sides, nobody thus far has undertaken any significant action to form effective alliances between the labor federations and the micro-entrepreneurial associations. It might have been prudent to follow up some lines of approach to an alliance, given the fact that the new members of the CONAMIC come from the ranks of public and private sector managerial and industrial workers who have been laid off, and have used their sever-ance pay as starting capital to set up a microenterprise.

In contrast to the Colombian situation, consecutive Peruvian governments since 1980 have shown, at most, a passive interest in creating legislation, development plans, and new policies with which to tackle the phenomenon of mass poverty and urban infor-mality as "normal" characteristics of national reality. The most direct activities have been, for the most part, delegated to recently created NGOs related to donor institutions, or to the "banks with a social face," which are related to the cooperative sector. The support programs have been seen basically as a matter for the attention of the private sector. Just as in Colombia and in other Latin American countries, most research programs and con-crete acts of intervention are directed towards the upper levels of the informal economy: the circuit of the "formalizable" micro-entrepreneurs, the élite of the poor. In Peru there is no national confederation of comparable significance to the Colombian CONAMIC.

Even so, the leading NGOs in the area of promoting small business have created their own institutional platform of business associations. The NGOs themselves have come together in what is known as the Consortium of NGOs Supporting Small Busi-ness and Microenterprise (COPEME), consisting of fifty affiliated organizations. Equal-ly, some local and regional small business organizations were created "from below." Since 1994 some government and public-sector programs – such as FONCODES (the Peruvian social investment fund), COFIDE (the National Development Corporation), and the municipal banks – have initiated new programs to provide credit to micro-entrepreneurs and the self-employed, and to promote the creation of associations among them.

Although it is commonly assumed that most businessmen and workers in the informal sector voted for Fujimori in the 1990 and 1995 presidential elections, no for-mal political links have been established. Yet at the organizational level, good working relations have at least existed between the Presidency and the organized segments of the informal sector. Máximo San Román, Fujimori's first Vice-President in 1990, was Chairman of APEMYPE, which at that time was the most important association of small businessmen and micro-entrepreneurs in Peru. Fujimori's First Vice-President after 1995, Ricardo Márquez, was previously President of the National Society of Industries, the spinal column of the formal economy. Márquez, nevertheless, had a personal history as a micro-entrepreneur and took charge of support programs for poor, informal and excluded businessmen.

Fujimori's government has taken the initiative in such matters as labor legislation, "flexibilisation," economic adjustment, and social compensation. As in the case of Colombia, the labor movement is responding passively to the restructuring of the country's economy and society. Moreover, as in Colombia, a considerable percentage of previous trade unionists have deserted to swell the ranks of the informals as micro-entrepreneurs and self-employed. Again, as in Colombia, no one at the level of trade union, federation, or confederation has offered any clear visions or alternatives for the future. Up to the present time, no serious action has been initiated to form functional alliances with micro-entrepreneurs' associations, nor with the immense atomized – or at best, semi-organized – mass of informal and self-employed workers. Whereas the Colombian Government developed an explicit strategy against poverty in the 1980s, aimed at supporting the micro-entrepreneurial sector (and the micro-entrepreneurs in particular), the Peruvian Government has assumed a more relaxed attitude towards poverty, and the struggle against poverty. In Lima, I had the honor of being received by President Fujimori's Minister for Labour and Social Affairs.[13] When an earthquake practice threatened to interrupt our interview, the Minister simply continued unperturbed with his presentation of the Peruvian policy regarding the war on poverty:

> "Poverty? You're asking me what we're doing against poverty? Well, to begin with, what is "poverty"? Poverty is a question of definitions. Ask five economists for a definition of poverty and each one will give you a different answer. Poverty is a relative concept; I have seen how they change it and use it in different circumstances. When you people talk about poverty you can be sure you're about to start an argument.
>
> The other day the Cardinal of Lima asked me – I happened to meet him at a reception – why we're doing so little about the poverty in the slums, which is getting worse every day. I answered him: 'Just a moment; who has the right to talk about this? Wasn't it the Church who allowed the exploitation of the Indians five hundred years ago? He didn't give me a straight answer, since, of course, he didn't have one. Peru has put up with poverty for five centuries, and survived. Our country has an enormous capacity to survive suffering.
>
> No, my friend, poverty can only be overcome by increasing productivity. First we must produce, then we can talk about what we want. And who should we talk to anyway, the old trade union leaders? The CGTP,

the CITP, the CLAT [the labor confederations], the politicians of the past?
They no sooner open their mouths than they start to complain…"

The new civil society has, nevertheless, other institutional actors on the economic, social and political stage. It is not the unions or other representative associations nor the national associations of commerce and industry that take the initiative of organizing or leaping to the defense of the poor and the excluded. Rather, it has been the emerging system of the NGOs that has understood the need to organize the informal sector. It has been the NGOs who have carried out systematic research into the feelings and aspirations of the micro-entrepreneurs and the self-employed, the families headed by women, street children and the direct and indirect victims of the civil wars that have ravaged countries of the Andean and Central American region.[14] In Latin America the public sector, too, is participating in the process of social dualization, within the unstable social and political order.

Informal citizenship?
Social integration alludes to the possibilities of constituting citizenship. Citizenship can be understood as the combined process of collective affiliation and identification, with access to certain rights. Ever since Marshall, citizenship has been conceived as the having at one's disposal a status of belonging to a community: "All those who dispose of such a status are equal with respect to the duties and rights that the status establishes" (Marshall (1992 [1950]: 18). When the citizenship in question is in a process of constitution or consolidation, it is presented as an ideal that establishes the desired horizon and against which one measures the degree of advance. On the basis of this definition Marshall identified three types of citizenship: (1) *civil*, which concerns particularly economic liberties (of property and work); (2) *political*, which refers to the right of suffrage; and *social*, which relates to the rights to livelihood, consumption, and welfare.

Reflecting on the seminal contribution of Marshall and its implications for the globalized international environment, Bottomore (1992) establishes the need to distinguish two levels of citizenship: the *formal*, relating to the fact of belonging to a community denominated nation-state, and the *substantive*, which integrates the three components of Marshall's typology. The distinction is important because in closely interrelated national planes, as is the case in the environment of globalization, one can have substantive citizenship rights even when one does not formally belong to a community (for example the social and economic rights of migrants). It is to be understood that social integration refers to the intensity of substantive citizenship, i.e. to the degree of development and fulfillment of civil, political, and social rights and duties.

The degree to which citizens' rights exist is unequal in every society because it reflects the results of historically conditioned processes of interaction between state and society. Consequently the levels of social integration – understood here as the degree of expansion of citizens' rights – will differ in every country, and their concrete weighting is important for social analysis. This weighing can be carried out using at least two different approaches. The first is a formal one in which the identification of statutory rights, on the basis of the examination of legal frameworks and institutional parameters (constitutions, codes), predominates. The second approach is of an empirical nature, and can be carried out through observations of the degree to which rights are being practiced. For example, the degree of electoral abstention can be used as an indicator of the consolidation of political citizenship; unemployment can be compared with rates of increase of output as an indicator of civil citizenship; or the percentage of the population covered by social security, and indicators of poverty, can be taken as expressions of the development of the social forms of citizenship.

To sum up, empirical observation of the degree to which the rights of substantive citizenship have developed facilitates a concrete approach to the dynamics of social integration. It would be a mistake, however, to assume that one is dealing simply with relations of a dualistic kind in which one either has or does not have rights. On the contrary, it is appropriate to consider the degree of satisfaction of the rights of citizenship as a process of construction, which may tend towards either social integration or disintegration.

Conclusion

The interesting thing about the thesis of exclusion, as outlined above, is that comprehensive observations enables one to combine social, economic, and political indicators so as to evaluate the dynamics of social integration. On the other hand, and as a consequence of them, these models do not lead to dichotomous models of integration, but rather to an opportunity to register the dynamics of the process of exclusion. Since civil citizenship is related to levels of economic liberty and employment, and in so far as social citizenship has to do with the degree of welfare, one should aim to study the degree to which social integration has been achieved (as an expression of the satisfaction of the rights of citizenship), as reflected in the magnitude of poverty and the problems of the labour market.

The central hypothesis that the evidence points to is that there is an advance towards the formation of an informal citizenship, this being understood in reference to the attainment of certain degrees of social integration on the basis of the "massification" of political and civil rights and liberties in an environment in which the precarious nature of the satisfaction of the rights of social citizenship is becoming more acute. In this sense, we may conclude that the precarious implantation of substantive citizenship that belies the existence of informal citizenship is the most recent expression of a model of economic reform that induces impoverishment and instability in labor markets.

Notes

1   In this contribution I make use of the argumentation published in other contributions such as Alba Vega and Kruijt (1994), Koonings, Kruijt and Wils (1995), Kruijt et al. (1996), and Kruijt, Sojo and Grynspan (2002: chapter I).

2   These reform measures included the devaluation of currencies, promotion of exports, liberalization of imports, reductions in government food subsidies, layoffs of public employees, cuts in social services, raising indirect taxes, measures for covering the costs of government, privatizations and reforms of public-sector companies, wage and salary freezes and the reining in of credit.

3   See, for example the World Bank Report 2000 (2000), the the Human Development Report 1997 (1997: 125 ff.), the ECLAC's *Social Panorama of Latin America* 2000-2001 (2002) and the ILO reports since the early 1990s, varying from the *Retrospectiva del sector informal urbano* (1991) to Chavez et al. (1998), Lagos and Arrigada (1998), Tokman and Martínez (1999), Egger and García (2000) and El trabajo decente y la economía informal (2002).

4   See especially Barrera et al. (1992,1993), Goldenberg and Acuña (1994), Menjívar and Pérez Sáinz (1989, 1993), Menjívar and Trejos (1992), Pérez Sáinz (1998, 1999), Pérez Sáinz et al. (1996), Pérez Sáinz and Menjívar (1991), and Tardanico and Menjívar (1997)

5   Rogers, Gore and Figuereido (1995). For Peru, the ILO recently published a solid empirical measurement study by Figueroa and Sulmont (1996).

6   Lima was described at that time in the geographical literature as one of the continent's most beautiful capitals.

7   See Ponce (1995: 130 -140), actualized by studies and data published by Social Watch (1999: 33 – 35).

8   For a more general analysis of the Latin American situation, see Foley and Edwards (1996), Roberts (1996), Stavenhagen (1997), Gideon (1998), Tulchin and Garland (2000), Friedman, Hochstetler and Clark (2001), and Foweraker (2001).

9   Data from *Panorama Laboral 1994* (1995).

10 DNP and DANE respectively. See *Plan nacional de la microempresa* (1994) and Rodriguez (1994).

11 Caro (1994).

12 Author's interview with Carlos Barrero, 25 May 1994.

13 Author's interview with Augusto Antonioli, Minister for Labour and Social Matters, to one of the authors on 31 May 1995.

14 Documented in the Peruvian case at the beginning of the 1990s by Bambarolo, Coscio and Stein (1992) and by Zolessi (1991).

Bibliography

Alba Vega, Carlos. 1987. *La petite industrie et les entrepreneurs dans une société dépendante: Le cas de Guadalajara, Mexique*. Paris: Ecole des Haute Etudes en Sciences Sociales, thesis doctorat nouveau régime.

Alba, Carlos and Dirk Kruijt. 1994. *The Convenience of the Minuscule. Informality and Microenterprise in Latin America*. Amsterdam: Thela Thesis Latin America Series # 3.

Bambarolo, Félix, Luis Pérez Coscio and Alfredo Stein. 1992. *El rol de las organizaciones no gubernamentales en América Latina y el Caribe*. Buenos Aires: FICONG.

Barrera, Yesid, Dirk Kruijt et al. 1992. *Informalidad y pobreza*. San José: FLACSO.

Barrera, Yesid, Dirk Kruijt et al. 1993. *La economía de los pobres*. San José: FLACSO.

Bottomore, Tom. 1992. *Citizenship and Social Class, Forty Years On*. London: Pluto Press.

Caro, Blanca. 1994. *Universo microempresarial*. Bogotá: DNP/Unidad de Desarrollo Social-División de Empleo e Ingresos.

Cartaya, Vanessa. 1994. "Informality and Poverty. Causal Relationship or Coincidence?" in Cathy A. Rakowski (ed.) *Contrapunto. The Informal Sector Debate in Latin America* pp. 223-249. Albany: State University of New York Press.

Chávez O'Brien. 1998. *Eliana et al. Perú: El sector informal frente al reto de la modernización*. Lima: ILO.

Chossudovsky, Michel. 1997. *The Globalization of Poverty. Impacts of IMF and World Bank Reforms*. London/Penang: Zed Books/Third World Network.

Cotler, Julio, ed. 1994. *Política y sociedad en el Perú. Cambios y continuidades*. Lima: IEP, (serie Perú Problema # 23).

Cotler, Julio, ed. 1995. *Perú 1964 – 1994. Economía, sociedad y política*. Lima: IEP, (serie Perú Problema # 24).

Egger, Philippe and Norberto E. García eds. 2000. *Apertura económica y empleo: Los países andinos en los novena*. Lima: ILO.

Egger, Philippe and Norberto E. García. 2002. *El trabajo decente y la economía informal*: Geneve: ILO (Conferencia Internacional del Trabajo 90.a reunión 2002).

Feliciani, F. et al. 1995. *Análisis de la exclusión social a nivel departamental*. Guatemala: Hombres de Maís for FLACSO/ UNOPS/PNUD.

Figueroa, Adolfo and Denis Sulmont. 1996. *Social Exclusion in Peru*. Geneva: OIT.

Foley, Michael W. and Bob Edwards. 1996. "The paradox of civil society." *Journal of Democracy*, 7(3):38-52.

Foweraker, Joe. 2001. "Grassrtoots Movements and Political Activism in Latin America: A Critical Comparison of Chile and Brasil." *Journal of Latin American Studies* 13(4):839-865.

Friedman, Jay, Elizabeth Kathryn Hochstetler and Ann Marie Clark. "Sovereign Limits and Regional Opportunities for Global Civil Society in Latin America." *Latin American Perspectives*

Gideon, Jasmine. 1998. "The Politics of Social Service Provision through NGO's: A Study of Latin America." *Bulletin of Latin American Research* 17(3):303-321.

Goldenberg, Olga and Victor Hugo Acuña. 1994. *Género en la informalidad. Historias laborales centroaméricanas*. San José: FLACSO.

Herrera, Javier. 2001. "Nuevas estimaciones de la pobreza en el Perú." *Economía y sociedad* 43:4-10.

Hobsbawm, Eric. 1994. *The Age of Empire*, 1875-1914. London: Abacus.

Hobsbawm, Eric. 1997. *Human Development Report 1997*. New York: Oxford University Press for the United Nations Development Programme.

Hydén, Göran. 1983. *No Shortcuts to Progress. African Development Management in Perspective*. London: Heinemann.

Koonings, Kees et al. 2001. El trabajo en fase de negociación. Evaluación de la política del VMP de CNV "Actie Kom Over" en Centroamérica 1995-2000. Utrecht/La Haya: CNV/DGIS-DSI.

Koonings, Kees, Dirk Kruijt and Frits Wils. 1995. 'The very long march of history.' in H. Thomas, ed. *Globalization and Third World Trade Unions: The Challenge of Rapid Economic Change* pp. 99-129. London: Zed Books,

Kruijt, Dirk et al. 1996. *Changing Labour Relations in Latin America. A Policy Evaluation of Labour Relations and Trade Unionism in Colombia and Peru*. Amsterdam: Thela Publishers for the Ministry of Foreign Affairs (DGIS) and the Netherlands Trade Union Confederation FNV.

Kruijt, Dirk, Carlos Sojo and Rebeca Grynspan. 2002. *Informal Citizens. Poverty, Informality and Social Exclusion in Latin America*. Amsterdam: Rozenberg/Thela Latin America Series.

Lagos, Ricardo A. and Camilo Arriagada (eds.). 1998. *Población, pobreza y mercado de trabajo en América Latina*. Lima : ILO.

Marshall, Thomas. 1992 (first edition 1950). *Citizenship and Social Class*. Cambridge: Cambridge University Press.

Matos Mar, José. 1984. *Desborde popular y crisis del estado. El nuevo rostro del Perú en la década de 1980*. Lima: IEP.

Mauro Machuca, Raúl. 2002. *Cambio en la pobreza en el Perú: 1991 – 1998. Un análisis a partir de los componentes del ingreso.* Lima: CIES/DESCO (Serie Investigaciones Breves).

Menjívar Larín, Rafael and Juan Diego. 1992. Trejos. *La pobreza en América Central.* San José: FLACSO,

Menjívar Larín, Rafael and Juan Pablo Pérez Sáinz eds. 1989. *Informalidad urbana en Centroamérica. Evidencias e interrogantes.* Guatemala: FLACSO/Fundación Friedrich Ebert.

Menjívar Larín, Rafael and Juan Pablo Pérez Sáinz eds. 1993. *Ni héroes ni villanas. Género e informalidad urbana en Centroamérica.* San José: FLACSO.

Moser, Caroline O.N. 1994. "The Informal Sector Debate, Part I: 1970-1983". in Cathy A. Rakowski (ed.) *Contrapunto. The Informal Sector Debate in Latin America.* pp. 11-29. Albany: State University of New York Press.

Moser, Caroline O.N. 1995. *Panorama laboral 1994.* Lima: International Labour Office.

Moser, Caroline O.N. 2000. *Panorama social de América Latina 1999-2000.* Santiago de Chile: ECLAC, (LC/G.2068-P).

Pérez Sáinz, Juan Pablo. 1996. "Los nuevos escenarios laborales en América Latina." *Nueva Sociedad,* 143:20-29.

Pérez Sáinz, Juan Pablo. 1998. 'TheNew Faces of Informality in Central America." *Journal of Latin American Studies* 30:157-179.

Pérez Sáinz, Juan Pablo. 1999. "Mercado laboral, integración social y modernización globalizada en Centroamerica." *Nueva Sociedad,* 164:106-121.

Pérez Sáinz, Juan Pablo and Rafael Menjívar Larín. 1991. *Informalidad urbana en Centroamérica. Entre la acumulación y la subsistencia.* San José: FLACSO.

Pérez Sáinz, Juan Pablo and Rafael Menjívar Larín. 1994. *Plan nacional para el desarrollo de la microempresa.* Bogotá: Departamento Nacional de Planeación,

Ponce, Ana. 1995. "Perú: perfil sociodemográfico (1972 – 1993)." en Gonzalo Portocarrero y Marcel Valcárcel, eds. *El Perú frente al siglo XXI.* pp. 127-155. Lima: PUCP/Fondo Editorial.

Portes, Alejandro. 1985. "Latin American Class Structures: Their Composition and Change during the Last Decades." *Latin American Research Review,* 20(3):7-39.

Rakowski, Cathy A. 1994a. "Convergence and Divergence in the Informal Sector Debate: A Focus on Latin America, 1984-92." *World Development,* 22(4):501-516.

Rakowski, Cathy A. ed. 1994b. *Contrapunto. The Informal Sector Debate in Latin America.* Albany: State University of New York Press.

Rakowski, Cathy A. 1994c. "The Informal Sector Debate, Part 2: 1984-1993." in Cathy A. Rakowski ed., *Contrapunto. The Informal Sector Debate in Latin America.* pp. 31-50. Albany: State University of New York Press.

Rakowski, Cathy A. 1991. *Retrospectiva del sector informal urbano en América Latina: Una bibliografía anotada.* Genebra: International Labour Office/PREALC.

Roberts, Bryan. 1996. "The Social Context of Citizenship in Latin America." *International Journal of Urban and Regional Research,* 20(1):38-65.

Rodriguez, Ana Luz. 1994. *Plan nacional para el desarrollo gremial microempresarial.* Bogotá: DNP.

Rogers, Gerry, Charles Gore and José B. Figuereido. 1995. *Social Exclusion: Rhetoric, Reality, Responses. A contribution to the World Summit for Social Development.* Geneva: ILO/International Institute for Labour Studies.

Rosanvallon, Pierre. 1995. *La nouvelle question sociale.* Paris: Editions du Seuil.

Salama, Pierre. 1995. "De quelques leçons économiques de l'histoire latino-américaine récente." *Revue Tiers-Monde,* 36(144):793-812.

Social Watch. 1999. "La democracia sigue en suspenso, la pobreza se mantiene." en Alberto Adrianzen et al. *El Perú realmente existente. Análisis y datos estadísticos sobre mujeres, niños, indígenas, descentralización, pobreza, mortalidad, desigualdad, derechos laborales.* pp. 31-42. Lima: CEDEP/Diakonia.

Social Watch. 2002. *Social Panorama of Latin America 2000 – 2001*. Santiago de Chile, (LC/G.2138-P.)

Stavenhagen, Rodolfo. 1997. "Las organizaciones indígenas: Actores emergentes en América Latina." *Revista de la CEPAL* 62:61-76.

Tardanico, Richard and Rafael Menjívar Larín ed. 1997. *Global Restructuring, Employment, and Social Inequality in Latin America*. Miami: North-South Center Press.

Tokman, Víctor E. ed. 1992. *Beyond Regulation. The Informal Economy in Latin America*. Boulder: Lynne Rienner Publishers.

Tokman, Víctor E. and Daniel Martínez eds. 1999. *Inseguridad laboral y competatividad: Modalidades de contratación*. Lima: ILO.

Tokman, Víctor E. and Daniel Martínez eds. 1999.*Flexibilización en el margen: La reforma del contrato de trabajo*. Lima: ILO.

Tulchin, Joseph S. and Allison M. Garland, eds. 2000. *Social Development in Latin America: The Politics of Reform*. Boulder: Lynne Reinner.

Webb, Richard y Graciela Fernández Baca. 2001 *Anuario Estadístico. Perú en números 2001*. Lima: Instituto Cuánto.

Zolessi, Mario (ed.). 1991. *La promoción al desarrollo en el Perú. Balance y perspectivas*. Lima: DESCO.

8

On the Very Idea of an Anthropological Study of Western Science

Diederick Raven

> In acquiring one's conception of the world one always belongs to a particular grouping which is that of all the social elements which share the same mode of thinking and acting. We are conformists ..., always man-in-the-mass or collective man. The question is this: of what historical type is the conformism?
>
> Antonio Gramsci (1971:324)

> Culture comes from schooling.
>
> Pierre Bourdieu (1967:340)

Introduction

In a recent essay Emily Martin (1988:25), professor of anthropology at Princeton University, asks 'What might a cultural anthropological study of Western science look like'. Martin's essay is part of a broader attempt by professionally trained anthropologists, like Hess, Rabb and Traweek, to catch up with the growing field of science and technology studies (STS for short) and especially with its sub-speciality the anthropology of science.[1]

With hindsight, it all seems so obvious to study working scientists as just another tribe. But the anthropologists did not arrive at the scene first but last. When they finally arrived they were not welcomed in the most friendliest of possible ways. Martin's question, however, signals a new-found confidence amongst the professional anthropologists active in STS. With 'considerable humility' (Martin 1988:25), they argue that they have something special to bring to STS. Predicably they concentrate on the notion of culture:

> I and a number of anthropological colleagues ... believe that we can make some important contribution to [STS] by bringing to the field the cultural perspective, critical questions, and ethnographic methods as they have been formulated in contemporary ... anthropology (Hess 1992:2).

In a similar vain Martin argues that the difference professional anthropologist can make is related to 'introducing the anthropological concept of culture ... a key concept of the discipline' (1998:28).

Culture may be anthropology's key theoretical notion, but going through numerous papers and books dealing with it always leaves one depressed and in despair. As one critique once remarked: 'The *discourse* of culture in the social sciences (...) does not dispel the lingering suspicion that the social sciences – particularly anthropology, ...– are more able to discuss what culture *does* than to identify or clarify what culture *is*' (Lee III 1988:115). I was reminded of this outcry when I tried to work out why Martin, Hess, Traweek c.s. suggest that 'from an anthropological vantage point' it makes sense 'to understand science as a form of culture' (Franklin 1995:165). So how is it intended? Franklin's essay is not much help. But I feel very uncomfortable when it is suggested in such a broad manner that 'X' needs 'to be reassessed as a cultural practice' (ibid:165). What is meant by this? Unless a theory specifies what makes human groups into cultures, I fail to see what is being said here. Even to the extend I do understand it – 'the study of culture should be based upon the fullest possible understanding of people's thought and actions from their own perspective' (MacDonald 1983:75) – there still is need for theoretical clarification and caution.

Just one short example of why clarification is needed. At one point in her analyses Traweek turns, without further theoretical justification, the differences between the American and Japanese particle physics community into 'cultural differences' (1993:400).[2] The American physicist community is characterized by competition, where organizational hierarchy is treated 'as the *natural* ranking of human talents' (ibid, emphasis in the original). In the Japanese community on the other hand, status is determined by age. It is striking that, in contrast to the American community, within the Japanese community there is no mention of a strict division of labour. Unlike the Japanese community, where the decisions are made by the leader, in the American community all members are able to contribute their point of view in discussions about decision making and planning. This picture is in line with other studies about differences between Japan and the USA and has a pedigree that goes back at least to Ruth Benedict's *The Chrysanthemum and the Sword*. Collectivism versus individualism and status based on age versus status based on merit. Interpreting these differences as cultural differences has been done before. Traweek, however, spoils much of her analyses when she writes in relation to a particular incident between an American and a Japanese physicist: 'Fortunately, the two physicists also share a culture – the culture of the particle physics community'. On the face of this suggests that one can at will switch 'allegiance' form one culture to another -which is an implausible suggestion and is need of further theoretical justification – or is she suggesting that Japanese or American culture and the culture of particle physics are of the same order, which is an equally implausible suggestion and requires theoretical elaboration as well. Traweek's fuzzy reasoning is caused by an insufficiently articulated concept of culture. Culture for Traweek (1988:ix) is a 'local strategies for making sense'. This allows her to be unspecific about the kind of resources that are utilized by the people making the sense. But there is an additional drawback to this kind of culture concept. Take the following quote:

A community is a group of people with a shared past, with ways of recognizing and displaying their differences from other groups, and expectations for a shared future. Their culture is the ways, the strategies they
recognize and use and invent for making sense, from common sense to
disputes, from teaching to learning: it is also their ways of making things
and making use of them and the ways they make over their world.
(Traweek 1992:438/8)

For an anthropologist Traweek is making here a very odd move: she subordinates the
anthropological concept of culture to that of the sociological concept of community or
group. Traweek is not alone in doing this. For Hess: 'the concept of culture in an
anthropological sense has more to do with the total knowledge and way of life of a
group of people' (1995:10). It is difficult not to read Hess and Traweek as turning
anthropology into a sub-discipline of sociology, and all other professional anthropologists tend to follow suit. Finally, this notion of culture tends to confuse the culture of
physics – what are the general ideas that constitute the practice of physics – with that
of the culture of the physicists – who is playing which political game with whom.
Traweek is without the theoretical resources to tell the two apart. Taking her inspiration from a Geertzian semiotic concept of culture, in which the name of the game is
'to explicate the webs of significance' spun by the actors being investigated, I am not
surprised by this. I do not believe, however, that an anthropology of knowledge should
be interested in the culture of scientists. It should primarily focus on the cultural nature
of the knowledge endeavour called 'science'. My suspicion is that Traweek and her colleagues think that proof of cultural differences between the physicists counts as proof
that physics is a cultural phenomenon. Well, it is not. The argument does not even
come close to proving that claim. How it needs to be argued is the topic of the remainder of this essay, which by necessity has to be rather programmatic.

Anthropology of knowledge: the key questions.
Anthropology is a comparative study of cultural differences. Anthropology of science is
the comparative study of the cultural differences of ... yes, of what exactly? If science
is in one way or another culturally specific, as I believe it is, it is not a straightforward
conclusion that in other cultures a counterpart to Western science exists. Several
options are open as where to go from here. One may make a distinction between science and ethno-science, (i.e. ethno-specific way of explaining the world). I am not particularly fond of this idea. The Western notion of science as the natural way- -of-know-
ing-the-world plays too dominant a role in the background; besides there already is a
branch of anthropology which uses that label and their research questions are different. My preferred option, therefore, is to take science for what it is in social terms: an
institution in which the way-of-knowing-the-world that is dominant in the West is
encapsulated. This looks like an innocent way of looking at science – and up to point
it is. But there is nevertheless a radical element to it. An implicit assumption of STS is

that science is the authentic way of looking at the world. This very assumption is what I want to challenge. I want to treat seriously the idea that science is just our locally preferred way of understanding the world. (This explains why I prefer to talk about anthropology of knowledge instead of the anthropology of science.)

Much to my surprise, this idea has hardly ever been taken up in a serious way. Refreshing exceptions to this are Andrew Cunningham and Perry Williams. In a jointly written paper they suggest that it is time to dispense with the idea that science is a universal human enterprise. They want to reject the idea that science is 'the expression of an innate human curiosity, a general and universal desire to understand the world, that [is] fundamental part of human nature and human thought throughout time and space' (Cunningham and Williams 1993:411/2). Instead, they suggest viewing it as a historically contingent enterprise 'embodying the values, aims and norms of a particular social group: one amongst a plurality of ways of knowing the world' (ibid:418). This seems to me to be absolutely spot on. This assumption is the core of a comparative anthropology of knowledge. A number of different research questions immediately suggest themselves. I only want to mention four:
(1) what other ways-of-knowing are there?;
(2) what is the difference between them?;
(3) how are they tied to cultural specific assumptions?;
(4) how and why did science become the dominant mode-of-knowing in the West only?

I take these as key questions for the anthropology of knowledge.

I am perfectly aware that this suggestion will not make me very popular with other professional anthropologists, or with certain post-modernists. Why the latter group will be uncomfortable is easy to see. I no longer seem to subscribe to their multi-cultural agenda of given each group its own perspective , its own standards, which are just as good as anybody else's. Looked at in a superficial way I seem to be rejecting their multi-cultural relativism because I am claiming 'Europe is somehow special'- they alone developed science. The professional anthropologists will be uncomfortable, for I neglect their key asset – fieldwork – and want to turn them into historians of science. Permit me to deal with the post-modernist first.

Following the late Ernest Gellner, I do not believe that 'in the name of expiation of past sins and inter-cultural inequality' (1992:6) much is to be gained by turning all other non-western ways-of-knowing into local versions of Western science by denying, as Hess (1995:67) does, that science is, in one way or another, different from indigenous knowledge practices. The point of much of the post-modernist critique, after all, was, that in the old days of colonialism the ethnographer was able to speak for the other and in doing so distorted the authenticity of the other. I fully understand the post-modern suspicion about an universalist projects harbouring imperialist and hierarchical structures. But this should not lead us to deny the veracity of stories in which 'the other' is suggesting that there is a difference between his indigenous way-of-knowing and the

Western scientific mode. The Indian born Raj has argued that 'even a cursory acquaintance with contemporary scientific practice in India is enough to convince one that it is different' from Western one, (1988:321). His fellow countryman Rai Choudhuri (1985), an astrophysicists who spent his graduate years at the University of Chicago to study theoretical physics, concurs with this picture when he analyses his experience as a physics student in India and in the USA, and tries to come to terms with what he and his fellow Indian students perceive as clear differences. I belief that an anthropologists of knowledge should take these experiences seriously, and should be able to explain them in terms of cultural differences.[3] These experiences – which are corroborated by other reports – may not suite the political agenda of some post-modernist, but that is not a particularly good argument for not taking them seriously. In my view they are crucial data that an anthropology of knowledge should be able to illuminate.

My answer to the professional anthropologists is as follows: when dealing with science, at some point the question arises of why scientists happen to talk like positivists about what they are doing. Most students of STS, confronted with this situation, opt for arguing that the scientist's own conception of their work is somehow mistaken. But this of course is not an option an anthropologist can take seriously, even for one moment. Lesson one, rule one, of any class on the methodology of fieldwork is: it is not for you in any way to judge what the people your are studying believe to be true or false. As Traweek puts it: 'Anthropologists have a habit of taking the mundane seriously. (...) If scientists believe in the difference between objectivity and subjectivity, between facts and stories, it is my job to listen to how they tell them part, how and when they use this difference, and maybe even why' (1992: 444). The implication is that an anthropologist needs to take the scientist's terms seriously and hence needs to explain why 'positivism is the organisational myth of science'. As Stephan Fuchs correctly argues, for STS 'positivism is something to be explained, not something to be defended or criticized on philosophical grounds' (1993:18). But this only makes sense if positivism is somehow special. It is my conviction that it is indeed special.

To get the gist of my argument, bear in mind that above I reject the idea that science is the universal desire to know the world writ large. Instead, my starting assumption is that what various cultures regard as knowledge, the status they assign to it and the way they transfer it, varies significantly (cf. Pinxten 1991: 218). Here anthropological field work becomes important. For the scientist, with his positivist's view of knowledge (i.e. justified true belief), truth is detached and impersonal; it is absolute, context free, and universal. Knowledge is seen as having an objective state and is gained through observations of reality, and by taking distance from it. What is central to this view of knowledge is the classical philosophical distinction between 'knower' and 'known'. But as Pinxten and Farrer (1994) have shown, this (for us) obvious and 'natural' dualism is completely absent in the knowledge conception of both the Navaho and the Apaches. They construe knowledge as 'those tenets or beliefs that are differently distributed throughout the universe' (Pinxten and Farrer 1994: 172). For the kKnowledge is dependent on the medium one chooses, hence each individual may have different perspectives on reality. Truth, therefore, is essentially dependent on time, place, and who one is interacting with. Besides, the 'higher' realms of knowledge are only accessible through non-discursive means such as rituals and visions. In short 'the detached, neutral or Aobjective@ status of knowledge in the western tradition, ... , is utterly foreign and even inappropriate for the Navajo' (Pinxten 1991: 219).

There is insufficient space here to add more examples of knowledge conception that are fundamentally at odds with the core idea of positivism. However, I take it that the point I wish to make is clear: there is ample empirical evidence that positivism is not only the working philosophy of the scientists, but also that this working philosophy is specific and unique to the Western conception of knowledge. So what an anthropologists of knowledge needs to understand is (a) what made positivism the source of preferred metaphors about how to do the science-game; and (b) what kind of cultural specific assumptions have brought this fact about.

Rorty once remarked '[a]n intuition is never anything more or less than familiarity with a language-game.. To discover the source of our intuitions is to relive the history of the language-game we find ourselves playing' (1980:34). This suggests that explaining why positivism is the working philosophy of knowledge can not be done without delving into the history of science and history of the philosophy of knowledge. Europe, after all, is a people with a history. In other words I do not see how the anthropologists of knowledge can avoid the history of science. In the kind of programme I envision for an anthropology of knowledge, field work is still of paramount importance. It clearly is not in the form of lab-studies that the professional anthropologists are currently doing. In my view it should be aimed at canvassing the various ways-of-knowing that are practised by the various people anthropologists normally study.

Learning the Islamic way: memorisation

'The whole of the first school course is the Qur'an, which has to be learned by heart before anything else can be done though little of it may be understood' (Meakin:1902:306). In Islamic education '[t]he memory is burdened with verbatim knowledge of the Qur'an and some outlines of theology and law, and the reason is exhausted in elaborate argumentation therefrom deduced' (MacDonald 1911:288/9). '... [E]ducation was commonly conceived as the teaching of fixed and memorizable statements and formulas which could be adequately learned without any process of thinking as such' (Hodgson 1974:438). Do these historical descriptions still accurately capture present-day Islamic education? This is a contested issue. The point is that Islamic education and religious education are no longer automatically the same. Islamic education differs from religious education by separating 'revealed' from 'human' knowledge and in doing so transformed Qu'ranic principles into formalized legal and moral codes. Following Eickelman (1985), Wagner and Lotfi (1980) and Huff (1995) I believe the religious education was still functional well into the latter half of the twentieth century. But I believe I can safely sidestep this debate, for in my understanding all participants acknowledge one thing: the religious mode of education is the indigenous mode of learning in the Islamic world. It is the paradigm of how education is done. The current day dispute over Islamic versus religious education is a discussion of *what* is to be taught, not about *how*. My point is that in Islamic countries there is an enormous impetus to make all educational practices consonant with a Qur'anic approach to education. (As Szyliowicz [1995:419] suggests, even in vocational and technical education memorization is commonplace.) This Qur'anic approach manifests itself first and foremost in how education is to be done. I am interested in this 'how' because the way an individual learns furnishes her with implicitly transmitted notions about the 'right' culture and the 'right' relation to that culture, as well as a 'right' mode of intellectual activity (cf. Bourdieu 1967:350).

Before I examine what the Islamic ideas of learning are, I first want to quote Hodgson at some length. He continues thus:

> A statement was either true or false, and the sum of all true statements was knowledge. One might add to the accessible sum of true statements to be found in one's heritage, but one did not expect to throw new light on old statements, modifying or outdating them. Hence knowledge that mattered, 'ilm, as against the facts of 'common knowledge' which even the illiterates picked up as a matter of course, was implicitly conceived as a static and finite sum of statements, even through not all the potentially valuable statements might be actually known to anyone at a given time. Education meant inculcating as many of these statements in as sound a form as possible. But the soundest form was naturally that in which the most knowledgeable authority for the statement had himself uttered them, though they might be rested more conveniently for popular use. Hence not only knowledge, in principle, a fixed corpus of statements; its authenticity was made to depend on the word of a limited number of great men, whose authority was not to be questioned, at least not by the student (1974: 438-439).

The passage suggests that the Islamic model of education is based on the memorisation of authenticated traditions. It evolved from the model of collecting and memorising chains of transmission of particular hadiths (original sayings) and is symbolically capped by the bestowing of the *ijaza*, the permission to transmit the authenticated knowledge.

What does this mnemonic mode of learning tell us about Islam? What kind of implicit assumption about the world and man's place in it are built into a meta-theory of learning that stresses memorisation and recitation? In Islamic thought, learning and religious veneration overlap. This, of course, is not a mistake but rather reflects some deeply held assumptions about mans relationship to Allah and Allah's relationship with the world. In order to unpack these assumptions some core aspects of Islamic knowledge need to specified.

Islamic education revolves around the Qur'an, the sacred book, considered by Moslims to be the literal words of God, and thus the basis for all knowledge. Religious knowledge constitutes the most culturally valued knowledge. The objectives of learning are to pass on the customs of the adult community, to teach children the knowledge and skills of the culture that they need to function effectively, and to instill beliefs about the relationship between the seen and the unseen in the universe, one of the objectives of learning. In other words religious righteousness, instilling community values, and social efficiency. This makes learning the Qur'an an integral part of socialization. Reason is seen as 'man's ability to discipline his nature in order to act in accord with the arbitrary code of conduct laid down by God' (Eickelman 1978:494).

Islam is built on the belief in the unity of all knowledge. All knowledge originates with Allah and is created by him. Man is incapable of creating it on his own. There is no separate human faculty a man can rely on in order to gain knowledge. Knowledge is to be had only in so far as it pleases Allah to bestow it on someone. But it is not just knowledge that is dependent on Allah; in fact the whole world is. Both man's capacity to understand the world and the existence of the world depend on a capacity that is distinct from man and nature. Huff sums up these two points in the following way: 'the patterns of nature appear as they do because of the prior action and the will of God: he holds the world together from moment to moment by his will' and 'man's physical and intellectual agency – his ability to create knowledge – is wholly dependent on God's prior action and man's "acquisition" of the capacity or knowledge from God' (1995:11).

The main point of this brief exposition of Islamic ideas is that the dominant Islamic meta-theory of learning, with its strict process of memorisation of a fixed set of statements, reflects 'the fusion of God in all acts of men'. The point is not that individuals have the ability to judge common matters or read the signs of nature, but that their endeavours can never be taken as an alternative to what already has been described in the Qur'an. All creativity, innovation and discovery are the prerogative of Allah. The individual can not share in this divine for Allah has no partner nor equal; man cannot share anything with him. This leaves to learning nothing but the 'teaching of fixed and memorizable statements'.

One final remark. I am not claiming that this Islamic tradition of learning and the set of ideas that have formed it are the only ones possible in Islamic thought. Nor do I suggest that Islamic culture is a homeostatic system without room for local variation. Historically, other options were tried. Take the Basra School of the Mu'tazila. They are, in fact, Islamic rationalists who grant 'that man is endowed by God with an autonomous power of efficient causality by which he is ... the originating author of his own acts'. They conceive man 'as having an innate desire to seek how own good, an innate power to act, and an innate understanding of the fundamental criteria of good and evil' (Frank 1971:12). They were even prepared to claim 'parity of reason and revelation' (Rahman 1966:90). For the Mu'tazilites the Qur'an was no longer the sole source of knowledge but 'a testimony to the veracity of the claims which they were making'(Rippin 1990:65). For a time, Mu'tazila thinking became the state-creed during the Caliphate of al-Ma'mun and of his successors. But ultimately its rationalist thrust was incompatible with the orthodoxy and in the tenth century (CE) they were defeated. With this the teachings of al-Ah'sari (d. 935) came to constitute the core of the ortho-dox tradition. What it suggests is that the Islamic indigenous mode of learning is the outcome of a local struggle and not the natural and inevitable result of Islamic think-ing.

Culture as a configuration of learning strategies

This excursion into Islamic learning suggeststhat the way people learn tells us some-thing specific about them, something that can be used to specifying their unique cul-tural way of doing things. I am not being very original in claiming this. Marshall Hodg-son made this point thus: 'At the core of any cultural tradition, ..., is its method of educating the young' (1974:438). In my view Hudgson is absolutely right. But why are learning strategies so fundamental? Lack of space prohibits a comprehensive theoreti-cal elaboration of this question so a short answer must do: learning strategies are com-manding practices which guide the life and learning of the freshman within their cul-tural context. Learning strategies mould an individual's initial psychological make-up, and hence shape one's outward material and social expressions of one's culture; they integrate the affective, the perceptual, and the intellectual. In other words strategies of learning tell us some very specific about a culture. Hence my suggestion to take them as the core for a theory of culture. I do not claim that this is the only theory possible but I do believe it is both a plausible and forceful theory. But I need to be a little bit more precise here. First, the question of *what* to learn – a question at the object-level – is different from *how* to learn – which is a question at the meta-level. This distinction is important because, as pointed out above, the way an individual learns furnishes her with implicit transmitted notions about the 'right' culture and the right relation to that culture, as well as the 'right' mode of intellectual activity. Since there are various, dis-tinct ways how to learn, it is important to canvas the various modes of learning and see how they are configurated. Cultures can be characterised by the configurations of learning strategies that are institutionalised by it. More specifically, I propose to take the dominant mode of learning as the distinguishing feature of a culture.

Western learning: theoretical explanation

In the case of the Islam the dominant strategy for learning clearly is memorisation. The dominant mode of Western learning is theoretical learning. Before arguing further, a caveat is in order. In the current research on learning a transformation is taking place from a conception in which 'learning is a naturally occurring, specific kind of cognitive functioning, quite separate from engagement in doing something' (Lave 1990:310) to that of a more ecological approach, which has come to be known as 'situated knowl-edge'. Within this new perspective cognition is 'stretched out across mind, body, activ-ity and setting' (Lave 1988:18), and takes place in a participation framework – as

opposed to an individual mind. Furthermore it is assumed that learning and understanding are socially constituted. I am perfectly aware of this trend, and I have even
used its key idea that knowledge is constituted in a interactionist relation between persons acting and the setting of their activity in a prior essay (Raven 1996). Still, I am
going to ignore it. The reason is as simple as it is fundamental, since this new trend
rejects what I believe to be the dominant mode of learning in the West: theoretical
learning. This tradition is institutionalized in Western schooling, and assumes that the
process of instruction is to be general and independent of what is learned.

I start with two observations: firstly, preaching and lecturing are homologous; secondly, the Christian religious world view and the secular world view are homologous.

In terms of historical continuity these structural similarities are obvious and are a
natural result of the subserviency of theology to philosophical reason in the early modern era. But what kind of continuity are we taking about here? What is it that does not
change when philosophy becomes what Funkenstein (1986:3) has dubbed 'secularized
theology'? Arguably, it is the Christian learning strategy and its built in metaphysical
assumptions. To show this I what to take a closer look at the Christian sermon.[4]

The homology of the sermon and lecture is not only obvious – once you give it
a thought at least – but is what you would expect because the lecture as a mode of
teaching is explicitly fashioned after the sermon. This well known historical point carries with it the key to what is characteristic of Western learning. First thing to note is
that the sermon, in its turn is, best seen as modelled after the relation God has with the
world recreated by him. The sermon is predicated upon soteriological knowledge. Sote-
riology is predicated on a persistent dualism between the imperfect and mundane
world and, as Rorty puts it, the 'nonidiosyncratic, atemporal, and universal' (1989:42).
The ultimate form of soteriological knowledge is revelatory, which is absolute and not
open to profane illumination.[5] Anyone familiar with the history of the early Christians
knows that one of the central question was – and would remain for a very long time
– 'can revelation be replaced by reason, and can reason be a source of saving knowledge?'.

Tertulians's famous lines 'What has Athens to do with Jerusalem?' captures the two
main positions: Jerusalem representing revelation and faith, and Athens representing
reason. Micheal Foster has described the Greek notion of reason as 'intelligent com-
prehension of form', which in his view 'is sufficient for the understanding both of what
is and what happens in the actual world'. He points out that 'sensuous experience represents no addition to, but only defect of understanding' (Foster 1934:455). The heritage of Greek rationalism, although absorbed in the Christian tradition, never completely integrated with its revelatory soteriological precepts. Hence the stage was set for
a prolonged controversy between reason and revelation. The challenges posed by the
hertics (such as the Gnostics – who were clearly on the side of reason with their claim
that all saving knowledge can be known by reason)- for the Christian orthodoxy (the
unbroken apostolic succession of bishops, and the consensus of those bishops) 'shaped
the agenda of early Roman Christian thinkers and that provided their Latin Christian

successors in the early Middle Ages with their intellectual self-definition' (Colish 1997:6). Tertulian's own view – 'I believe because it is absurd' – although less radical than the Gnostic position and clearly on the side of the orthodoxy, already carries with it the seeds of the rationalist option that was in the end to win.

The resolution of this conflict is what is called 'secularization'. The victory of reason signifies the first step in this long and drawn out process. Secularization is the process whereby profane notions become the structural equivalents of scared ones, while at the same time retaining the religious characteristic of transcendence. The 'revelatory truth of religion is transformed into the singleness and absoluteness of truth achieved by rational human reasoning' (Cohen 1988:208). To put in differently, the idea of redemption was preserved and replaced by revelatory knowledge with reason as the source of saving knowledge. This displacement was the work of medieval theology. Medieval historians, like Chenu (1997), Haskins (1927), Levine (2001), Moore (2000), Southern (1997), and Stiefel (1985), have firmly established that the twelfth and thirteenth centuries marked a turning point in the history of the West (for a summary of the argument see Blockmans and Hoppenbrouwers (2002)). In this period the nature of the powers man possesses was determined in favour of 'reason', while at the same time the nature of God's work was determined in favour of 'lawfully whole, largely controlled by natural causes'. This, at least, is what unities Adelard of Bath (d.1146), William of Conches (d. 1154), Thiery of Chartes (d. 1156), High of St. Victor (d. 1142), William of Saint-Thierry (d. 1148) Alan of Lile (d. 1230) and Bernard Sylvester (d. 1136). While by no means agreeing on all philosophical and theological issues, these philosophers nevertheless 'argued that the world is a single whole, a *universe*. By this term they referred to the natural domain that was thought to be rational and lawfully ordered, and which included humankind. It was further assumed that the human species possessed a divine attribute, that is, reason and this empowered it to discern truth and falsehood both with regard to the Scriptures and nature' (Huff 1995:5).

Medieval theology transformed reason into the basic organizing principle of knowledge, and the sermon into discursive revelation, and made it into the paradigm case of knowledge. There are two features of religious knowledge that are important for the question at hand. First, there is the notion that religious knowledge is knowledge of God. Second, the belief that God is a transcendental Being; hence knowledge of God is transcendental knowledge. Transcendental knowledge is conceptual knowledge. The crucial question then becomes: how does one learn conceptual knowledge? In the Western tradition the answer is: in a theoretical way, by outlining the first principles (the ground-work of the theoretical frame work) and expanding understanding from there. 'Understanding' as meaning able to see how the various different theoretical notions are linked to one another and as able to envelope the external world into a web of meaning. The suggestion here is that the sermon conditions one to experience the world as something in need of meaning, as in need of being ordered. But as Balangagadhara rightly pointed out nobody has 'ever experienced a chaotic world, outside and independent of an experience of the world as-an-order' (1994:454). In other words, descriptions of the world in terms of 'chaotic', etc are not reflections of some 'primal' or 'primitive' experiences, but are concepts that structure them. The fundamental experience for everyone born into the Western world that the world is somehow chaotic, and desperately in need of being ordered, is the result of taking the sermon as the paradigm of what knowledge is, and must do. Its meta-message, after all, is that the world is hostile unless interpreted and woven into an explanatory tale, and that God is the explanation.

Two metaphysical assumptions – (1) an individual human being is endowed with the divine attribute of reason and (2) nature is an intelligible entity – help to make the sermon what it is today: a paradigm of conceptual explanation, an exercise in patient textual analyses and logical refinement. It is not that difficult to see reflected here the principles and assumptions of the scholastic method of 'analysis of words and meanings, of general concepts and individual instances, and of forms of argument' (Southern, 1997:11). It set the example of how one was to learn: theoretical. Understanding amounted to conceptual clarification. Theoretical understanding and conceptual clarification became indistinguishable. This dominance of the theoretical forced other forms of understanding – for example experimental – to a second tier position; and as Van den Bouwhuijsen (1996:122) rightly pointed out, this dominance of the theoretical mode of understanding forced them to express themselves as some form of theoretical understanding, for example to construe practice as applied theory.

Science a cultural phenomenon

It is not difficult to see that these metaphysical assumptions are part and parcel of Western Christianity. Hence my working hypotheses that Christianity, with its theoretical way of learning – modelled after the sermon as the Western paradigm of transferring conceptual knowledge – is not only of fundamental importance for the 'invention' of science, but is essential to it as well. Christianity provided Europe with the conceptual resources to develop the scientific ethos, i.e. the formation of an identifiable community of people who roughly share the same ideal of natural inquiry. This specific way of understanding nature is embodied in the notion of science as a generic truth-securing institution. What an anthropological study of science needs to understand is why such an institution emerged only in modern Europe, which (a) conceived nature as a *naturae universalis* constituted by laws of nature; (b) linked knowledge of these laws to experimentation, and (c) combined this with new attitudes towards the progress of knowledge as well as new forms of human cooperation.

In this view science only came into being when the artisan tradition of learning through acquisition of skills, of learning through doing and the scholarly tradition of learning by grasping the underlying theoretical principles merged. (This reformulation of the famous Zilsel thesis [Zilsel 2000] is argued for in Raven 2003). The artisan tradition of learning by tinkering can be found in any culture and as such qualifies as a universal. The scholarly tradition, however, is unique to Europe, is a uniquely Western endeavour and is crucially dependent upon notions and ideas about the universe, God and mankind that are specifically Christian. It is the later aspect that makes science a specific Western cultural phenomenon.

At this point I also want to touch briefly on the limits of an anthropological understanding of science. One limitation is linked to the fact that a culturological explanation of science can only point to the cultural resources that are utilized in science. It is unable to answer why these resources were allowed to flower at time X and place Y. Historical sociology of the kind done by Weber, Nelson, and Eisenstadt to name just the most well-known is needed here. Another limitation is linked to the fact that not all ideas that go into the science-game have a cultural origin. For example, Toby Huff (1997) makes a very convincing case that there is at least one institutional element to the science-game that is both essential to it and which is historically unique to Europe as well; but it is sociological in origin, not cultural. I am referring to the creation of a 'neutral space' where one can speculate about anything 'free from the incursions of political and religious censors'(Huff 1993:11).

Conclusion

This programmatic essay is the outcome of a deeply felt personal uneasiness about the current ideas about what constitutes a proper anthropology of science. I found myself in the situation the historian Collingwood (1961:248) once described when he suggested that every new researcher, not content with giving new answers to old questions, must rewrite the questions themselves. I understand that the professional anthropologists are not contend with STS as it stands. I agree that STS has never seriously explored the potentials of the notion of culture. But I fail to understand to what kind of question their work is an answer. If the question is to show that science is a cultural phenomenon, then I am on their side. But as indicate I do not believe their way of answering it is satisfactory. Worse still, often I fail to understand what kind of question relevant to STS they are trying to answer. I can see that the work done by Martin, Rabb c.s. is relevant to understanding a multicultural world in which everything has become fragmented, and in which policy makers and the like no longer know what effect their decisions have on all kinds of people or why certain policies have no effect. To the extend that science is an important source of information about and transformation of society, this kind of work has relevance to STS. But I do not fail to see what in fact they have to offer STS.

An important impetus for STS has always been to provide a much broader conception of knowledge – , broader that is, than the traditional philosophical one. I believe that my suggestion for an anthropology of knowledge can contribute to that project by elucidating why there is scientific knowledge in the first place. This all important question is too often simply passed over in STS; one assumes that there is such a phenomenon as scientific knowledge without seriously wondering why that is the case. I want to bring this question into the STS research programme, and have suggested a line of research which may answer it. The comparative anthropological analyses that is the core of this endeavour does, of course, incorporate the work the late

Joseph Needham did on the so-called 'science question' in China. I have always wondered why neither Latour nor the professional anthropologists touched on the so-called Needham question. Why was the kind of comparative analyses Needham pursued never incorporated into the kind of pursuit of the so-called anthropologists of science? I can not answer this question, for I seriously do not know the answer. I only wish to point out that whatever anthropology is, it is a comparative science, and inclusion of the Needham question into an anthropology of science only seems natural.

Notes

1. Although there are minor difference between the positions of the professional anthropologists like Hess, Martin, Traweek and Rabb and various others, for the purpose of this paper they can be ignored. For lack of a better term I will refer to this group as the professional anthropologists; they are thus named in contrast to the amateur anthropologists like Latour, Woolgar, c.s. Anthropology of science was initially developed by people like Latour and Woolgar, i.e., the amateur anthropologists. In this essay I shall answer Martin.
2. A couple of times I have in this essay I called for a theoretical clarification of the use of the notion of culture. My insistence on a theoretical justification is motivated by a simple truism: 'No amount of individual particles of observed data will suffice to represent "culture" until one has a theory of their systematic interrelations. This principle may appear self-evident, but it creates a galling dilemma for a rigorously empirical science of the kind that classical anthropology ... aspired to be, a science of "concrete, observable facts" (Radcliff Brown) for relationships are not observable phenomenon' (Herbert 1991:10). In other words discussions about culture without having a theory of culture at hand gets you nowhere. How this position squares with the current trend – see, for example, Kuper (1999) and Sandall (2002) – to be very critical of the concept of culture and try to come as close as one can get to eliminating it. I applaud what these 'culture debunkers' are doing. But then my reading of what they doing is different from what they themselves think they are doing. Much of the current malaise is to a large part due to the prominence of the Geertzian semiotic notion of culture. Geertz himself may have always argued for a notion of culture that is cut down to size, but, in the hands of others the opposite is what happened: the inflation of the notion of culture. This inflated notion of culture is behind new academics specialities like cultural studies – see Barker (2000) for one of the best introductions to this field – which take culture to be 'overlapping maps of criss-crossing discursive meaning which form zones of temporary coherence as shared but always contested significance in a social space' (Barker 2000: 283). What, to my mind, Kuper quite correctly and convincingly argues is that the idea of construing culture as the way communities envelop their local knowledge practices into a web of meaning, and how these local practices are intertwined with meaning and power, gets you nowhere. This 'definition' is embarrassingly vague and non-informative; it includes too much and is too diffuse either to separate analytically the twisted threads of human experience, or to interpret the designs into which they are woven. (In case these words have a familiar ring to it that is correct. These are the very words with which Keesing (1974: 73) once criticized the proposal Kroeber and Kluckhohn produced after having examined over 150 definitions.) Where I disagree with them is that the solution is not additional and more nuanced fieldwork, but that, instead, anthropologist should recognize that the only way out of the current intellectual stalemate is by developing a theory of culture.
    Just a few closing words on what should be expect from such a theory. Anthropology is the science of difference, but clearly not all differences are cultural. Differences in wedding pat-

terns between different social groups are a case in point. Generally we view these differences as due to sociological processes and hence social in nature. And rightly so. It is a truism that anthropological data clearly show that 'elsewhere things are different'. This easily gives rise to the idea that all difference that anthropology deals with are cultural in nature. But only sloppy thinking would allow you this inference. One problem with this line of reasoning is that it makes internal differences, for example within the Islamic world between say the Sunni and Shiites, cultural in nature. I my view this a wrong. As is well known, the difference between these two communities does not hinge on a doctrinal mater, but rather is best construed as political in nature. What a theory of culture should be able to do is to direct one to differences between societies that are constituent aspects of that society, and are incommensurable with constituent aspects of the other society. It should follow from the theory as a matter of course that these differences are *sui generis*.

3.   The way Rai Choudhuri puts the problem (in terms of having the proper psychological gestalt) is only helpful if one construes this gestalt in terms of a culturally imposed disposition, or habitus. Raj comes close to doing this when he tires to explain the noted differences in terms of 'images of knowledge', which he construes as a 'culturally determined doctrine' of knowledge and links to the Vedic concept of knowledge. As marking features, he lists equations of science and erudition, solitary approach to knowledge, formal encyclopaedic education, a disdain for manual work and a distaste for collaborative experiments, and a stress on theoretical understanding. As will become clear Raj's approach is very close to the kind of explanation I belief an anthropologists should give.

4.   The sermon is in my view the embodiment of what is the dominant conception of knowledge in the West (i.e. that real knowledge is theoretical knowledge and its ultimate aim is theoretical illumination). Clearly the sermon is a central part of Christianity, but that is not to say that Peter the Chanter's axiom that 'the discipline of Holy Scripture comprises three things: the exposition by the lecturer, disputation, and preaching ...' *(Verbum Abbreviatum* PL 205, 25 as quoted by Lawrence 1989: 145) had always been central to the Christian conception of knowledge. Clearly it had not. Before scholasticism introduced a revolutionary change in the method of study and made the lecture system the main form of teaching in the universities, the *lectio divina* had centre stage. Central to it are two things. First Biblical exegesis aimed at elaborating the 'spiritual', as opposed to the literal sense of the text. In other words the aim was to extract an allegorical or moral significance from person, things and events referred to in the Holy Book. Second, religious 'knowledge' consisted of a fixed body of moral principles, and thus was considered to be unchanging and unchallenged. The *lectio divina* as the main form of monastic learning aimed at prayer, not at conceptual illumination.

5.   I am not saying that the sermon is only known in Christianity. Clearly it is something that the Islam uses as well, it is part the routine of Friday prayer. Its key element, however, is always to tell those present about the right a proper way of dealing with the world; the Islamic sermon is about living as a true Muslim and the routines of live, and as such is completely devoid of this typical Christian attempt of explanation and cognitive system building. Remember that 'Islam' means 'submission' which clearly highlights the traditional way of acting and living

Bibliography

Balagangadhara, S. N. 1994. *'The Heathen in His Blindness...': Asia, the West and the Dynamic of Religion.* Leiden: Brill.
Barker, C. 2000. *Cultural Studies: Theory and Practice.* London, etc: Sage.
Benedict, R. 1973, [1946] *The Chrysanthemum and the Sword: Patterns of Japanese Culture.* London: Routledge Kegan and Paul.
Blockmans, W. and P. Hoppenbrouwers. 2002. *Eeuwen des onderscheids: Een geschiedenis van middeleeuws Europa.* Amsterdam: Prometheus.

Bourdieu, P. 1967. 'Systems of Education and Systems of Thought' *International Social Science Journal* 19:338-58.

Bourdieu, P. 1977. *Outline of a Theory of Practice*. Cambridge: Cambridge University Press.

Bouwhuijsen, H. v. d. 1996. *Play-Fellows of God: Towards an Anthropology of Science*. Utrecht: Academisch Proefschrift.

Chenu, M.-D. 1997. *Nature, Man and Society in the Twelfth Century: Essays on New Theological Perspectives in the Latin West*. (Selected, edited and translated by J. Talor and L. K. Little) Toronto, etc: University of Toronto Press.

Cohen, E. 1988. 'Radical Secularization and the Destruction of the Universe of Knowledge in Late Modernity', *Knowledge and Society: Studies in the Sociology of Culture Past and Present* 7:203-24.

Colish, M. L. 1997. *Medieval Foundations of the Western Intellectual Tradition 400 – 1400*. New Haven and London: Yale University Press.

Collingwood, R. G. 1961. *The Idea of History* . Oxford: Oxford University Press.

Cunningham, A. and P. Williams. 1993. 'De-centring the 'Big Picture': The Origins of Modern Science and the Modern Origins of Science', *British Journal for the History of Science,* 26: 407-32.

Eickelman, D. F. 1978. 'The Art of Memory: Islamic Education and Its Social Reproduction', *Comparative Studies in Society and History* 20:485-515.

Eickelman, D. F. 1985. *Knowledge and Power in Morocco: The Education of a Twentieth-Century Notable*. Princeton, N.J.: Princeton University Press.

Foster, M. B. 1934. 'The Christian Doctrine of Creation and the Rise of Modern Natural Science', *Mind* 43:446-68.

Fox, R. G. and B. J. King (eds.). 2002. *Anthropology Beyond Culture*. Oxford, etc.: Berg.

Frank, R. M. 1971. 'Several Fundamental Assumptions of the Basra School of the Mu'Tazila' *Studia Islamica* 33:5-18.

Franklin, S. 1995. 'Science as Culture, Cultures of Science' *Annual Review of Anthropology* 24:163-84.

Fuchs, S. 1993. 'Positivism is the Organizational Myth of Science', *Perspectives on Science,* 1, 1: 1-23.

Funkenstein, A. 1986. *Theology and the Scientific Imagination From the Middle Ages to the Seventeenth Century*. Princeton, N. J.: Princeton University Press.

Gramsci, A. 1971. *Selections from the Prison Notebooks*. London: Lawrence and Wishart.

Haskins, C. H. 1927. *The Renaissance of the Twelfth Century*. Cambridge, Mass.: Harvard University Press.

Herbert, C. 1991. *Culture and Anomie: Ethnographic Imagination in the Nineteenth Century*. Chicago and London: University of Chicago Press.

Hess, D. J. 1992. 'Introduction: The New Ethnography and the Anthropology of Science and Technology'. *Knowledge and Society: The Anthropology of Science and Technology* 9:1-26.

Hess, D. J. 1995. *Science and Technology in a Multicultural World: The Cultural Politics of Facts and Artifacts*. New York: Columbia University Press.

Hodgson, M. G. S. 1974. *The Venture of Islam (Vol 2:The Expansion of Islam in the Middle Period)*. Chicago and London: Chicago University Press.

Huff, T. E. 1993. *The Rise of Early Modern Science: Islam, China and the West*. Cambridge: Cambridge University Press.

Huff, T. E. 1995. 'Islam, Science and Fundamentalism' Journal of Arabic, *Islamic and Middle Eastern Studies* 2(2):1-27.

Huff, T. E. 1997. 'Science and the Public Sphere: Comparative Institutional Development in Islam and the West' *Social Epistemology* 11(1):25-37.

Keesing,R. M. 1974. 'Theories of Culture', *Annual Review of Anthropology,* 1974, 3, pp. 73-97.

Kuper, A. 1999. *Culture: The Anthropologists' Account*. Cambridge, MA: Harvard University Press.

Lave, J. 1988. *Cognition in Practice: Mind, Mathematics and Culture in Everyday Life*. Cambridge: Cambridge University Press.

Lave, J. 1990. 'The Culture of Acquisition and the Practice of Understanding' Pp. 309-27 in *Cultural Psychology: Essays on Comparative Human Development* J. W. Stigler and et al. (eds.). Cambridge, etc.: Cambridge University Press.

Lawrence, C. H. 1989. *Medieval Monasticism: Forms of Religious Life in Western Europe in the Middle Ages.* second edition, London and New York: Longman..

Lee III, O. 1988. 'Observations on Anthropological Thinking about the Culture Concept: Cliffird Geertz and Perre Bourdieu' *Berkeley Journal of Sociology* 33:115-30.

Levine, D. 2001. *At the Dawn of Modernity: Biology, Culture, and Material Life in Europe after the Year 1000*. Berkely, etc.: University of California Press.

MacDonald. D. B. 1911. *Aspects of the Islam*. New York: Macmillan.

MacDonald, M. 1983. 'Anthropological Perspectives on the History of Science and Medicine', Pp. 61-80 in *Information Sources in the History of Science and Medicine,* P. Corsi and P. Weindling (eds.). London, etc: Butterworths.

Martin, E. 1998. 'Anthropology and the Cultural Study of Science' *Science, Technology, and Human Value* 23(1):24-44.

Meakin, B. 1902. *The Moors: A Comprehensive Description*. London and New York: Sonnenschein and Co. and Macmillan.

Moore, R. I. 2000. *The First European Revolution c. 970-1215*. Oxford and Malden, Mass.: Blackwell.

Pinxten, R 1991. 'Geometry Education and Culture' *Learning and Instruction* 1:217-27.

Pinxten, R. and C.R. Farrer. 1994. 'On learning and tradition: A Comparative View', Pp 169-184 in *Sociogenesis Reexamined* W. de Graaf and R. Maier (eds.). Springer Verlag; New York, etc.

Rahman, F. 1979. *Islam*. second edition Chicago and London: University of Chicago Press.

Rai Choudhuri, A. 1985. 'Practising Western Science Outside the West: Personal Observations on the Indian Scene' *Social Studies of Science* 15:475-505.

Raj, K. 19881. 'Images of Knowledge, Social Organisation, and Attitudes to Research in an Indian Physics Department' *Science in Context* 2(2):317-39.

Raven, D. 1996. 'The Enculturation of Logical Practice' *Configurations* 3:381-425.

Raven, D. 2001. 'How not to Explain the Great Divide', *Social Science Information,* 40(3): 373-409.

Raven, D. 2003. 'The Cultural Roots of Science' in *A Reappraisal of the Zilsel Thesis.* W. Krohn and D. Raven (eds.) (Boston Studies in the Philosophy of Science), Dordrecht, etc: Kluwer Academic Publishers.

Rippin, A. 1990. *Muslims: The Religious Beliefs and Practices (Vol I: The Formative Period)*. London and New York: Routledge.

Rorty, R. 1980. *Philosophy and the Mirror of Nature*. Oxford: Blackwell.

Rorty, R. 1989. *Contingency, Irony, and Solidarity*. Cambridge: Cambridge University Press.

Sandall, R. 2002. *The Culture Cult*. Bolder, Col.: Westview Press.

Strairs, A. 1991. 'Learning Processes and Teaching Roles in Native Education: Cultural Base and Cultural Brokerage' *The Canadian Modern Language Review* 47,2:280-94.

Southern, R. W. 1997. *Scholastic Humanism and the Unification of Europe*. Oxford and Cambridge, Mass.: Blackwell.

Stiefel, T. 1985. *The Intellectual Revolution in Twelfth Century Europe*. London and Sydney: Croom Helm.

Szyliowicz, J. S. 1995. 'Educational Methods'. in *The Oxford Encyclopedia of the Modern Islamic World (Vol I)*, J. L. Esposito ed. New York and Oxford: Oxford University Press, 1995.

Traweek, S. 1988. *Beamtimes and Lifetimes: The World of High Energy Physicists*. Cambridge, Mass. and London: Harvard university Press.

Traweek, S. 1992. 'Border Crossongs: Narrartive Strategies in Science Studies and Among Physicists in Tsukuba Science City Japan' Pp. 429-66 in *Science As Practice and Culture* A. Pickering (ed.). Chicago and London: University of Chicago Press.

Traweek, S. 1993. 'Cultural Differences in High-Energey Physics' Pp. 398-407 in S. Harding (eds.). Bloomgton and Indianapolis, Ind.: Indiana University Press.

Wagner, D. A. and A. Lotfi. 1980. 'Traditional Islamic Education in Morocco: Sociohistorical and Psychological Perspectives' *Comparative Educational Review* 24:238-51.

Part II

Discourses and Arenas of Identity

9

Meeting Cultures, Merging Cultures
Reflections on Nation-Building and 'Mestizaje' in Mexico

Wil Pansters

> "So the 'unities' which identities proclaim are, in fact, constructed within the play of power and exclusion, and are the result, not of a natural and inevitable or primordial totality but of the naturalized, overdetermined process of 'closure'."
>
> Stuart Hall (1996:5)

> "The fundamental project of the state …is to elaborate and resolve the contradiction of differentiation and unity."
>
> Michael Kearney (1991:55)

Introduction

Against the background of the various changes affecting society generally referred to as globalization, localization, and multiculturalization, a great deal of interest is focused on the issue of identity. The idea is that in an internationalizing economy and culture, migration and the decline of old political and other dogmas and ideologies might well be why people are increasingly confronted with the need once again to define their *place* in the social and cultural world (Beck et al. 1995; de Ruijter 2000a:14-19). Some anthropologists feel that the prevailing conceptualization of the relation between *place* and *culture* has been overtaken by changes in society, and that theoretical innovation is thus called for (Olwig 1997). Others turn the notion of cultural roots into a topic of debate (Malkki 1992; Gorashi 1997). Due to the erosion of the traditionally meaningful frameworks of church, state, and politics, people are looking for new sources of identity. In some cases, this pursuit manifests itself as a renewed interest in old cultural identities, imagined or otherwise. De Ruijter (2000a:19) alludes in this respect to a new defensive orthodoxy: a sense of self is manufactured to protect oneself from others. The attention devoted to the idea of authenticity should also be viewed in this context. I am mainly referring to the yearning for originality, bonding, and purity in a world often perceived as turbid, superficial, and unpredictable.

My approach to this set of problems is guided by a constructivist view of identity and authenticity. This means that I view these issues as the result of particular historical circumstances, institutional arrangements, power relations, and discursive contexts. They are the product of the demarcation of difference and not of the conscious articulation of essences that exist in themselves (Hall 1996:4; see also de Ruijter 2000b:38-40). It is more constructive to devote attention to authentication rather than to authenticity. The constructivist shifts attentions from what *is* authentic to how something *becomes* or is *made* authentic.

Something is viewed as authentic if it does not or no longer bears any traces of "alien" influence. Authenticity is consequently linked to such concepts as homogeneity (vs. heterogeneity), unity (vs. fragmentation), uniformity (vs. pluralism), and purity (vs. mixing and hybridization). In Hall's terminology, an authentic identity can only result from "[its] capacity to exclude, to leave out, to render 'outside'" (1995:5), i.e. by "resolving" difference. Difference does, however, play a central role in the definition of hybridization. Something is hybrid if and when it consists of heterogeneous elements. Nederveen Pieterse (1998:104-105) notes that hybridization refers to an amalgamation of phenomena that are different and separate. In his view, some authors nostalgically define hybridization as a loss of purity, totality, and authenticity. In post-structuralist and postmodern thinking, though, hybridization is venerated for its ability to counteract essentialist conceptions of identity and authenticity. Angie Chabram Dernersesian sees herself as a *Chicana-Riqueña*, but this hybrid identity is not appreciated by one of her university colleagues at the *Chicano Research Center*, who feels that Chabram can be either one or the other, but not both – "certainly not a hybrid, hybrids aren't authentic, they have no claim to a fixed set of ethnic categories" (Chabram Dernersesian 1995:271).[1]

Authenticity and hybridity are generally viewed as being diametrically opposed. In this article I would like to examine this suggested opposition and demonstrate that it does not always hold true. For this purpose, I analyze the emergence and nature of the authenticity discourse on "Mexico" and "the Mexican" in the first half of the twentieth century. I show that a new and authentic Mexican national identity was constructed by means of a hybridization project. A constructivist interpretation of the issue of national identity requires that attention be devoted to negotiations and interventions of various actors in a given nation-state on the contents and legitimacy of the distinctive and homogeneous elements of a national culture (Williams 1990:128).[2] In this article, I concentrate on one of these groups, the intellectuals (philosophers, anthropologists, historians, artists, politicians and writers) who took part in the construction of a discourse of the authentic national identity in the period from 1920 to 1940.[3] According to many of them, this identity was primarily based on a hybrid amalgam of ethnic elements. Before I analyze some key texts, I will briefly outline the social context in which they were produced and received.

Revolution and nation-building

The first great social revolution of the twentieth century took place in Mexico. From 1910 to 1917, Mexico was the site of an armed struggle between peasant armies and government troops, and especially between rival revolutionary factions, concerning the nature of the social, economic, and political reforms. After the bloody civil war, the country was characterized by thorough fragmentation in every societal domain. In 1917 the pronouncement of a new Constitution, one that was extremely progressive at the time, marked the end of the civil war and the start of a period of approximately twenty-five years when repeated efforts were made to overcome the deeply felt fragmentation and to construct a new unity and consensus. But after years of revolutionary struggle, the transformation of the military, political, and ideological power relations into a new social order was no simple matter. In an arena of this kind, there are always winners and losers. Actors who did their best to reinforce the centralist tendencies did so in defiance of the groups who took cover behind their local or regional domains of power.

Especially in the 1930s, the administrative competence and legal jurisdiction of the central state and the presidency were reinforced at the expense of the provinces and the towns. The nationalization of the oil industry at the end of the 1930s gave the federal state a powerful economic base that was further expanded in the decades to come. In the field of party politics, an important step towards unification was taken in 1928 when one large national party was founded that was to expand in the following years into the *Partido Revolucionario Institucional* (PRI), which was to rule Mexico at the national level up until 2000. The party was modeled along corporatist lines in the 1930s, as was manifested in the huge organizational efforts to unite into one party as many social groups as possible, ranging from cattle farmers, Indians and students, to mariachi musicians, electricity workers, and housewives. Without underestimating the counter-movements, there was clearly an ample movement to think and act in terms of unity. This stimulation was not completely devoid of coercive pressure. Dissidents were not tolerated. After the Second World War broke out, this trend was converted into the policy of *unidad nacional* in the face of the threat from abroad (Niblo 1999).

What possibilities were there for developing a binding identity that could erase the memory of the recent disruption and fragmentation of the Revolution, and so allow people to move beyond the social heterogeneity and diversity inside and outside the dominant party? It is easy to guess the answer: *the nation*. The developments described above can also be viewed as part and parcel of a process of nation building and state formation. The education policy, for example, was not only used to support peasants or persuade them to take part in land reform operations; it was also used, and perhaps to an even greater extent, to promote national integration and cultural homogeneity. The importance of the nation as a category that helped provide identity was articulated in the emergence of a nationalist ideology. Since it was largely the result of the revolutionary upheaval, it not surprisingly came mainly to be known as *nacionalismo revolucionario*. This revolutionary nationalism became the ideological adhesive of the Mexican political system, at least up until the end of the 1980s.

But what is the subject of Mexican nationalism? The obvious answer, of course, is *the Mexican*. But this does not really solve the problem, since heated discussions raged in the first half of the twentieth century about who or what exactly a Mexican is, and about the underlying essence of Mexican-ness, or *mexicanidad*. One key theme in the debate on national culture has been the relations between racial groups, such as *criollos, mestizos,* and Indians.[4] Although the Revolution did not include any project expressing an Indian consciousness, many Indians nevertheless had taken part in the battle. As a result, there was now a greater variety of interrelations between the various segments of the population. After the armed struggle had ended, the Indian issue (i.e. the position and integration of the Indian community into society and nation, which is referred to below as *indigenismo*[5]) was incorporated into the official discourse of the state.

The mission of the *mestizo*

The need to resolve the strong divisiveness resulting from the Revolution greatly stimulated the process of nation building. In 1937, the revolutionary Ramón Beteta notes that "with the Revolution, our greatest force, we have discovered ourselves; analyzing the Revolution, we have understood our heterogeneity, our lack of unity" (quoted in Benjamin 1990:321). The Indians constituted a major challenge for the nationalist project. They were generally viewed as passive subjects to be transformed into active Mexican citizens. The desire to give substance and an actual shape to this new nationalism is evident in the writings of such thinkers as Manuel Gamio, José Vasconcelos, Luis Cabrera, and Andrés Molina Enríquez. The aim in mind was to integrate the multifarious Mexicos and shape a new unity where the Indian community would also be given a proper place, and not simply be relegated into separate corporative spaces or onto reservations. The fact that there was space in the new nationalism for Indian symbols, myths, and history did not necessarily mean anyone was denying the importance of "European" culture in Mexico. On the contrary, it was the process of cultural mixing that was emphasized. This is how a break was made with the Eurocentric ethos of the *ancién régime*. The English historian Knight makes the following comment on this important change: "According to the emerging orthodoxy of the Revolution, the old Indian/European thesis/antithesis had now given rise to a higher synthesis, the mestizo, who was neither Indian nor European, but *quintessentially* Mexican" (1990:84-85. My emphasis). The response given by several important thinkers to the question regarding the subject of the new Mexican nationalism was unambiguous: the authentic Mexican is a *mestizo* (or ought to be). An effort was thus made to construct an *authenticity* (Knight's quintessence) based on a *hybrid* identity.

One of the most influential authors in this regard is Andrés Molina Enríquez (1868-1940). This barrister, journalist, author, and historian got most of his intellectual and political education during the heyday of the *ancién régime* of dictator Porfirio Díaz (1876-1910). For the most part, however, he gained fame in the period just after the end of the Revolution. His main work, *Los grandes problemas nacionales,* was published a year before the Revolution broke out in 1910. All his life, Molina wrote about the nature of the relationship between nationality and race. His thinking always centered on the idea it is the struggle between different racial groups that is the engine of history. When he engaged in diagnosing Mexico's problems at the turn of the century, Molina was not just an armchair scholar who was influenced by Spencer. He was also an activist who incessantly warned against the damaging consequences of sharp inequalities. Socioeconomic inequalities, political coalitions, ideological projects, property relations, class formation – to Molina they all resulted from how racial groups interacted with and fought against each other. In turn, the inequality was at the root of the instability and heterogeneity so typical of nineteenth-century Mexico, and did not serve as a good foundation for a viable nation. Even an authoritarian form of government – applauded by Molina as a necessary evil – was not forceful enough to end the continuing instability and turmoil. In his view, only the elimination of racial differences could be effective.

In *Los grandes problemas nacionales* these views are systematized further and a link is drawn with the social problems at the time. In Molina's view, in the course of the history of Mexico a racial and socio-economic stratification emerged with the following features: a concentration of wealth in the hands of a *(criollo)* minority, inefficient large land ownership, the oppression of the peasants, and industrial stagnation due to a limited internal market. Using the metaphor so commonly used by social Darwinists of society as a body, Molina depicts the situation as follows:

> "At the moment our social body is disproportional and deformed. From the chest up it is a giant, and from the chest down a child. The upper part weighs so much the body can hardly stand erect. There is even the danger of it falling over; the feet are growing weaker every day" (quoted in Basave 1992:64).

One remedy for this objectionable situation might be to form a new balance by way of ethnic integration and mixing. According to Molina, the *mestizo* is the progeny of all the Indian races modified by Spanish blood. Since the Mexican Indian lived in isolation for so long, he has learned to adapt to his natural environment.[6] This explains his enormous forcefulness and perseverance and ability to bear and cope with injustice. This forcefulness is passed down to the *mestizo* because in his veins he has, after all, a drop of Spanish and an abundance of Indian blood. What is more, the mixing process has continued between *mestizos* and Indians.

The *mestizo* is thus predestined to exercise power. In Molina's view, this only really began in the mid-nineteenth century, when progressive groups (i.e. *mestizos*) convincingly seized power for the first time. The political influence of the *mestizo* was consolidated by the rise to power of Porfirio Díaz in 1876. During the lengthy mandate of Díaz, who was not driven out until 1911, certain processes and government policies impeded, at least in Molina's view, further racial unification and socio-economic development. The main problem was that Díaz continued to protect the large land ownership of the criollo elite – mainly at the expense of the Indians and the *mestizos*. Molina's conclusion, then, was that the large haciendas had to be dismantled and divided up. He also proposed introducing a credit system that would increase the purchasing power of the *mestizos* and make it possible to initiate irrigation projects to improve the peasants' agrarian productivity. With small-scale land ownership, credit and water, the *mestizo* could take control of the land and the nation, and these would constitute a solid basis for his political power. Even so, Molina holds that if there was to truly be a nation or fatherland, it required racial, cultural, and moral unity. This is why he called for steps in various social fields to create homogeneity via the process of *mestizaje*. The common roots, frames of references, and aspirations to be generated in that way were to serve as the basis for "a true nationality, strong and powerful, with one life and one soul" (Molina as quoted in Basave 1992:70).

The political and scientific program Molina Enríquez had in mind would lead to the banishment of difference and the reduction of racial pluralism and multiculturalism. Mexico could only become a nation-state by means of mestizaje, i.e. hybridization. The agrarian reform he propagated and his espousal of a strong regime (that is, a powerful presidency or an authoritarian form of government) were no more and no less than preconditions for creating the *México mestizo*.

The emancipation of the Indian

These developments coupled with the role that Molina's line of reasoning played in the process were well suited to the broad political and cultural framework of the 1920s and 1930s. It was also an era when the theoretical views that Molina's ideas were founded upon were slowly but surely replaced by new approaches and new ways of thinking. The ethno-essentialist and evolutionist *mestizophilia* of the late nineteenth century was criticized and endangered by the rise of modern anthropology in Mexico. Manuel Gamio (1883-1960), who got his PhD in New York under Franz Boas, played a key role and his *Forjando patria* (1916) was of particular importance in this regard. The very title of the book *(Forging a Fatherland)* evokes a powerful image that was elaborated upon as follows:

> It is this struggle [between various ethnic groups] for the creation of a fatherland and a national identity that has now been going on for a century....Now it is the Mexican revolutionaries' turn to pick up the hammer and don the garb of the smith so that on the magnificent anvil the new fatherland can result from a mixture of iron and bronze (Gamio 1916:5-6).

The metaphor used here does not immediately suggest that Gamio is trying to dissociate himself from racial essentialism in his work. He cannot completely let it go, but he does take a few important steps towards cultural relativism. With an explicit reference to the work of Boas, Gamio refutes the idea that certain ethnic groups are inferior to others. The differences between these groups are no longer explained in racial terms, but are now approached using historical, sociological and geographic characteristics. Nor is it feasible to speak of a superior culture, and aesthetic criteria are not made absolute. There is no room in this view for Eurocentric standards or a linear course of development as regards morality, art, wealth or democracy. Whether the Indian is judged in a negative (a brute) or a positive way (a *noble savage*), according to Gamio both views are based upon unscientific prejudices: "The Indian has the same capacity for progress as the White man, he is neither superior nor inferior" (1916:24).

So there is evidence in Gamio's work of a shift from a racial to a cultural focus. In so far as the aspiration of mestizaje is involved, it is purely cultural. Gamio's formulation of his own *mestizophile* variant has to do with what he sees as the inadequate social and cultural homogeneity of Mexico. A truly national society can only emerge after several preconditions have been met with: ethnic homogeneity, a common language, shared aspirations, aesthetic and moral standpoints, and a common historical consciousness. Can Indians and the descendants of European immigrants aspire to one and the same fatherland and give rise to a nation in a comparable fashion? According to Gamio, it is unfeasible. The deep socio-economic inequality only reinforces the absence of unity. The remedy to this situation would be to mix the groups and thus reduce the inequality between them. Being an urban *mestizo*, Gamio acted as the champion of the socio-economic, political, and cultural emancipation of the Indian. The Indian should not be simply left to his fate, as had been the case ever since Mexican Independence in 1821. Instead, he should be involved in the national enterprise.[7] It should be the *mestizos* themselves who take the initiative. "You will not simply wake up spontaneously. Friendly hearts will have to make an effort to work towards your liberation" (1916:22), Gamio paternalistically informed the Indians. The Indian communities in Mexico did produce some significant cultural works, but in the twentieth century they exhibited an enormous developmental lag vis-à-vis the rest of the society.[8] The various civilization offensives of the past failed because they were enforced from above. Gamio consequently made a proposal that was quite unprecedented at the time: "Let's become a bit more Indian and show him [i.e. the Indian] a civilization that is 'diluted' with his own which he shall therefore no longer consider exotic, cruel, bitter and incomprehensible" (1916:96). It was the *mestizos* who ought to take responsibility for this approach to the "pure Indian." If they wanted to partake of the "banquet of modernity," the Indians would have to don the mask of the *mestizo* (Basave 1992:126).

In *Forjando patria* a number of steps and ideas are formulated for achieving this project of unification by way of mixing. According to the author, the conditions were favorable for this at the end of the armed stage of the Mexican Revolution (1910-1917). As he wrote the book, new power relations and ideas were emerging that would make it possible to come closer to solving some of Mexico's historical problems. The innovative power of the Revolution would clear away the obstacles to wellbeing for a majority of the population, and clear the way for a process of national development (1916:79-83, 168-170).[9]

To promote this development, a thorough knowledge was needed of the Mexican people and the processes unfolding in Mexican society. There was however very little of this knowledge in Mexico, or in most of Latin America for that matter. That is why Gamio spoke of the need to professionalize the social sciences, accumulate reliable statistical material, and use it for policy development (1916:15-19, 27-36). This is why his words in favor of an official agency for anthropology did not go unheeded. Not so long afterwards, the Anthropology Division was founded at the Ministry of Agriculture. Gamio himself was appointed director, a position would hold until 1925 when he became Assistant Secretary of Education.[10]

Mexican unity could only be built if steps were taken towards that end in various social fields. In the field of art, the aesthetic criteria of the Indians and the middle classes could come together in such a way that "national art" could emerge that would be "one of the main cornerstones of nationalism." In literature each socio-cultural group had its own genre, but the European oriented literary tradition was the only one to be acknowledged as such. Gamio consequently proposed improving the production and distribution of other literary forms such as oral traditions of the Indians and *mestizos*, including those of the poorest of them. Only in this way could a "literature be born that would nourish the national soul." The school system, imbued with the diversity of languages and cultures, would have to be comprehensively reformed. In the political field, steps would have to be taken to adequately represent the subordinate social groups in the legislative bodies. In the economic field, the preferential treatment of foreign products and production processes would have to be reduced and efforts would have to be made to combine local traditions of craftsmanship with foreign technology (1916:37-40, 113-118, 159-161, 75-78, 143-148).[11]

Gamio's pursuit of homogeneity ultimately manifested itself in the form of a huge project of mestizaje. Eliminating difference by mixing the native and European influence was to lead on the one hand to a strong nation state, and on the other, to the abolition of inequalities that particularly affected the Indian population. This was the motivation behind the forceful words at the end of Forjando patria:

> RACIAL MIXING, CONVERGENCE AND FUSION OF CULTURAL EXPRESSIONS, LINGUISTIC UNIFICATION AND ECONOMIC EQUILIBRIUM BETWEEN THE SOCIAL ELEMENTS... are concepts ... that ought to characterize the Mexican people so that the people will found and embody a powerful Fatherland and a coherent and clearly defined Nationality (Gamio 1916:183, capital letters in the original).

Mestizaje as liberation

Manuel Gamio may have got his inspiration from the social inequality mainly affecting the Indian population, but the controversial work by José Vasconcelos (1882-1959) was rooted in philosophical and mystical studies. This does not necessarily mean Vasconcelos was a scholarly recluse. On the contrary, from the very start Vasconcelos was active in the political and later the military resistance to dictator Díaz, and was a close friend to Madero, the first great revolutionary leader. Vasconcelos spent various periods in forced exile in the United States, a country he was extremely critical of his entire life. When he returned to Mexico in 1918, he was appointed the first Vice-Chancellor of the National University. He achieved his greatest fame as Minister of Education from 1921 to 1924. He has gone down in history as an extremely active Minister with a great deal of expertise. He also stimulated and protected the arts in Mexico. As a result in part of his active support, the murals by Rivera and other artists flourished as a new art form. Due to political problems, he decided to leave his country once again, but in 1929 he ran for the presidency, which turned out to be an unfortunate fiasco. During his numerous trips and periods in exile, Vasconcelos wrote a sizeable oeuvre consisting of a cycle of philosophical studies, political essays, novels, and studies on the culture and history of India.

In the context of the analysis of the ideology of *mestizaje*, it is mainly his essay *La raza cósmica* (1925) that is of importance.[12] The central thesis of the essay is that the various peoples and races of the world will gradually mix more and more so that a new type of human being will emerge – the *cosmic race*. The continent where this racial and cultural mestizaje will first unfold is Latin America. In keeping with this line of thought, Vasconcelos tried to revitalize Pan-Ibero-Americanism. This notion of a struggle between Latin and Anglo-Saxon culture on the American continent is a major element in his reasoning, with the Anglo-Saxon unification strategy serving as an example for the parochialism of Ibero-Americans. The influence and power of the United States symbolize one of the peaks of the civilization of the Whites, one of the four races that, according to Vasconcelos, shape world history.[13] Each of these groups has a mission, and the mission of the Whites has almost been played out. With their expansionist drive, they have laid the foundation for a new era, an era of the mixing of the peoples that will generate a fifth race. Vasconcelos explains why Ibero-America is the ideal spot for this development by alluding to its history and its experience of *mestizaje*. Since they decimated the Indian population and developed a monoculture, White North Americans will taste defeat (1925:56-62).

His analysis of the process of *mestizaje* is very different from Gamio's or Molina's. Gamio makes little effort to conceal his paternalistic sympathy for the Indian, but Vasconcelos leans more towards the Spanish element.[14] Barely any references are made in *La raza cósmica* to the situation of the Indian at the time in Mexico, or in Latin America for that matter. Nor is there much appreciation for the culture and the level of development of pre-Columbian society. In an effort nonetheless to give the continent a place in world history, Vasconcelos alludes in one of the most striking passages of the essay to the myth of Atlantis, which he situates in America: "The Aztec and Inca empires are scanty remains and completely unworthy of the ancient and superior culture [of Atlantis]" (1925:49). Vasconcelos' *mestizophilia* is based on the pragmatic observation that most of the people are already *mestizos*. According to Basave (1992:134), Vasconcelos tries to give this empirical fact a mythical dimension, partially in an effort to promote Latin American integration

Another important principle in the essay, and perhaps the major structuring one, is the idea of three stages in the evolution of mankind. The first stage entails material necessity and warfare; the second is the stage of reason and politics, and the third of spirituality and aesthetics. The criticism Vasconcelos formulates of the second stage bears an unexpected resemblance to the post-modern criticism of the modernity project: "Reason prevails in this stage … its main feature is the belief in the formula … all this period does is standardize intelligence, reduce freedom to act, restrict the nation and suppress the emotions. Rules and regulations, norms and tyranny, that is the law of the second period we are imprisoned in and must escape from" (1925:69). The last period, however, which coincides with the creation of the fifth race, will be ruled by good taste, beauty, and freedom. A society that has proved via *mestizaje* that it is characterized by openness and pluralism will serve as the home base for spiritual and sexual liberation. His support for the notion of *mestizaje* is a strategy or route to escape from what Nederveen Pieterse calls an "inward directed conception of culture" (1998:119) and what Vasconcelos himself refers to as "ethnic closure."[15] *La raza cósmica* plays a role of great importance in the ideology of the Mexican national identity.

Vasconcelos' work can be viewed as the culmination of ethnicity-oriented *mestizophilia*. The odd mixture of pragmatism, metaphysical thinking, and visionary view on hybrid Latin America could hardly be anything else (Basave 1992:136). Together with the efforts of others, the most important of which are analyzed here, it stimulated Mexicans to focus on their uniqueness and their own worth and continue to expand upon them. Molina, Gamio, and Vasconcelos were all skeptical about an outward-directed perspective (Spain, France, and the United States) that usually amounted to an imitation of foreign ideas, political ideologies, and development models. The unproblematic application of models of this kind – like republican federalism and democracy – to their own reality only generated numerous new problems. These ideas have been very prominent in Mexico and Latin America. Decades later the leading intellectual, Antonio Caso (1924:28), noted that an effectively functioning democracy required ethnic unity and social uniformity, which were definitely not in evidence in Mexico.[16]

The politics of *la mexicanidad*

Ever since the publication of *La raza cósmica,* the discourse on the *mestizo* as the authentic embodiment of the national identity and vanguard of the nationalist ideology has undergone important changes. The search for the characteristics and core values of the "true Mexican" has gone on ever since the 1930s, but later took a different route. Ethnocentric *mestizophilia* gradually made way for social-psychological analyses. The programmatic aspects still in evidence in the work of Molina and Gamio in connection with promoting the *mestizo* largely disappeared at the start of the 1930s. This is why a group of younger thinkers focused so intensely on the "soul" of the mixed Mexican, which does undeniably exist. While the key concept for the older generation was mestizaje, the younger generation became more interested in *mexicanidad*, a concept that covers the whole gamut of images and metaphors thought to characterize the essence of the (*mestizo*) Mexican. *El perfil del hombre y la cultura en México* (1934) by philosopher Samuel Ramos heralds the start of this new stage. In this study, the author holds that the Mexican has an inferiority complex going back to the traumatic experience of the *conquista*, when the native population was subjugated and humiliated, and therefore the mixed descendants of the conquistadors feel humiliated by their lowly position vis-à-vis the Europeans. The Mexican who is still young tries to compensate for the sense of inferiority by way of compulsive behavior. *Machismo* is an example of this kind of behavior. It is time for the frustrated young man to grow up, and according to Ramos he can best do so by viewing himself as a branch of the European race. Ramos does not think much of the Indian people and their culture. In the following years, other comparable books were published such as *El mexicano: su dinámica psicosocial* by Francisco González Pineda, using concepts from the field of psychoanalysis, and *El mexicano: psicología de sus motivaciones* by Santiago Ramírez, both published at the end of the 1950s. *El laberinto de la soledad* (1950) by Octavio Paz deserves separate mention; this essay later became world famous. He differs from Ramos in that he notes that the Mexican does not hide behind masks, for he himself is the mask. Behind the mask lies only solitude. In his book, Paz tries to break through the Mexican solitude by abandoning the strongly inward-directed perspective and looking for links to Western culture.

These literary and scientific (or semi-scientific) publications yield a set of images that are supposed to sketch the Mexican (national) "character": a culture of an easy death, of "slow" time and the "typical" sense of time that goes with it, of the violent lumpenproletariat (the *pelado),* the macho, and of *México bronco,* the rough and tough Mexico associated with the countryside and the unfathomable Indian soul. From the perspective of the urban middle classes and elites, this Mexico is sinister and menacing.[17] These images and stereotypes can also be observed in the movies of the 1950s and 1960s and in other forms of art and folk art, and have gradually expanded into a whole mythology of *lo mexicano* in Mexico as well as abroad. Even a quick analysis of the depiction of Mexico and Mexicans in American mass culture products reveals a one-sided picture of violence and corruption, but also of a leaning towards the noble savage.

The observation of the contours of the *homo mexicanus,* especially in the 1950s, cannot be viewed as a purely literary matter. At the beginning of this article I noted the important role played by nationalism in consolidating and legitimating the post-revolutionary regime. Although memories of the divisiveness of the Revolution ebbed after the Second World War, the rapid and comprehensive process of socio-economic and demographic change that mainly manifested itself in impressive industrialization and urbanization generated new forms of inequality, divisions, and grievances. In the political field, the administrative and economic elites were by now entrenched in a one-party system, a corporatist apparatus, a sizeable governmental bureaucracy, and above all an extremely powerful presidency. Democratic practices appeared to be mainly of a formalist nature. The *dramatis personae* and its character traits from the myth of the Mexican national identity were given meaning now against the backdrop of the numerous imperfections and injustices of modernity (Niblo 1999). The discourse of *la mexi-canidad* is consequently a political one. The definition of "the" Mexican "is predominantly a description of how he is dominated." According to Roger Bartra, the subject of the studies about Mexico's national character is an imaginary construction by the authors themselves. They are biting their own tails (1987:16). The shrewd and pertinent criticism of Bartra reveals the arbitrary and sometimes absurd nature of the stereotypes from the gallery of national culture. In Bartra's view, the discourse of Mexican-ness is a crucial component of the dominant political culture. In the post-revolutionary period the *mestizo* became the official protagonist of Mexican history, while there was a certain extent of appreciation for indigenous culture and history.

This interpretation of the national identity had an anti-imperialist connotation and legitimated the formation of a strong national state that could serve as a buffer against foreign influences – especially in an economic sense – while at the same time redefining Eurocentric development aims. It also propagated an active state role in regulating the market so as to favor the national community, which could best be served by an all-powerful party that represented the various social sectors in a hierarchical and corporatist fashion. In short, the core of the ideology of the Revolution was nationalism, particularly *mestizo* nationalism. This ideology supported the strong state and the corporatist party (PRI), whose aim was to include the entire society and represent it as one entity. There is not much room for plurality in a mind-set of this kind. The cultural logic of homogeneity corresponds with the political logic of the one-party state.

Conclusions

Cultural diversity has recently come to play a prominent role in the public and academic debate in post-industrial societies. With the Mexican case study, I would like to demonstrate that comparable debates have also been going on in other parts of the world, and often for quite some time now. Devoting attention to them makes it possible to guard against Eurocentrism and can yield conceptual insights.

At the beginning of the twentieth century the limited cultural homogeneity of Mexican society was viewed as an obstacle to building a viable nation. The devastating effects of the Revolution on the society only reinforced the pursuit of a new national identity. In the first few decades of the twentieth century this endeavor led to the construction of an authenticity discourse focused on the *mestizo*. Paradoxically enough, the Mexican interpretation of authenticity has to do with hybridization *(mestizaje)*. Although authenticity and hybridization are generally viewed as diametrically opposed, the analysis of the Mexican case demonstrates that this is not always the case. In the Mexican authenticity discourse, the tension between the two is eliminated because the pursuit of purity, which is linked to the whole idea of an authentic identity, is attained by *including* and resolving existing heterogeneity and difference. Authenticity and purity can, however, also be sought and attained by *excluding* heterogeneity and difference. This is what might be referred to as the "Balkan solution." Whereas in the Mexican case, authenticity is the result of assimilating or inclusive – be it asymmetrical –

hybridization, in the Balkan case there is evidence of exclusive authentication. Despite this crucial difference, in both cases there is evidence of the "invention of purity," which suppresses whatever difference there might be.

In this contribution I have distinguished three variants in the construction of the discourse of national identity, each using different core concepts and conceptual frameworks. Racial concepts play a central role in the first variant. The second variant is a culturalist one, and the third is mainly (socio-)psychological. All three do, however, share a common pursuit of unequivocalness and purity in the respective fields of race, culture, and psychology. In recent years, the pursuit of the purity of the hybrid *mestizo* culture has been undermined by a new politics of difference, predominantly set in motion by various neo-indigenous movements. The struggle to construct new identities continues, but that is another story.

Notes

1   Chicana refers to Mexican or Central American roots, whereas Riqueña refers to Puerto Rican ones.

2   In her study of the debate pertaining to the authenticity of a cultural festival in British Guyana at the beginning of the twentieth century, Williams also very emphatically refers to the positioning and evaluation of national individuality in a field where international forces interact. The international is also a significant factor in the case of Mexico – one should bear in mind its complex relations with the United States – but I am not in a position to go into that question in detail here.

3   I am well aware that with this approach I am deviating from the usual modern-day analyses of processes of nation-building and cultural politics in Mexico. There the attention is not focused so much on the big story of the state and the nation and the role that certain thinkers and key texts play in it as on how the discourse on the nation is embedded in local daily practices and contexts and they way these local practices play a role in constituting the nation. Some extremely interesting and important studies have been conducted on the negotiations by for example peasants, Indians and Catholics on the contents and the meaning of the post-revolutionary state and nation from a local and regional perspective. One important publication in this connection is Joseph et al. (1994). See also Aitken (1999) and Bantjes (1997, 1998).

4   In Mexico the term *criollo* is not used to refer to a mixed identity, but to someone of Spanish descent who was born in Mexico. The criteria that were and still are used to determine whether an individual or a community is categorized as Indian are extremely diverse. Some people view the language as the predominant criterion, whereas others prefer indicators that might be more comprehensive but are also more unclear, such as clothing, customs, and social and religious modes of organization. In the administration practice of colonial Latin America, the *Indian* was already far more of a fiscal than a racial or ethnic category. From a biological as well as a cultural perspective, after centuries of Spanish rule and racial mixing, a *pure Indian* is rare in Mexico if not totally non-existent. The racial idiom has nonetheless continued to play a role of importance, even among the authors and thinkers of the first half of the twentieth century whose stance as regards these groups was positive and benevolent. As Knight concludes, "… these theorists could have dropped the use of 'race' altogether or at least they could have made it clear that for them 'race' denoted a social category. Instead, they remained prisoners of the preceding racist discourse, and continued to scatter references to 'race' among their ostensibly antiracist *indigenista* writings"(1990: 87).

5   In Spanish, *indigena* roughly means indigenous inhabitant., which in Latin America is equiv-

alent to Indian. The Spanish word *indio* has a pejorative connotation.

6   Here Molina shows that he is indebted to Haeckel, who defines a race in terms of the relations with its physical environment.

7   According to Gamio, the Indian population was better off in colonial times than in independent Mexico. This has to do with various factors, such as the abolition of the colonial legislation that allowed the Indian communities to have autonomous regions. Afterwards , in particular the liberal reforms of the mid-nineteenth century greatly harmed the survival chances of the Indian communities.

8   Gamio's main focus is on scientific progress in this regard. This is evident, for example, from his repeated emphasis on the importance of collecting scientific knowledge for the purpose of policy development.

9   Basave (1992: 128-129) has noted the ill-reputed differences between this work and *Hacia un México Nuevo*, which was published in 1935. This book evokes an atmosphere of disappointment. Twenty years after the end of the Revolution, a new elite was in power that proved to be just as corrupt as the leaders of the *ancièn régime*.

10 Gamio was also active for what he believed in any number of other ways. He was the director of the *Instituto Indigenista Interamericano* from 1939 to 1960, and the director of *Escuela Internacional de Arqueología y Etnologia* and founder of the journal *Ethnos* (Basave 1992: 125).

11 It is striking that no mention is made of religion in this list. Gamio holds that there was a non-problematic merging in the colonial era in this field between Catholic and pre-Columbian religious practices because there was a strong analogy between the two. He holds, however, that Protestantism differed greatly from the pre-Columbian "paganism" (1982 [1916]: 85-88).

12 This essay has attracted a great deal of attention ever since. A new bilingual edition was recently published in the United States with an extensive introduction.

13 The other races are the Blacks, the Indians, and the Mongolians.

14 Vasconcelos himself was more of a *criollo*, i. e. someone of direct European descent but born in America.

15 The author uses this metaphor to describe the attitude of northerners and compare it to the *sympathy* of the southerners. Could he have had a premonition that seven decades later, the northern neighbours would indeed start building a wall on the border between the United States and Mexico?

17 This not only holds true for Mexico or even Latin America. The same comment was recently made by Paul Scheffer in a bibliographic analysis of the situation in the Balkans: "Ethnically more homogeneous countries such as Poland, Hungary or Slovenia have more of a chance of becoming a stable democracy … than ethnically divided countries like Slovakia and Serbia. The minority issue … appears to serve as a stepping stone towards nationalism and an authoritarian form of rule"(1999).

18 The occupation of the large cities by the triumphant armies of peasants led by Zapata and Villa in the Mexican Revolution are often cited in this respect as an example of the mobilization of *México bronco*. The short-lived occupation of San Cristóbal de las Casas by the neo-Zapatistas in 1994 evoked similar fears among the local elites.

Bibliography

Aitken, R. 1999. *Localizing politics. Cardenismo, the Mexican state and local politics in contemporary Michoacán,* Leiden. Unpublished dissertation.

Bantjes, A. 1997. The eight sacraments: nationalism and revolutionary political culture in Mexico. In W. Pansters, ed., *Citizens of the Pyramid. Essays on Mexican Political Culture,* pp. 131-146. Amsterdam: Thela Latin American Series.

Bantjes, A. 1998. *As if Jesus walked on earth. Cardenismo, Sonora and the Mexican Revolution.*

Wilmington: Scholarly Resources.

Bartra, R. 1987. *La jaula de la melancolía. Identidad y metamorfosis del mexicano.* México D.F.: Enlace/Grijalbo.

Basave Benítez, A. 1992. *México mestizo. Análisis del nacionalismo mexicano en torno a la mestizofilia de Andrés Molina Enríquez.* México D.F.: Fondo de Cultura Económica.

Beck, U., et. al. 1995. *Reflexive modernization. Politics, tradition and aesthetics in the modern social order.* Cambridge: Polity Press.

Benjamin, T. 1990. Regionalizing the Revolution: The Many Mexicos in Revolutionary Historiography. In T. Benjamin and M. Wasserman, eds., *Provinces of the Revolution. Essays on Regional Mexican History, 1910-1929,* pp. 319-357. Albuquerque: The University of New Mexico Press.

Caso, A. 1955. *El problema de México y la ideología nacional.* México D.F.: Libro-Mex Editores. (Originally published in 1924.)

Chabram Dernersesian, A. 1995. "Chicana! Rican? No Chicana-Riqueña!." Refashioning the transnational connection. In David T. Goldberg, *Multiculturalism. A critical reader,* pp. 269-295. Oxford/Cambridge: Blackwell.

de Ruijter, A. 2000a. *De multiculturele arena.* Tilburg: Catholic University Brabant.

de Ruijter, A. 2000b. Globalization. A challenge to the social sciences. In F. Schuurmanm, ed., *Globalization and Development Studies,* pp. 31-43. Amsterdam: Thela Thesis.

Gamio, M. 1916. *Forjando patria.* México D.F.: Editorial Porrúa. (1982 edition.)

González Pineda, F. 1961. *El mexicano. Su dinámica psicosocial.* México D.F.: Esditorial Pax-México.

Gorashi, H. 1997. Shifting and Conflicting Identities: Iranian Women Political Activists in Exile. *The European Journal of Women's Studies* 4: 283-303.

Hall, S. 1996. Introduction: who needs 'identity'? In Stuart Hall and Paul du Gay, eds., *Questions of cultural identity,* pp. 1-17. London: Sage.

Joseph, G., et. al., eds. 1994. *Everyday forms of state formation. Revolution and the negotation of rule in Modern Mexico.* Durham/London: Duke University Press.

Kearney, M. 1991. Border and boundaries of the state and the self at the end of empire. *Journal of Historical Sociology* 4(1):52-74.

Knight, A. 1990. Racism, revolution and indigenismo: Mexico, 1910-1940. In Richard Graham, ed., *The idea of race in Latin America, 1870-1940,* pp. 71-113. Austin: University of Texas Press.

Malkki, L. 1992. National Geographic: The Rooting of Peoples and the Territorialization of National Identity among Scholars and Refugees. *Cultural Anthropology* 7(1):24-44.

Nederveen Pieterse, J. 1998. Der Melange-Effekt. Globalisierung im Plural. In Ulrich Beck, ed., *Perspektiven der Weltgesellschaft,* pp. 87-124. Frankfurt on.Main.: Suhrkamp.

Niblo, S.D. 1999. *Mexico in the 1940s. Modernity, politics and corruption.* Wilmington: Scholarly Resources.

Olwig, K.F., and K. Hastrup, eds. 1997. *Siting culture. The shifting anthropological object.* London/New York: Routledge.

Paz, O. 1950. *El laberinto de la soledad.* México D.F.: Fondo de Cultural Económica. (1967 edition)

Ramos, S. 1934. *El perfil del hombre y la cultura en México.* México D.F.: ESPASA-CALPE Mexicana, Colección Austral, no. 1080. (1965 edition.)

Ruy-Sánchez, A. 1995. Approaches to the problem of Mexican identity. In Robert L. Earle and John D. Wirth, eds., *Identities in North America. The search for community,* pp. 40-55. Stanford: Stanford University Press.

Scheffer, P. 1999. Verzoening of vergelding. *NRC Handelsblad,* 11 June, p. 31.

Vasconcelos, J. 1997. *The Cosmic Race/La raza cósmica.* Translated, with an introduction by Didier T. Jean. Baltimore / London: Johns Hopkins University Press. (Originally published in Spanish in 1925.)

Williams, B. F. 1990. Nationalism, traditionalism, and the problem of cultural inauthenticity. In Richard G. Fox, ed., *Nationalist ideologies and the production of national cultures,* pp.112-129. American Ethnological Society Monograph Series, No. 2, Washington.

10

Crossing Borders, Meeting Gender
The 'Quinceañera' in Mexico and
the United States

Gerdien Steenbeek

This essay deals with a ritual by which young Mexican and Mexican-American females in their fifteenth year move from girlhood to womanhood, and in the process are integrated into the social and moral community. The celebration of *quince años* (fifteen years) can be described as a rite of a passage – a girl's journey into womanhood, though as yet not into the full status of woman.[1] Moreover, it is a practice in which gender is constructed with, and through, notions of sexuality.

The ritual of *quinceañera* (the name refers both to the ritual event and to the fifteen-year-old individual), however, is not only a practice that relates to the creation and re-creation of the identity of woman. Like other passage rites of this kind – whether they are Jewish bar and bat mitzvahs, Masai circumcisions, or fraternity hazings – it also functions to create or re-create the identity of her social group, and to enhance the solidarity of participants (see Davalos 1996, Fried and Fried 1980, Turner 1974). In this case, the ritual transforms the fifteen-year-old female into a virtuous, marriageable woman, yet it also reinforces the collective identity of the family and the community as morally incorruptible, unified, and strong.

In the first part of this essay I will describe and analyse the key elements of the quinceañera event as celebrated in Mexico. In particular I will refer to the way it is celebrated by the working class families of Irapuato, a provincial town in the Catholic heartland of central Mexico.[2] The second part focuses on the this rite as it has drifted across the border into the United States, where it today continues to flourish in Mexican and other Hispanic migrant communities, and particularly among second- and third-generation Mexican-American girls.[3] The argument I wish to propose is that north of the border between Mexico and the United States, it would appear that the *quinceañera* has become a practice that plays a crucial role in constructing, enacting, and embodying an ethnically specific gender identity by ritualistically emphasising what can be called an *"axis of difference."*

A study of the *quinceañera* as practiced in Mexico and the United States provides me with the opportunity to understand the process by which different identities are articulated within a transnational context. To this end, I intend to concentrate in particular on the complex connections that, in the process, are constructed between cultural practice, gender, and identity. My analytical premise is that definitions of cultural and/or ethnic "Otherness" are mainly based on the ways in which women's sexuality and reproductive capability are socially controlled. In a much disputed essay about the troublesome relationship between group rights and the interests of women in multi-cultural societies, Susan Okin (1999:12-13) has pointed to important connections between culture and gender. An important fact that is commonly overlooked is that the cultural practices and rules that constitute cultural identity often focus significantly on the personal, sexual, and reproductive spheres of life. The obvious conclusion from this is that the cultural rules and practices that influence the construction of cultural identity will likely also have a great impact on the lives of girls and women. Furthermore, emic notions of motherhood and womanhood – although often undervalued in male-hegemonic contexts – nevertheless generally play a crucial role in drawing the boundaries of cultural belonging and membership in a group. In short, the construction of cultural identity, ethnic belonging, and Otherness – complementary outcomes that they are – is thus a gendered process.

Among Hispanics in the United States, this gendered process takes on an extra dimension because it also accrues meaning against the multicultural backdrop of the construction and definition of ethnic communities. Malkin, for instance, has studied the implications of transnational migration for Mexican women and the reproduction of gender ideologies. Based on a study of a suburb of New York City suburb, Malkin concludes that the active creation there of a Mexican identity placed emphasis on the family. That the discourse should refer to the family has implications for the women migrants since they are portrayed as the very symbolic nucleus of community. This can be a source of pride for some women, but it can also become a double-edged sword in as much as it presents the problem of having to challenge not only the roles and identities of gender norms, but also the ethnic identity that is being constructed on the basis of predetermined ideas of "the family" and its supposed unity (Malkin 1999:492). This essay on the *quinceañera* aims to make a modest contribution to the study of the "transnationalisation" of cultural practices, and their changing meaning for the actors involved.

Gendered purity and shame in the Mexican family

Although growing up in Mexico is a process constantly accompanied by gender differentiation (e.g. homosexuality is generally still looked down upon), it would be a mistake to assume that the construction of gender is directly associated with sexuality. It is said that a girl looses her innocence upon her first menstruation. From this critical moment onwards, values that are related to the female gender acquire a sexual dimension. The onset of menstruation turns girls into *"señoritas"* or "young ladies," even though they will not be called this until they have reached their fifteenth birthday. *Señoritas* have an ambiguous gender position, for as long as they are unmarried they are not yet considered to have assumed the full status of women. As *señoritas* they have lost their childhood innocence, they have become sexual, fertile beings. Yet they are expected to keep their virginity intact, for it is only in so doing that they preserve their virtue and moral integrity as young women.

Moreover, chastity is not only a concern for the women themselves; above all it is a family matter. The integrity of the virgin stands for the integrity of the family. As a member of the family, a virgin daughter shows that the unity of the family is tight, and that the boundaries within are intact. The girl's chastity, and hence her dignity and the honour of her family, is guaranteed by the presence of family at her side, especially her father. All such decent, young women are affectionately referred to by her parents as *hija de familia*. A "daughter of the family" stands for a woman who is honourable, who belongs to and is protected by her family. When a young woman is surrounded by her family, it means that her virtue is protected and her virginity is intact.

As in other cultures (see Beck and Keddie 1978), the emphasis on chastity as something that must be protected and controlled is expressed through the idiom of honour and shame. In Mexican culture, the discourse of honour depicts women as beings who, because of their sexuality, are in constant danger and must therefore be patronized and protected. Honourable women respect the shame of their body by preserving sexual purity. However, it has been argued that what is actually being protected is not so much the integrity of the female body as the honour, status, and power of the patrilineal group (Pomata 1987:100).

Preparing for the *quinceañera*

One's fifteenth birthday is very important for most Mexican girls, and one that they look forward to for many years beforehand. It is unthinkable for them not to celebrate their *quinceañera*, or to exchange it even for a holiday to Cancún, for it is the day that she will be "presented to the community."

Given their required minimum of extravagance, the celebration often constitutes at least some financial burden for working class parents. Nevertheless, its significance is such that parents are willing to go to great lengths to give their daughter – and themselves – this important celebration by saving for years and/or by borrowing money.

The fiesta is organised by the family, with the help of one or more godparents *(padrinos)*. As with many rites of passage in the life cycle of Roman Catholics in Latin America, such as baptism, first communion, confirmation etc., the *quinceañera* requires the physical presence and the moral and financial (however small) support of godparents. One's financial means is an important consideration in selecting godparents. However, their moral integrity and reputation are considered more significant. The most important godparents of the *quinceañera* will be married individuals. If these cannot be found, then the role will pass to the most important available *madrina*. Godparents are often chosen from one's patrilineal relatives, although this is not obligatory. In Irapuato it was the parents who arranged the food for the party while the godparents paid for the clothes of their *ahijada* (goddaughter), the mass, and all the necessary paraphernalia for the ceremony, such as a golden medallion, a special prayer book, and a rosary.

Depending on the financial situation of the parents and godparents and the size of the fiesta, other godmothers may be asked to contribute to the cost of the festival by paying for the cake, the musicians, or the dance hall. (There were a number of madrinas at the festivals I attended.) It is always the "first" *madrina*, however, who must foot the cost of the sacred paraphernalia that are used in the *quinceañera* ceremony.

The ritual of the *quinceañera*

When describing the ritual of the *quinceañera*, one should keep in mind that there is no such thing as a "typical" performance. Indeed, by its very nature, *performance* is fluid, never static. Additionally, the social class and the financial and social resources of the family will determine the actual character of the celebration. Nevertheless, there are certain elements that appear in almost all *fiestas de quince años*.

On her celebration day, the 15-year-old wears a glamorous long dress, which sometimes is white (symbolising her virginity), though is more often pink. According to many 15-year-olds, pink is a soft, romantic colour. Their mothers think this colour is suitable, because it is both feminine and "girlish." The style must be as romantic as possible: a tight bodice of shiny satin and a pleated distended skirt adorned with ribbons and bows. On this day the *quinceañera* receives her first pair of lady's stockings and high-heeled shoes. The metamorphosis is complemented by a visit to a local hairdresser, who arranges her hair and applies make-up. Not coincidentally, at the end of it all the *quinceañera* looks very much like a bride.

The young lady is chaperoned to the fiesta by a young man of approximately the same age, known as the *chamberlán*. Traditionally, he is the girl's brother or a young man to whom the family (particularly the father) places great trust. Some people told me that the ideal is for the *quinceañera* to be accompanied by 14 *chamberlanes* and 14 *damas* (ladies), but nobody of the working class could ever afford that. The *chamberlán* escorts the girl to church, but does not walk her down the aisle to the church altar. His role also includes dancing the first waltz with her at the fiesta that follows. In the socio-religious rite of *quinceañera*, the mass and the formal sequence of dances are the most important recurrent elements.

Religious and social ceremony

The rite of *quinceañera* begins with a church mass, which is especially dedicated to the fifteen-year-old. Beforehand the priest has heard the young woman's confession. Thus, free from sins, the *quinceañera* stands as a *"una señorita pura,"* a "pure young woman," next to her father at the altar. The priest then proceeds to commemorate her happy and, above all, *innocent* childhood, for which God is thanked and her parents are blessed. However, the priest emphasizes that that period of time is now over. From now on she is a *señorita*, and it is her duty to be a virtuous and religious daughter so that she can in the future once again stand with purity at the altar, next to her groom. The priest sermons her on her responsibility to preserve her (sexual) purity until her wedding day. At the end of the mass the *quinceañera* goes and kneels down in front of the statue of the Virgin Mary, where she lays flowers, and prays for guidance. As we can see, the religious ceremony focuses on the relationships between parents and daughter, between God and the family, and between the Virgin Mary and the young woman.

A party given at the home of the *quinceañera's* parents or at a party salon follows the religious ceremony. It is attended by many guests, most of whom are relatives, and, of course, by the *padrinos de los quince años,* who are now the *quinceañera's* spiritual relatives. In addition, the attendants include neighbours, friends, and acquaintances of the *quinceañera* and her family. On average, *quinceaños fiestas* of the working class in Irapuato are attended by at least eighty guests.

The *quinceañera* and her *chamberlán* open the ceremony by dancing a waltz. For this moment the dance floor is solely for them alone. The dance has been carefully choreographed and practiced with the help of the *madrina,* or the *quinceañera's* mother or sister. The young woman is the "centre of the show," while the *chamberlán* is just an "accessory." After a while the *quinceañera's* father joins his daughter and takes his turn to dance with her this first dance of the party, while the *chamberlán* discretely retreats into the circle of spectators.

When the dance is finished, the *quinceañera's* father gives a short and often emotional speech, in which he praises his daughter's virtue, and ends by presenting his daughter to the community with the words: *"les presento mi hija."* These words can be taken to mean both "I introduce my daughter to you," and "I offer my daughter to you as a prospective bride." After the father has delivered this speech, other men are permitted to ask the *quinceañera's* for a dance without first having to ask her father's permission, which etiquette normally demands at ordinary fiestas. The other guests are now also permitted to come on to the dance floor.

During the celebration a meal is served to all the guests, consisting preferably of rice, beans, and chicken in *mole* sauce, which is the most important dish offered Mexico at festive occasions in Mexico. The meal confirms the solidarity of the social group and the bonding of the community. Those who have arrived after the meal has been served will be the first to be offered food.

The cutting of the *pastel,* the cake, is another recurring element of the social ceremony. The cake has different layers and looks like a wedding cake, the only difference being that there is a little figure of a solitary woman on top, rather than of a wedding couple.

The *quinceañera*: a rite of passage

As I have already suggested above, the celebration of *quinceaños* can be considered a rite of passage. It is true that with the ceremony the 15-year-old leaves her childhood behind, but that is not to say that she now has the status of an adult. Adulthood is not a generic stage of the life cycle, but rather is embedded in Catholic expectations of womanhood (see also Dávalos 1996:100). In other words, the *quinceañera* is not really mark the complete transition from a girl to an adult woman, from *niña* to *mujer*. For being an unwed woman, she cannot yet be fully considered as a woman. A *quinceañera* is a "woman" on the threshold. She is a *jovencita* (young woman), at most *mujercita* (little woman), who is only just beginning to enter the responsibilities of womanhood. As such, the rite of *quinceañera* may be viewed as both a rite of passage in and of itself insofar as it marks the transition from girl to young woman, and as an entry into a *liminal phase* – to use Turner's (1974) term – in the larger and more protracted passage towards full womanhood and, eventually, motherhood. As is characteristic of being in a liminal phase, the *quinceañera* occupies an ambiguous social position between girl and woman. Hence, it may even be said that the ritual of *quinceañera* represents a particular rite of passage (i.e. transition from girl to young woman) within a larger and more extended rite of passage (transition from girl to a "full" status woman). As such, it provides, on the one hand, an interesting commentary on anthropology's theoretical conceptualisation of the dynamics of rites of passage within the larger context of the individual's life cycle, and on the other hand, insight into the fundamental contrasts in the passage to adulthood between girls (i.e. more drawn out, happens in gradual stages, defined by end-state: a married woman, and eventually a mother) and boys (i.e. a more straightforward change in social status from boyhood to manhood, often defined by one's (preferably) early loss of virginity) in Mexico and elsewhere in Latin America.

In addition, it is also important to recognize that the ritual evokes the construction of femininity (and so of gender) with and through meanings of sexuality. It is through the ritual that the 15-year-old is acknowledged as a sexual being, and her receiving her first nylons, high heels, make-up – all attributes commonly associated with mature women – is symbolic affirmation of her sexual being. After having celebrated her *quinceañera*, honourable men are now permitted to court her. Indeed, even at the party itself, the presence of the *chamberlán* may even be interpreted as a catalyst to provoke men to focus their attention on the *quinceañera*. Dressed up like a bride – an impression that is accentuated even more by her "aesthetic counterpart" in the person of the male *chamberlán* – the message to all eligible suitors is clear: she is now a "candidate" on the "marriage market."

That this new phase in a young woman's life can indeed be spoken of as a liminal phase is borne out by the apparently contradictory situation whereby the acknowledgement of her sexuality is nevertheless checked by a denial of sexual activities. That is to say, the young woman may now be presented as a sexual being, but not as a person who engages in sexual intercourse. In fact, she must now learn the correct behaviour expected of a chaste and virtuous young woman. These attendant values for a *quinceañera* were already clearly expressed during the church ceremony. For example, her escort accompanies her (protectively) to the church, but he is not the one to lead her down the church aisle, nor does he stand beside her at the altar. That symbolic gesture is reserved for her future husband to be. For all its similar appearance to a wedding, the *quinceañera* must also take care to omit the crucial parallels because of what a wedding ceremony and marriage implies: subsequent sexual consummation and regular sexual activity (cf. Dávalos 1996). The correct behaviour expected of the *quinceañera* is also expressed in the priest's sermon, in which the keywords are "purity," "virginity," "dignity." Furthermore, during the mass her moral relation with the Virgin of Guadalupe is symbolically and publicly emphasised. The girl prays to the Virgin for guidance on her journey to full womanhood, and seals this spiritual connection by giving the Virgin an offering of a bouquet of flowers. In short, it may be argued that the religious aspects of the *quinceañera* rite enacts and celebrates the (re-)creation of a gendered sexual identity that relates the status of the young woman with the Virgin, while at the same time also reaffirming the strength of her bond with her family.

Presentation to the community

It is not only the *quinceañera*, but also the moral reputation of her family, that is presented to the community. The celebration makes her publicly available for the "marriage market," and shows that she is a good candidate for marriage because she is a *"hija de familia."* As stated before, being a "family daughter" reaffirms her virtue and guarantees that it will be protected by her male family members and relatives throughout the duration of her journey to womanhood. Moreover, the religious aspect of the celebration serves to place a sacred seal that guarantees the young woman's virtue, for the priest is regarded as the respected guardian of the moral community par excellence. The young woman is regarded as virtuous not just because her virtue is guarded by her male kin, but also because she shows respect for and obedience to those who protect her, particularly her father. The presence of her male relatives throughout the rite is also meant as a promise to the public that the young woman will also be protected in the future up until her wedding day.

As in other cultures, the virtue of Mexican women is generally regarded as decisive for the honour of the family at large, especially for the men who represent this honour. It is primarily in their interest – or rather in the interest of their own reputation – to protect the virtue of the young woman. By showing this protection during the *quince años* celebration, the community is warned: this woman is not freely available. She is a member of a group, and if you touch her you touch the family. By protecting women, the honour and integrity of the family is also defended.

The transnational nature of the contemporary *quinceañera*

I have thus far sought to show that the celebration of *quinceañera* is a performance of budding womanhood in which gender is created and recreated with and through (a symbolically exhibited yet actively denied) sexuality. In addition, up till now I have concentrated on explaining the *quinceañeras* as it is celebrated in provincial Mexico. The reality, however, is that the fiesta of the quince años has crossed physical and virtual borders.

This special celebration is not restricted simply to those parts of the United States and Mexico that are situated along their common border. Norma Cantú (1996:3) states that in the borderlands of the United States the tradition has existed for generations (certainly since the 1920s). Acording to Cantú, Chicanos perpetuate all kinds of fiestas that have often been ongoing since before 1848 when the United States took possession of a large part of the Mexican north. However, until recently the objects that were worn or given at a *quinceañera* were unavailable in the United States, and instead had to be bought in Mexico. Nowadays, however, they are easily available in bridal and gift shops wherever U.S. Hispanics live, and religious convenience stores consequently enjoy a lively trade because of this. Karen Davalos (1996) notes that owing to the intensification of migration in recent decades, the celebration of the *quinceañera* has become popular among Mexican and other Hispanic transmigrants living in other parts of the U.S., like Chicago, New York etc. Moreover, the event enjoys much attention in the media.

The widespread and rising popularity of the *quinceañera* among Latins living in the United States can also be inferred from the large amount of websites on the Internet dedicated to the topic of *quinceañera*. As a "virtual" anthropologist who also does fieldwork in cyberspace, I travelled to numerous Internet *quinceañeras*. It was a fascinating trip. One search engine – Google – produced over 147,000 hits for the term quince años, plus another 43,500 for the term "quinceañera". The majority of these sites belong to shops that sell the special paraphernalia for the *quince años,* at exorbitantly high prices one might add. The variety of commodities offered is impressive. More interesting is the fact that many of these objects are claimed to be features of the event as it has been "traditionally celebrated," although I have never seen them in Mexico.

The growing popularity of the *quinceañera* in the United States, and the lucrative market it has given rise to, is made more evident by the fact that the multinational toy manufacturer Mattel, which introduced the hugely successful Barbie doll over four decades ago, brought out on of its newest dolls in 2001 – the *quinceañera* Barbie. It was launched nation-wide, with limited distribution abroad, including Mexico and Puerto Rico, in the light of market research that showed the celebration of the *quinceañera* was even more popular in the U.S. than in other countries.[4]

Besides these commercial sites, the Internet also contains many sites where young women can give a full account of their own *quinceañeras* and display their photos, which are all presented with great pride. Some use the Internet to thank their parents or family for their "unforgettable" *quinceañera*.

Apart from these personal sites and web pages, there are also other sites which urge girls to celebrate their *quinceañera*. For instance, on the Chaffey High School's web site, female students of Latin background are encouraged, "If you have a Hispanic heritage, have reached the age of 15, and have maintained your virginity, it's an honor your parents celebrate."[5] I even came across sites that hold contests for the most beautiful *quinceañera*, or for the most touching party reports. There are even *quinceañera* Planner Worksheets with a complete itinerary for "a perfect celebration." A site devoted to "Planning Your Special Day" offers a list of "Special Traditions for Your Quinceañera." The obviously huge marketability of the *quince años* celebration "as traditionally celebrated" is clear evidence that the idea and the activity fulfil certain needs in the population.

On the basis of approximately 200 sites I visited in June 2002, I have been able to distinguish at least two patterns. The first concerns the transformation of the celebration of the quinceañera in two ways. Firstly, the vast commercialisation of the fiesta is striking. It feeds an entire industry of dressmakers, florists, photographers, choreographers and event organisers, who are kept busy serving the needs of this market. Secondly, a comparison with the *quinceañeras* in Mexico demonstrates that many new elements have been added to the celebration as it is commonly given in the United States. Three elements recur very frequently. It is depicted as customary, firstly, for the mother of the quinceañera to place the tiara upon her daughter's head, secondly, for the father to change her flat shoes to high heels before or after the first dance, and thirdly for the quinceañera to give her porcelain doll to her youngest sister In itself, the transformation of the celebration due to commercialisation and the addition of certain elements is in itself not surprising. These changes merely show that the quinceañera is very much alive. It may be regarded as astounding for those who have a static, bounded, and hence essentialist conception of culture and cultural phenomena. However, any attempt at establishing traditionality or of freezing the performance of the quinceañera in any such way would deny the dynamic and fluid nature of cultural performances in general. All celebrations of the quinceañera (in the United States as in Mexico) and the communities who celebrate this fiesta are socio-historically (and politically) constructed and in constant flux.

Constructing new boundaries

More important than the performance of the *quinceañera* itself is the symbolic meaning it has for people. In the first part of this essay I stated that the ritual of the quince años enacts and celebrates the creation and re-creation of a gendered sexual identity. The Internet sites from the U.S., however, show that Mexican and other Latino transmigrants celebrate the passage into adulthood of young women also as a way of holding on to their cultural roots. A lot of sites represent the celebration of the *quince años* as a quest for and (re-)creation of a cultural tradition.

The Internet sites that urge girls to celebrate the event emphasise the value of the *quinceañera* as a way to transform them and physically connect them with their Mexican or Hispanic cultural heritage. As such, for a Hispanic-American girl to celebrate her fifteenth birthday in this manner is depicted by these Internet sites as "a way to declare your heritage to the world and to say goodbye to your girlhood." Some sites claim that the *quinceañera* is a Mexican tradition with historical roots in Aztec and Mayan culture, while others appeal to the surfer's sentimentality to "Do your *quinceañera* the Mexican way."

Marcela, a divorced mother of two daughters born in Oakland, California, tried to teach them about their heritage. She loves cooking Mexican meals and speaks Spanish at home. But as her girls grew older, they preferred to speak English. She took her daughters several times to Mexico and showed them the celebration of the *quinceañera*. However, Jennifer and Christina were not impressed. After they moved to Hampton Roads, Virginia, Marcela gave up on her dreams of one day giving them a *quinceañera*. Besides, this event is very rarely seen in Virginia, which in 1989 had only a small Hispanic population. But as more Hispanics moved to Hampton Roads, *quinceañeras* grew more common and more popular. Two years ago, her daughters gave their *quinceañeras* on the same day. Marcela's ex-husband shouldered his responsibility and took care of all the financial costs. Jennifer and Christina prepared themselves seriously, for they had become aware of the importance of the celebration. They practised their Spanish and took special classes at the Catholic Church.[6]

Young women like Jennifer and Christina, who commonly write about their *quinceañeras* on the Internet, describe not only their discovery of their gender identity through the *quinceañera*, but also of their cultural and ethnic identity. The same holds true for those who have attended a *quinceañera*. A mother once explains, almost with embarrassment, "I did not grow up with my culture...so it was an educating and enlightening event for me to have experienced my daughter's quinces [sic]. I learned a lot about myself, my values, my culture, my faith, and the value of the family unit."[7]

The *quinceañera* brings families together as it is common for guests to come from all over the U.S., or Latin America. José Armas and his daughter travelled 2000 miles to be part of the *quinceañera* of his niece Felicia. He values the celebration of *quinceñeras* in the U.S. in that "[t]hey symbolize the transition of the older to the young generation – now becoming known as the "ñ" generation; of bonds of family and friends. There is the passing of knowledge and heritage, like a bridge from the past to the present with a promise for the future."[8]

Conclusions

Even though the rite of passage is present in the descriptions of the *quinceañeras*, for the participants the celebration is often more about reaffirming – sometimes even reinventing – their culture. And for migrants who "live lives across borders," the fiesta evokes multiple identities (Grillo 2002:136). As such, the ritual of the quince años enacts and celebrates the (re-) creation of not only gender, sexual and religious identities, but also of cultural and ethnic identities. The *quinceañera* is an event that transforms a girl into a young (though as yet incomplete) woman; but for those who live in the United States, it is also an event that makes a girl into a Mexican woman (cf. Davalos 1996).

It is not only Mexican-American girls, however, who remake themselves through this cultural practice. The celebration of the *quinceañera* in the United States encompasses the presentation of families that claim to belong to a particular community that respect their cultural heritage. In other words, the *quinceañera* is an event that turns migrants of Mexican descent into *Mexican*-Americans or *Latino*-Americans. Thus, the fiesta is also an act of community building, for celebrating the *quinceañera* is an active construction of a community's culture.

According to Cantú, the celebration has enjoyed resurgence and is alive and well, not just along the border. She suggests that the spread of the celebration among Chicano and immigrant Latino groups in the U.S. could be attributed to their growing strength of Hispanic cultural nationalism in recent decades. The border communities, she argues, "continue a tradition that stretches back into our cultural history as conquered region whose population refuses to abandon its traditions and customs" (1996:18). This element of the *quinceañera* as an act of resistance is also asserted by Davalos in her work on Chicago as a place where "*mexicanas* encounter political and social institutions that promote, organize, and normalize assimilation through the erasure of their history or appropriation of their experience" (1996:123). Against this background, the *quinceañera* may even be viewed as having become a political act of cultural and ethnic affirmation (not unlike the return of many so-called "modern" Muslim women in the West to wearing head scarves). Hence, invitations for a celebration of a *quinceañera* become "a call to alliance," to which people throughout the land give ear (de Ruijter 2000:19).

It is also important to note, however, that culture construction is given impetus from outside the community as from within. In this case, one must also recognise the important impact of changing national values over the past two decades, if not more. The American ideal of the "melting pot" has gradually shifted to the idea of cultural diversity within the unifying and overarching fold of American patriotism. Hence, it's now OK to call oneself a *Mexican*-American. In addition, the growing political importance of the Hispanic-American community in recent decades has not escaped the notice of politicians, and this in turn has helped fuel and to vindicate a resurgence of pride in being an American of Hispanic background. Furthermore, it is also important to recognize (though seldom examined by anthropologists) the overriding impact that popular youth culture has on the attitudes and opinions of the young. Hispanic role models have emerged in the hugely popular figures of such pop entertainers as Jennifer Lopez, Shakira and Marc Anthony, and the valoration of the Latin "Other" has been hugely boosted by actors like Antonio Banderas and Salma Hayek. Moreover, other non-Hispanic role models from youth pop culture may also have influenced a change in values of young Americans. In the age of AIDs, a role model like Brittney Spears is able to articulate the virtue of remaining a virgin until one is married, without dire consequences to her popularity and her image as a sex symbol. Thus, one is left with the interesting question of to what extent the growing popularity of virtue-emphasising rites like the *quinceañera* has (also) been influenced by the changing values and definitions of what is "cool" in popular youth culture.

Thus the image emerges of a situation in which the ritual of the *quinceañera* obeys to the drive to reaffirm Hispanic identity and mark community boundaries in a societal context that has become more receptive to such attempts. The issue of the reaffirmation of ethnic boundaries has received much attention in recent debates on globalisation, localisation and transnationalism (e.g. de Ruijter 2000a:14-15; de Ruijter 2000b:32-37). In this paper I have tried to demonstrate that the role of gender has often been neglected in these discussions. Ritual practices like the *quinceañera* play a crucial role in the making of ethnic identity. Different feminist authors have observed that in many cultures group identities are constructed through rules for women (Lutz et al. 1995; Saharso 2000). The growing popularity of the *quinceañera* in the U.S. seems to confirm this. At the same time, this process contributes to the reproduction of gender identities according to hegemonic "traditional" patriarchal rules and regulations.

Christina and Jennifer, the two sisters from Virginia who celebrated their *quinceañera* together, learnt Spanish only so they would be able to declare before God and the priest that they promised to remain virgins until their wedding day. However, Maria, another girl, describes her experience as follows: "The only thing I didn't like was my escort. I had to come out with my brother because he's the only boy in the family and the oldest. So, unfortunately I couldn't come out with the guy of my dreams." These and other testimonies illustrate that the reaffirmation of cultural boundaries can coincide with the subordination of the desires and needs of girls to those of the family and the Catholic Church.

Notes

1   The origins of the *quinceañera* are unclear, and there are differing views on the subject. Some trace the history and origins of the rite to pre-Columbian civilizations. Others trace it back to European roots because elements of the *quince años* ritual are similar to those found in French and Spanish court dances. But ultimately, these theories are all just conjectures as there is no conclusive evidence to suggest any particular root origin for this fiesta (Cantú 1996; Davalos 1996).
2   For this part of the paper I will draw heavily on Steenbeek (1995).
3   WWW.GALEGROUP.COM/FREE_RESOURCES/CHH/ACTIVITIES/QUINCEANERA.HTM
4   WWW.SANCHEZ-ASSOCIATES.COM/BARBIE.HTML
5   WWW.CHAFFEY.ORG/STUDENTS/TIGERRAG/1998-09/QUINCE.HTML
6   HTTP://CARIBOU.CC.TRINCOLL.EDU/~APEREZ/QUINC.HTM
7   HTTP:///WWW.HISPANICONLINE.COM/1STYLES/FAMILY/WINNER.HTML
8   HTTP://WWW. IMDIVERSITY.COM – Felicia's Quinceañera

Bibliography

Beck, Lois, and Nikki Keddie, eds. 1978. *Women in the Muslim World.* Cambridge, Mass. and London, England: Harvard University Press.

Cantú, Norma (n.d.). *La Quinceañera: Towards an Ethnographic Analysis of a Life Cycle Ritual.* HTTP://COLFA.UTSA.EDU/CANTU/QUINCEAERA.HTML

Davalos, Karen Mary. 1996. La Quinceañera: Making Gender and Ethnic Identities. Frontiers. *A Journal of Women's Studies* 16(2/3): 101-128.

de Ruijter, Arie. 2000a. *De multiculturele arena.* Tilburg: Katholieke Universiteit Brabant.

de Ruijter, Arie. 2000b. Globalization. A challenge to the social sciences. In F. Schuurman, ed. *Globalization and Development Studies,* pp. 31-43. Amsterdam: Thela Thesis.

Fried, M.N., and M.H. Fried. 1980. *Transitions: Four Rituals in Eight Cultures.* New York: Norton.

Grillo, Ralph. 2002. Transnational migration, multiculturalism, and development. *Focaal. European Journal of Anthropology* 40:135-148.

Lutz, Helma, Ann Phoenix, and Nira Yuval-Davis, eds. 1995. *Crossfires: nationalism, racism, and gender in Europe.* East Haven: Pluto Press.

Malkin, Victoria. 1999. La reproducción de relaciones de género en la comunidad de migrantes mexicanos en New Rochelle, Nueva York. In G. Mummert, *Fronteras fragmentadas,* pp. 475-496. Zamora: El Colegio de Michoacán.

Okin, Susan. 1999. Is multiculturalism bad for women? In J. Cohen et al, eds., *Is multiculturalism bad for women?* pp. 9-24. Princeton: Princeton University Press.

Pomata, Gianna. 1987. De geschiedenis van vrouwen: een kwestie van grenzen. In *Socialisties-Feministiese Teksten* 10:61-113.

Saharso, Sawitri. 2000. *Feminisme versus Multiculturalisme?* Utrecht: Forum.

Steenbeek, Gerdien. 1996. *Vrouwen op de drempel. Gender en moraliteit in een Mexicaanse provinciestad.* Amsterdam: Thela Publishers.

Turner, V.W. 1974. *The Ritual Process.* Harmondsworth, England: Penguin.

11

Cultural Identity and Psychosocial Traits in Regionalism

Menno Vellinga

Introduction

The subject of regionalism has been a hot topic already for quite some time. All over Europe, national states appear to be giving in to regions that claim their independence from the state center, emphasizing in the process a cultural identity that in their view sets them clearly apart from the center and from neighboring populations. In Eastern Europe the disintegration of the socialist regimes left an economic, political and ideological vacuum that was rapidly filled by movements that mobilized on the basis of regionalist sentiments that under previous regimes had often been violently suppressed. But also in other parts of Europe, regionalism has come to play an important role. Spain represents a very interesting case (Borja de Riquer 1994). The granting of regional administrative autonomy to the Catalans and the Basques after the demise of the Franco regime motivated other regions to claim similar status. Furthermore, these developments created work for anthropologists as regional administrations began to enlist their services in a search for a specific regional identity that would support the claims for administrative autonomy.

In Africa and Asia, regionalism – most often religiously and/or ethnically inspired – has been rampant. In Latin America, regionalism has always been an important phenomenon. It had its roots in the centrifugal tendencies that resulted from the bureaucratic-patrimonial organization of the colonial state, although it acquired in many instances a different cultural lading in subsequent periods.

Regions and regionalism

Regions are mostly products of history. They are "processual" spaces that have emerged over the course of time through the projects of various economic and social actors seeking to secure a territory of their own. These spaces cannot always be defined in a strictly geographical sense. The boundaries are often not clearly delimited and may shift with the changes in the development process. The formation of these regions results from the development of material interests, and of related social classes and power relations in a socio-spatial context. This process will often also involve a formation of communities of belief and identity that we mentioned above. In turn, such communities of belief and identity tend to turn the region into an object of identification, and a context or arena for competing loyalties to one's local community, social class or nation state.[1] These sentiments and identifications can be mobilized and manipulated by regional power-holders, which has been a frequent historical phenomenon as exemplified by Northern Italy, Catalonia and Basque Country. In this way, cultural-ideological complexes may become a driving force in regional development projects. They may also 'style' the region's response to globalizing tendencies and projects of economic integration, in addition to forming a crystallization point for movements emphasizing regional identities.

The discussion on the phenomenon of regionalism has received inputs from debates on national or social character or identity, national stereotypes and the like, issues that have been suspect for a long time. They have often been characterized by a reactionary tinge. Moreover in the 1930s, these notions were incorporated in theories of society with racist underpinnings. Consequently, in subsequent decades it was often difficult to debate the subject, let alone research it. Yet, the presence of such phenomena and their importance in conditioning human behavior cannot be denied.

There is something "in the air," so to speak, that one may call national, regional or social character, labels that we stick to complexes of norms, values, institutional structures, behavioral patterns and the like, and that differ from one country or region to another. Notions that the people of different countries or regions share certain distinctive psychological and or behavioral characteristics are common. These observations figure dominantly as stereotypes in "small-talk," but it is obvious that these often can make a claim to a reality that supersedes that level. One does not always have to go so far as to assume similarities in personality structure among people sharing a territory. It is easier to accept the influences of culture on cognition and perception. We know that every culture – including the regional ones – has a different "tuning." They model behavior and prescribe patterns that make people behave differently from others; and that, we could say, is what gives them a distinct "social character." Although on an impressionistic level these phenomena are easily observable, it has been notoriously difficult to show their presence in a systematic and scientific way. We still lack a methodology to research it adequately, and a paradigm to explain it consistently. Through the years, the explanatory factors for national or regional cognitive and behavioral differences have varied from environmental ones, to ones based on genetic or 'racial', religious, ethnic, economic, social-historical, or social-cultural factors. Several of these would probably need a simultaneous place in any explanatory scheme, but this is rarely done. Anthropologists, sociologists, and social-psychologists have generally treated factors that deal with the relationship between individual and society in terms of basic personality patterns or as culture-personality relationships. They have focused on the way society's norms and values, its family structure, basic institutions, have contributed to the development of patterns of personality traits that "style" the behavior of people. Researchers of social character have often assumed congruence between these norms, values, psychosocial traits, and the more general socio-cultural environment. They have done so in the more conventional culture and personality studies, but also in the "national character" studies in which basic and modal personality studies were applied to the territory of the national state.

Recently, cross-cultural comparative studies have become increasingly popular (Hofstede 1980, also Williams et al. 2002) based on trait lists of customs, researched according to each country and compared against the date for others. The analyses of such studies are characteristically rather general, and remind one of the studies based on Parsons's pattern variables and that were popular in the 1960s. The studies using the individualism-collectivism continuum, which we find commonly used in studies of the Japanese idiosyncrasy, are cases in point. The idea of a one-to-one correspondence between a type of personality structure (ideal, basic or modal) and a culture or society has been rejected, and the ideas of Ruth Benedict, who tried to demonstrate the isomorphism of cultural patterns with personality structures, were abandoned. Cultural factors, it has been recognized, are not the only ones influencing personality. It is true that certain cultures support traits and patterns that are discouraged by others, but we are dealing with very broad and general differences between one society and the other in which many other factors are involved.

Region and cultural identity: Northern Mexico

"The behavioral differences which can be noted between the people in regions like Jalisco, the North, Veracruz, Oaxaca or Yucatán should be systematized by some learned persons who would be able to assemble the data into a psychological map of Mexico."

José E. Iturriaga

We will now explore a few of the aforementioned notions in a general discussion of regionalism in Northern Mexico. This is an example of a region where the combination of location, economic activities, history and cultural patterns have produced a very distinctive complex of values, norms, and beliefs that has 'styled' behavioral action, and, at times, has even inspired collective action (Carr 1973; Vanderwood 1992: 167-189). Northern Mexico presents an excellent case for the study of the relationship between cultural identity and the role of psychosocial traits and behavioral patterns in regionalism.

The strong differences in cultural patterns between regions has fascinated researchers for a long time ever since the "culture and personality" studies of the 1950s and 1960s.[2] The object of research was the way in which regionally distinct cultural traits have become "roles" that over time have become integrated into personality structures. These studies produced regional patterns of distribution of the traits that model behavior. However, these often appeared to be stereotyped, and the results of the studies are sometimes quite inconsistent. For instance, "national character" research in Mexico has indicated that the *Norteños* tend to picture themselves as serious, hardworking, straightforward, brave, aggressive, loyal, sincere and entrepreneurial people. When distinguishing themselves from their neighbors, the *Norteños* view the *Costeños* as lighthearted, good humored, open, communicative, humorous, brave, but also as chaotic, corrupt and bad-mannered. The people of Central Mexico were pictured quite negatively, as fanatic, egoistic, exploitative, malicious and abusive. This image is undoubtedly part of the generally negative view of the national political center, which forms part of the regionalist sentiments in the North (Bejar Navarro et al. 1986, 1988, 1990, 1997).

The self-images that are mentioned here have been researched by way of rather superficial attitude and opinion studies. Their methodology – dominated by large-scale survey research and scaling techniques – leaves much to be desired. Yet, as much as these results can be criticized, there are some psychosocial peculiarities – and I limit myself to the North of Mexico – that can be observed in the behavioral patterns of the population, and that resemble some of the characteristics mentioned above. In this respect, the *Norteños* are different, as VanderWood (1992) noted. This is easily observed but difficult to explain (Vanderwood 1992: 169). The question arises whether one group has modeled one's own behavior in order to conform to the regional stereotypes. In any case, it is obvious that these regionalisms – including positive auto-stereotyping – have grown within a cultural complex that has been internalized, has been styling behavior patterns, and (as in the case of Northern Mexico) has been producing ide- ologies that have lent themselves to manipulation by regional bourgeoisies, and have even served as the cement of multi-class regional movements that support the repro- duction of the phenomenon (De la Peña 1981).

How has this happened? Obviously, in the Mexican North, socio-cultural institu- tions have, through history and societal development, evolved that have left their imprint on the attitudes and behavioral patterns of the inhabitants (Tinker Salas 1988). An inquiry into this phenomenon should take its point of departure in the study of the heritage left by the colonial regime and societal development in the 19th century. The main thrust of the Spanish colonial effort was directed at Central Mexico. Most of the population in those days lived along the Guadalajara-Mexico-Puebla-Veracruz axis, where the activities in the economic, political, social and cultural spheres were con- centrated. In the second half of the 19th century, Oaxaca (birthplace of Juarez and Por- firio Díaz) emerged as a new regional focus. The North, however, lagged behind. At the end of the 19th century the region around Monterrey experienced rapid develop- ment. But the significant transformation in the status of Mexico's outlying Northern areas did not occur until the Mexican Revolution, when there emerged a number of revolutionary *caudillos* who were characterized by "radicalism and an anti-clerical affil- iation, [by] vigorous nationalism bordering on xenophobia and by an highly creative opportunism" (Carr 1973: 320).

The northern provinces of New Spain were immense, and were situated within a harsh and inhospitable geographical area. Communication with the other areas in Cen- tral Mexico was made difficult by the geography, and the region occupied a marginal position within the Spanish colonial empire. The North was integrated into the colonial state through colonization, rather than through conquest *(conquista)*. The absence of a large sedentary Indian population there made it a region of Spanish and *mestizo* settle- ment. The region counted a reasonably large nomadic Indian population, though, whose hostility towards the colonization process served to discouraged large-scale settlement. Its most important urban settlement – Monterrey – was founded in 1596, in the fertile *Valle de la Extramadura,* which was seen as the ideal area to provision the silver mining regions of Zacatecas-Durango-San Luis Potosi with agricultural products. The valley was originally colonized by Spanish settlers who came from the Iberian region with the same name, located along the border between Spain and Portugal. The colonization of the valley encountered considerable problems due to the continuous raids mounted by bands of nomadic Indians. Its main importance was agricultural, and the mining activities that took place in the region were small-scale. Societal development was quite different from the one that we find in southern and central Mexico. The general shortage of labor meant a softening or even disappearance of institutions that in other regions had bred servility and dependence in the population. The geography of the region, the enormous distances and the isolation it often implied, furthered an independent mentality just as it had done in the frontier areas of the American West (Carr 1973).

These characteristics, combined with the scarcity of the population, meant that the colonial government had difficulties in asserting its full jurisdiction over the region. Further to the North, the provinces operated in a situation of semi-desolation. The 2,205,639 km^2 which were ceded to the United States by the Treaty of Guadalupe (1848) were, at the time, inhabited by an estimated 75,000 *mestizos* and some 250,000 Indians.

From its foundation in 1596 until the first half of the 18th century, the *Nuevo Reino de León* was ruled by governors who took their orders from the central colonial government. They were assigned the tasks of expanding the colony to the North, and supporting the interests of the cattle ranchers and mine-owners. The character of the colonization process and the incessant war with the Indians would have a great influence on the social and cultural make-up of the region. These influences became even more important after the Spanish occupation of territories in the Northeast (Texas) in order to block French penetration. Mining activities along the Center-Northeast axis of Mexico also helped to stimulate cattle ranching and meat production in this region. In turn, cattle ranching became instrumental in the growth of the *latifundia* in the region, which were mostly owned by absentee landlords.

The reforms of the Bourbons at the end of the 18th century enabled the colonial government to increase internal production, to accelerate the establishment of new settlements, and to increase its income through taxes and other sources. These changes modernized the colonial economy. However, they also led to a greater emphasis on the centralization of political power and a greater concentration in the economic sphere. These tendencies prepared the groundwork for the political conflicts in the 19th century between centralism and federalism. In the far-away Northern provinces, the cattle haciendas responded in the first instance to local interests, rather than to those of the absentee landlords, most of whom lived 800 km away, south of the *Nuevo Reino.* Particularly active was contraband trade, which provisioned the mining areas while avoiding the monopoly of Veracruz. There was a general expansion of commercial activities. The great herds of sheep stimulated the wool trade up North. Horse trade was carried on with San Antonio, Texas and with Louisiana.

There was also violence. The expansion of the cattle ranching and the commercial activities along the Northern frontier generated constant conflicts with the Indian tribes that roamed the region. Settlers, soldiers, and traders took to capturing, enslaving, or annihilating Indians they came across. By the provisions made in the article in the Law of the Indies, which permitted the enslavement only of those Indians who had engaged in war and aggression against the Spaniards, Indian slaves – the *Chichimecas* of the *Nuevo Reino de León* – were sold in the mining regions of Zacatecas or Sombrerete, in Puebla, or even in Mexico City. However, the Indian population of this region was not incorporated into the *hacienda* system, as occurred in Central Mexico.

Since the end of the 17th century, there was a gradual flow of regular colonists to the Northern territories. The influx did not merely consist of vagabonds, soldiers of fortune, and of adventurers, as in previous periods. The fertile valleys attracted farmers, and stimulated the rapid growth of small- and medium sized holdings, where maize, grains, and sugarcane were harvested. These settlers were to form the nucleus of a rural middle class, characterized by assertiveness and egalitarianism in thought and action that gave then an idiosyncrasy very different from the population in other areas of Mexico (Vanderwood 1992: 169).

The mining activities in the far North could not compete with those of Zacatecas or San Luis Potosi. For one thing, silver was not found in great quantities. Rather, most of the minerals mined were lead and copper. Lead mined in the region through small-scale mining endeavors was exported to Mazapal, Sombrerete and Zacatecas, or to Parval and San Luis Potosi. The main economic activity in the region remained cattle ranching.

The absenteeism of the landlords meant that the surpluses that the sector generated benefited only the *criollo* aristocracy of New Spain; that is to say, the owners of the *latifundia* in the region. This specific pattern of landownership – in combination with the modest possibilities for the development of mining – accounts for why there did not emerge in this region a class of the well to do and the powerful, living in the region and spending their riches there, as did in Zacatecas, Guanajuato, Taxco, San Luis Potosi, Sombrerete.

The reforms of the Bourbons brought important changes in the colonial economy, principally in terms of greater possibilities for furthering local interests in the cattle ranching and commercial sectors. These reforms likewise created the possibilities for a modest accumulation of capital by local and regional groups, beginning a process that would pick up steam after independence.

The Catholic Church, which had such strong identification with the Spanish colonial effort, had a weak presence in the North. Its control over lands and mines was never so pronounced as it was in the South and in the Center. In the North secular ownership prevailed. It was not until 1777 that a bishopric was grated to the region, in Linares. This was moved to Monterrey in 1787. Not until then did the region feel a marked influence of the Church.

Liberalism had always been strong in the North. The conservative alliance between a subservient Indian population and the Catholic Church, which was so typical in other parts of the colonial empire, did not come into being in the North. Even today, it is still very common to see in the central plaza of the Northern villages a Masonic temple – a meeting place for the Liberals – right next to a Catholic Church.

Thus, a society of a rather idiosyncratic nature – at least when compared to the rest of the Republic – by the start of the 19th century. In the rest of the Republic, its inhabitants were associated with traits generally recognized as typical of the *Norteño* "personality." The region's conditioning factors include:

- the characteristics of the process of colonization, instead of *conquista*, leading to the establishment of a frontier society. The violent encounters with the nomadic Indians led to violently independent, "trigger-happy" orientations similar to those found in the American West;
- its distance from the colonial center, its complex geography, and its lesser economic significance as compared with other regions of Spain's New World empire. This meant that the full weight of the Spanish colonial administration (including the influence of the Catholic Church) was not brought to bear in this northern region. The large landholdings were governed by absentee landlords who did not leave an imprint on the region, unlike in other parts of Mexico where their presence – along with that of the colonial administrators, military men, top clergy – led to the emergence of an aristocratic culture superimposed upon a deeply hierarchical society (Mannheim 1956). The other economic activities in the region were connected with the interests of local ranchers, miners, and medium- and small-sized agriculturists. This peculiar economy and society generated a strong sense of individualism and independence in local affairs. This historical experience meant that major factors were lacking which in other regions had promoted the evolution of economic, social, and ideological structures that, later in history, limited the possibilities for development;
- its proximity to the United States and the development stimuli resulting from that location. During the Porfiriato period (1876-1910) major development in the sectors of agriculture, mining, industry, and in communications changed the face of Northern Mexico. Large-scale agricultural property burgeoned; big mining projects were exploited; a railway network was constructed which linked Northern Mexico with the United States. Given its characteristics, the region easily adopted capitalism, and the region's proximity to the United States gave an important boost to its capitalist development. In the region of *Nuevo León,* the foundations were laid, with important politico-institutional support, for a spectacular process of industrialization that would contribute to the formation of an economic and political bastion that, in later years, would challenge the central government for power.

In the case of Northern Mexico, "nationalism," defined as a sentiment of "nationhood," including an identification and readiness to defend the perceived entity of "nation," does not appear to have been strong enough to supersede regionalist sentiments (Vanderwood 1992: 169). Neither did the development of a national capitalist market manage to substitute national interests for regional ones. This situation remained relatively unchanged until the last quarter of the 20e century. In the 1970s, however, massive socioeconomic changes altered the socio-demographic map of Mexico (Monsivais 1992: 248-252). The intensified and combined processes of migration and urbanization changed the composition of the population in the North and integrated zones that were once isolated into a wider regional framework. Regionalisms consequently changed in their content. Increasing development brought American-inspired lifestyles within reach, certainly for the expanding middle class. However, the dialectical nature of such cultural processes has again become apparent. The constant pressure of American influences has strengthened the trend towards an affirmation of regional identities; and in this aspect the population, despite its heterogeneity in origin, has increasingly come to share the same regional identity. What is typically *Norteño*-Mexican is not a pure product of the "culture industry," as Carlos Monsiváis maintains (Monsivais 1992: 250-251). That thesis negates the strength of the tendency to defend *lo regional* and to develop counterpoints against the socio-cultural pressures emanating from the other side of the border.

In this process of defense and resistance against what is experienced as totalizing or homogenizing processes, the *Norteño* personality – fruit of the internalization of beliefs of regionalism's higher values and norms – may also spread among those segments of the Northern Mexican population with a migratory lifestyle. The fact that this personality, in its dominant psychosocial traits, agrees with the basic elements of the capitalist mentality is an additional element that explains the success with which the North has adapted to processes emanating from North America by integrating "foreign" elements into their cultural framework while maintaining a strong, unique cultural identity.

Conclusion

When discussing the question of regionalisms and cultural identity, and their impact on the sense of self, what comes to mind is Eric van Young's remark which he made in reference to the phenomenon of regions, but which is equally applicable to the subjects that we have dealt with in this essay: "they are like love, they are difficult to describe, but we know them when we see them" (Van Young 1992: 3).

Northern Mexico offers a good example of the importance of regionalist value and norm complexes in forming self-image, and in "styling" behavior patterns. This cultural dynamics has led to significant regionally-specific social and socio-cultural practices. In some cases, it has also played an influential role in the purposive politically significant actions of regional power holders that are directed toward the development potential of the region and the possibilities of its realization within an international context (Vellinga 2000). The dynamics of the *ambito regional* – or sphere of influence – of the North Mexican industrial city of Monterrey is clearly a case in point. Here, the mobilizations in support of regional projects have often been community-oriented, and have ordinarily operated across class lines using collective "self-other" representations strongly based on *Norteño* sentiments and identities. These projects have often been politicized by regional and local power holders in the North, who have been active in these mobilizations of the various sectors of society while also meeting the challenges of the globalizing processes that have intensified under the impact of NAFTA. This phenomenon has shown that regions and localities are not just passively producing responses to these influences, but actively reworking them, or reintegrating them selectively into their regional culture in combination with regional elements. The *Norteño* complex has shown itself to be multidimensional: it has facilitated functioning under capitalism, but it has also done so while emphasizing its own socio-cultural idiosyncrasy. In the course of this, it has resisted the cultural invasion that accompanies globalization. This process has underlined the importance of cultural differences in things that people consider to be psychologically important. Ideas concerning self-image – even when stereotyped – are part of these differences and remain important in the mobilization – and often also subsequent politicization – of regionalist sentiments

Notes

1. The theme of regionalist identities and its relation to phenomena of self image and social character has been studied in reference to the Mexican North by R. Bejar Navarro and Manuel Capello (1986; 1988; 1990; 1997).
2. Any social psychology textbook will provide a long list of such studies; an effort to put these studies on more modern footing, is presented in the studies by Bejar Navarro and Capello (1986; 1988; 1990; 1997).

Bibliography

Bejar Navarro, R. & M. Capello. 1986. 'Diagnostico de la Identidad y Carácter Nacional de México', in: *Revista de Psicología Social*, 1(2):286-312.

Bejar Navarro, R. & M. Capello. 1988. *Identidad y Caracter Nacionales en Cd. Juárez, Chihuahua y El Paso*, Austin: Center for Mexican Studies, University of Texas.

Bejar Navarro, R. & M. Capello. 1990. *Identidad y Caracter Nacionales en el Centro-Norte de México*, México D.F.: Comisión Nacional para la Cultura y las Artes.

Bejar Navarro, R. & M. Capello. 1997. *Identidad Nacional y Caracter en Socio-Politico en el Norte de México*, México, D.F.: CONACYT.

Borja de Riquer i Permanyer. 1994. *Nacionalidades y Regiones en la España Contemporanea*, Barcelona: Universidad Autónoma de Barcelona, mimeo.

Carr, B.. 1973. 'Las Peculiaridades del Norte Mexicano', in *Historia Mexicana*, 22:320-346.

de la Peña. G. 1981. 'Los Estudios Regionales y la Antropología Social en México', in *Relaciones*, 8:43-93.

Hofstede. G. 1980. *Culture's Consequences: International Differences Work-Related Values*, Newbury Park: SAGE.

Mannheim. K.. 1956. *Essays on the Sociology of Culture*, pp. 206-239. London: Routledge & Kegan Paul.

Monsiváis, C. 1992. 'Just Over that Hill', Notes on Centralism and Regional Culture', in: Van Young, *Mexico's Regions: Comparative History and Development*, pp. 248-254. San Diego: Center for U.S.-Mexican Studies, University of California.

Tinker Salas, M, 1988. Under the Shadow of the Eagle: Sonora, The Making of a Norteño Culture, San Diego, PhD-Dissertation, University of California at San Diego.

Van Young, E. 1992. 'Introduction: Are Regions Good to Think?', in: Van Young, *Mexico's Regions: Comparative History and Development,* pp. 1-36. San Diego: Center for U.S.-Mexican Studies, University of California.

Vanderwood, P. 1992. 'Region and Rebellion: the Case of Papigochic' in E. van Young ed., *Mexico's Regions: Comparative History and Development,* pp. 167-189. San Diego: Center for U.S.-Mexican Studies, University of California.

Vellinga, M. 2000. 'Toward an Actor-Oriented Approach in the Study of the Globalization Process', in M. Vellinga, ed., *The Dialectics of Globalization; Regional Responses to World Economic Processes,* pp. 281-292. Boulder: Westview Press.

Williams, J.E., R. C. Satterwhite & J. L. Saiz. 2002. *The Importance of Psychological Traits. A Cross Cultural Study,* New York: Kluwer Academic Publishers.

12

Beau Hunks
Musicians Making their Lives
Spanish Arawak in the Northwest District of
Guyana

Fabiola Jara

Las Mañanitas

The morning haze was still hanging above the river when we boarded the 25 h.p. motorboat. The whole family was at the beach in their best Sunday clothes. The girls sat at the far end of the boat wearing white satin laces in their hair and starched, pink organdie dresses. The boys who were helping to accommodate our luggage, were having difficulties in keeping their neatly ironed trousers dry as they jumped from boat to boat. We were leaving Santa Rosa. This last trip to Charity and Georgetown would end my month-long period of fieldwork in the Northwest District.

I suspect that Nicolas was hiding, waiting, until we were all aboard. I had been looking out for him so I could say one last goodbye, and I was very disappointed not to see him there. He appeared on the beach at the very last minute, with his violin, playing a beautiful farewell serenade.

Nicolas had planned to travel with us to Charity. But the night before, we heard that the owner of the boat, his son-in-law, refused to take him along as a passenger. Obviously, Nicolas was very upset by the situation. He wanted to show us La Lancha, the spot where the battle between the old people and the Venezuelan patrol boat had taken place.

The entire episode of that battle may have lasted about 15 minutes, but it enveloped the whole of my fieldwork experience in Santa Rosa,[1] the eventual focus of which was to find a satisfactory answer to the question: How do these people that call themselves Spanish Arawak relate to Spanish?

My attention was drawn to various types of names, of villages like the Santa Rosa mission, and family names like Mendonza, Rosa, Castro. I also came to concentrate on the fact that crucial incidents in the epic narratives appeared to be in described in Spanish, like *el poste* (the border marker), and *La Lancha* (the deportation episode that leads to the definitive settlement of the old people across the Guyanese border). The titles of the songs were also all in Spanish: *"Las muchachas de Moruca"* (Morucan girls), as were the names of dances like *Joropo* (waltz rhythm), *la culebra* (the snake), *el gavilán* (the chicken hawk), *la sapa* (the she-frog). The elocutions intercepted in narratives and songs or during dances were also expressed in Spanish: *"vamos compadre tómese paiwari, baile la mari-mari"* ("come on godfather drink your beer, dance the Maria Mari"). I also discovered a vast repertoire of Spanish jokes, which are customarily told by the musicians during feasts. I got the impression that while English was the language of everyday life, most of the important names and a large repertoire of expressive elocutions were in Spanish. For all I heard I could not make out how the Spanish Arawak were different from the rest of the villagers. Nor did I understand what kept them different other than their use of Spanish words and elocutions. What is in a word? To whom could I direct my questions? I was advised to enquire from Nicolas; he could be the right person to talk about these "Spanish" matters, so people told me. He knew the stories and the songs, and he was also the eldest member of the Mendonza family in the village.

My encounter with this singer had, like everything that had to do with him, the air of a dramatic performance. In answer to my message asking if he would talk with me about Spanish Arawak tales and music, he wrote back that he would be at home the following morning after breakfast. As I walked down the path under a bamboo avenue I heard violin music. I followed the sound and found Nicolas sitting in his veranda. He looked at me, smiled, and continued playing until he finished the melody. His appearance was just as fascinating as his personality: blue jeans and a worn out short sleeved red T-shirt; immense, black Nike shoes that were too large for his feet; a black sailor kepi. "This is the Mari-Mari tune you will hear all over the Moruca and far over de Venezuelan border," he told me. "They play it everywhere the same way, *con el violín. Venga cumpa baile el joropo!* [..., like this with the violin. Come on godfather, dance the Joropo!]. This is my music, Spanish Arawak music."

For Nicolas music was his dearest passion; it was his way of life. He has been singing and playing the violin ever since he was a seven-year-old boy. And now in his eighties he never goes to sleep without first playing something. Every morning, just before dawn, the village wakes to hear his violin once again. His farewell serenade expressed the way he felt about goodbyes. Just the night before he told me that considering his age, every time he says goodbye to a person the chances are that he would never live to see him or her again. That last talk with him also concluded a long series of conversations we had had about Spanish Arawak things. In a very short period of time he had shared with me vast repertoire of tales, his personal story with music, and we tape-recorded his songs. The remainder of this essay will attempt to arrive to some understandings of the way Nicolas related to the "Spanish" in Spanish Arawak.

Across the borderline

According to local historians, priests, and teachers who have documented the history of the Santa Rosa Mission since its founding in 1817, the label "Spanish Arawak" refers to a group of people who are the descendants of refugee families that came from Venezuela at the beginning of the nineteenth century. Their main settlement, the village of Santa Rosa, was built over a group of islands in a sand bank, in a wet savannah flooded by the Moruca River.[2] From this perspective Spanish Arawak marks a distinction between Arawak/Lokono, whose grandparents were born in Catholic missions in Venezuelan territory, and those born in Arawak villages on Guyanese territory. This distinction was crucial for the missionary, for the Spanish Arawaks were regarded as "civilized" Christians. One archival source notes:

> Father Hymes paid a visit to Santa Rosa on St. John's day, June 24th 1830....He was impressed by the behaviour and the sobriety of the people and the cleanliness of their homes and persons – the men in their Spanish hats, trousers and loose shirts – the women robed in white with necklaces of coral and silver, their hair neatly dressed with combs tipped with gold. They had well cultivated farms with all sorts of vegetables and poultry. They caught and cured fish. Their only liquor was the juice of the sugar cane (quoted in Atkinson 1990:145).

The Spanish Arawaks became a model for the protectionists, who insisted that with proper guidance Amerindians were capable of learning high moral standards The migrants were at first only reluctantly granted asylum, but later they received land and a Catholic priest was permitted to run the Mission (Menezes 1979: 216).

For a long period the missionaries mediated contacts between the Arawaks and the British colonial administration. This was to change, however, at the end of the ninetieth century, for gold was discovered over a large area along the border. The Northwest territory was claimed by both the Venezuelan State and the British colonial government. The borderline was then renegotiated and redrawn.

The people living along the Moruca River, while not aware of the dispute, were nevertheless deeply affected by the outcome of the negotiations. The new frontier was drawn and the native population in the area were assigned to either nation, according to their adopted language. Colonial history presumes to convey the whole array of experiences of indigenous populations with the colonial powers. In this case, part of the population in the Moruca were assigned to Venezuela on account of the fact that their grandparents had lived in Capuchin Missions before 1817, the year they migrated to Moruca. Within this context an ethnic construct, the "Spanish Arawaks," emerged and was given a heuristic value. However, colonial history and local histories are, in my experience and in that of numerous anthropologists, largely incommensurable. Therefore I suspend judgment on the question of what Spanish Arawak is, and I propose to see how the local histories produced by Morucan musicians offers an alternative, interesting view on what Spanish Arawak can be.

Listening to Nicolas and his fellow musicians it became clear to me that the "Spanish" in Spanish Arawak referred much more to speech than to language, more to narrative than to history. Nicolas is renowned as a storyteller. His narratives have a distinctive rhythm and dramatic punctuation. He has a keen feeling for the phrasing and the climax. What is special about his style is that he uses language shifts to convey meaning and dramatic intensities in his stories. He uses Guyanese English when he recreates the dialogues of daily life, or when he gives rhetorical emphasis; he uses standard English to make explanatory remarks; he lets Spanish characters speak Spanish, and uses Spanish expressions to add passion and whit to his tales. Some short fragments of Nicolas's narrative on the Launch serve to illustrate his style:

> It all happened during the season of the Crab [August-September]. All the people were going out for crab and to bring catfish too. All that was going well, but there was this order that they had to move and they knew nothing about it. The wife and the children, very well, they stayed at the house. The man, he was going for hustle for bring the things for the feast and the other women were going to make the drinks and so. People were to eat crab and to drink. They were preparing for the pai-wari. They were living happy you know. So now. All ain't gone for catch crab. They don't go all of them because them who can't go to catch crab they are going to trap fish and the other make the paiwari, and so on, you know? So that was the mistake they made.

In his introduction Nicolas puts a special emphasis on the *paiwari*. In the narrative this serves various purposes. The first is a rhetorical one, as the *paiwari* sets the mood of the people against the background of the mood of the military for the events to come. It shows his perspective as a storyteller, for Nicolas' own life history is linked to his performances in the *paiwari* feasts. He used to travel from village to village following the festivals. Secondly, the *paiwari* is also a situational device, mentioned in order to distinguish the main characters as Arawak. The information serves also as a counterpoint to the local missionary history, in which the old people are depicted as pious Christians who had abandoned their native festivals. The story goes on:

> *Nicolas:* They came now, those people, the military, who came [from Venezuela]. They had left La Lancha [the boat] at Barabarra, the water was shallow and they came in a small boat to Santa Rosa. So they [the soldiers] came to the beach and they called the people. They don't know about the others that were hustling for the Grabfeast. They [the villagers] fought them. So, the Españoles [the Venezuelan] said, *"si no se va conmigo les doy un tiro. Si tu esposo no está aquí, no importa tu te vienes ya, caramba!"* so they say, "You know your husband is not here but we came for you. So, if you don't go we are going to shoot you."

The story, as told by Nicolas, lasted about one hour. He indulged in the details of daily life, in the extensive dialogues between the characters, and in long descriptions of places and moods. The narrative of the Launch is an epic tale. It does not constitute the social reality of the group, but of a speech style. The tale emits itself as content: the hydride/syncretic quality of the language in which it is told, is the message. The story is a speech event. So too are the musical performances of the Morucan Musicians, as I hope to demonstrate. The repertoires of songs, narratives, jokes, and the short elocutions and some of the names used in Moruca, are the ways in which Spanish is incorporated as part of Morucan life. This Morucan way of relating to Spanish is mainly accomplished by the creative work of musicians like Nicolas and his fellow band members.

Three short musical biographies

The following conversations were tape-recorded in 1994. Nicolas talked with a sense of marvel about how music, the passion of his life, had led him down his life path. Paul Henry, the *shak-shak* man (called *"maracas"* in Spanish) has a similar story to tell. Like Nicolas he is a "professional musician," a title meaning that he could earn his living by playing, and that he had a fairly good reputation in Moruca. Paul is a man of fewer words than Nicolas. A reserved man, he talks easier about things than about himself. His story tells us valuable things about the musicians' scene in Moruca, and about their relationships with the missionary. Justine Josephs, almost as eloquent as Nicolas, is the band's second player. Justine plays the banjo. His life story does not begin but ends in music. Like his buddy Nicolas, Justine is a real *"Beau Hunk,"* an adventurer. He did not settle until he was an "old man" in his mid thirties. His travels, and the fact that he earned his living by joining wood and gold prospectors and border expeditions, are at the root of his friendship with Nicolas and Paul. As musicians, they also have lived "on the road." Justine regrets the fact that not until very late in his life did he get the opportunity – with the help of the right friends – to follow his innate musical inclinations. Only after his marriage and after settling in Santa Rosa did he begin to play music. Through these short biographical descriptions, I intend to show the interplay of individual and collective agencies in the ongoing creation of Spanish Arawak in the Moruca. The life stories of Nicolas and of his musical friends, and a (very limited) sample of their repertoire of songs, are presented below.

Nicolas Mendonza
Ever since the death of his wife in 1984, Nicolas has lived alone in a house some 200 meters from the main family house. From that moment his son-in-law, Adrian Rose, became the head of the family. The family property stands at the Curiapito landing, one of the biggest islands of Santa Rosa. Nicolas eats with the family but spends most of the days visiting his friends Justine and Paul. His eyesight is extremely poor, but he knows the village by heart and goes everywhere by himself. He values his independence, which he can still maintain by working as a musician. He performs frequently at the village feasts and house parties with his band. He is also directing a group of young people who are learning from him the Spanish Arawak dance repertoire.

>   *F:* Tell me Nicolas, how did you get that music in you?
>   *Nicolas:* I born with that. I know because when I hear music... well, it is like it

comes from my own, inside… My father was a musician. He used to play the violin. I used to hear him every morning. And I used to trouble his violin. Once I burst up the string. That day me gone and take the violin. But it burst and I put it down. When daddy came to play again the following day. "Ah, ah, what is wrong man? This thing's burst". He said: *"Uttah, quién tocó el violín?"* [Shit, who touched the violin?]. *"Yo no sé"* [I don't know], said my mother. Oh boy! I stay away from him now and me do something else. But at last me go talking with the old man. "So, it was you, no?" All right, me done it! And I run away. I got me beating now. But, I did it again.

Once me mother tried to help me. She used to carry me to the farm, where we got a tree named hicha tree. The skin of the tree curls up. Me are going to take one hicha skin and me going to bore four holes and... String no there! Me mother got origa [domestic cotton species] thread. Me gone at me mother where she got the cotton... Me got two threads and upon this: kling, kling, kling. Ayy, that is the chap..! …with the cotton thread instrument [ ]. I go study that. When I done with it, I got the tune already!

Soon after, daddy goes to the Kamwatta (a Warrao settlement upriver) that side and he meets up with the Warao buckman [trader]. This man was making these things. And he buy me a ukulele, made of cedar wood, with iron strings. He was going to give me that before I burst up his violin string again, and so I stopped troubling me mother's thread.

He buys that for three dollar. He said: "Boy, look me bring this, take it, this is your own. When you come from school and throwing the book, you play kling, kling, kling."

While in the process of looking for the antecedents of Arawak music, what I found quite helpful was work of Stiffler (1982), an ethno-musicologist who made a systematic recording of the musical repertoire of the northwest district of Guyana. He introduces his work with the following words: "The music is simple, the singers and players imply rather more melody with their intonation than their voices can convey with pitch, the instruments (even when store brought) are primitive, but there is charming musical phrasing and ebullient native spirits on display" (Stiffler 1982:1). The author is caught between conflicting feelings. He seems charmed by Morucan music, but he listens from a perspective of a loss. He points out the blurring of the borders between the musical traditions in the region. As a concerned individual, he comments on the impact of Afro-American and Latin-American music on the repertoire, musical techniques, and the instruments used by Amerindian musicians. His ethno-musicological diagnosis of the Arawak was as follows:

The acculturation of the Arawak has made its effects upon their music. These are [Spanish Arawak] the Amerindians who remember the fewest of their ancestral songs and who show the most indulgence of the Euro-

pean presence in the songs they do remember and in the way they perform them. Homemade instruments are not used significantly by these
people, who use purchased instruments, including drums, in preference.
The native pentatonic scale also, has been a casualty, and the singers
and instrumentalists among the Arawak usually perform in the Europeans' 8-note idiom (Stiffler 1982: 3. My emphasis).

As the life histories of Nicolas and his musician friends unfold, it will become clear that
Stifflers understanding of the things appertaining to the Spanish Arawak music is eth-
nologically inadequate and analytically unsound. Why unsound? Namely, because
Stiffler establishes as an a priori what the Morucan music should be, calling it by the a
name "the Arawak musical tradition," which he then moves on to compare with what
the musicians actually do. In other words, he creates a model and then proceeds to
explain how the musicians' performances deviate from it. As can be expected, he concludes that there is breach between these two things, and he gives the breach a name:
acculturation. In so far as he also has gained knowledge of the musical scene and
enjoys the novelty of the Morucan music, he ends up double bound, hence his ambivalent feelings for the music he is presenting: new, effervescent, ebullient, and at the
same time a sad reminiscence of a forgotten and damaged cultural heritage.

> *Nicolas:* Once we were cutting wood for other man, at a kayapa [collective
> work] a Mashramanni [Lokono word] they call it here. We call it in Spanish kaya-
> pa. This is a come-together help party. In the afternoon we just go make me
> coffee, but then he said 'it is time to start boy. I go show you one cord. Put your
> finger so and put your finger so and strong and go ...at one time... quick'. I was
> 10 years old.
>
> In time I became daddy's second player. When he go play the violin me
> coming along now. When I stand near daddy, he goes with his violin. After
> school some time I go behind me daddy, to the kayapas, or someone's funeral,
> or birthday party. After a while I started to go out by meself. So when then I
> became more and more advanced and I left school.

Most households need to organize *kayapas* to repair or to make a new roof for a house,
or to clear and burn the undergrowth for a new farm. Extra workers are usually necessary in order to finish the tasks in time, before the rains.[3] The villagers are engaged,
all at the same time, in several time-consuming activities, all at the same period of the
year, often at the height of the dry season (October/November). At this time of year,
Kayapa feasts are constantly being celebrated, and the musicians travel from village to
village to perform. Additionally, from the beginning of August to mid-October, musicians travel to entertain those gathered to celebrate the crab season.[4] During the rest of
the year musicians are asked to perform at funeral ceremonies, and nowadays it has
become common in Moruca to celebrate birthdays.

In Moruca the knowledge of musical repertoires is specialized. There are roughly two distinctive repertoires: one is associated with healing and funeral rites; the other is associated with seasonal feasts and family parties. The repertoires are kept separated by individual specialists but are nevertheless commonly performed at the same occasion, and sometimes even at the same time. For instance, during funerals women choirs and shamans perform chants dedicated to the dead; at the same time and in the same space bands like Nicolas' sing secular *paiwari* songs.

Paiwari tunes, *el joropo,* as Nicolas called this kind of music, are his specialty. Joropo leads the dances during the Crab feast. The dances are based on the themes of animal hunting and mating behaviour, and are performed by men and women playing different roles in the choreography. The music played at *kayapa* gatherings and family parties is composed on the basis of the *joropo* rhythm. During most of the twentieth century, Spanish Arawak music played by travelling Spanish Arawak musicians was the standard repertoire in the *Kayapa* and *Paiwari* feasts of Moruca. Nicolas performed for miners, wood propectors, and border tracking expeditions. During this period he expanded his repertoire and became acquainted with new instruments. His passion for music grew fast through contact with other musicians he met on the road.

> *Nicolas:* It was time for me now to go about working. I see that they [other musicians] got guitars. Some boys bring those in from Brazil, they played Brazilian guitar. I wanted to play it too. There was this nice one, man! Me took that in me mind, to have my own guitar. So, me get a job. I go and join the government, a travelling party. They were tracking the borders and also making prospections I joined. I wanted that big guitar. I am going to buy me own guitar. A real homemade guitar and I start to play[] I start to practice this guitar, listening and get to know the accords. After a while I said: "Me all right now".
>
> I was about 20 years old by then. There was this store, at Fogerty (in Georgetown) there I get a book that shows the cords and so, I take that and develop meself. I begin to play three or four notes and so. But I wanted a violin, just like my father. I said: -"man I going to buy violin"-. So went working again, I joined the mine prospectors. In the evenings I played also for the men. After a while I had enough money so I send to make local violin and also banjo and thing. This is it I love it and I still keeping up to my father to this time.

Nicolas' involvement with music is not only the measure of his passion; it also reveals the intensity of the musical activity itself in the Moruca region. This activity is not residual but, indeed, very central to social life. Nor is it a dying or a weak expression of more powerful "traditions" of the past. Rather, it is the activity of people creating music as part of their lives, here and now. The view of Stiffler can be sustained only from a dissociated perspective. Engaged subjects such as Nicolas cannot experience a sense of loss and at the same time compose and perform his music. In other words, acculturation is only instrumental to ethno-musicology, as the product of a detached (mis)understanding.

When new musical instruments were introduced to the area, small-scale aggrega-
tion levels provided more relevant insights into Spanish Arawak music than larger-scale,
detached analytical perspectives. In the story of Nicolas, his violin indeed tells us an
interesting story. In older ethnographic sources (e.g. Roth 1924) there is a mention of
a native violin: a string instrument with a body made of bark, or of armadillo shell, with
strings made of palm fibres, and played with a bow. Nicolas mentions his mothers'
experiments in crafting a "house" violin. Apparently, that toy instrument was based on
the old native model. This means at least that the old, indigenous sort of violin was not
completely forgotten, nor that the incorporation of the new model of violin interrupted or disrupted the production of music for this kind of stringed instrument. The new
violin may have interrupted the production of the old ones, but were simply adopted
as a modern variant. From Nicolas's perspective, his violin was not imported at all. A
Warrao craftsman made such instruments, and Nicolas had bought his in a village nearby. Paul Henry brings us further into the matter as he tells his own story.

Paul Henry
Nicolas has already been playing with his new band for four years, along with Justine
Joseph and Paul Henry, both of whom are well into their seventies. In Nicolas's band,
Paul is the *shak-shak* man and Justine is the second man who plays the banjo. Paul
Henry's father was a *shak-shak* man, a *maraca* player. Paul suffers from rheumatism
and some form of arthritis. His hands are almost paralysed and he gave up playing the
violin 15 years ago. In fact, he used to play the *bandola*, a kind of large violin commonly found in Venezuela. Paul learned to play by listening to his father.

> *Paul:* In those days [1940's] these kind of musical instruments were scarce in
> Moruca. They were imported from America through the priest. Mainly through
> the missionaries. When we need something we go to the priest: "I want a vio-
> lin". But you got to be with the priest! You can't get it just so. You got to be
> with the priest. If you don't belong to the priest you don't get the violin through
> him.

Paul Henry was not with the priest; he did not need to be because he learned to make
his own musical instruments:

> *Paul:* You did not buy your instruments you had to made them yourself. Those
> were made as a whole body from solid wood, you know. The rear is the cover.
> Natural carving out. Nowadays, you might meet one or two but, it hardly got
> people doing this carving anymore. But not because they don't know how to do
> it. It got people who know how to do it. It is because now the music is on tape;
> they don't bother to learn anymore. Well, I had a little one [violin] first. I had a
> little of meself made. And that way I practice more to build up meself.
>   My father was a fisherman, and he was going to start to dig gold. Life was

very hard some time ago, a little money that can't support your family. So he was thinking to do something else. So he began to play music. I learned from him. Later on I began to play the bandola. It is just like this violin, but bigger. They play it in Venezuela. You play it in the C note. I learned by meself. Just like Mr. Justine. I just watch when they are playing. All this string go moving. This is C and this is D. I just watch and time after time me learn. When you know the song and you practice how you could do this. But you have it in mind. I going to start to play and me get one accord; well you practice from that.

The story of Justine's instruments is enlightening. He made his own *bandola*, he says because he did not "belong to the priest." Music was and still is a conflictive subject in Moruca. The missionaries, Catholics and Presbyterians alike, have been crusading against the *paiwari* festivals since the moment of their first contact with the Amerindian population. The texts condemning the rituals indulge in uninhibited ethnocentric language. Walter Roth provides a summary of the ethnographic reports made by nineteenth century chroniclers: "Every Indian party,…is practically a drinking bout, intercepted with more or less music, and its necessary corollary, a dance.…In the drinking of *paiwari*, the Indian is never satisfied, and here also the dance and song, if one can still apply that name to a dissolute row, continues until the intoxicating liquor is drained to the last drop. (SR, I, 207)" (Roth 1924: 470).

The chroniclers express deep moral outrage when they describe the rituals. The music and the dances are portrayed with the same scandalous undertone:

> …In general terms it may be stated that without drink there is never any dancing, which will continue so long as the former lasts, and thus a dance may often continue a couple of nights, including the intervening day (WER, IV, 197). The whole affair furthermore, usually ends up with a sexual orgy, or, as Barrere naively puts it (PBR, 253), 'to wind up, they all intermix'.…No sooner were their brains muddled with drink, and the shades of night had closed in, than all the dark places were turned by the couples into kennels, after which they would stealthily rejoin the dance, just as if nothing had happened (BER, 23) (Roth 1924: 470-471).

The use of musical instruments and song, along with the performances of dances, are central in all the rites of passage among the Amerindians, as is the ritualistic use of tobacco and manioc beer. The *paiwari* is an alternative name for the Crab feast that is believed to cause the seasons to change, the rains to cease, and the drought to endure. There are intricate links between native musical performances and cosmology – too complex to go into in this article, but which explain the resistance of the Arawak to the efforts of the missionaries to ban or control their production of music. In some Amerindian villages, missionaries were known to have imposed penalties, including the withholding of medical aid from those who doggedly continued to perform *paiwari* rituals or organized dances after the *kayapa* gatherings. Furthermore missionaries actively recruited musicians for the church services. A musician that "belonged to the priest," as Paul Henry puts it, would receive imported instruments free of charge. In turn, the musician refrained from participating in *paiwari* ceremonies. Thus, musicians had to make their choices. Paul Henry and his father, like Nicolas and his father, remained independent musicians. The pressure exercised by the missions through the school, the health services, and the church is undeniable and it certainly affected the musical universe of the area. However it should be clear that the Spanish Arawak music in Moruca is not the result of the cultural encroachment by the missions, but rather the product of the creative genius and endeavours of people like the Mendonzas and Henrys.

Individual choices and compromises, which imply the election of one way of life above anther, affect the musical landscape of the Moruca. The travelling musicians are a product of the attempts to ban *paiwari* ceremonies by the missionaries. In the same process the nomadic life of the musicians has shaped the kind of music they create; it expresses their encounters with other musicians and musical forms, the diversity of their frontier audiences, and the fact that they could make money as musicians. The instruments they play, the techniques they use, the inspiration for their tunes and their lyrics, have been picked up on the road.

Justine Joseph

Justine Joseph's introduction to music was very different from those of mates. He had a difficult youth. He left his parent's village [also in the Northwest district] when he was about 14 years old. He found himself wandering from job to job, from village to village. He was always alone and always very poor, until he met his wife just 28 years ago. Justine then moved to Santa Rosa and settled down. He tried to change his way of life and went, now as an adult, to school. He took lessons in religion from the priest at the Santa Rosa mission. After a while he and his wife ended up singing in the church choir. The priest put them in charge of the children's choir. Eventually he met and became friends with Nicolas. He began playing the banjo just five years ago and was introduced to Spanish Arawak music by Nicolas.

> *Justine:* I born and grown to the place they call Parikis, my parents were dead before I was four year old. I grew up with my uncle. I was twelve years old when I first left Moruca. I go away all about in Essequibo, Demerara. After a long time, I think over meself and I say: - 'man but this thing can't go on' -; your uncle and auntie are old. So I came back here. I was 35 years. Single, a bachelor.
>
> So you know, some people give advice to you: "The best I could tell you is marry and settle down yourself, properly, and bless you with children and one day there will come help to you, in your old days"-. A man he introduced me to the family of the girl that later became my wife. Her family is Warrao. I

go like a blind man. I come to ask for this lady. I want her to make my wife. They think it over, if they agree. And after the few days they say yes.

Me have this idea or this feelings of music from ever long. But I never get the proper opportunity to say well you know. So I actually cut out the interest of mine. Then Nicolas he brings back these feelings again by inviting me to practice. I like the banjo, I think I could try with that very well, through like we say with the seven accords, A, B, C and you know. The natural accords. I learn meself just like that, from the sound and watch Mr. Mendonza playing this music. I try all three. I try the violin, no, no, no. I try the guitar, no, no, no. And I try the banjo and I see a little progress with that now. So I continue that and then I get this. I see this mandolin and I like this. When I see the shape. I say: "Oh man". Feelings come to me, and me say: "You could do it?"

Goodnight Irene, Morucan Gal, Johnny and other tunes

According to Nicolas the story of Justine is just like one of his compositions. It is life along the Moruca that forms the ingredients for his songs. The Johnny songs are a good example, of which Nicolas has composed a trilogy.

> *Nicolas:* That is one of my compositions. The name of that is Johnny that's the lad. A little boy who used to hide, you know? A small boy, Johnny passing to school. And he was always buying a lolly. Sometimes he is bursting firewood and so on. Every day. But, he ain't going to school you know. He had the sense, he is thinking of a girl. So he rimes out. I hear the story and I make a thing I match it so suit the music. So I compose like that.

"Johnny One" begins on Monday: "It is Monday morning, Johnny was going to school. He me say as he tells me that he wants to make love with you," and then goes on day by day. Johnny marries the girl on Sunday. In "Johnny Two," he does not succeed. In "Johnny Three," the boy is seduced by the girl. "Johnny" is originally a Guyanese song. Nicolas is the proud composer of the *joropo* arrangement of "Goodnight Irene." Inspired by the title, he also modified the text of this American tune thereby turning it into an entirely new composition.

> *Nicolas:* That is a song right! "Something had been happened that caused me to come back to you". The story goes like this: the old lady's man who is working in the bush, in the mines. He ain't got it with him, he is unlucky. And he gets some money. He sends a million dollars now through the post. What happened? He wants to hear if she got the money. So nothing. Till he writes a letter now concerning that, no reply as a little line. He writes again, nothing. Wondering about this now, if the money is lost or what. So he writes another letter again now. Where is the money gone, he's wondering now. Sometimes this postman. Something happen so I got to go down now. She got the money. The postman

and the girl were so. So they cut the money between them. That is the story. That I put into rimes inspired by the music of "Irene Goodnight".

The texts of the songs are not fixed. They change with Nicolas's the mood. "The words are just come to my mind," he once explained to me. If he is feeling funny he goes on with some kind of silly rhymes. If he is feeling melancholic then the song will be about love and the misery of love. The length of the songs is kept flexible. "When people are dancing you have to go on improvising." This, according to Nicolas, is what distinguishes him from other musicians who only play one song all the time. "They don't have the gift!"

Nicolas calls his arrangements of music and texts, his compositions. The newest items of his repertoire were once heard on the radio, or from a tape-recording. The songs talk about his world and the music is arranged according to the standard rules of the "tunes":

Morucan Gal
Morucan girl me love you for truth....
Morucan girl me love you for truth....me going to marry you now.
I been to Kaituma, I walked through savannah and I ... Kanaima [spirit] girl
come on let we go now. ...[etc.]
(Fragment of a ten strophes long song. Text and music by Nicolas Mendonza)

Morucan gal is Nicolas's most successful composition. It is a long Joropo tune and the lyrics are devoted to love's pathways in Moruca. The Spanish version, also composed by Nicolas, is shorter. Both versions are regarded as his *pièce de résistance*. The tune is played for a very long time, and the English and Arawak lyrics are intercalated.

Las mocitas de moruca
Las mocitas de Moruca [the girls from moruca]
dicen que yo soy feito [say that I'm an ugly man]
Pero ellas me gustan [but they like me]
porque yo no soy mesquino [because I'm generous] ...[etc.]
(Text and music by Nicolas Mendonza)

According to Nicolas Morucan girls are both gay and shy, but they all have Kanaima. Kanaima is literally the power of the shaman to transform himself into an animal in order to take someone's life force (soul) from him or her. When talking of love Kanaima refers to sexual passion. Another version of the Morucan Girl elaborates further on the kanaima theme, beginning with the lines: *"If you trouble a Moruca girl you get type of fever you get fever until you go to the doctor."*

Nicolas' and Paul's lives have been shaped by their musical inclinations. At least that is

the way in which they now are composing their autobiographies. They began their carriers playing on the road, and subsequently became well known in the region. During
the time when he travelling with the prospectors and the government border mission,
Nicolas was a courier; he began performing for the crew simply for amusement. After
a while he was being called by villages all around to come and perform at funerals,
kayapas, for the girl's initiation ceremonies, and for weddings. He managed for quite
a long time to obtain his living through performing. Paul did similarly well. Their
incomes were limited, but they managed to maintain their families. Musicians are held
in very high esteem. Wherever they went, whether they were performing or not, they
always got some money to take back home. Nicolas is still one of the most requested
musicians in Santa Rosa and in the nearby villages.

Nicolas presents himself as a musician, but his profession is more complex. He is
an animator. His playing is embedded in a larger act. He leads the dances, tells jokes,
and during nightly pauses he is asked to tell old stories. Through his mouth, the language of his father and other independent Spanish Arawak musicians has endured as
a speech form in Moruca. Spanish Arawak is what these musicians and storytellers do.

How can you get moving (unless you migrate too)

Let me conclude with a couple of short remarks. The Moruca received migrants from
over the border of Venezuela almost two centuries ago. These people shared their way
of life and their cosmological framework with the local population they encountered.
Their most particular feature was their mastery of the Spanish language and, according
to the missionary history, their Catholic Christian upbringing.

My impression, however, is that neither the language nor the schooling conveys
the way in which Spanish Arawak exists in Moruca today. Much more relevant are the
living narratives that maintain the memory of once-shared experiences: namely, escap-
ing the war and the epic of the fight against the intended deportation. There, Spanish
has become a dramatic instrument in the mouth of gifted performers. The hybridism of
the language is a constitutive element of the narratives and of other oral performances.

Spanish Arawak is not necessarily a group; in this context it is primarily a speech
form. The existence and persistence of these forms of speech is entangled with the life
of independent Morucan musicians. The life stories of these musicians take them up
and down the Moruca area. They have performed Spanish Arawak music during at least
the past 60 years. In a very literal sense, musicians like Nicolas, Paul, and Justine are
creating Spanish Arawak in the Moruca.

Notes

1   In 1994 during a short visit to the Arawak village of Santa Rosa, in the northwest district of Guyana, I and one of my graduate students from Utrecht University, M. Reinders, managed to record a vast repertoire of songs composed and arranged by Nicolas Mendonza, then an eighty-three-year-old man.

2   Forte (1990) has made the most recent systematic survey of the Amerindian villages in the Northwest district.

3   For a recent description of daily life and subsistence activities in Santa Rosa, see Jara and Reinders (1997).

4   The crab feasts are known as *Paiwari*. This name derives from a special kind of manioc beer prepared for the occasion. For a treatment of the yearly ritual cycle of the Arawak, see Jara (2000).

Bibliography

Atkinson, H. 1990. *The History of the Catholic Church in Santa Rosa in the North-west District of Guyana. 1817-1990*. NSJ July 1990.

Forte, J. 1990. The populations of the Amerindian Settlements in the 1980's. *Timeheri: The Journal of the Guyana Society* 46:38-51.

Jara, F., and M. Reinders. 1997. Kin and Cash. Ecological and Social Consequences of the Changes in the Sexual Division of Labour in Santa Rosa, An Amerindian village in the Northwest District of Guyana. In M. De Bruijn, I. Van Halsema, and H. van den Hombergh, eds., *Gender and Land Use. Diversity in Environmental Practices*, pp.49-69. Amsterdam. Thela Publishers.

Jara, F. 2000. Arawak Constellations: In search of the Manioc Stars in Tropical South America. A Bibliographical Survey. *Latin American Indian Literatures Journal* 16(2):114-151.

Menezes, M.N. 1979. *The Amerindians in Guyana 1803- 1873. A Documentary History*. London: Wheaton and Co.

Proceedings of Amirang. 1994. *National Conference of Amerindian Representatives "Amerindians in Tomorrow's Guyana. President College*, Eats Coast Demerara. Guyana.

Roth, W.E. 1924. An Introductory Study of the Arts, Crafts and Customs of the Guiana Indians. *38th Annual Report 1916-1917 of the Bureau of American ethnology*. Washington, DC: Smithsonian Institute.

Stiffler, D.B. 1982. *The Music of the Coastal Amerindians of Guyana. The Arawak, Carib and Warau*. Recorded and annotated. Folksways Records Albums no. FE 4239.

13

Social Exclusion and the Structural Symbology of Sports: Soccer and Formula 1 in Brazil

Kees Koonings

The significance of social structure

Looking at Arie de Ruijter's academic and professional achievements, one particular and yet complex core concern stands out: the study and management of social contradictions and the way social agents try to bridge these through discursive practices and strategies of classification and interpretation. These practices and strategies can offer at the same time the building blocks for scientific interpretation. During the many years in which Arie de Ruijter managed to combine scholarly and managerial responsibilities, he himself often gave proof of the art of merging action and interpretation. Few others have mastered the subtle skill of "management by meaning" more than he did.

Early indications of this fascination and capability can be found in de Ruijter's doctoral dissertation (1977). One of the reasons he gives for analysing the structuralist anthropology of Claude Lévi-Strauss is the effort of the latter to "reduce empirical reality to a foundational system of a limited number of determinations and principles" (de Ruijter 1977:1). This foundational system is construed on an abstract level and transpires into human agency through the cultural classification of symbols and meaning, often in the form of binary oppositions or triads within an overriding structure (de Ruijter 1977: 194ff.).

How can these early reflections be related to the contemporary problem of social exclusion? For de Ruijter, social exclusion became a central scholarly concern, and one of the core issues studied by the CERES research school he founded and directed for many years. Lévi-Strauss himself has never been explicitly concerned with the problem of social exclusion as one of the "consequences of modernity" (Giddens 1990). Still, his method and system approach, as it sets out to grasp the intrinsic reality and logic behind empirical manifestations, may offer a tool to understand the ways in which people give meaning to and come to terms with social exclusion. These strategies may well reveal the underlying structure of social exclusion. At the same time, the underlying structure may give social agents clues not only to understand it but also to mitigate or transcend it. From a structuralist perspective, it can be precisely ritual representations or re-enactments that serve the purpose of transforming the more manifest institutional forces of social exclusion.

In this essay I want to look at this general problem through the lens of sports in

Brazil. I will draw extensively on the insights of the well-known Brazilian anthropologist Roberto DaMatta. DaMatta explicitly builds upon a structuralist perspective to generate categories for the interpretation of what he calls "Brazilian reality" (DaMatta 1983, 1987). DaMatta suggests a specific triad with which to give meaning to social and cultural life in modern Brazil. This "meaning" not only serves the purpose of the social scientist, but also of ordinary Brazilians in daily life as they try to cope with the hardships of living in a basically unequal and unjust society. DaMatta's triad consists of the domains of the "house" *(a casa)*, the "street" *(a rua)*, and the "other world" *(o outro mundo)*. His basic aim is to offer an alternative perspective for interpreting the "hybridity" of social categories and relations in modern Brazil. He rejects Eurocentric approaches that see Brazil either as pre- or non-modern with respect to the North Atlantic or "Western" norm, or as structurally deformed by some sort of peripheral, hence incomplete, capitalism (DaMatta 1995). Instead he seeks to understand the complex articulation of modernity and non-modernity, citizenship and exclusion, and the public and the private. The domains of the triad not only explain the intrinsic reality or structure of Brazilian society, but also generate pathways for social agents to try to mediate or supersede the consequences of inequality and exclusion by means of symbolic practices.

Sport constitutes a particularly valid social field (Bourdieu 1984) from which to study these matters. Aside from the fact that Arie de Ruijter himself was a dedicated and skilful soccer player in his time – a quality that he put to work to inspire colleagues and students (see photo) – sport can readily be seen not only as a specific pastime in modern societies but also as a field of social practices with a high level of symbolic

Arie de Ruijter (sitting, second from left) with faculty and student team mates in the line-up for an indoor soccer tournament in 1982. This team actually won the tournament. (The author appears standing on the extreme right-hand side.)

content. Anthropologists, DaMatta (1988) included, have pointed at the possibility to see sport as an example of ritual or social "drama" that serves to validate or to inverse social relations and practices through symbolic re-enactment of social behaviour.

In Brazil in particular, sport systematically serves the purpose of social re-enactment through mass mobilisation, mass sentiment, and the imputation of meaning. According to DaMatta (1988), sport can teach us things about Brazilian society, but at the same time it also shapes social life and the cultural categories that constitute the intrinsic reality on which the manifestations of social practice are based. The wider the popularity enjoyed by a specific sportive discipline, the more valid this sport becomes as a metaphor for social reality. When large masses rally to a sport and identify with it, sentiments are generated that transcend the particular sport in question, thereby reflecting wider relations and processes in society. In Brazil, two sports surpass all others in terms of structuralist significance: soccer *(futebol)* and Formula 1 racing. In the remainder of this essay I will compare both sports for their social-symbolic significance. As I will show below, such a comparison makes perfect sense from a structuralist point of view despite the enormous differences between the two sports in terms of intrinsic characteristics and social embeddedness.

Soccer and society in Brazil

Soccer hardly needs clarification in this respect. Although not invented in Brazil, soccer has been perfected there. I do not mean the physical and tactical perfection à la Rinus "Broer" Michels, Louis van Gaal, or the Ukranian success coach Lobanovski, but rather the perfection demonstrated by Garrincha, Pelé, Zico, Falcão, or Romário. In Brazil it is the players, not the coaches or managers, that guarantee superb performance. The "one touch" soccer propagated by the "Dutch school" of trainers was invented in the *favelas* by poor individualists that play by intuition. They are widely known by the public – in Brazil and abroad – under nicknames that they often carried since boyhood, and are embraced by the crowds to strengthen the sense of closeness and intimacy that is so important in the mass sentiment provoked by soccer.

This characteristic of Brazilian soccer is important in order to understand the social and cultural significance of this sport. Three aspects of Brazilian society are important in this respect. These aspects relate to a sense of modernity that often seems to elude Brazilians as they experience their daily life. First we have *individualism*. In Brazil, networks of personal ties and dependency – which DaMatta (1983) calls the "relational universe" – are still very important. Therefore, the soccer field offers a singular opportunity to display individual skills, creativity, and ambitions. The crowd *(a torcida)* can identify with particular samples of individual brilliance or with the singular biography of a soccer star.

Secondly, there is the crucial issue of *equality*. As is well known, Brazil ranks among the most unequal and hierarchical societies in the world. This inequality is not only based on systematic social exclusion on the basis of class and colour, but also on the practical failure of formally existing non-discriminatory institutions and rules. However, on the playing field and also on the grandstands in the stadiums everyone is equal in principle. Soccer was the first sport in which the exclusion of black people and *mulatos* came to an end. Soccer is not a sport that can only be accessed by the wealthy and the privileged. In soccer, equality means equality of rules and therefore of opportunities. Unequal results are determined by the quality of individual players and teams, in which case success is also extended to the supporters. An additional factor is good fortune *(sorte)*, something that cannot be influenced directly but can be prayed for (DaMatta 1988). As a result soccer is owned by the masses and soccer stars are popular heroes (Willemsen 1994). Soccer stars are often coloured. The status of "megastar" that has befallen Pelé, Falcão, Romário, and most recently Ronaldo, does not diminish their aura of ordinariness. They speak a popular language, identify with popular pleasures, and demonstrate ambitions befitting of successful *favela* youngsters, such as taking care of their family and setting up welfare facilities for the underprivileged youth. Only Falcão, aristocratic, white, a playboy and later fashion tycoon, offers an exception to this principle. And of course Pelé developed into a class of his own: amiable, businesslike, he turned into an international sports icon and was appointed Minister for Sport by the former president Fernando Henrique Cardoso.

Ronaldo, for instance, shows respect for his family, is concerned about the poverty in the country, is thankful to God for his good fortune and wealth, and – in the early years of his international career, hoped modestly to be able one day to meet the Brazilian television star Xuxa. At the time when he was engaged in the 10 million dollar transfer from PSV Eindhoven to Barcelona, he stated:

> I am a good lad. I never harmed anyone. I am not presumptuous. I like to be with my friends and I try to help whomever I can. Some people seem to think that idols have to be different; I don't think so. I want to be a good lad forever (quoted in Torras and López 1997:164).

The quintessential popular icon of Brazilian soccer was, of course, that famous right-winger considered by many in Brazil the greatest player of all times: Manuel dos Santos, a.k.a. Mané Garrincha (Castro 1995). This unique dribbler with the curved legs (one leg was even shorter that the other due to a disease he suffered as an infant) presented himself to the world at the World Cup of 1958 in Sweden, together with the 17-year-old Pelé. Four years later Garrincha single-handedly led Brazil to its second world championship title in Chile. (Pelé was absent due to an injury.) After that, Garrincha's knees were definitely worn out, and he glided slowly into oblivion. Unfortunately, the naïve soccer star proved unable to deal with fame; destitute and forgotten, he died of alcohol abuse in 1983. He stands as a symbol for all those Brazilians that in the end don't make it despite talent and hard effort. The soccer universe of equal opportunity has its limits beyond the direct domain of the teams, the matches, and the grandstand crowds. As Eduardo Galeano observed, "[Garrincha was] a loser with good luck. And good luck does not last. In Brazil they say that if shit would have value the poor would be born without an asshole" (1996: 119).

Recently, Garrincha was rehabilitated by his hometown, an insignificant place called "Pau Grande." The town council decided that the name would be changed into Cidade Mané Garrincha. One should bear in mind, however, that Pau Grande means not only "big stick," but also "big dick," so a change of name was advisable in any case.

This brings me to the third aspect of Brazilian society, one closely related to the first two, namely *social participation* and *national identification*. In Brazil, despite the fact that the country shows all the trappings of a modern, urban-industrial and unitary mass society, social participation in the sense of citizenship and sharing in national identity is never certain for the underprivileged 50 to 60 percent of the population. In and around soccer however, these – and indeed all Brazilians – are able to be a part of national life. Since 1950, when Brazil barely failed to secure the World Cup victory during the tournament it hosted, success of *a seleção* in the field has been closely related with the fate of the nation as a whole. The dramatic defeat against Uruguay in a Maracanã Stadium packed with 200,000 flabbergasted spectators (Willemsen 1994:151-152) was followed a few years later by President Getúlio Vargas' suicide, marking the end of an era. Four years later Brazil won its first World Cup in 1958, in the midst of the euphoria being stirred up by Juscelino Kubitschek's developmentalist administration that was driven by the adage to advance "fifty years in five." The third championship, won by probably the best national team of all times, marked the heyday of the Brazilian economic miracle. Yet the title also fed the antagonism between opponents and supporters of the military regime. The latter prevailed using the slogan *"Brasil, ama-o ou deixa-o"* (Brazil, love it or leave it). After that, the general decline of Brazil's economic health and the turmoil of a protracted democratic transition seemed to spill over into the disappointing World Cup results during the 1974-1990 period. Each time, the road to the final and hence the Coupe Jules Rimet was blocked by Holland, Argentina, Italy, France, and again Argentina.

Only in 1994 was the link between soccer success and national well-being restored. On Sunday 17 July 1994, Brazil won the final against Italy in Pasadena's shimmering hot Rose Bowl Stadium after a series of penalty kicks. The narrowness of this victory resembled the uncertainty of national recovery heralded by the new currency (the real) introduced only weeks before by Fernando Henrique Cardoso to end fifteen years of hyperinflation. The match was a nervous one and of mediocre quality, and the penalty series was dramatic. After the failed kick of the Italian star Roberto Baggio the Brazilian people went crazy. Brazil became the only country to have ever won the World Cup four times: *tetracampeão!* (The fifth title in 2002 was subsequently received in an almost matter-of-fact way.) In 1994, indeed, a whole new generation could relish in the glory of a nation reborn, 24 years after Mexico 1970. This was the generation of the new urban Brazil that had no conscious experience of the 21 years of military rule, and knew the 1970 final only from videotapes and the stories of their parents. The weekly magazine IstoÉ wrote, "A country of the future dances the samba and cannot resist the temptation to have faith in the future" (20/7/1994). A fan was quoted: "This was a victory of the people, so that the elite can see what love for our country means." The success of the *canárias* managed to push poverty and violence to the background for a while, and gave the people its proper due.

Formula 1 and its heavenly heroes

The competitions for the Grand Prix of formula 1 racing are almost as popular in Brazil as soccer. On the Sunday of a Grand Prix race there will hardly be a house in which the direct transmission of the race is not watched. This must have started in the early 1970s when television sets were trickling down even to the poor as a spin-off of the economic *milagre* and became a mass consumer item. At that time, Emerson Fittipaldi won his first Formula 1 world championship title.

Since those days, Brazilian pilots like Fittipaldi, Nelson Piquet, and the best of them all, Ayrton Senna, have risen to the absolute top of the international Formula 1 circus, gaining several world championships and winning many individual Grand Prix races across the globe. Mass sentiment and identification is directed at these impregnable heroes. They are just a distant appearance on the television screen or even from the grandstands of São Paulo's Interlagos racing circuit, encapsulated beyond recognition in their suits, helmets, and frail bolides. Apparently there seems little ground for sentimental identification by a mass public. Display of passion by the practitioners is rare: one fist in the air, or the national flag upheld during the victory round at snail pace.

Yet mass sentiment for Formula 1 is very much alive in Brazil. How can this be explained? In almost every aspect Formula 1 is the antithesis of soccer, particularly in Brazil. Soccer is cheap and accessible. Everyone can play it. For Formula 1, by contrast, "expensive" is a bizarre understatement. Soccer has millions of practitioners from every class and colour. The handful Formula 1 pilots only reach this status after years of achievement in carting, formula Ford, formula 2000, etc. This trajectory is only accessible, in Brazil at any rate, for the sons of the well-to-do. The sport itself also has a distant tinge to it from the perspective of o povo. The winner of a race sprays the runners-up and a small in-crowd of bystanders with the content of a thoroughly shaken magnum of champagne. The pilots are not of the people but belong to the international jet set; they earn salaries in the millions of dollars and move around the world in private airplanes. Ayrton Senna lived part of the year in Monte Carlo. In Brazil he belonged to "high society," running a business empire built around merchandising his fame and image, as symbolised by the cartoon figure and doll "Senninha" (little Senna). Senna was not a lad from the people. Unlike Ronaldo he did not have to dream of meeting TV celebrities; Xuxa Meneghel (who had been the wife of Pelé for a while, nevertheless) was a close friend.

The massive reality of sentiment provoked in Brazil by Formula 1 appeared unmistakably after Senna's tragic death on the first of May, 1994. On that fateful day, at the Grand Prix of San Marino, he crashed his car into a wall in the Tamburello curve of the

Imola circuit (see Longmore 1994). The official cause was a broken steering rod, but Senna had had premonitions and was impressed by the earlier deadly accident of the Austrian driver Ratzenberger during training for that same contest. Senna's death sent a shock wave through Brazilian society. It overshadowed for a while the preparations of the national soccer team for the World Cup tournament in the USA. The focus of mass sentiment was the burial of Senna on Thursday 5 May 1994 in São Paulo. It was a state funeral in which all public dignitaries were present at the wake and the funeral procession. Stunt pilots from the demonstration team of the Força Aérea Brasileira performed in the sky. The coffin, covered with the Brazilian flag, was carried on a fire brigade truck along the boulevards of the huge city on its way to the cemetery in the elite district of Morumbi. Hundreds of thousands from all ranks and classes lined the route. During the previous day and night, kilometres-long queues had formed around the palace of the state legislature so that people could pay their final respects. Weeks, even months later, Brazilians continued to show their sadness for this national loss.

Mass sentiment and ritual re-enactment of equality and salvation

How can it be explained that two sports that are so different can stir up similar forms of mass sentiment and belonging in Brazil? As far as soccer is concerned, I follow the lead of Roberto DaMatta in order to get at the social significance of mass sentiment and identification. According to DaMatta (1988) soccer can be seen as a dramatic condensation of Brazilian society as a whole. However, this refers to a quite specific dimension of Brazilian society, a dimension that is most of the time distorted in normal everyday life. I mean the notion of equality, social justice, and citizenship rights that are supposed to be grounded on stable public rules and institutions. DaMatta sees the significance of soccer as a collective ritual in the possibility it offers to experience "permanent structures"; equal rules for all so that success is the fruit of effort and merit. DaMatta stresses the significance of this experience for individual expression and the foundation of citizenship – a scarce article in a society he sees as a "relational universe." The arrogance of the *"você sabe com quém está falando?"* (do you know who you're talking to?) does not hold on the soccer field or in the grandstands (DaMatta 1983). But I also think the problem has a collective dimension. Soccer forms the Brazilian *societas*, the civil community Brazilians want to be part of. Soccer cements togetherness and national identification, not only in the streets of Brazilian cities and towns but also in the diasporas of Los Angeles, New York, London, Paris, and Amsterdam. After the final world cup victories in 1994 and 2002 Brazilians danced and embraced each other regardless of class, gender, or origins.

As such, soccer is a part of DaMatta's (1987) domain of the "street." In real life the street means inequality, injustice, a permanent struggle for survival. It is the domain of anonymity, abandonment, and exclusion. As such it stands in opposition to the "house," which is the domain of security, compassion, intimacy, and trust. In soccer, the street is ritualised, or re-enacted, in a way that turns the street on its head: festive instead of violent, equal instead of unequal, universal rules instead of the privileges of a minority.

Formula 1 has none of this. At best the successful Brazilian *pilotas* serve as fancy ambassadors for their country in the international glamour world. At best they use part of their fame and fortune for charitable ends, thus reproducing the old hierarchical practice of aloof patronage. Why then that the inhabitants of the *favelas* and *vilas*, or of the middle-class condominium blocks for that matter, would care about Formula 1? I suggest that the explanation can be found in the third domain of DaMatta's structuralist metaphor: the "other world." This is the domain of spirituality and reflection where the contradictions between house and street can be mitigated. It is, of course, also the domain of the many gods, saints, and spirits Brazilians honour (Droogers 1988). These deities are often called upon to intervene in house or street to offer good fortune *(sorte)* through faith *(fé)* for a better destiny *(destino)*.

As the saying goes, God is a Brazilian, but it is often hard to find him amidst the hardships of everyday life. Therefore, the Formula 1 heroes offer occasional but very tangible substitutes. Proof of this can be found in the way Senna's death, funeral, and memory have been ritualised and re-enacted. It is clear that rituals that relate to the *outro mundo* differ from the euphoric carnivals that celebrate soccer victories. Senna's funeral was solemn, introverted, and the people were nostalgic. A housemaid that went to the wake, in thinking about the national flag that covered the coffin, said, "...it seemed Brazil itself had died" *(IstoÉ*, 11/5/1994:46). Senna's death and funeral was not that of a popular hero, but it nevertheless brought the people closer to the other world, to the realm of the gods.

One may might even say that Senna, in fact, was bestowed the status of Jesus Christ, the son who had sacrificed himself for the salvation of the masses. At the same time there was the sense of loss of a brother or a son, familiar in so many living rooms because of television. Here we see the approximation of house and other world, the sacred and the private, a role fulfilled in Christendom by the figure of Jesus. I do not mean to blaspheme, but the parallels are undeniably strong. Senna was, away from the racing contests, a quiet, somewhat shy person. He was deeply religious and righteous. Longmore (1994) calls him "...sensitive, gentle, thoughtful, courageous, intelligent, loyal, honest, hunble. He was also temperamental, arrogant, ruthless, single-minded, opinionated, obstinate and possessed of a frightening will to win." Jesus of Nazareth must have had roughly the same qualities. In his works of charity, Senna favoured poor children. According to Rendall, his "charitable work and donations were, like his private life, shrouded in secrecy and linked with his religious faith" (1996:131).

A final parallel is provided by his untimely death, at the summit of his fame and glory. As in the case of Jesus, this fact validated his superhuman status. Relics of Senna now circulate and are traded, often for lofty sums. Just like Jesus, Senna has become transnational – worshipped not only by Brazilians but by people all over the world. Also Senna had his Pilate: in Italy a criminal investigation had been conducted against the boss of Senna's team, Frank Williams, for possible criminal negligence. Of course Williams washed his hands and proclaimed his innocence. The cemetery of Morumbi has become a place of pilgrimage. From all corners people still come to pay tribute to the fallen driver. The conspicuous tomb is adorned with a plaque that states: *Ayrton Senna da Silva, 21.3.60-1.5.94. Nada pode me separar do amor de Deus.* (Nothing can separate me from God's love.)

And to remove all remaining doubt about Senna's rightful place in the other world, let me end my reflections with an extensive quotation of Ayrton Senna himself. These words are taken from a statement he gave in 1988 after winning the Grand Prix of Japan, thus securing the first of his three world titles (taken from *A fé do campeão,* www.africanet.com.br/senna/fe.html, 1997):

> I was asking HIM to let me win. GOD gave me the hard-fought [victory in the] championship, conquered in the penultimate race of the year, the dream of every pilot. It was a wonderful gift. Even when I was praying, I was super concentrated, I prepared for a long curve of 180 degrees, when I suddenly saw the image of Jesus. He was so big, so big...He was not standing on the ground. He was hanging in the air, with the clothes he always wears, surrounded by light. His whole body rose into the sky, high, high, filling all space. And as I saw this incredible image, I was driving a racing car. I drove with precision, with power...That is far out, isn't it? That is far out.

Bibliography

Bourdieu, Pierre. 1984. *Questions de Sociologie.* Paris: Les Éditons de Minuit.

Castro, Ruy. 1995. *Estrela solitária – um brasileiro chamado Garrincha.* São Paulo: Companhia das Letras.

DaMatta, Roberto. 1983. *Carnavais, Malandros e Heróis. Para uma Sociologia do Dilema Brasileiro.* Rio de Janeiro: Rocco.

DaMatta, Roberto. 1987. *A casa and a rua. Espaço, cidadania, mulher e morte no Brasil.* Rio de Janeiro: Guanabara.

DaMatta, Roberto. 1988. Soccer: Opium for the People or Drama of Social Justice? In Geert Banck and Kees Koonings, eds., *Social Change in Contemporary Brazil,* pp. 125-134. Amsterdam: CEDLA.

DaMatta, Roberto. 1995. For an Anthropology of the Brazilian Tradition; or "A Virtude está no Meio. In David J. Hess and Roberto DaMatta, eds., *The Brazilian Puzzle: Culture on the Borderlands of the Western World,* pp. 270-292. New York: Columbia University Press,

de Ruijter, Arie. 1977. *Claude Levi-Strauss: een systeemanalyse van zijn antropologisch werk.* Utrecht: Instituut voor Culturele Antropologie

Droogers, Andre. 1988. Brazilian Minimal Religiosity. In Geert Banck and Kees Koonings, eds., *Social Change in Contemporary Brazil,* pp. 165-176. Amsterdam: CEDLA.

Galeano, Eduardo. 1996. *El Futebol a Sol y Sombra.* Santiago: Pehuén.

Giddens, Anthony. 1990. *The Consequences of Modernity.* Cambridge: Polity Press.

Longmore, Andrew. 1994. "Weekend in Hell." Originally written for the *London Times,* 31/10/94, taken from www.xs4all.nl/~donjanus/hell.html.

Rendall, Ivan. 1994. *Ayrton Senna, a Tribute.* London: Pavilion.

Torras, David, and Marcos López. 1997. *Ronaldo: retrato de un niño.* Barcelona: Ediciones Grupo Zeta.

Willemsen, August. 1994. *De Goddelijke Kanaries.* Amsterdam: Thomas Rap.

14

Talking Food in an Indo-Dutch Home for the Elderly

Geert Mommersteeg

Introduction

To anthropologists, eating is never "just eating," and food is never "just food." For as Counihan and Van Esterik note, "because everyone eats and many people cook, the meanings attached to food appeal to many more people than do the meanings attached to more esoteric objects and practices" (1997:2). Food and eating habits are constructed culturally and are passed on culturally. What we eat says something about us as an individual, but also about the group we belong to. As Farb and Armelagos put it in their book *Consuming Passions. The Anthropology of Eating,* "because of values that go far beyond filling the stomach, eating becomes associated, if only at an unconscious level, with deep-rooted sentiments and assumptions about oneself and the world one lives in" (1980:97). Studies by anthropologists like Lévi-Strauss and Mary Douglas, to name but two of the best known, show how eating habits mark our cultural identities. We eat pork; they don't. They eat insects; we don't. By defining certain things as edible, we differentiate ourselves from others who don't. Shared eating habits indicate shared membership in a group. In many contemporary anthropological and sociological studies about food and eating in western societies, a preoccupation with "food as a marker of difference" is notable (Caplan 1997:9). Variables like gender, age, class and ethnicity on the one hand, and different eating habits on the other hand, can be (and often are) interlinked.

For example, how food is used as a marker of "Dutch identity" can be illustrated with two striking, recent examples. The first one is a poster from "De Rijksoverheid" [The Government], on which a large plate of mashed potatoes with curly kale, and sausage is shown. Next to the plate, a dark-skinned hand is holding a gravy spoon, about to pour brown gravy into the hole in the middle of the pile of kale. The background of the poster is filled with the embroidered front of a *djellaba*. The caption at the bottom of the poster reads: "When has someone sufficiently settled in *(ingeburgerd)*?" The second example is a VVD (the Dutch Liberal Party) televised campaign ad for the upcoming (January 2003) elections for the Lower House of Parliament. Together with a portrait of a black female asylum seeker the following words are projected: "Does she have to like Brussels sprouts? No." "Does she have to learn Dutch? Yes." The message is clear. Our identity as Dutchmen can be linked to our national cuisine. We eat curly kale and Brussels sprouts; "the others" don't. Moreover we don't even expect them to do so.

In so far as eating habits mark the boundaries between groups, they distinguish insiders from outsiders. As such, they model processes of inclusion and exclusion (Mennell et al. 1992:115-118). Social-scientific research has shown that immigrants and ethnic minorities often attempt to retain their own cooking and eating habits for as long as possible.[2] To groups of migrants, eating habits often may serve as a cohesive and stabilizing factor. Harbottle (1997a, 1997b), for instance, considers the issue of ethnic identity and food among Iranians in Britain and shows how amongst these migrants considerable continuity is demonstrated with regard to the "flavor principles" of the traditional Iranian cuisine.

According to the structuralist Lévi-Strauss (1963, 1965) the categories of the culinary field offer insight into both the structure of a particular society and the fundamental structures of human thinking. Food, he therefore argues, can be "good to think." It is this famous quote from Lévi-Strauss to which Harris (1986) referred when he entitled his book about the "riddles of food and culture," *Good to Eat*. From a cultural materialist perspective, food is first and foremost "good to eat." In this contribution I want to show that food can also be "good" for a third purpose – "good to talk," and that in this way it can also serve as a "distinguishing marker." The ethnographical material I shall use to illustrate this was collected through anthropological research in a home – which will hereafter be referred to as "The Home" – for Indo-Dutch elderly.

"With a little imagination, salty fish tastes like herring"

Late in the afternoon, when I go down to the foyer of The Home, I see Mr. and Mrs. Arends and Mrs. Bekker sitting together at one of the small tables.[2] We exchange greetings and when they invite me to join them, I pull up a chair. They continue their conversation. They talk about the past, about games they used to play when they were children. About how little they needed to be happy, and about all things you could get for only one cent. It used to be a good time, in the East Indies, they tell me. "At least, before the war," Mrs. Bekker is careful to add. "The war changed us."

Now that the war has been mentioned, the conversation turns to life in camps. During the Second World War all three were detained in internment camps in Java. One memory after another is pulled up. Now and then they turn to me to explain something. Mr. Arends, who dominates the conversation, intersperses his stories with imitations of Japanese camp guards, and a couple of phrases in Japanese. Once or twice he ends an anecdote by mimicking a slap given by "the Jap."

When there is a brief silence, Mrs. Bekker remarks that they should be glad they lived to tell the tale. The stories may sound funny, but a slap like that could really hurt. Then Mr. Arends suddenly remembers a fellow detainee, a man who used to pretend he was an opera singer. "And then he sang like this...." Holding a finger above his Adam's apple and quivering it up and down, Mr. Arends imitates him with exaggerated vibrato in his voice: *"With a little imagination, salty fish tastes like herring."*

I ask if they had herring in the East Indies.

"Oh, yes, pickled herring," says Mrs. Arends.

"And salted herring?" I ask.

"Absolutely," says Mrs. Bekker. "They used to come in those barrels."

"Really nice," remarks Mr. A, adding that it tasted best when his wife covered the herring with egg and baked them: *haring goreng*. Or when she used them to make *pèpèsan* [a fish dish prepared with a lot of spices, onions, and sambal].

"Herring, using herring to make *pèpèsan?*" asks Mrs. Bekker, astonished.

"Yes, but first you have to dry the fish on the ...." Mrs. Arends does not complete her sentence, but points to the central heating.

"But you didn't have that then, did you?" Mrs. Bekker asks.

"On the stove, on the stove," Mrs. Arends continues. "I took three of those plates from the East Indies, three of those enamelware plates. Put them on the stove and turned the herring now and then. Next you cut it into pieces and ...."

"And the smell?" interrupts Mrs. Bekker.

"Oh, I always take ... from coffee, coffee grounds, right? I put that in a small saucepan, with some water. I put it on the stove and everything smells of fresh coffee."

Mr. Arends says they also used to dry *trassi* [fermented fish or shrimp paste] on the stove. When they did this the neighbors would always start complaining and asking where that stench came from.

It isn't until Mr. Arends mentions his complaining neighbors that I notice their memories have shifted to their first years in the Netherlands. Which also explains the stove. Mr. Arends tells me they once offered their neighbors a plate of *bami*. It was only after they had finished eating it and announced that they liked it, that Mr. Arends would then tell them that cooking this dish produced the "stench" they used to smell. Later, when their neighbors figured out that *bami* wasn't the same as *trassi*, so Mr. Arends concludes, "we already got acquainted with each other."

"But curly kale and Brussels sprouts also smell bad when they're being cooked," Mrs. Arends remarks; and she adds, "We're talking about food again."

"But that's nice, isn't it?" says Mrs. Bekker. "When you talk about food, you will never quarrel. After all, tastes do differ."

It looks like Mrs. Bekker has given some sort of signal with this. An animated conversation ensues in which the two old ladies do most of the talking. The names of all kinds of dishes from the Indo-Dutch cuisine fly back and forth across the table. They discuss different ways of preparing them, whether something should be boiled, fried, or steamed in *pisang* leaf, the correct ingredients and spices for the dishes, and what they taste like. When both of the ladies can't think of the name of a dish, Mr. Arends helps out.

Mrs. Bekker repeats, "you'll never quarrel when talking about food. Because tastes do differ."

"And you learn something, too," Mrs. Arends adds.

Mr. Arends starts on a new anecdote. All this talk about food has stirred up this memory, as we are all about to find out. He tells us that in the army, where he found a job after his repatriation, he and the other boys from the East Indies always used to sit together. One time when they were sitting outside on a cold day in wintertime the captain asked why they would not join the others in the canteen. He asked why they were sitting apart.

"Who taught us that, sitting apart?" Arends rhetorically asked the captain, and then immediately provided the answer to his own question: "You Dutchmen! Who always used to sit together at the club, at the *Concordia* Club, De *Harmonie* Club?"[3] The captain dismissed the matter with a shrug and an "Oh well."

"Besides," Arends continued to say, "if we sit with the other men, we'd just be listening to conversations about Tom, Dick, and Harry. But here we talk about *sajoer lodeh* [a dish of various vegetables and meat prepared with spices and coconut milk] and *goelé kambing* [a dish of goatmeat prepared with curcuma and coconut milk]. And that's why we're sitting here, cozily, together."

"We always talk about food"

Mr. and Mrs. Arends, both well into their seventies, and the octogenarian Mrs. Bekker, are part of a group of about 300,000 Dutch people who came to the Netherlands from the Dutch East Indies – now Indonesia – between 1945 and 1968. Defining this heterogeneous group of "repatriates," as the Dutch government labeled them although many of them had never before set foot on Dutch soil, is a rather complex problem. On the one hand, the Indo-Dutch immigrants shared a common past. On the other hand they were distinct from one another, owing to differences in parentage, and their social and class status in the former colony. The largest group were descended from European fathers and native Indonesian mothers. Alongside these there also were the so-called *"totoks"* – referring to both European newcomers and full-blooded Europeans who had lived in the East Indies for generations. Although these differences, which were expressed on a social level, definitely did not disappear after these people came to the Netherlands, they did become less functional in their new context. Due to internal as well as external circumstances, a process of community construction began, and hitherto differentiated people began to regard themselves as a single community, with a common history and a common fate.[4]

Since the early 1950s government policy focused mainly on assimilating the repatriates. The subsequent integration of Indo-Dutch people went so well that even before 1970, the promulgation of explicit policies to achieve this was already deemed unnecessary. Certain factors, such as the repatriates' willingness to adapt, their familiarity with Dutch standards and values, the fact that they could not return, in addition to a good job market where the newcomers quickly found their places, contributed to a successful integration of this population (Robinson 1992:24). Therefore, present Dutch policy does not consider Indo-Dutch citizens as an ethnic minority.

However, the government's assimilation policy made exceptions for one group of repatriates: the elderly. These elderly people, mostly single women of sixty years and older, were considered unable to adapt to Dutch society and continue their life here independently. Special homes were founded for them, where they could maintain their own daily habits.

In 1953 the first home for Indo-Dutch elderly people was set up in the province of Noord-Brabant. It was followed by similar homes being opened in the central, southern, and eastern parts of the country. By 1958 these facilities included twenty homes, and by 1965 the number of residents had risen to a total of 1,600. As their number of residents gradually declined over the years, however, the number of homes has correspondingly diminished. There are now only three homes left in the whole of the Netherlands, with a total number of about 250 residents. These homes are so-called "categorial" care and nursing homes, in reference to the fact that only those who fall into a certain category of infirmed, elderly people are eligible to be admitted. These homes are distinguishable from regular old age homes by the care they provide, which in several respects cater specifically for a specific target group.[5]

As Van Dongen (1983) and Robinson (1988,1992) point out, the fact that there is still a need for special homes for Indo-Dutch elderly can be seen as a marginal comment on the story of the successful integration of the first generation of Indo-Dutch people in Dutch society. The assimilation has obviously not been as complete as is often assumed.[6]

Vriezen (1993:151) observes that there was a revaluation of ethnicity at a higher age among Indo-Dutch elderly. In the approximately thirty extensive interviews I had with residents of The Home, I asked them if they could describe the "Indo-Dutch character" of their home. Most replies first mentioned the residents and their background. However, emphasis was often put on the diversity of individual backgrounds, and it was the common past of the residents that gave the home it's special character. Furthermore, the past that one shares with others is a cohesive factor and makes associating with one another that much easier. As one resident put it, "People from the East Indies come together and then you have all kinds of things in common... things you can easily understand, things you can talk about.... So that...well ...you can enjoy everything together. That's it."

Besides the characteristics of the residents themselves and their common past, in virtually all the conversations a second feature was mentioned as being specific to the character of the home: the *food*. It was common for the residents to say:

> "Yes, the surroundings, really, the fact that the people are from the East Indies. That – and also the food! Well, and talking about the past with everyone, because we all experienced it."

> "Well, the fact that all the residents are from the East Indies. And because you all have the same background, you can talk about anything. And also the food is familiar."

> "Yes, everything, really: the food, you talk to Indo-Dutch people here, and sometimes you hear someone speaking Malay. And that makes it pleasant, yes."

Clearly, when asked to describe the specific character of The Home, the residents not only referred to their common past, but also "the food." Without further explanation, it was clear that they referred to the Indo-Dutch meals which three times a week are served in the home. In a randomly chosen week during the time I spent in the home, the Monday menu was *babi tuta gutu ruga, sajur tjampur,* served with rice and fruit. On Wednesday, *katoprak, tempeh goreng,* rice, *emping,* and fruit. And on Friday, *ikan bali, tumis taugé,* with rice and fruit was served. It was with meals such as these that the residents emphasized what they regarded as the special character of The Home. This service was – as some emphatically told me – the foremost reason why they chose to live in this particular home.

But food not only characterized the very nature of The Home; it also often determined the topic of conversation between its residents. The excerpt from a conversation between Mr. and Mrs. Arends and Mrs. Bekker, which I presented earlier, already illustrated clearly. Yet, residents themselves also indicated that in their conversations food is the one thing that almost always comes up. When, for instance, I enquired about Mrs. Coenraad's contacts with other residents of The Home, and asked her whether she ever discussed the past with them, she replied, "Yes, yes, ... when we get together, right. When I go downstairs around six or six-thirty, I sometimes talk with the people there. And then we always, almost always, discuss the past. And almost always the food.... Yes, I know, it's a habit of ours. But we always start out just discussing a little dish, so to say, and it grows more and more, and then you get a whole meal, in a manner of speaking. We always talk about food."

Especially illustrative in this respect was what Mrs. Diederiks – who was different from most other residents of The Home because she was of European birth and only left for the Dutch East Indies after her marriage, where she stayed for twenty years as a *totok* – brought up when I asked her if she talked to her fellow residents a lot about the East Indies. "If you want to talk to the people here, everything you hear is about the cuisine, about spices and cooking, because there, in the East Indies, it's a gastronomic culture. They all know 'You have to use those spices for those dishes,' and 'for those dishes you need those spices.' And, fortunately, I know all of those spices because I tried to make "rice table" myself. If you don't know what to talk about, you ask someone 'Do you know how to make such and such dish?' Oh, and then you don't have to say anything anymore."

Mrs. Diederiks made talking about food a strategy to revive a conversation when everyone had fallen silent. Mr. Ekkers, on the other hand, often didn't feel much enthusiasm for the subjects of conversation his fellow residents chose. Most conversations in the home didn't really interest him. "When you talk to people here," Mr. Ekkers told me, "in the end they are going to talk about food. But a real conversation about life in the East Indies, about the history, the plantations etc., you don't hear people talking about that....Most of it comes down to the same old thing. So you start to tell them something, a travel story, where you've been, what it was like there, where you worked, and so on and so forth. But however you tell your story, at some point they will say: 'Oh, were you there? ... Then you must know this and that food.' Then there it is again. The food crops up again."

"I think it's because we miss it"

In her article about the historical development of ethnic cuisines in the Netherlands, Van Otterloo remarks:

> Although there was widespread uncertainty as to the "Indo-Dutch" identity, it was clear that the common eating habits were indisputably their own, and are still (or again) now experienced as binding....The art of cooking had its origins in many traditions (Chinese, Indonesian and also to some extent Dutch) which had influenced each other over a long period, and this had produced a great variety of refined dishes. The now well-known 'rice table,' consisting of among other things rice with chicken, pork and beef dishes, is an example which is typical of the Indo-Dutch group (1987:128).

According to the authors of a small volume about "flavor and history of the Indo-Dutch cuisine," this cuisine – which as they declare belongs "to the richest gastronomic cultures in the world" – can be characterized as follows:

> It is not just the great variety of dishes with varying flavours, but also the refined combination of spices and ingredients that makes every dish, however simple, unique. We learned the recipes, as they are still being used, from our mothers, grandmothers and great-grandmothers. But they probably go back for centuries, and they have been influenced by many nationalities: the Portuguese, the Spanish, the French – and let us not forget the Indonesians and the Dutch. And it is also impossible to imagine the Indo-Dutch cuisine without Chinese and Indian dishes. In short, the Indo-Dutch cuisine, like the Indo-Europeans, is of mixed origin (Derksen et al. 1994).

In the spring of 2001, staff of The Home took part in a training program that was intended to "let staff of homes for elderly people from the East Indies get acquainted with, and receive training in, the characteristics of the Indo-Dutch and Moluccan cultures." In the collection of course material used in this training I came across a poem under the title of *"Een Indo blijft een Indo"* ("An Indo stays an Indo"). The first of the five stanzas of the poem read:

> An Indo stays an Indo,
> Always ramé ramé: koempoelan.
> Nasi goreng, bami, soto,

> Sate babi, gado-gado,
> Talking on about makanan.[7]

As Mrs. Coenraad once told me, "We always talk about food," and so the poem claims that "Indos" talk on and on about eating and food *(makanan)*. Indo-Dutch people are not just obviously part of a joint culinary culture – a cuisine that, like the people themselves, is of mixed origin - their very act of talking about food is something that is shared by all members of the group.[8] Mr. Arends' anecdote about life in the army vividly illustrates how talking about food can mark the boundaries of a group, and how processes of inclusion and exclusion can be expressed in this way. Mr. Arends and his Indo-Dutch mates sought each other out to talk about the fabulous dished of the Indo-Dutch cuisine; and with this topic they explicitly separated themselves from their Dutch colleagues who spent their time gossiping.

Several residents of The Home contrasted gossiping with talking about food. Talking about others was considered to be one of two aspects that were typical for the conversations of the Dutch. The other is talking about the weather. They impressed upon me that whenever the Dutch would talk about the weather or about others, Indo-Dutch people would talk about food. And although the weather also came up regularly in conversations in The Home, and although residents certainly did not refrain from gossiping, it was food, eating, and cooking that frequently were the favorite topics of conversation among them.

Usually Mrs. Franken skips taking tea. But this afternoon, at the insistence of one of the attendants, she is there. After sitting herself down in the common room of the ward, where the other ladies are staring somewhat aimlessly over their cups of tea, she suddenly blurts out: "You are so quiet here!"

"Well, what is there to talk about?" Mrs. Groeneveld replies with a sigh.

"Anyway, nothing happens here," adds Mrs. Harting.

"Well, talk about food, for instance," says Mrs. Franken. It makes Mrs. Immink laugh. It's no wonder that comment came from Mrs. Franken; she always has food on her mind.

Mrs. Jansz, who seldom says anything, suddenly opens her eyes and quips, "Talk about food? When I think about food, I get a stomachache. Food ... the food here in The Home.... If you'll excuse me, and tastes do differ, but I think it's ...."

"Then maybe you're ill," says Mrs. Franken, "I almost always think the food here is very tasty."

One of the other ladies supports that statement, pointing out that, after all, she is very happy not to have to cook for herself anymore.

"I suppose you want *saté udang* [prawn satay], right?" Mrs. Harting asks Mrs. Franken, upon which Mrs. Franken immediately and enthusiastically starts to tell her how she would like to eat that.

"Now they've started," Mrs. Immink says to me.

Almost all of the eight ladies present are talking at once, and to each other. Even Mrs. Klein, who isn't normally so talkative, joins in. I hear Mrs. Harting say, "And Mrs. Lantzius just ate that for her birthday, yesterday, didn't she?" Mrs. Lantzius doesn't answer the question, and instead starts to tells the two ladies who are sitting close to her all about her birthday dinner. She celebrated her eighty-ninth birthday yesterday in an Indo-Dutch restaurant, with all her children, grandchildren and great-grandchildren. She bemoans that all her grandchildren wanted were French fries.

"So, don't they like rice?" asks Mrs. Harting, who is sitting a little further away, but has obviously been keeping track of the conversation. "Hardly," replies Mrs. Lantzius.

After the ladies have finished discussing some more dishes from the Indo-Dutch cuisine, I use a brief moment of silence to again ask something that I have asked before, at other occasions: why do Indo-Dutch people talk so much about food?

"I think it's because we miss it, because we miss our country," says Mrs. Harting. Meanwhile, Mrs. Franken continues musing over other dishes: "... and with that sauce! Oh, delicious!"

While one resident expressed her discontent with the quality of the meals served in The Home,[9] one of her fellow residents, a known gourmand, talked ardently about several tidbits and dishes from the East Indies, and another pointed out that her grandchildren preferred fries.[10] Talking about food may be done in many ways. However that which attracts the most attention in this passage is the reply Mrs. Harting gave to my question. She feels that Indo-Dutch people talk about food so much because they miss it.

I remarked once to Mr. Arends that I heard people in The Home talk about food so often, and he suggested that this wasn't really so difficult to understand. "That's how it is in Indonesia," he told me. "Food is sold at the door. And there are certain places where you find all those food stalls arranged in lines along the side of the road. And then at night – because in Indonesia we lived outside, so to speak, and here in Holland, we live inside, which makes sense, because you don't walk outside in the cold – but there, at night, you go outside because of the heat, and you look and see food. 'Hey, that's nice! Let's have a taste.' And you have another taste. You go into a little restaurant and tuck into it. And then, ... suddenly, you're in Holland, and we have to get used to it."[11]

When I asked Mrs. Groeneveld whether she could tell me more about why they all talked so much about food, she said, "I don't know why we do that. But we always do it. Although in Indonesia we did not do that!" I asked her to explain. "It's because we actually ate more native dishes than Dutch ones because Dutch food was more expensive. You couldn't plant potatoes just anywhere; you had to do that in the mountains, where it's cold. And you could...eat on the streets. They go from door to door, sometimes with entire hot meals, carrying them on their backs, in a *slendang*, a sling. You can call over someone like that and buy hot rice dishes."

It has been noted before that we can attribute a group-binding function to talking about food. Just as food itself can mark group boundaries, talking about food can also have a distinguishing effect. It is partly due to that phenomenon that Indo-Dutch people, and certainly the elderly among them, distinguish themselves as a group within the wider Dutch society. As has been stated already, talking about food is to Indo-Dutch people what talking about the weather is to the Dutch.

Looking closer at what Mr. Arends and Mrs. Groeneveld had to say about this, and remembering Mrs. Harting's remark, we find that one of the principal reasons why the residents of The Home and other members of their generation talk so much about food is that it, in fact, is a reflection of an experience of deprivation. To them, talking about the food from the past means, in a manner of speaking, the opposite of what the well-known Madeleine biscuit meant to Proust. It's not, as in the Proustian way, taste that calls the past to mind, but rather reminiscing that brings back taste – the flavors of the past. Here, *flavors* stand for a whole culinary culture in all it's aspects, including not only the great variety of refined dishes but also the food stalls and the food-selling peddlers associated with it. Of course all of this is easily linked to the function of talking about food that was discussed earlier. Talking about the flavors from the past, the deprivation of which only people who share that same experience can understand, clearly does have, after all, an including and excluding effect.

Notes

1   See Calvo 1982 for an overview of such studies.
2   All residents of The Home who are quoted in the text, are referred to with pseudonyms. I chose these names randomly from common family names from the Dutch East Indies, as recorded in "Janssen's Indisch Repertorium" (www.igv.nl/jir/jirnmgr.html).
3   In colonial days both *Concordia* and *De Harmonie* were fashionable society clubs in Batavia (now Jakarta). See Cress 1998:66and100.
4   For the history of the arrival, receptions, and settlement of Indo-Dutch people in the Netherlands, see especially the standard book by Willems 2001.
5   The homes are *Dennenrust* in Wageningen, *Patria* in Bussum, and *Rumah Saya* in Ugchelen/Apeldooorn. Included in the federation *Bersama Kuat* (Together We Are Strong), founded by these care and nursing homes, is also the Rafy home in Breda, which is specifically for elderly people from the Moluccan Islands. In order to limit chances of identification of the home where I conducted the research on which this article is based, certain characteristics – such as the number of residents, specific facilities etc. – are not specified. The research was commissioned by the institution itself, the purpose being to gain insight into the question of how the residents evaluated the care, and how the care services could be more fine-tuned to the desires, needs, and feelings of this specific group of elderly people. Central to the project was the application of qualitative research methods, through direct observation of, and participation in, the daily lives of the residents. For this purpose I stayed in the home for a period of three months in the first half of 2001. The research results were made available in a confidential report. This is the first published article based on the data collected during this research, and as such marks my first steps in a new research field. I consider it a pleasure to be able to contribute in this way to a *Festschrift* for Arie de Ruijter, who was one of my tutors in cultural anthropology, and has long been a passionate advocate of anthropological research into our own multicultural society.
6   See also Van Overbeek and s'Jacobs 1992, Rijkschroeff, The and Wu 1993, and Feirabend et al 1998. See Cottaar and Willems 1985 for more general comments on the so-called success

story of the assimilation of Indo-Dutch people.

7   The poem was printed without any mention of author or source. *Ramé* = busy, but especially busy in a cosy way; *koempoelan* = meeting, association, club; *makanan* = food, to eat; the other terms are all names of Indo-Dutch dishes. Of the other four stanzas, one was completely dedicated to spicy food (sambal and *boemboe*). The remaining characteristics of "an Indo," as mentioned in the poem, were being fond of country and *krontjong* music, sleeping with a bolster or so-called 'Dutch wife' *(goeling)*, using tiger balm *(obat matjan)*, frequently using "uncle" and "aunt" as forms of address, and the use of a number of typical exclamations like *Adoeh sèh* (expresses pain, surprise or astonishment), *Soedah* (expresses resignation), and *Kassian* (expresses pity). Translations of Indo-Dutch terms are taken from Cress 1998.

8   A striking example of the fact that Indo-Dutch people always talk about food can be found in Yvonne Keuls' biographical novel *Mevrouw mijn moeder* (Madam my mother), where she vividly describes how even during the funeral of a relative her Indo-Dutch aunts animatedly kept talking about a new recipe (1999:229-230).

9   In his anthropological study of life in an American nursing home, Savishinsky remarks that it is always important to view the complaints of individual residents concerning the quality of the meals in the institution in light of the fact that "meals were a convenient place for many residents to displace their other displeasures with life" (1991:19).

10   With her remark concerning her grandchildren, who prefer potatoes to rice Mrs. Lantzius, implies that the third Indo-Dutch generation has become "dutchified." The binary opposition of "potatoes : rice" is often used as symbolising the opposition "Dutch : Indo-Dutch" (see, for instance, Van Otterloo 1987 and Vriezen 1993). In the 1960s, social workers used the distinction between potatoes and rice as being a determinant for group boundaries. An "oriental" family – a so-called "oriental orientation" was seen as one of the main complicating factors in the integration of repatriated families in Dutch society – was characterized, among other things, by "mainly eating rice instead of potatoes" (Willems 2001:189). Also compare Feirabend et al.'s remark about the residents of a home for Indo-Dutch elderly: "One elderly person says he has been 'dutchified' more than others ("We eat potatoes"), but no one has left 'being an Indo' behind" (1998:54).

     Another way in which ingredients of the Indo-Dutch and the Dutch cuisine are opposed, is of an olfactory nature: the smell of garlic and *trassi* is compared to the smell of curly kale and Brussels sprouts. In the early period of the settlement of Indo-Dutch people into Dutch society, when they began to prepare their own meals, the smell of *trassi*, garlic and other (then unknown) spices was used as a stigma against them – something that happened, and happens still, to other groups of newcomers as well (see Van Otterloo 1987:129). The quoted remark of Mrs. Arends, "But curly kale and Brussels sprouts also smell bad when they're being cooked," should be seen in this particular context. Also compare what has already been observed in the first paragraph about curly kale and Brussels sprouts with regards to the Dutch "identity".

     Cottaar and Willems (1984:112-114) describe, how in the 1950s, Indo-Dutch immigrants in the boarding houses where they were lodged after their arrival in The Netherlands were forced, "for their own good," to eat potatoes and, curly kale!

11   Compare this with Van Otterloo's statement: "The centrality of eating in Indonesia manifested itself in other ways as well, such as the extensive street sale of prepared foods" (1987:128). Also compare Cress 1998:226.

Bibliography

Calvo, M. 1982. Migration et alimentation. *Information sur les sciences sociales* 21(3): 383-446.

Caplan, P. 1997. Approaches to the study of food, health and identity. In P. Caplan, ed. *Food, Health and Identity,* pp. 1-31. London/New York: Routledge.

Cottaar, A., and W. Willems. 1984. I*ndische Nederlanders. Een onderzoek naar beeldvorming.* Den Haag: Moesson.

Cottaar, A., and W. Willems. 1985. De geassimileerde Indische Nederlander: mythe of werkelijkheid? *De Gids* 148(3/4): 257-270.

Counihan, C.M., and P. van Esterik eds., 1997. *Food and Culture: a Reader.* New York/London: Routledge.

Cress, R. 1998. *Petjoh. Woorden en wetenswaardigheden uit Indië.* Amsterdam: Prometheus.

Derksen, E., L. Ducelle, and E. van Geleuken. 1994. *Met kruiden en een korrel zout. Smaak en geschiedenis van de Indische keuken.* Den Haag: Stichting Tong Tong

Farb, P., and G. Armelagos. 1980. *Consuming Passions: the Anthropology of Eating.* Boston: Houghton-Mifflin.

Feirabend, J., A. Meyer, R. Wolff, and R. Penninx. 1998. *'Het lijkt wel of ze geen wensen hebben...': oudere Indische Nederlanders en zorg. Een verkennend onderzoek.* Amsterdam: IMES/Den Haag: Stichting Pelita.

Harbottle, L. 1997a. Taste and embodiment. The food preferences of Iranians in Britain. In H. Macbeth, ed., *Food Preferences and Taste. Continuity and Change,* pp. 175-185. Providence/Oxford: Berghahn Books,.

Harbottle, L. 1997b. Fast Food / spoiled identity: Iranian migrants in the British catering trade. In P. Caplan, ed., *Food, Health and Identity,* pp. 87-110. London/New York: Routledge.

Harris, M. 1986. *Good to Eat: Riddles of Food and Culture.* New York: Simon and Schuster.

Keuls, Y. 1999. *Mevrouw mijn moeder.* Amsterdam: Ambo.

Lévi-Strauss, C. 1965. Le triangle culinaire. *L'Arc* 26:19-29.

Lévi-Strauss, C. 1962. *Le Totémisme. Aujourd'hui.* Paris: Presses universitaires de France.

Mennell, S., A. Murcott, and A.H. van Otterloo. 1992. *The Sociology of Food: Eating, Diet and Culture.* London: Sage.

Rijkschroeff, B.R., G.T. The, and S.M. Wu. 1993. *Bij leven en welzijn: de positie van oudere Chinezen en oudere Indische Nederlanders vergeleken.* Capelle a/d IJssel: Labyrinth Publication.

Robinson, G.B. 1988. Pegangan Indo. Een explorerend onderzoek naar het niveau van etniciteit en de betekenis daarvan in het leven van twee generaties Indo's. Katholieke Universiteit Nijmegen. (Unpublished PhD dissertation.)

Robinson, G.B. 1992. Indische ouderen in Nederland. In M. Bakker, ed. *Oud in den vreemde. Over allochtone ouderen,* pp.12-46. Houten/Antwerpen: Bohn, Stafleu, Van Loghum.

van Dongen, P. 1983. Suara Mereka (Hun Stem). Een explorerend onderzoek naar het integratieproces van bewoners van Indische verzorgingstehuizen. Katholieke Universiteit Nijmegen. (Unpublished PhD dissertation.)

van Otterloo, A.H. 1987. Foreign immigrants and the Dutch at table: 1945-1985. Bridging or widening the gap? *Netherlands Journal of Sociology* 23(2):126-143.

van Overbeek, H.J., and R. R. s'Jacob. 1992. *Indië, ons t(e)huis: een onderzoek naar de behoefte aan Indische verzorgingshuizen.* 's-Gravenhage: NIMAWO.

Vriezen, J. 1993. *Rijst of aardappelen? Indische en autochtone ouderen in Nederland.* Universiteit van Amsterdam. (PhD dissertation.)

Willems, W. 2001. *De uittocht uit Indië 1945-1995.* Amsterdam: Bert Bakker.

15

Comparing Sources in African Surinamese History
The Maroons of Granman Broos

Wim Hoogbergen

Introduction

In his scientific writings, Arie de Ruijter has paid much attention to the topic of multi-cultural society, and the problems of identity and self-determination. In 1999, he and I published an article in *Caribnet. Journal of the Caribbean Studies International Network* on the topic of comparing sources in anthropology and history. In it we discussed the methodological point of view that we all have an implicit theory of the reality in which we live. We argued that since perception and conception are based on inter-woven expectations and experiences, we in fact do not discover facts but rather construct them from reality with the help of particular tools, which are our concepts. Facts are not so much encountered they are produced. So, the view that anthropological or historical facts exist independent of the anthropologist's or the historian's perception of them, and are somewhere "out there" waiting to be discovered, may be appealing in its simplicity. But such a vision would be totally and fundamentally mistaken.

In our 1999 article we pointed out that the activity of comparison does not only have to do with phenomena and events, but also with sources – the aids with which the anthropologists or historians use to describe and analyse. Results are, after all, always the upshot of an interaction between "empirical reality" and the instruments used to describe that reality. We illustrated our argument using some events from Surinamese history, mainly from the history of the Surinamese Maroons.

One of the most profound problems faced by the slaves who were brought to Suriname was the issue of multicultural society. The Africans brought to Suriname and auctioned off in Paramaribo, the capital, had different ethnic origins. Once they arrived in Suriname, the slaves went through different developments. The most important distinction today within the African-Surinamese population originates from the fact that during slavery times, a great number of slaves fled the plantations and created new societies in the interior of the country. There they had to deal with ethnic complexity in the process of building new societies. In this article I will focus on the issue – also relevant to the work of de Ruijter – of the methodological complexity of combining evidence from oral history with archival material dating back to colonial times.

Historians mainly base their work on those of other historians, and on information retrieved from archives. To a lesser extent they also use what we anthropologists call "oral history." It is a lucky coincidence that both types of sources are amply available in the case of the Suriname Maroons. Their history can be largely reconstructed by means of archival material. The Suriname Maroons themselves, however, are masters in passing on oral tradition. They constantly ask themselves how, for God's sake Africans ended up in the Suriname jungle. The central story that unfolds begins with the cruelty of slavery, which prompted many slaves to flee into the forest; the narrative then relates the struggle against the Whites and the way in which gods and ancestors helped them in this fight. The importance of oral history in Maroon societies is a main reason why anthropologists engaged in its study are often also specialists in historical anthropology.[1]

The examples I have collected for this article relate to a specific Maroon group called Broos, after a nineteenth century chieftain. The Broos-Maroons were a small group that in 1860 comprised around 200 individuals. The group was formed in the nineteenth century by runaway slaves from plantations situated along the Suriname and Commewijne Rivers. They found a suitable hiding place in the marshy area between those rivers. These Maroons subsequently often got into fights – particularly in 1830, 1831, and 1862 – with soldiers sent to destroy their villages, to kill or to recapture them. In contrast to other Maroon groups, the Broos-Maroons did not stay in the bush after slavery was abolished in Suriname in 1863. They left their Maroon villages in the marsh and went to live on an abandoned plantation, called Roorak, situated along the Suriname River (see Hoogbergen 1996a).

For some 50 years they lived peacefully and harmoniously on Roorak. However, in the 1920s the Whites returned after they discovered that the land contained bauxite; the plantation was subsequently sold to Americans. So that the mining could begin, officials came to Roorak to evict the Broos-Maroons. They were compensated for the loss of their land and their houses, and with that money Jansi Babel, Broos's eldest son and now chieftain of the group, bought the plantation Tilifo[2] situated some ten kilometres south of Paramaribo. Some of his descendants still live there. Since the 1920s the Broos Maroons have mixed with local Creoles. Many have also immigrated to the land of their former colonial masters and enemies, the Dutch.[3] Some families (particularly the Babel and Landveld families) cherish their Maroon heritage, and take great care to transfer their culture to following generations.

Carrying slaves to Suriname
"Ma Fanny came from Africa," Edwin Landveld told me in 1981.

> Ma Fanny was my great-grandmother. How she ended up in the hands of slave hunters is unknown in my family. However, it is said that on board the slave ship to Suriname, she wasn't the only one from her family. Three of her brothers also were captured. When the slave ship arrived in Suriname, they were all sold to different owners.[4]

Nowadays, inhabitants of African descent count for around 220,000 of Suriname's inhabitants, which is roughly 45 percent of the country's population. Another 100,000

African-Surinamese live in the Netherlands. In French Guyana live some 50,000 blacks of Surinamese descent. Postma suggests that between 1668 and 1795, around 185,443 slaves were sold to Surinamese planters (1990:186-212). In the period between 1796 and 1827, another 28,000 slaves were imported (Van Stipriaan 1993:314). Until 1735, more than 70 percent of the imported slaves were male. Even after the planters became more serious in encouraging breeding as a replacement strategy for the plantation population, the proportion of female slaves imported never rose above 40 percent.

Most African-Surinamese people know hardly any specific about their African background because, according to the oral tradition (and as far as I know), no stories had been handed down to their predecessors in Africa before they were captures and brought as slaves to Suriname. Even though, of course, the Afro-Surinamese cultures have deep African roots, a cultural tradition is not the same as a personal story. Thus, for the African-Surinamese, oral history began in Suriname. Even the oral history of the Surinamese Maroons does not tell us anything about the African background of the founding mothers of their society. Did they come from Angola or Kongo, or perhaps from northern regions like Senegal? Only in the archival documents are the ethnic origins of Surinamese slaves revealed.

After analysing extensive quantitative data, Postma (1990) came to the conclusion that before 1725 more than half of the Surinamese slaves originated from the Slave Coast, i.e. the area between the estuary of the Volta and Cape Lopez. Over the next ten years, the area that supplied slaves became much larger, and came to include not only the Slave Coast, but also the Gold Coast and Loango-Angola. In the period, from 1736 until 1795, however, the focus of the Dutch trade on the Guinea Coast moved gradually and steadily westwards, such that by the end of the century, half of the slaves were coming from the Sierra Leone area, known as the Windward Coast. We do not have exact data at our disposal about slave imports in the period after 1795.

By 1808, however, the Atlantic slave trade had become prohibited in many of the former slave owning and slave trading European and American states. Nevertheless, thousands of slaves continued to be brought to Suriname until 1826.[5] Not much research has been done into the ethnic origins of slaves that entered Suriname after 1795, but they probably had been imported from the same harbours on the Windward and Gold Coast as in the second part of the eighteenth century.

For a long time Surinamese slaves were very aware of their ethnic origins. They made a clear distinction between Africans (slaves who had been born in Africa) and Creoles (slaves born in Suriname). The first group was subdivided into *Gangu-slaves* (from the Windward Coast), *Kormantins* (from the Gold Coast), *Papa* and *Abo Slaves* (from the Slave Coast), and *Luangus,* Bantu-slaves from Kongo and Angola. However intermarriage eventually caused the disappearance of ethnic differences in slave society. The ethnic African languages evanesced and were replaced by English-based Creole languages.

By 1705 there were 10,000 Africans slaves in Suriname. In the next 60 years, the slave population grew steadily, with some 750 persons born each year. In 1770 there were around 50,000 slaves living in the colony. The majority lived in Paramaribo city, were most of them were servants, or on one of the 533 plantations throughout the country (Van Stipriaan 1993: 71). However, by 1863 the number of slaves had diminished to a mere 36,000 persons. And even though slavery was officially abolished that same year, there nevertheless continued to function as many as 216 plantations.[6]

There were other developments taking place. Owing to the shortage of European women in the colony, some female slaves became the concubines of their masters: planters, soldiers, administrators. These unions produced mixed offspring: the mulattoes. Being born a mulatto sometimes brought with it a ticket to freedom. However, through legal manumission, slave-owners also sometimes freed slaves. We do not exactly know the number of freed slaves until 1832. From archival records, we do know, however, that between 1832 and 1863 6,364 slaves were manumitted. In 1863 the free black or mulatto population of Suriname numbered 14,000 persons (Ten Hove and Dragtenstein 1997).

The Maroon camp of Broos

Ma Fanny was one of the roughly 80,000 female slaves imported in total into Suriname. As the great-grandmother of Edwin Landveld, the period of her forced immigration can be situated around 1800. In Suriname she became one of the 45,000 slaves living there at the time. By the time slavery was abolished Ma Fanny was still alive; but she had already ceased being a slave for some time beforehand, not through manumission, but by running away from her plantation.

Slaves in Suriname did not have official family names. The plantation registers only mention the names that the owners had given to their slaves. In March 1863, three months before Abolition Day,[7] a commission visited each plantation to register the slaves' newly chosen or given family names. The *Emancipatie Register* records the names of all the 36,484 slaves who were emancipated in 1863.

In the *Emancipatie Register* we find a section, appended some months after Abolition Day, with the names of 133 "runaway" slaves from the Maroon village of chieftain (or captain) Broos. There we can read that a sixty-year-old grandmother, Mofina, chose "Fanny" for her first name, and "Landveld" for her family name.[8] The community in which Mofina (Ma Fanny) was a member was located in the expansive swamps at the upper course of the Surnau creek, a small tributary of the Suriname River.

When we compare the stories preserved in the form of oral tradition with data written down in the archives about the Maroon village of chieftain Broos, we immediately find a discrepancy. Edwin Landveld told me that Broos was the son of Ma Fanny. However, according to the *Emancipation Register*, Broos was the son of another woman: Ma Amba, who was born in 1804. In that register we find three founding mothers of the runaway community: first Ma Fanny, second Ma Amba, and her younger sister Ma Antje. In 1863, when the list was written down, these three "founding mothers" were already grandmothers. Ma Fanny had seven children (four sons and three daughters), Ma Amba had eight (four sons and four daughters), and Ma Antje, six (five daughters and one son). In that year those three founding mothers already had twenty-eight grandchildren, of whom eighteen were daughters. After abolition all the decedents of Ma Fanny took the name Landveld, but all the children and grandchildren of her sisters Amba and Antje were registered under the name Babel.[9] Oral tradition emphasizes that all the Babels and the Landvelds lived together, as one large family. "Therefore we nowadays do not know exactly if someone was the mother, or perhaps the mother-in-law," Edwin Landveld replied when I brought his attention to the discrepancy contained in the archival record.

Maroon societies

There does not exist something like a history of *the* African Surinamese. As we have already seen, Africans brought to Suriname to be sold as slaves came from different ethnic nations. Furthermore, once they were in Suriname, the Africans lived different experiences. As already mentioned, a great number of slaves were able to escape from their plantations, and create new societies in the interior. These runaway slaves were commonly called *Businenge* or Maroons, and today the largest population of Maroons in the Western hemisphere is found in Suriname.

Price estimated that by the year 2000, the total number of the Maroon population had reached 79,000 (2002: 82). For a long time the Maroons remained in the interior of Suriname, where they had built their relatively isolated villages above the impassable waterfalls. Over the past thirty years, however, they have increasingly immigrated to the coastal area, and after the civil war (1986-1992) also to French Guiana. This total of about 80,000 Maroons is encompasses six ethnic groups which, in spite of the fact that they were formed under the same historical and ecological conditions, show considerable differences in terms of language, religion, marriage patterns, art forms, and the degree of dependency on the economy of the coastal area. All these groups share a similar political structure and agricultural system, however. The Saramaka and the Ndyuka are the largest groups, consisting of 32,000 people each one. The Matawai (4,000), the Paramaka (5,000) and the Boni or Aluku (5,500) are smaller populations, while the Kwinti (the smallest one) has no more than 600 members. (For a further bibliography about the history and the anthropology of the Suriname Maroons, see Price 1976; Brana-Shute 1990.)

In the life history of Ma Fanny, we find all the same episodes as in Suriname history: slave trade, slavery, rebellion and marronage, and abolition. As already mentioned, she began her life in Africa but was later taken to Suriname in slavery. There, somewhere (we do not know the exact location), she worked on a sugar or coffee plantation. The white administrators registered her as a *negerin* (female Negro) because all slaves were called *negers* (Negroes). (If you were black but not a slave, your status was that of a *Vrije Neger* (Free Negro). One day Ma Fanny fled into the bush, thus becoming what are called Bosch Neger – a *Bush Negro* in Businenge.[10] There she remained for a long time, a runaway slave with the name Mofina. But, thanks to abolition, she died a free black woman: Fanny Landveld.

Oral history

Along with some 50,000 slaves, Suriname also had two segments of free people: name-ly, the manumitted blacks and mulattoes,[11] and the Maroons. Let us now return to the Maroons, and particularly to Ma Fanny.

I met Edwin Landveld for the first time in 1981, and he proved to be a renowned expert in oral history. He died in 1994 at the age of 87. I spoke with him several times. Before our conversations Edwin used to wash his hands with rum, splashing the liquor on his neck and shoulders. His audience, whether it was just me alone or with others, were given little glasses of rum to drink. The oral tradition – as related by Edwin Land-veld – concentrates on three themes: the escape of the ancestors from slavery, the destruction of their village after an Indian had betrayed its location to the Whites, and the ensuing battle against the Whites.

Anthropologists are well aware that oral history has a structure that is different from that of formal history (see for example Henige 1974 and 1982; Hoeree and Hoog-bergen 1984; Hoogbergen 1985; Vansina 1969 and 1985). The most important charac-teristic of oral history is that it is based on some central stories that usually are not chronologically ordered. Furthermore, the stories that make up oral history commonly focus around a few central characters, and a kind of epical condensation occurs. This literary phenomenon is not unheard of even in European history, as the stories based on the Frankish king Charlemagne, or the English King Arthur, attest. Another charac-teristic of oral history is that events are often combined. Incidents that historically occurred consecutively are presented in oral history within a short – and sometimes even the same – span of time. Moreover, oral history often has a mythical nature.

In the historical accounts of Edwin Landveld, epical condensation occurred around the characters of the two sons of Ma Fanny: the brothers Broos and Kaliko. It is recorded in the archives that Broos was born in 1822, and that Kaliko was thirteen year younger.[12] By around 1860 Broos was the chief, the *granman,* of his village. In the archives he is called a *boschcreool* (bush creole), which in Suriname is the name for someone who was born in the forest, not on a plantation. Oral tradition emphasizes very strongly the (probably fictional) collective background of the inhabitants of the vil-lage of Ma Fanny.

> On the slave ship to Suriname, Ma Fanny wasn't the only one of her fam-ily to make the trip. She and her three brothers were sold to different owners upon arriving in Suriname. In the course of time the brothers and Ma Fanny escaped from their cruel plantation lives and met each other again in the forest. Since there was a long lapse of time between their arrival in Suriname and their reunion in the forest, the siblings didn't know each other anymore. At that point, one had to ask the spirits to help recognize: is this your brother; is this your sister? The people them-selves knew nothing of their collective backgrounds, but the geesten (spirits)[13] that had come with them from Africa did.

The escape from the plantation

It is recorded in the Suriname archives that in September 1862 slaves ran away from a sugar plantation called Rac-à-Rac. According to the oral tradition, they did this in a rather spectacular way. The slaves organized a big dance party on a Saturday night; by the following morning they had all disappeared (Hoogbergen 1996; Hoogbergen and de Ruijter 1999; Hoogbergen 2001). Those slaves fled to the Maroon camp of Ma Fanny. This is how Edward Landveld described to me what then happened after the escape:

> In the woods, the Negroes gathered at a big lake. It was just like an ice lake, covered with moss. The Negroes called it *Kaaimangrasi* (cayman grass). Crossing the lake was difficult, like crossing ice. Ice breaks when it is not strong enough. Moss is the same. You walk on it and you fall through. But the Negroes were being driven forward by the Whites toward Kaaimangrasi, and now they thought, `How can we cross it?' They called on the gods, who showed them a path on which to walk. But it was not a road; it was one large cayman. It looked like dry wood. This cayman made sure they got to the other side.
>
> At *Kaaimangrasi* the Negroes had a place of sacrifice, where they lived at that time. They called this place of sacrifice *posu magremu*. *Magremu* is [a word in the] *Kromanti*-language. It means 'I stand like a rock; nothing can go past me.' At this place a white and a black flag [the flag of the dead] was waving. There was a big white rooster running around and there were potions. It was a fort and a place of sacrifice at the same time. Some sacrificed rum, others cola or wine. If you go there now, you can still see the stone bottles that contained the different potions.
>
> There was a large tree there. It was as big as the forest giant *Kankantri*. The tree was called *Mama Ondro*. The Negroes poured rum and beer on its base. The tree was also a place of sacrifice. They wrapped the tree in white cotton. Then they sprinkled it with rum and talked to it. The tree would move, even when there was no wind. The people made their sacrifices there and talked about God.
>
> Besides the cayman there was also the *aboma*, or boa constrictor. This snake was larger than a cobra, but it was not a real boa. It was a *winti*. The Negroes called it *jaja ma dunga*. The cayman and the aboma were the *winti* that stood by the Negroes, when they fought against the Whites. This was at the location called *posu magremu*. While the Negroes fought a battle against the Whites there, they sang:

> > *a mi ni go magremu*
> > *a mi ni go magremu*
> > *posu magremu*
> > *a mi ni go magremu*
> > *a mu ma he, a mu ma ho*

> *a mi ni go magremu*
> *posu magremu*

'*A mi ni go*' is Kromanti-language. It means "Spirits of this place of sacrifice, help us."

Before our ancestors lived at *Kaaimangrasi*, Amerindians already came to hunt there. One of them, named Mankaw (bull), was hunting when he discovered the village. Mankaw was the one who guided the Whites to the village. One morning Broos and Kaliko discovered that Whites were in the vicinity. "How did they cross the lake?" Broos asked. Fortunately our *kromanti*-men gave forewarning. In those days you had a jere-man, that is a *kromanti*-man, who can hear anything. He put his ear to the ground and the *gromna* (Mother Earth) told him how far away the Whites were. When the Whites came close, the Negroes started to shoot. The whites shot dangerous dumdum bullets. The Negroes shot with ordinary lead bullets, but had washed them in herbs. So those bullets were guided by the *Wintis*, who could aim extraordinarily well. Every bullet was a spirit that could kill 30 to 40 men. You might think, "How is it possible?". But it happened because it was purely spiritual.

When the Whites arrived at *Kaaimangrasi*, they wondered, "What is this?" They decided to cross it anyway. A whole battalion went down in it. And we Creoles[14] can hear them speak. The soldiers now belong to the ones who are there under the moss in the water. Spiritually they became *watra-wintis* (water spirits). So *Kaaimangrasi* is not a restful place. Without exaggeration!

When the Whites fought their battle there, a few musicians were present who all went under: tambourine, trumpet players, etc. The Whites were constantly bested because they could not cross the moss. The Negroes kept on hitting them with their bullets. The Whites could not find cover. The Negroes had at their disposal a herb to put in their ears when they were scared. Not many were afraid, but sometimes a few were. When the bullets would come by, they would only hear *zing!* next to their ears, but they could not be hit.

Broos and Kaliko said to their fellow warriors, "Are you scared? Do you hear the bullets? Think of the gods, the *obias* and the *Kromanti*. When you think of them and have faith in them, nothing will happen to you. When you don't pray and do nothing, you will die!"

A prince was fighting on the Dutch side. He was armoured. He never fell down and kept on chasing the Negroes. They asked themselves, "Who is this man?" They didn't know the armour and they thought it was a *kromanti*, a spirit coming towards them. The armoured man came closer and closer. The Negroes had the herbs that prevented them from being hit. Kaliko, my grandfather, got scared. After he had taken the herbs, he started to stutter. Now he became too courageous. However, the Negroes also had the herbs to temper courage. Otherwise you could have a heart attack. After taking that, Kaliko had just enough courage. He stormed towards the Whites with his machete. He heard the bullets whiz by his ears. One dumdum bullet hit him in his chest. He did *wgra* to make it go away. He saw the herbs there, and some slime, and a little bit of blood and the dumdum bullet fell on the ground. Kaliko ran toward the prince and hacked at him like a madman. The prince shot at Kaliko but could not hit him. My grandfather said: *"He a bun...sana obia."*

After the war, when my grandfather went to sleep, he sometimes jumped up and screamed, "The Whites are coming!" When the Whites had surrounded Kaliko, he disappeared into a column of smoke and from this pillar he shot at the Whites. They fell on the ground and Kaliko was able to keep on fighting.

The capture of the Maroon village

The oral tradition mentions that the Whites captured the village of Broos after the Amerindian Mankaw betrayed its location. In the archives I found documents that record that the villages of the Maroons had been discovered and destroyed on various occasions. This was especially true around 1830. In this period the Maroons were led by a chief called Sambo. In 1829, a slave escaped from a plantation and joined the Maroons; but he later regretted this and returned. To avoid punishment, he offered to reveal the location of the Maroon village. The punitive expedition was a partial success. The runaway slave took the soldiers to the Maroon village, which is called *Pasop* ("Look out!") in the archives. However, the soldiers started to shoot prematurely, and that is why almost all the inhabitants were able to escape. The village contained 31 houses, and was inhabited by around 100 people.

In the months following, expeditions were sent again and again to find the Maroons, but the soldiers never found out where they had fled. Since the Amerindians had a reputation for finding their way through the woods, the governor put twenty Amerindians in one of his patrols to act as trackers. However, they were unsuccessful at finding the Maroons. After a disagreement with the military commander, they even decided to stop with the operation and to return to their villages.[15] In January 1830, another effort was made to find the new hiding place of the Maroons, again with the help of the Amerindians. The now cramped Amerindians lived in the same area as the Maroons, so they should have been completely familiar with the woods and the swamps of the Surnau. But, again, they could find no trace of the Maroons.[16]

After a year it was discovered that the Maroons were living much further to the east, in two villages called *Kopie-Hij* and *Potikondre*. These hamlets were found with the help of an old Maroon, who had been captured by the Whites during an earlier expedition. He was forced accompany them as a guide. At first he was not very enthusiastic about the situation, but after some time he began to cooperate. The archives do not mention whether he was physically coerced into helping. After a couple of days the man announced that he knew the area well and said that the Maroons called it *Aboma-bee*. During the battle for the village, two Maroons were killed and three were captured. The other inhabitants got away. One of the men killed in combat was chief Sambo.[17]

In 1862, some Amerindians again played a role in locating the Maroon village. I found only a brief mention of this event in the archives. A letter, dated 28 January 1863, mentions that a certain Telting, a White overseer on the plantation of Livorno, near to Rac-à-Rac, was to receive a reward for locating the runaway camp, behind Rac-à-Rac (that is, the camp of Broos), with the help of some Amerindians.[18]

It is not clear from the historical records whether the Amerindians played an important role in the capture of the Maroon villages. It also remains unclear to what extent the aforementioned events, in which both Amerindians and Maroons played a role in bringing the Whites to the villages, have influenced the story around Mankaw. Amerindians were employed by military patrols, but from the chronicles it would seem that they did not play a very important role in the search for Maroons. Between 1829 and 1831 the Maroon villages were discovered, often after former inhabitants betrayed their locations.

The battle against the Dutch

Although the inhabitants of the village of Broos had fought battles with the Dutch on various other occasions, the stories about the skirmishes fought by Broos and his younger brother Kaliko are undoubtedly based on the fights of 1862. Why was it so important to the colonial government to fight, just half a year before the abolition of slavery, against a group of Maroons who, for most part, had lived peacefully in the woods for a long period time? One reason has already been given: the mass desertion of the slaves from the plantation Rac-à-Rac and their flight to the Maroons in that year. The other reason was precisely the impending abolition itself.

In 1848, the year in which the Netherlands became a constitutional monarchy, a parliamentary discussion arose regarding the question of slavery. It did not take long for the decision to be made that slavery was morally contemptible, and so must be abolished. Even so, parliament could not decide on the best manner in which it should be stopped. In 1859, the government appointed the liberal Reinhart van Lansberge as Governor of Suriname. The task fell to him to prepare for the abolition. The main problem, however, was that after abolition and the ensuing days of celebrations, former slaves still had to get back to work, preferably at their plantations. In other words, after abolition the former slaves became contract labourers. They were granted the legal status of free people, but every former slave had to enter a working contract. This transitional period lasted ten years.

Governor van Lansberge was obviously afraid that the transition from slave-owning society to the consolidation of emancipation would not be seamless. In May 1862, four months *prior* to the escape of the slaves of Rac-à-Rac, he wrote a letter to the Minister of Colonies in which he expressed his apprehensiveness at the disturbances caused by the inhabitants of the "runaway camp" near the Surnau Creek. He suggested the construction of a road between the Rivers Suriname and Commewijne, which would cut right through the area where the Maroons lived. Such a road would make it possible to destroy Maroon villages and their provision grounds at any time. To increase the chance that the escaped slaves would return to their plantations, the Governor suggested granting amnesty to the Maroons, permitting them to return to their plantations without being punished.[19]

In Holland, Loudon, the Minister of Colonies, did not see very much wisdom in the proposal of Governor van Lansberge. He did not believe in amnesty without an accompanying display of power. He wrote to the King, expressing his view that few Maroons would react to the promise of amnesty if it were not accompanied by military patrols. If the runaways could be dislodged and their villages destroyed, it would then be much easier to force them to accept the amnesty, so the Minister argued. The King sent the letter of the Governor, along with the advice of the Minister, to the Council of State. This organization, however, had no taste for a display of military power. They thought the hunts for runaway slaves were outdated, and so their advice was in favour simply of the suggested amnesty.[20]

The Minister, though not happy with the advice of the Council of State, could not do much more than send the order through to the Governor. In a cover letter, he wrote that he was personally in favour of a display of power. However he would leave the final decision to the Governor.[21] Van Lansberge, for his part, had to manoeuvre between the ambiguous advice from Holland and the wish of the Surinamese planters to launch an old-fashioned bush patrol. In their view, the more slaves that came back to their plantations the better, for a visitation commission, registering the slaves, was expected in November – and every registered slave meant *f*300 for the plantation owners. In those days this was a sum equal to two years' wages of a lower civil servant.

On 20 October 1862, Governor Van Lansberge promulgated the amnesty decree. He announced, furthermore, that a "communication path" – as he called it – between the Rivers Suriname and Commewijne would be constructed. The members of the Colonial Council were satisfied by this. For them there was not much difference between the construction of a communication path by military men and launching a "bush patrol," as the hunting of runaways used to be called. However, I think that for Van Lansberge, a difference did exist. He told the leader of the patrol, one Captain Steenberghe, that the expedition was to avoid bloodshed. The purpose of the patrol was, first and foremost, to make the runaways familiar with the proclaimed amnesty.[22]

Captain Steenberghe did not quite know what to do with his orders. He decided to encounter the Maroons armed, but he did not give his men any ammunition. So the soldiers marched through the swamps with unloaded rifles. The inhabitants of the village of Broos did not know this, of course. They expected a "normal, old-fashioned" patrol. Accordingly, Broos and his Maroons lured the soldiers into an ambush, and opened fire.[23] After five soldiers had been the slave porters accompanying the patrol dropped their goods in the water and fled. The soldiers soon followed them. When the Governor heard what had happened in the swamps, he travelled immediately to Rac-à-Rac. Steenberghe was given reinforcements and sent to back to the Broos' camp. Once again, however, the soldiers walked straight into an ambush. Another soldier was killed died and five heavily injured. This expedition, the very last mounted by the

Dutch against Suriname Maroons, became a fiasco. The Governor subsequently withdrew the marching orders.[24]

The failed expeditions of Captain Steenberghe brought the Maroon Wars to an end in Suriname. Slavery was abolished in Suriname on July 1, 1863. The slaves celebrated for a couple of days before returning to work without protest as contract labourers. Some months after abolition, Broos contacted the government through a missionary. He apologized for what had happened to Steenberge's bush patrol, and explained that he did not know that the soldiers were unarmed. During an audience with Governor Van Lansberge, it was agreed that all the slaves who had escaped to the Maroons since 1860, including the runaways from Rac- à-Rac, would return to their former plantations (Zeegelaar 1871:70; Vlier 1881:224). The other Maroons were allowed to settle as free blacks at the abandoned plantations Roorak and Klaverblad, where they lived in harmony, according to a note that appeared in the Herrnhutter *Missionsblatt aus der Brüdergemeine* in July 1872. Of Broos it was said that he never set foot in a church, was engaged in polygamy, and had seven wives. The Maroons lived at Roorak and Klaverblad until 1920. After that they migrated to Paramaribo, and in recent decades many left for the Netherlands.

Maroons and oral history: a discussion as gift

In researching the history and society of Surinam Maroons, we have a whole range of sources at our disposal. During the past twenty years, considerable use has been made of oral traditions to reconstruct the history of Surinam. Richard Price (1983 and 1990) presented the history of the Saramaka in a post-modernistic way. He lets the various sources speak to us as "voices" printed in different typefaces. For the rest, Price casts very few doubts on the oral tradition stories. To him they are sources having the same empirical weight as any other source of information. In his view, they enhance other information and provide the emic version of Maroon history, which for the most part has largely been written on the basis of etic-data (i.e. archives of the colonial powers).

In an article on Boni's death, Silvia de Groot (1982) makes a methodological plea for recognising the value of using oral tradition in reconstructing the past. More than anything else, De Groot wants to convince historians working with written sources of the significance of oral history. She writes that oral traditions can be used very well to get at the truth: "Are there possibilities to discover when, where and how the story of an informer deviates from the truth?" she asks herself, before concluding: "Actual data can be retrieved just as well from oral history as from written sources, sometimes even better" (1982:14).

The emphasis that De Groot places on getting at "the truth" does not seem very useful to me. Returning to my introduction, it should be pointed out that for a long time (and certainly since Freeman) anthropologists have held a number of doubts on what constitutes the "truth," and they now avoid the term. In De Groot's defence, however, we might say that post-modernism, with its negation that anything can be known, did not become popular before the 1980s.

My discussion of the history of the Broos Maroons clearly shows that the combination of archival data and oral traditions has resulted in scintillating information. Yet both sources should not be used in an uncritical way, as mere supplements to each other. Reconstructions based on archival material, and stories contained in oral tradition, hardly ever match when considered critically. It would be a very obvious conclusion to state that they are two complementing versions of one particular event. Oral versions are stories in themselves. When we compare oral and archival versions systematically, it becomes apparent that there are many more discrepancies than similarities. From a methodological point of view, it is arguably not the similarities that are most important, but explaining how the discrepancies have come into being.

Notes

1   In the case of Surinam we see the combination of work based on archival sources and oral traditions in Richard Price (1979, 1983, 1990), in De Groot (1982), in Hoeree and Hoogbergen (1984); in Hoogbergen 1985, 1990, 1996 2001), and in Thoden van Velzen and Van Wetering (1988).
2   Tilifo is the Sranantongo (Creole) name of the plantation. The official name is Tout-lui-Faut.
3   The independence of Suriname in 1975 brought a huge migration of Surinamese people to the Netherlands. More than 300,000 persons (first, second and third generation) of Surinamese descent live nowadays in the Netherlands (as against 450,000 in Suriname).
4   Edwin Landveld, March 16, 1981.
5   In that year the registration of slaves made an end to illegal imports.
6   The number of slaves in Suriname in 1706 was 9,988. In 1726 there were 16,547. In 1752 the number was 37,835. In 1774, 59,923. In 1794 there were 48,155. In 1813, they numbered 44,084. By 1836 there were 46,879. In 1854, there were 38,545 slaves, and in 1862, 36,484. (Sources: 1706 and 1726: Nationaal Archief Den Haag: *Archief Sociëteit van Suriname,* other years: Van Stipriaan 1993: 311.)
7   The first of July 1863, Abolition Day, is also known as keti koti, which means "break the chains."
8   *Emancipatie-registers. Burgerlijke Stand* (Civil Register) Paramaribo, Suriname.
9   *Emancipatie-registers. Burgerlijke Stand* (Civil Register) Paramaribo, Suriname. It appears from the Emancipatie-registers that in the colony there was already a person with the family name Babel. This was Jan Hendrik Babel, born on the coast of Africa, illegally imported into Suriname in 1828, and manumitted by the government. He was the owner of the small plantation Argentcourt, on the Orleane Creek, and had four slaves and a child. It was not common practice to give existing family names to the freed slaves, but perhaps this rule did not apply to black family names.
10 Businenge is Sranantongo, the language of the Black Surinamese.
11 In 1762 the total number of free coloureds and blacks in Suriname was 330, of whom 298 (90%) lived in Paramaribo (Vrij 1998: 136). That number should be viewed in the population context of around 50,000 slaves and 2,390 European whites (planters, administrators, merchants and military). Twenty years later, the free coloured population of Suriname had almost doubled. In 1781, 739 free coloureds and blacks were listed as living in Paramaribo (Vrij 1998: 136). The European segment of the Suriname population declined in the years between 1750 and 1863, in contrast to the number of free blacks and colored, which increased during this period from 1,760 individuals in 1791, to 2,889 (1,031 blacks and 1,858 colored) by 1805, to 3,075 by 1811 (Wolbers 1861: 442-3; Einaar 1934: 72, 98). In 1830 the number of free colored

persons already outnumbered that of the Europeans in the colony. In that same year the
colony counted 2,638 (European) whites, 1,094 free blacks, and 3,947 free coloreds (Einaar
1934: 72, 98). The vast majority of them lived in Paramaribo. On 31 December 1862, six
months before abolition, the population of Suriname numbered 52,963 persons, of which
16,479 were free (8,338 men; 8,141 women, 90% of whom were black or colored). The slave
population at that point in time numbered 36,484 persons: 17,162 men and 19,322 women
(Hoogbergen and Ten Hove 2001).

12 *Emancipatieregisters. Burgerlijke Stand* (Civil Register) Paramaribo, Suriname. Remember that
only in the oral tradition was Ma Fanny the mother of the two boys. Based on the archives we
can conclude that she was more likely their mother-in-law.

13 Edwin Landveld spoke about *geesten* (spirits). He never used the much modern word *winti*.
Dini Grootfaam, his female cousin, (whose information is not included in this article) always
uses the term *winti*.

14 In Suriname, the descendants of slaves call themselves "Creoles" so as to distinguish themselves from the Hindus and the Javanese. "Us Creoles" also means "Us, and not you Whites."

15 ARA-*Archief van het Nederlandsch West-Indisch Bezit, 1828-45*, 736: 13 November 1829
no.138, and 803 no. 411.

16 ARA-*Archief van het Nederlandsch West-Indisch Bezit, 1828-45* 804: 11 January 1830 no. 20E.

17 ARA-*Archief van het Nederlandsch West-Indisch Bezit, 1828-45*, 807 no. 569.

18 ARA-*Archief Ministerie van Koloniën 1850-1900*. Gouvernementsjournaal January 28, 1863.

19 ARA-*Archief Ministerie van Koloniën 1850-1900*; Verbaal, 26 June 1862, no. 21.

20 ARA-*Archief Ministerie van Koloniën 1850-1900*; Verbaal, 26 June 1862, no. 21.

21 ARA-*Archief Ministerie van Koloniën 1850-1900*; Verbaal, 26 June 1862, no. 21.

22 Nationaal Archief-*Archief Ministerie van Koloniën 1850-1899*, Government resolution of 20
October 1862, in Verbaal, 26 June 1862, no. 21.

23 November 2, 1862.

24 Nationaal Archief- *Ministerie van Koloniën 1850-1900*, Secret deposition, 13 February 1863 Y.

Bibliography

Brana-Shute, Gary ed. 1990. *Resistance and Rebellion in Suriname: Old and New*. Studies in Third
World Societies, number 43. Williamsburg, Vi: The College of William and Mary.

Einaar, J.F.E., 1934. *Bijdrage tot de kennis van het Engelsch tusschenbestuur van Suriname 1804-1816*.
Leiden: M. Dubbeldeman.

Freeman, Derek, 1983. *Margaret Mead and Samoa; the Making and Unmaking of an Anthropological Myth*. Cambridge, Ma: Harvard University Press.

Groot, Silvia W. de, 1975. 'The Boni Maroon War 1765-1793, Surinam and French Guyana.' *Boletin
de Estudios Latinoamericanos y del Caribe* 18: 30-48.

Groot, Silvia W. de, 1982. 'An Example of Oral History: The Tale of Boni's Death and of Boni's
Head.' *Karibik. Wirtschaft, Gesellschaft und Geschichte*. Referate des 4. Interdissiplinären Kol-
loquiums der Sektion Lateinamerika des Zentralinstituts 06. Im Auftrag herausgegeben von
Hans-Albert Steger und Jürgen Schneider. München: Wilhelm Fink Verlag.

Henige, David, 1974. *The Chronology of Oral Tradition*. Oxford: Clarendon Press.

Henige, David, 1982. *Oral Historiography*. Essex: Longman Group Ltd.

Hoeree, Joris and Wim Hoogbergen, 1984. 'Oral History and Archival Data Combined: the Removal
of the Saramakan Granman Kofi Bosuman as an Epistemological Problem.' *Communication
and Cognition* 17(2/3): 245-289. Gent (Belgium).

Hoogbergen, Wim, 1985. *De Boni-oorlogen, 1757-1860; Marronage en guerilla in Oost-Suriname*.
Bronnen voor de studie van Bosnegersamenlevingen, deel 11. Universiteit Utrecht: Centrum
voor Caraïbische Studies.

Hoogbergen, Wim, 1990. *The Boni-Maroon Wars in Suriname*. Leiden: E.J. Brill

Hoogbergen, Wim, 1996. *Het kamp van Broos en Kaliko. De geschiedenis van een Afro-Surinaamse familie*. Amsterdam: Prometheus.

Hoogbergen, Wim, 2001. 'De basya: de zwarte opzichter op plantages in Suriname; Een veranderde visie.' *Kleio, Tijdschrift van de vereniging van docenten in geschiedenis en staatsinrichting in Nederland* 42(5): 14-18.

Hoogbergen, Wim and Okke ten Hove, 2001. 'De vrije gekleurde en zwarte bevolking van Paramaribo, 1762-1863.' *Oso, Tijdschrift voor Surinaamse Taalkunde, Letterkunde, Cultuur en Geschiedenis* 20(2): 306-320

Hoogbergen, Wim and Arie de Ruijter, 1999. 'Comparative Dimensions in Social and Cultural Anthropology: Conflicting Views, Comparing Sources – Examples from Surinam.' *Caribnet; Journal of the Caribbean Studies International Network* 1999(2): 75-105. London: University of London, Goldsmiths College and Amsterdam: University of Amsterdam.

Hove, Okke ten and Frank Dragtenstein, 1997. *Manumissie in Suriname. Bronnen voor de studie van Afro-Suriname*, deel 19. Utrecht: CLACS and Stichting IBS.

Postma, Johannes Menne, 1990. *The Dutch in the Atlantic Slave Trade 1600-1815*. Cambridge: Cambridge University Press.

Price, Richard, 1976. *The Guiana Maroons. A Historical and Bibliographical Introduction*. Baltimore and London: The Johns Hopkins University Press.

Price, Richard, 1979. 'Kwasimukamba's Gambit.' *Bijdragen tot de Taal-, Land- en Volkenkunde* 135: 151-169.

Price, Richard, 1983. *First Time; The Historical Vision of an Afro-American People*. Baltimore: The Johns Hopkins University Press.

Price, Richard, 1990. *Alabi's World, Coersion, Colonialism and Resistance on an Afroamerican Frontier*. Baltimore: The Johns Hopkins University Press.

Price, Richard, 2002. 'Maroons in Suriname and Guyane: How Many and Where.' *New West Indian Guide / Nieuwe West-Indische Gids* 76 (1and2): 81-88.

Stipriaan, Alex van, 1993. *Surinaams contrast. Roofbouw en overleven in een Caraïbische plantagekolonie 1750-1863*. Leiden: KITLV Uitgeverij. Caribbean Series 13.

Thoden van Velzen, H.U.E. and W. van Wetering, 1988. *The Great Father and the Danger. Religious Cults, Material Forces, and Collective Fantasies in the World of the Surinamese Maroons*. Caribbean Series 9 (Kon. Instituut voor Taal-, Land- en Volkenkunde). Dordrecht: Foris Publications.

Vansina, Jan, 1969. *Oral Tradition, a Study in Historical Methodology*. London: Routledge and Kegan Paul, Ltd. [traducción de : De la tradition orale; Essai de methode historique.]

Vansina, Jan, 1985. *Oral Tradition as History*. London [etc.]: Heinemann.

Vlier, M.L.E., 1881. *Geschiedenis van Suriname*. 's-Gravenhage: C. van Doorn en Zoon.

Vrij, Jean Jacques, 1998. 'Jan Elias van Onna en het 'politiek systhema'. *Oso, Tijdschrift voor Surinaamse Taalkunde, Letterkunde, Cultuur en Geschiedenis* 17(2): 130-147.

Wolbers, J.(Julien), 1861. *Geschiedenis van Suriname*. Amsterdam: H. de Hoogh [1970: Amsterdam: S. Emmering].

Zeegelaar, J.F., 1871. *Suriname en de opheffing der slavernij in 1863*. Amsterdam: Gebroeders Binger.

16

The Killing of the Snake
Reflections on a Bukusu Mytheme

Jan de Wolf

Arie de Ruijter's many and diverse interests include a long-standing love of myths and legends. It is a pleasure to be able to present him here with a previously unpublished narrative, which I recorded in 1969 during my fieldwork among the Bukusu in West Kenya (see de Wolf 1977). It was told to me by Noa Kitanyi and transcribed and translated by Jackson Khisa. First I present this text with a few minor changes, which bring the transcription more in line with the original recording. I have also followed the advice of the editors by making the translation less literal, although some of the flavour of the oral performance is lost in this way. Next I note a number of parallels in motifs and plots from other tales collected from the Bukusu and neighbouring peoples. I conclude with some reflections on the possible relationship between this tale and the unconscious self.

The story

Long ago there were two people, a mother and her child. The mother just stayed at home and the son used to go fishing. One day he trapped a bird, which spoke words like a person. And when he had caught that bird it said: "I am like one of your people, do not kill me." And he said: "I have caught a different kind of bird which speaks just like a human." Then that particular bird told this boy: "Return home and go and tell your mother to close the door, and shut it tightly because wild animals eat people. When you have done so, you should come back to the place where you trapped me, and I shall guide you to a place where you can get what you want."

Well, this boy left the bird there. He went home and told his mother: "Mother, I am going to a dance of unmarried people. You should close the door and shut it tightly. And if you do not hear my voice, you should not open it. If you open it the monsters will eat you." When he had locked her in, he went and found that bird which had been waiting for him and told him: "Let us go, I am bringing you to a place that I know." And he agreed, saying: "Yes, where you want me to go, I will go." They went together, he and that bird. The bird slept in a tree and he also climbed up a tree and slept. There were plenty of wild animals. Then they reached a certain town. There were built many houses, which surrounded a shining metal house. But that bird told the man: "You ought not to touch this metal house, you should not even do so with one finger. There is something bad inside." And the young man said, "Alright." When they had stayed there for some days the bird suddenly just disappeared and left the man alone.

And the man said to himself, "Although that bird has left, look at what he gave me. He brought me to where there is food in plenty for cooking: even meat and sesame seed. Everything that is desirable to eat, bananas." While he remained there, he said, "When I left my mother, when I locked her in, she just had to stay in the house. I must go back and bring her here, because there hunger will kill us. She must also come to eat this food." And he cut a big banana bunch and cooked it. He carried the mashed bananas on his head. He carried them together with a fresh bunch of bananas. He arrived home at night, and when he called his mother she said: "Perhaps the one who calls me is he who

Noah Kitanyi, the narrator, 1969 Sirisia, West Kenya.

wants to eat me. My child got lost, where do I see him?" But her son said: "No mother, it is me. You can open the door." When his mother opened the door she saw the big banana bunch and the mashed food. She asked her son: "Where did you get it from?" But he replied, "Do not ask, just eat the bananas and I shall tell you later on." They sat down and he just told his mother: "Cook this green bunch of bananas which I brought, we are going to leave." She cooked the green bananas. They tied them up into a parcel, which they took with them on their trip. They went a long way and walked until they had reached the town. When they got there the young man told his mother, "You can enter all these houses, but you ought not to touch this metal house in the middle. There are bad things inside." His mother said, "Yes."

Now her son would always go to the lake to catch fish, which they ate. It was their daily food. Every day he went fishing and brought the fish home. His mother got her food and was just sitting in that place and was afraid of the metal house. She said, "That house is like that. But Mwambu told me, 'Do not go and touch it even with a finger. A bad thing is inside.' I will not go there for sure." But one morning, the young man had left to catch fish. The woman, however, had been eating food and had become fat, and the power of the hunger had disappeared. Now she became restless. She said, "Whatever Mwambu says, the house is clean, it is just clean. It is not as if it is a bad house with bitterness inside. Let me walk carefully over there so that I can see for myself." Well, she tiptoed slowly towards it, and peered. She said, "Aaah, did Mwambu by any chance say that there is something bad inside?" Well, she arrived at that house. When she stood there she said, "Let me go and touch it with a finger. It looks perfectly clean without any dirt." She moved nearer and when she stretched out a finger. Her finger actually touched the door, which opened. It flung open. She burst into the middle of the house and was very astonished: "Eeh, it is true what this child told me, it is really true." When she looked she saw a snake. Its coils spiralled upwards, and the head was breathing up there under the roof. Fear caught her, her body was shaking. She said: "Ooh!" She was about to run outside, but the snake said, "If you go outside, you will die. Do not move. Come back here. Just climb and come to where I am." Well, she took courage and when she climbed she stepped on the coils. The coils squeezed. Then she said when the coil made the sound *khwoaa*, "Sister, sister, sister, that big snake is really something very dangerous." Then she raised her foot and stepped on another coil. "Ohoo, aaa, hmn." And the snake said, "Just persevere until you have climbed the entire way. But if you do not persevere, you will fail." She persevered. She stepped in that way on the coils until she arrived to where the head of the snake was. Then the snake told her, "Now look around you that you may see the whole interior."

When she looked around she saw only good things inside the house: cooked meat, groundnuts, ripe sesame seeds, which were just right. Everything she want-ed, which her heart wanted to eat. "Now just eat, everything which you see among these things is yours." The snake spoke to her and she became the friend of the snake. When she now stepped on the coils she just ran as if she were running on the smooth surface of that house. She said, "Actually I was just afraid. But when you said that I could have the things, the food, really there was no fear, it was no longer there." And, because she talked like that to the snake, it became her friend. When the snake had become her friend he told her, "Now you are my friend, and you should not tell Mwambu. If you tell Mwambu, that is a bad thing. You may come here alone when Mwambu is not at home, but you must go back quickly before Mwambu returns home again. And if he should come and find you here and see you, he would fight with you and harm you. Well now, you come quickly and leave again soon. You come quickly and leave again soon." And that woman came every day to visit the snake, and she subsequently became pregnant. Yet she always returned to the house of Mwambu.

But one day when Mwambu came back from catching fish in the lake he found his mother seated near the fireplace. He asked her, "Mother, you had no big stomach. Why then has your stomach become fat?" But his mother replied, "It was the hunger that killed us, but now I am eating sweet things, and my body is grow-ing fat." "Is that so?" " Yes, it is so." He said, "Well, perhaps." But in fact, she was pregnant. She had already been pregnant for nine months. When Mwambu had gone away to catch fish, she gave birth to a child, a small snake. The child came out of her belly in the shape of a small snake. Then it just slid away outside. It went to the lake where Mwambu was catching fish. It passed along and it came around a hill to the hill where Mwambu was catching fish with a hook. When Mwambu saw him it changed from being a little snake to something resembling a human person. He saw the little snake. He came nearer. Mwambu looked at it and looked at it, and he left that hill and looked at himself in the water. Then he looked again at that little snake, and said, "Truly, if you have seen his bones, they are like mine, and if you go an see his hair, they are like mine, and if you go and see all his teeth, they are mine. His whole body is exactly like mine, and how does he talk? It has changed itself to resemble a human being." He said, "Wow."

He left that spot, and resumed fishing. The little snake remained where it stood. It stood there where the fishes were kept, in a small gourd. Mwambu saw it there and looked again at himself in the water and said: "I have seen a person who looks like me, what shall I do with him? I cannot remain unknowing, I must ask him. I shall know whether we understand each other, or whether we do not understand each other. And if we understand each other, that means that he is a person like me." When Mwambu reached that person and they stood eye to eye, and he asked him: "My friend, whose person are you?" Then that particular little snake told him: "I am the child of your mother. From now on, I am your friend, we can catch fish together." Mwambu asked: "You and I, are we both children of our mother, is that true?" "It is so," said the little snake. "Then you are really my friend." They went home. Although his mother knew, Mwambu himself had been unaware. His mother knew already who it was when they came home. She cooked food and they ate. Mwambu told his mother: "This is my friend, whom I found near the river."

They became friends. In the morning they always went together to catch fish for many days. They became accustomed to each other, for if you walk together with one another, do not you get accustomed to one another? And that small snake asked Mwambu, "My friend, do you know what they are doing in that house?" He said: "No." The big snake had told Mwambu's mother, "You should kill Mwambu so that we can be on our own together with the little snake, you alive and Mwambu dead." But the small snake was now asking Mwambu, "Mwambu, do you know what is in that house there?" Mwambu said, "No." The little snake told Mwambu, "The basket from which you always eat, today you should not eat from it. Leave it and we eat from mine. If you eat from yours, you will die. Do not even smell it or touch it with a finger." They left, and when they got home his mother said, "I have cooked your food. There is Mwambu's, and here is your friend's." Mwambu knew what to expect, but his mother did not know that. He said, "We shall eat the food of my friend." They ate the food of his friend and left his own food untouched. Looking left and right, Mwambu took it and quickly threw it away.

One day when they were catching fish at the lake, the small snake asked Mwambu, "My friend, do you want to kill your mother, or would it be bad if we kill her? Mwambu said, "She treats me badly, and when you know how to kill her, my heart has also finished with her." The little snake said, "Now, catch a fish with a hump, a fat fish." When Mwambu threw the hook into the lake, he pulled out a fat fish, with a hump, and sweet looking, fat. He brought the fish to his friend, who asked, "Have you seen this fish? Go and give it to your mother, so that she eats this fish. You should not even smell it. Even I cannot try to eat it." She ate that fish, and she ate her fill. When she had finished, illness struck her and she died. For in fact it was poisoned.

Well, then, who remained? There remained the snake, high up in the clean house, that metal one. And then the small snake told Mwambu that they would be going there, saying, "My friend do you know what thing is there around?" Mwambu answered, "No." He said, "Well my friend, I shall tell you so that you know. There is a thing which is just watching you; and he is your enemy, up there." "My enemy?" The snake said, "In that house. And in it is something bad. And it comes to cause you misery." "Is that so?" "Yes, it is." The little snake said, "I will take you where you can have spears forged for you so that you may go and fight with the thing which is in that house, as there are only the two of us, and that thing which is there will not leave you alone." Well then, he sent Mwambu to forge spears. They forged, and forged, and forged. That little snake sent him there. When they finished forging spears he went and had a gun made with lightning. Then the little snake said, "When we arrive in the home then I am just far away, I am just there in hiding. When you see the big one coming out then I will show you where to stand, when that one comes out to fight with you with all his might." Well then, that little snake went into hiding, far away. Then they saw the big snake arrive. It spit poison against Mwambu's shield. *Kwaa*. It spit poison against his shield. Kwaa. He stabbed with a spear; it was bent; he threw it away. He stabbed with a spear; it was bent; he threw it there. When the snake spit poison he took his shield for protection. Well, he fought and fought and fought with the snake. He fought with him very much, until he took the gun. Then he shot and killed the snake. As it died it was finished, it was completely finished.

Now two people were left: Mwambu and his friend, the small snake, together, on their own. As they were on their own they cultivated food crops and Mambu remained for a long time with that friend of his. After a long time that little snake came and told Mwambu, "Mwambu, bake bread, cook food which we can take with us on a journey. I am going to take you on a trip. I am going to show you something else and we shall end it well." Well then, they cooked that food; they cooked and cooked and cooked. Well, they put it into a bag; they went on their way. They set off, actually they climbed a hill with cultivated fields, just on the other side of the river. He took Mwambu there just to survey all the four corners of the country. He measured the country with his eyes for Mwambu. "Now let us look as far as we can see. Have you seen anything wrong?" So they took measure of all the four directions. He said: "Have you seen everything? I will leave you here now. I am going to occupy the house that belonged to that snake, because if his relatives, the brothers of that snake, come and they find us both there they can kill us because you killed their relative. I am now grown up; I am like my father. When I occupy his house the other snakes will believe that I am truly the owner when they come and see me, whereas in fact we killed my father. But you are fine."

Well, that story ended there like that.

Parallels

There are several themes in this story, which we also find in other published folktales from this part of East Africa. The Luo have a story in which a girl is forced to spend a night in the abode of a python, but is rewarded with a most magnificent scarification, making her more beautiful than all her girl-friends (Onyango-Ogutu and Roscoe 1974: 22; Oguda K'Okiri 1970: 32-46). The story resembles a Bukusu version, with the difference that instead of a python a monster or ogre figures in it (de Wolf 1995: 40-2). The clue to the plot in both the Luo and Bukusu version is that the girl is not allowed to show her scarification, or else dire consequences would follow. In the Luo version her suitors persuade her; in the Bukusu version it is her newly married husband and her own brother. However, she only does so on the condition that they prepare for a battle. During the battle the snake (Luo version), or monster (Bukusu version) is killed.

The motif of a snake that changes into a human person after taking off his skin is found in a Bukusu story in which the skin is worn by a bridegroom who lives as a snake in the river. The bride colludes with the mother of the snake/man, who makes some good beer that puts him thoroughly asleep. Thus, it becomes possible to take away the skin and burn it. The man/snake then becomes an ordinary husband (de Wolf 1995: 24-7).

Conflict between mother and son is mentioned in a Bukusu story at the beginning of which a woman promises a monster her unborn child in exchange for food during a famine. She delays the transaction until her son has grown big. He escapes being caught several times until finally the mother tells the monster to come at night. It will recognise the boy because he will be smeared with oil, while the mother will be covered with ashes. The boy overhears this arrangement and changes places with his mother who is devoured instead. Subsequently, his sister and brother-in-law want to take revenge, but they fail and are also killed by the boy (de Wolf 1995: 72-7).

The most important reference to the killing of a snake occurs in the myth accounting for the origins of circumcision. Early on in my fieldwork my assistant wrote for me the following text in LuBukusu with translation (cf. Were 1967: 172-3).

How circumcision started

Mango was the ruler of the Bukusu at Mwiala and he had two sons: (1) Malaba, (2) Wanyanja. As he arrived in Mwiala, a snake had lived there and had killed cattle and many people. It killed the son of Mango whom they call Malaba. Next it killed Wayanja. Mango saw that it had killed his favourite children. The Barwa [Uasin Gishu Masai] told him: "The snake has just killed your sons, go and kill it for us."

Mango took a big knife, left and said: "Today I die or the snake dies." Really he went, reached Mwiala and saw where it usually slept. But it was not there. And Mango took a log to sit on and placed it at the door where the snake sleeps. As it came and reached there, Mango went on looking at it and thought: "Today I die or it dies." Just as the snake entered and moved his twisted body completely into the hole, the head remained outside [on the wooden log]. And Mango did not wait. He cut it with his sword. Mango had killed it. He took the head and placed it on top of a spear, showing it to the people. When the people saw that, they said: "Now you are a brave person, today you will be initiated." Their chief leader also said the same. They brought Mango to the river and they sang siyoyao [the circumcision song]. They brought Mango back home and they circumcised him. They also circumcised his children. And their chief leader, whom they call Wakhulunya, gave that circumcision age group the name of Kikwameti. This very Mango started the circumcision age groups in Bukusu country. From that moment they continue until this time.

Nowadays circumcision ceremonies for boys are held every second year and coincide with the school holidays in August. Candidates are normally between 14 and 16 years of age. Although they take the initiative, they need the permission of their father. The ceremonies begin with a period of dancing and singing. They boys wear hand bells, which they beat against iron rings around their wrists. They also wear strings of beads, which they get from female relatives, across back and chest. Two or three weeks before the actual operation they start going around to invite their relatives. Two days before the circumcision this stage is ended with preparation of beer during which boys have to assist their mother with threshing or grinding millet and fetching water. On the next day the mother's brother is visited to receive his blessing. At home sacrifices are made to the ancestors. During the night there is much dancing and singing. When dancing the boys stand in the middle and ring their bells while the rest of the people shuffle around in a fairly wide circle and sing the chorus to the songs sung by the song leader. The boys are admonished and scrutinised repeatedly to see whether they know how to stand properly as required during the operation.

Early the next morning the boys go to a river accompanied by a large crowd. Here they are smeared completely with mud while women and children wait at a distance. The party goes home along a different road and people sing the appropriate circumcision song. This describes how a leopard (the circumciser) waits for the boys and tells cowards to go to Luoland (where they do not circumcise). Everybody may watch the operation, which should be endured without any signs of pain. Close paternal relatives are often initiated together. They are circumcised in order of genealogical seniority. Boys often steady themselves by gripping a stick, which they hold across their shoulders. Spectators watch silently until the operation has been completed. Then women start rejoicing and bring baskets of food, which are put in front of the novices. Many well wishers put coins into the mud on top of their heads or thrust bank notes into

Admonition is an essential part of the circumcision ritual, 1968 Kimilili, West Kenya.

their hands. They move backwards into the hut where they will spend their convalescence. Here they wait for the circumciser who will give them some food after which they may start eating again. He comes again to bless the boys when they have recovered sufficiently to wear ordinary clothes. Later they will be blessed by their fathers and receive a new name and new clothes.

The ceremony marks the sexual maturity of the boys. This aspect is emphasised when the mother's brother kills a bull, which he should do for at least one of the sons of his sister with whose bridewealth cattle he himself acquired a wife. A piece of skin to which the testicles are attached is slit and put around the shoulders of the boy. Adorned in this way he has to walk home. Branches, which ostensibly are brandished by grown up men to prevent the boys from running away during such ceremonial occasions, can also be seen as phallic symbols. Once initiated the boys will have to build separate huts and can no longer sleep in the same house as their parents (see also de Wolf 1983; 1994).

Reflections

In the following interpretation I follow Johnson and Price-Williams, who view folktales in some sense as the voice of the unconscious:

> [T]hey speak both for and to the unconscious self that exists in everyone. For the
> human self is created out of the struggle between innate impulses and cultural rules,

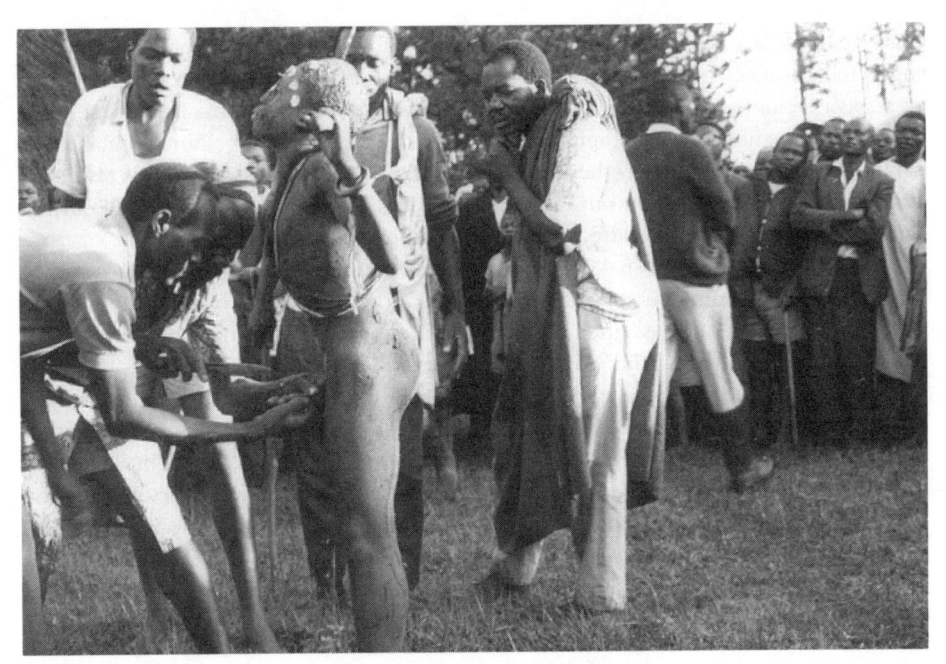

The circumcision operation is a public event, 1968 Kimilili, West Kenya.

and seems inevitably to contain a fundamental split. Humans have the ability, and this must be an important part of their capacity for impulse control, to create self-awareness (a conscious self) that does not acknowledge or avow all attributes of the person it inhabits.

These disavowed attributes of the person are not bits and pieces relegated to a dump or snake pit called the unconscious, but are still properties of a larger, whole, supra-ordinate self. That self, or the unconscious aspect of it, or an unconscious self - words for this are difficult because the whole situation is intrinsically paradoxical - is a listener whenever folktales are told. (1996: 102-3)

Suzette Heald suggests that for the neighbouring Gisu, who also have circumcision rites, the traumatic experience of weaning may give this initiation of boys at puberty some of its emotional force (1994: 199). Weaning is, of course, necessary when a new baby arrives. This is also connected with the role of father as destroyer of the mother/child bond. At circumcision the mother is idealized as the one who supports the rebirth of her son as a grown-up person, with adult responsibilities. The suppressed aggression is transferred to the father, who may oppose his son's circumcision (1994: 200).

In the story presented here we also find some of these themes. It all starts with a paradisiacal peacefulness in which mother and son live harmoniously together. That

this situation does not last forever is due to the disobedience of the woman. Her yielding to the advances of the snake has paradoxical results. The snake becomes the father
of a second child and the parents now want to exclude the first-born. This is also what
happens at weaning. The children then eliminate the treacherous mother and make war
on the father whose authority the snake child usurps. One may also note that Mwambu
does not kill his own father, but rather a being that is associated with the role of the
father as competitor for the affections of the mother (respectively, of the wife).

Yet, the killing of the snake may be read in another way as well. In this story the
snake stands for forbidden sexuality, disruptive of ordinary social relationships. At the
end of the coming out rites after circumcision, Bukusu boys are not only blessed but
also formally warned that the closed door is forbidden to them. This means that now
they have achieved sexual maturity they must take care not to enter the huts of married women, as this would be taken as evidence of adultery. In the story the mother
went inside the house of the snake, although this was forbidden. Mwambu killed the
snake that seduced his mother in the same way that Mango gained a victory over the
destructive forces of wild nature by cutting off the head of the snake at Mwiala. If the
cutting of the foreskin may also be a symbol of the socialisation of the sexuality of the
boys at circumcision, this adds yet another dimension to the meaning of the story of
Mwambu and the snake (cf. Heald 1994: 205).

Conclusion

Readers familiar with the biblical story of Adam and Eve and its various interpretations,
to which we may safely reckon Arie de Ruijter, may discover interesting parallels. The
same occurred to the storyteller who, before he started, announced: "This one, which
we are going [to tell], is the story of Adam *[Adamu]*, but of long ago, as WE [with
emphasis] used to be telling, as we told it." Noa Kitanyi, then in his sixties, apparently
felt that he had to mark this story off from the three previous stories that he had been
telling at that session, and which were recognisably "traditional." He himself belonged
to the Anglican Church, which put much emphasis on literacy and education, and provided at an early date vernacular translations of important parts of the bible. So it is not
surprising that he noticed the similarity with the beginning of the book of Genesis of
the Old Testament.

Although many folktales tend to be repeated in more or less the same manner, the
hallmark of the creative artist is the way in which he combines existing motifs and plots
in new and unexpected ways (cf. Scheub 1975). In my opinion, and in that of the audience that was present when I made the recording, the narrative that I presented here
is a good example of the latter type of tale.

Bibliography

de Graaf, W. and R. Maier eds. 1994, *Sociogenesis reexamined*. New York etc.: Springer Verlag.

de Wolf, J.J., 1977, *Differentiation and integration in Western Kenya: a study of religious innovation and social change among the Bukusu*. The Hague: Mouton.

de Wolf, J.J., 1983, 'Circumcision and initiation in western Kenya and eastern Uganda: Historical reconstructions and ethnographic evidence', *Anthropos* 78:369-410.

de Wolf, J.J., 1994, 'Circumcision and psychogenesis: Concepts of individual, self, and person in the description and analysis of initiation rituals of male adolescents'. In de Graaf and Maier pp. 261-279.

de Wolf, J.J., 1995, *Bukusu tales: collected around 1936 by research assistants of Dr. Günter Wagner (1908-1952)*. Lit: Münster.

Heald, S., 1994, 'Everyman a hero: Oedipal themes in Gisu circumcision', in *Heald and Deluz* [1994: 184-94].

Heald, S. and A. Deluz eds. 1994, *Anthropology and psychoanalysis: an encounter through culture*. London: Routledge.

Johnson, A.W. and D. Price-Williams, 1996, *Oedipus ubiquitous: the family complex in world folk literature*. Stanford: Stanford UP.

Oguda K'Okiri, L.G. 1970. *So they say*. Nairobi: East African Literature Bureau.

Onyango-Ogutu, B. and A.A. Roscoe, 1974, *Keep my words. Luo oral litarature*. Nairobi: East African Publishing House.

Scheub, H., 1975, *The Xhosa ntsomi*. Oxford: Clarendon Press.

Were, G. S., 1967. *Western Kenya historical texts*. Nairobi: East African Literature Bureau.

17

Bounding, Relating, Mixing
Identity Formation at a Christian school

Jeroen Vermeulen

This essay is about identity. To be more precise, it concerns the formation of identity at a Christian school for higher vocational education in the Netherlands. As part of the more general process of "depillarization" of Dutch society, the school is struggling with the problem of redefining its Christian identity. In this piece I want to interpret the local process of identity-formation at the school from the point of view of three theoretical notions taken from actor-network theory: the notions of (1) "region," (2) "network," and (3) "fluid" (see Mol and Law 1994). Each of these three notions offers a different perspective on the process and the outcomes of redefining Christian identity. That is, each concept gives a different understanding of the identity formation process, provides a different *locus* for it, and leads to a different description of the process. In showing this I will make use of semiotic analyses of actions, statements, fragments of text, and physical objects that I gathered as data from the school (Vermeulen 2001).

The school

In the city of Zwolle, situated in one of the northern provinces of the Netherlands, stands the country's biggest protestant-Christian institution for higher vocational education (see Vermeulen 2001). It has around 10,000 students and over 900 employees. The school comprises six faculties: Economics, Journalism, Social Work, Organizational Studies, Education, and Technology. These faculties were formerly autonomous organizations of Protestant denomination, but merged into one institution in 1987 (with the exception, however, of the technical faculty which joined the school in 1996 but was not of Christian denomination). The campus is situated next to a relatively new residential area.

Entering the campus by foot or bicycle, alongside the students, teachers and other employees of the school, it might not be obvious to a newcomer where the main entrance of the school is. Although all of the buildings are connected, there are ten of them. Most striking is the difference between the original buildings, and the newer buildings built in 1993. One of the differences is that the older buildings are primarily used for regular educational activities while central management and administration use the newer ones. The differences between the buildings are the main cause of confusion as to where the main entrance of the school is. And linked to that is the question of which is the central building of the school, and what can be regarded as the institution's central activities.

The name of school is attached to the wall next to the entrance: *Windesheim*. The name refers to an Augustine monastery that was located to the south of Zwolle and was founded in 1387 by members of a movement under the leadership of Gerard Groote (cf. Broderick 1976). Holes and plugs in the wall above the name "Windesheim" attest to the moment in 1997 when the words *"christelijk"* (Christian) and *"hogeschool"* (school) were taken down from the wall. The removal of the word "Christian" reveals something about how this school has chosen to deal with, or to redefine, its (Christian) identity. The question, however, is: how can this action be interpreted? Does it reveal a disintegration of Christian values, within this institution or even within Dutch society as a whole? There are voices that would confirm this (Sap et al. 1997). Is it a way of expressing that the school has become accessible to non-Christian students? Or was it simply an esthetic purpose that was behind the action? Whatever its significance, what I noticed during my research was that although the removal of the words was inter-preted in various ways both by members of the school and by myself, it nevertheless provoked discussion about the Christian identity of the school. As such, the action func-tioned as a sign, as part of meaning-giving, semiotic processes.

Meaning-giving processes, such as this example, need to be contextualized. (Christian) identity is considered as a relational phenomenon. This means that identity is not defined in terms of an invariable essence, but in terms of its relations with other social phenomena and processes. Identity is indexical in that its relations with other things in a local context define it (see Hall 1996; Hanks 1996:47). Because identity is the outcome or effect of relational processes (see Gergen, 1991; Michael, 1996), it can-not be located other than via other "things" that stand in some sort of semiotic relation to it. These "things" (that function as signs) can be anything: words, actions, people, objects. Thus, to understand identity in the context of the Christian school means try-ing to find what "other things" are relevant, what kind of indexical relation these "things" have to identity, and where these are located. The answers to these questions about relevance, relation, and location are, of course, highly dependent on the way these issues are framed or contextualized. Again, meaning-giving processes need to be framed or "contextualized." Mol and Law (1994) argue that this framing can be done spatially, in different ways, through a regional approach, as a network, or as a fluid.

They argue that framing is based on the performance of spatial presuppositions. There are "regions" "in which objects are clustered together and boundaries are drawn around each cluster" (1994:643), and there are "networks" which are series of elements having well-defined relations. These are well-known, preferential ways of framing social phenomena. However, Mol and Law identify a third type of space, which is dif-ferent from the first two: fluid space. In fluid space, there are neither boundaries nor stable relations. In fluids things "tend to stick together" (ibid:661). These three types of space frame social phenomena in certain ways that have consequences for how we can understand them. In the following I want to explore the use of these spatial framings in the context of the formation of (Christian) identity at a Dutch Christian school for higher vocational education. A regional approach to identity formation would emphasize (the construction of) boundaries that divide "us" from "them" (for instance, "Christians" versus "non-Christians") and that define one's own identity by opposing and negating the identity of the others. Thus, the meaning of identity is constructed spatially by way of drawing sharp lines between inside and outside. A network approach affirms the regional "identity work" of creating insides and outsides, but would itself emphasize processes of formation that define the inside. It looks for elements of meaning (signs such as "words," "texts," but also physical objects like buildings, or the interiors of buildings) that together form a more or less coherent and stable relational network. The third type of contextualizing, the fluid, is quite different in character from the former two. In the fluid, identity is not formed by way of boundaries, nor by stable relations within a network (the inside of identity). On the contrary, identity is being formed by the juxtapositions of things (signs, elements) that don't fit together. Identity formation turns out, then, to be an unstable and heterogeneous process that can have unforeseen and even undesirable outcomes.

Thus, identity formation can be considered as a process of bounding, of relating and of mixing. In the remaining of this chapter I will provide all three of these framings of identity formation with empirical illustrations.

Regional identity

The regional manner of approaching a social problem is to provide a local phenomenon with a context that transcends the particularities of the local. The attempt here is to create a broader, more general and generalizing frame that has the power to explain all kinds of other related problems with different time and space co-ordinates. In the case of the construction of identity at a Christian organization in Dutch society at the end of the twentieth century, there is a powerful story available, namely the (de)pillarization of Dutch society. One of the most influential books on the topic is that of Lijphart (1976). According to this popular view, Dutch "civil society" in the past century was split into three "pillars": the Catholic pillar, the Protestant pillar, and the non-denominational pillar (divided into a socialist and a liberal pillar). Pillars were, according to Lijphart, simply, certain groups of the population (1976:35). "A pillar is an integrated complex of public organisations or institutions based on an ideological view of life" (ibid.). Every pillar had its own network of public organizations, which met the needs of education, healthcare, press, politics etc. The inherent organizational character of each was of great importance to the stability and coherence of the pillars. The organizations held the pillar "in place," so to speak. Yet at the same time the pillars were the embodiment of sharp religious and social-economic dividing-lines in Dutch society. These divisions enabled groups and individuals to construct a well-defined identity through the organizations of one's pillar. As Righart (1996:10), a Dutch social scientist, once put it: the pillars gave their members "symbols, rituals, antagonistic images and vocabularies" with which to construct their separate identities. An important role was played by a "pillarized" education system that not only divided "the youth into separated social circles," but also engendered "differences in values" (Lijphart

1976:65). According to Lijphart, since the 1960's a process of "depillarization" has occurred. The dividing lines grew steadily blurred. "As a consequence the ties between pillar organizations of every pillar have been weakened", Lijphart noted (ibid:12).

The above analysis of Dutch society, and the position of Protestant-Christian organizations in it, is principally guided by the metaphor of the pillar, which in itself has spatial connotations. The metaphor emphasizes verticality and division. Identities are taken as stable, homogeneous, clear-cut, centered, and organized. The identity of an individual or a group is clearly delineated by its contrast to that of others of another pillar. The boundaries, then, are well defined. Using a term from Mol and Law, identity construction in this context was "regional." The use of the metaphor of "pillar" is possible because a regional spatiality is presupposed. This regional framing leads to an analysis of "the social," and consequently of that of identity, in which difference and similarity are un-problematically discerned. "So it's possible to build a version of the social in which space is exclusive. Neat divisions, no overlap. Here or there, each place is located at one side of a boundary. It is thus that an 'inside' and an 'outside' are created. What is similar is close. What is different, is elsewhere" (Mol and Law 1994:647).

The "region" favors a view from above, a perspective from outside, instead of from below and from within a pillar. As such, it does not talk about differences *within* a pillar, nor about actions of "real" groups and individuals. It misses activities that cross the borders of the "pillarized" groups of the population. Crossings and multiple identifications cannot be easily accounted for within this framework because this would undermine not only the pillar, but also the perspective on identity construction itself. As such, it misses dynamic and change, and it is unable to present an alternative to a regional construction of Christian identity. The process of de-pillarization assumes the same premises.

What, then, is the alternative to a regional construction of Christian identity? The regional type of space seems to have nothing to say about situated activity. It carries the danger of "being historically over-privileged in social science and blind to their own embedding in tacit, locally and historically situated activity" (Rampton 1998:13).

Even so, does this criticism of the "regional" construction of identity mean that we should dismiss it altogether as being of little value in providing us with insight into local processes of identity-construction? I would say, no. In fact, one may argue that Lijphart's analysis of Dutch society is itself based on regional presuppositions, and as such are situated activities. His analysis provides a framework for understanding Dutch society at a general level. It even provides a possible explanatory framework with which to account for the removal of the word "Christian" from the name of Windesheim school. Moreover, Lijphart's conceptualization of the structures of Dutch society provides common people with a framework and a vocabulary to give meaning to their own situation. This is what Anthony Giddens said about analytical concepts that are formed in an academic context: "The concepts that sociological observers invent are 'second order' concepts in so far as they presume certain conceptual capabilities on the part of actors to whose conduct they refer. But it is in the nature of social science that these can become 'first order' concepts by being appropriated within social life itself...." (1984:284).

This certainly applies to the regional framing of identity-construction. In my research on the identity of Christian organizations (see Vermeulen 2001), I found that individuals gave accounts and carried out discussions concerning identity by framing it in a regional way (despite Lijphart's characterization of Dutch society as having become "de-pillarised"). For instance, at a conference on the Protestant-Christian identity of schools for lower vocational education, participants always brought the discussion back to the question "but how are we different from schools based on a humanistic view of life?" This regional framing seemed to determine very much their way of thinking and talking. In that sense it can be seen as expressive for their own identity: the way people talk about the construction of their identity can be seen as part of their identity. It is part of their own expressive repertoire.

Mol and Law (1994), however, argue that regional presuppositions are not spatially neutral, but rather are the product of another kind of spacing based on a network. (Lijphart mentioned this already in his analysis of the pillarized society by suggesting that a pillar exist as a network of organisations.)

Network identity

The existence of a network is illustrated with a short discursive analysis of a policy text produced by the management of Windesheim. Here, the network is constructed by means of language. This does not mean that the substance of networks is solely or predominantly linguistic. In fact, its elements can comprise all sorts of heterogeneous semiotic material (see Law 1994).

The chapter of the Windesheim text in which the identity of the school is defined begins with a discussion of current society, regionally framed. Two sentences stand out in particular. One begins, "In the economic-technological domain we see: an insufficient dedication to a durable environment [and] the persistence of immense differences in opportunities for living between a rich minority and a poor majority of the world population." The other states, "In the social-cultural domain we see: ongoing processes of individualization, together with social and ethnic fragmentation of society...[and] increasing confusion about questions of sense making." A number of observations can be made about these sentences. Firstly, the metaphor of "domain" fits into the regional framing. Secondly, the wording of societal "problematics," stated in rather static terms and in a negative tone, as appears here, is strikingly similar to well-known sociological analyses of late-modern western societies. Moreover, the regionally framed analysis of society functions as an element in the network that is constructed in the text, which aims to define the school's identity.

The negative and static analysis of society appears to be the backdrop against which a positive construction of the school's identity can subsequently be made. This is evident in so far as the sentences continue thus: "For many the school is seen only as supplier of knowledge and manpower in service of the economic-technological process. By that society is does not do justice to itself. Windesheim cannot accept having to function as a kind of knowledge-factory exclusively." Here, Windesheim, characterized as a "knowledge-factory," is treated in relation to the earlier regional analysis of society. The argument is being constructed as one of differing views as to the role of the school (namely Windesheim) in society. Now, in the following step of the argumentative network, the rejection of the image of Windesheim as a "knowledge-factory" can be translated in positive terms – as the *alternative*. "The societal responsibility that is accepted by Windesheim is the recognition that ethics and economics, respect and technics ought to be connected in a vital manner." Clearly, the positive terms used in the text are "societal responsibility" and the pedagogic concept of "learning to learn."

This last sentence is a response to the one that preceded it, as is clear from the verbal play regarding what Windesheim does and does not accept. The word "connected" is used in relation to the underlying regional analysis of society. Furthermore, the pedagogy of "learning to learn" introduces into the school new relations between students and teachers, and between students. The student is expected to learn by way of self-study, and the role of the teacher is transformed into that of a supervisor of the learning-processes of the student. Many schools in the Netherlands at that time were already beginning to introduce this unique pedagogy.

In this text, the concept of "learning to learn" is related to other phrases and words that have religious associations: "[A] Human being is a relational being and, thus, his personal learning-process is a socially determined process. In meeting the other, he learns to develop himself and to know himself deeply. In meeting the other, human being is at the same time meeting that Other." Clearly, it is from this point that the identity of Windesheim as a school is being constructed in positive terms, by opposing the self-created (or at least self-chosen) analysis of society. The negative influences of contemporary economic and cultural processes are overcome by presenting Windesheim as a "meeting place," based on "societal responsibility" and the concept of "learning to learn." In other words, the regional framing has created the space for a network which defines Windesheim as a kind of meeting place. Concomitantly, the construction of the network affirms the regional boundaries (see Law 2000:7). This is the point that Mol and Law are making when they state that "...[the region] is an effect or product which depends on another quite different kind of space, the space of networks. This isn't regional in character, but is generated within a *network topology*. A network is a series of elements with well defined relations between them" (1994:649). Moreover, the "meeting" mentioned in the text above alludes to the religious identity of the school. The next step in this process of identity construction is to explicate the content of the religious inspiration, and this is stated in the following manner:

> We do not choose for a certain theological current or ecclesiastical direction. We do join the broad stream of 'Gods people on its way', throughout time. Our partners are all those who, whatever their philosophy of life, stand for the striving towards justice, peace and a durable world. That is the quest. None of us owns the (whole) truth.

What is remarkable here is the fact that the text suggests that the school opens its doors to all students, including non-Christians, "whatever their philosophy of life." Everyone that strives for justice, peace, and a durable world is welcome to participate in the quest. No regions are created between Christians and non-Christians, as was the case in pillarized society. There are no regions delineated along religious boundaries. In this sense, the view on religion that is expressed here fits as an element of the network that identifies Windesheim as a "meeting place."

On the following page, however, it is written: "For Windesheim the biblical notions with regard to justice, peace and the concern for a durable society are normative. These notions are not ready-made blue-prints, but functions as beacons, that lay out the course for our quest." Thus, in order to be included in the meeting place, that Windesheim aspires to be, the *biblical* notions of justice, peace, and a durable society must be endorsed. Not just any notion will do, and this clearly performs an exclusionary function. The regional presuppositions underlying the construction of identity in Christian organizations are being preserved, but my discursive analysis shows that the network is of a spatial type than is different from that of region. They may mutually support, or even implicate, each other; but they are not the same. The network-presuppositions enable us, as students of social theory, to open the regions and go inside. There we can see the nature of elements and relations that produce the region as an effect. The region is then shown as a construction, not as some sort of objective reality. Within the spatial frame of the network there is no inside or outside, as in the frame of regions. Rather, there is relational variety. As Mol and Law suggest, "'here' and 'there' are not objects or attributes that lie insides or outside a set of boundaries.... It is a question of the network elements and the way they hang together" (1994:649).

Fluid identity

The construction of identity involves a process of distinguishing between what it is and what it is not, and of defining elements and relations between them in a network. In both cases the result is a concept of identity that is stable, though not necessarily homogeneous because both similarity and difference exist within a network of relations. Mol and Law propose an alternative spatial metaphor that deals differently with the performance of social difference and similarity – *the fluid*.

As I said at the beginning of this paper, the main entrance of Windesheim is beset with confusion. It is not clear what really is the main entrance of the school. The ambiguity is related to the differences that are created between the original buildings of the school and the newer ones. When entering the doors of the original main building, this ambiguity is not solved. The "central canteen" is located here. It is an open space in which various activities take place and which is full of heterogeneous objects: the reception of the school, the dining place, a cafeteria, a central place for chairs and tables, the "silence center" (*"stiltecentrum"*) of the student parish, a place for playing table football and table tennis, a selling-point for office-equipment, readers and copy machines. The place as a whole was originally intended as a multifunctional space. The first chairman of the school favored the idea of using the space for all sorts of communal activities, including the organization of religious services. The Christian identity of the school formed the inspiration for the architectural design of the "central canteen." A series of eleven paintings hang on the circular wall of the "central canteen," in a circle. The artwork as a whole is called *Alpha et Omega; Jacob and the Angel?* Both the beginning and the ending point of the circle of painting is formed by the "silence center" of the student parish. It is a small chapel inside the canteen. It is freely accessible and meant to serve as a public space for small groups and individuals who want to retreat for short moments of meditation. (The title of the artwork refers to the biblical story in Genesis (32:22-32) about the wrestling during the night between Jacob and an unknown man. It is the night before Jacob's renewed confrontation with his brother Esau. After the fight, in the early morning, Jacob is blessed by the man. He is given a new name: Israël, which means literally "he who fights with God.").

The circle of paintings and the centrality of the silence center tried to impose a certain religiously inspired order on the meaning and use of the "central canteen," located in what was originally, unambiguously, the central building of the school. Yet, this order, or this intention to order, has changed over the years. The circle of paintings is still in its place, as is the "silence center." The placing of Coca Cola and Mars vending machines and of posters and advertisements in juxtaposition to the paintings has interrupted the original order of things. And the centrality (in a material as well in a symbolic sense) of the "silence center" has been encroached upon by the juxtaposition of a new, colorful commercial cafeteria called *Jack and Judy's*. The ordering of the "central canteen" has become "heterotopic": "an ordering that takes place through a juxtaposition of signs that culturally are seen as not going together, either because their relationship is new or because it is unexpected" (Hetherington 1997:9).

The point I want to make with this description and analysis of the canteen's interior is that the respective elements do not establish well-defined relations, as is the case in a network. The heterotopic relations are of a fluid type. There are no clear relations between the elements. Instead, there is ambiguity. But still the elements go together, in one way or another. The juxtaposition of contrasting elements does, in its own way, define the 'central canteen' as a kind of meetingplace. But it does so in a way that is quite different from the idea of 'meetingplace' that is described in the policy text. Consequently, what Mol and Law have to say about fluids seems to apply here: "In a fluid space it's not possible to determine identities nice and neatly, once and for all. Or to distinguish inside from outside, this place from somewhere else. Similarity and difference aren't like identity and non-identity. They come, as it were, in varying shades and colours. They go together.... A fluid world is a world of *mixtures*" (1994:660).

Framed in terms of a fluid, the Christian identity of Windesheim now appears less stable and clear-cut than both the regional and the network framing would otherwise suggest. As such, it also appears much less problematic, for in a fluid contextualization, contrasting objects may nevertheless appear together in albeit "strange" concordance.

Conclusion

In this essay the notions of region, network, and fluid were explored in relation to identity formation at a Christian school. Because identity is a relational and context-dependent concept, identity formation should be understood as situated activity. Following this position, the data used to gain insight into identity, are grounded – localized – in their context of production. The data, the linguistic (text) as well as the material (physical objects), were interpreted as *signs*. This means that they stood for something else, namely for "a way of redefining Christian identity at the Windesheim school." They referred to Christian identity in a way that is not self-evident. Semiotic analysis of textual and other signs in this essay revealed their meaningful relation to the process of identity formation. The way the concrete signs are contextualized or framed, however, determines their interpretation. Three ways of framing were discussed: regional, as a network, and fluid. Regional framing understands formation of Christian identity in terms of the differences with other denominations in Dutch society; the *locus* of identity formation is in the boundaries between different identities. The network framing sees Christian identity as a constructed, though coherent and stable, meaningful "meeting place" defined by relations between societal views, pedagogy, and bibical notions. The *locus* here is to be found in the substantial elements of identity and their relations. The fluid framing, lastly, conceives of Christian identity as a heterogeneous set of contrasting elements, which lead here to "strange" and unexpected connections between religious and commercial objects and activities; the *locus* is the juxtaposition of heterogeneous elements.

There is no one-liner that concludes this essay. But at least it can be argued that there is no single ("best") way of dealing with identity formation, or with the redefining of Christian identity at Windesheim The three framings discussed here must be seen as contemporaneous. Probably each situated activity of identity formation is a matter of bounding, relating, and mixing.

Bibliography

Blommaert, Jan, and Jef Verschueren. 1998. *Debating diversity. Analysing the discourse of tolerance.* London: Routledge.

Broderick, Robert C. 1976. *The catholic encyclopedia.* Nashville: Nelson.

Gergen, Kenneth. 1991. *The saturated self. Dilemmas of identity in contemporary life.* New York: Basic Books.

Giddens, Anthony. 1984. *The constitution of society.* London: Routledge.

Hall, Stuart. 1996. "Introduction: who needs identity?" In Stuart Hall and Paul du Gay, eds. *Questions of cultural identity*, pp. 1-17. London: Sage Publications.

Hanks, William F. 1996. *Language and communicative practices,* Boulder, Colorado: Westview Press.

Hetherington, Kevin. 1997. *The badlands of modernity. Heterotopia and social ordering,* London and New York: Routledge.

Law, John. 1994. *Organizing Modernity,* Oxford: Blackwell Publishers.

Law, John. 2000. "Objects, spaces, others" (draft), Center for Science Studies/ Department of Sociology, Lancaster University.

Lijphart, Arend. 1976. *Verzuiling, pacificatie en kentering in de Nederlandse politiek.* Amsterdam:

J.H.De Bussy.

Michael, Mike. 1996. *Constructing identities. The social, the nonhuman and change.* London: Sage Publications.

Mol, Annemarie, and John Law. 1994. Regions, networks and fluids: anaemia and social topology. *Social Studies of Science* 24:641-71.

Rampton, Ben. 1998. Speech community. In Jef Verschueren, Jan-Ola Östman, Jan Blommaert, and Chris Bulcaen, eds., *Handbook of pragmatics 1998.* Amsterdam/Philadelphia: John Benjamins Publ. Co.

Righart, Hans. 1996. Religie en de perceptie van moderniteit. In Dirk Jan Wolffram, ed. *Om het christelijke karakter der natie. Confessionelen en de modernisering van de maatschappij,* pp.7-14. Amsterdam: Het Spinhuis.

Sap, J.W., A. Soeteman, and W.J.M. van Veen, ed. 1997. *Identiteit en fusie. De spanning tussen overheidsbeleid en het behoud van sociale verbanden.* Utrecht: Lemma.

Vermeulen, Jeroen. 2001. *De naam van de school. Worstelen met identiteit op een christelijke hogeschool* [The name of the school. Wrestling with identity at a Christian school for higher vocational education]. Baarn: Ten Have.

18

Emancipation of Women and Organized Crime

Frank Bovenkerk

Crime is a male business. Irrespective of time, place and culture, crime rates of men are always higher and often much higher than those of women. In prison, the number of women incarcerated seldom exceeds 5 to 10 per cent of the total incarcerated population. In the Netherlands, 700 incarcerated women comprise no more than 6% of the total prison population. Traditionally, women have most commonly only been convicted for very specific categories of crime and misdemeanours, such as murdering their husbands with poison and shoplifting, or for prostitution and abortion (acts that typically tend to be decriminalised and considered victimless crimes). In the figures of burglary and assault (which constitute the bulk of all police arrests and criminal convictions) women are statistically virtually absent. The body of criminological theory explains why younger, lower class males get into trouble with the law and why some of these develop life-course persistent criminal careers. If women figure in these theories, it is possible they are discouraging men from crime. There seems to be no better crime-stopper than "the decent girl friend"! Theory on the background of female crime itself is largely non-existent. In individual cases she has never done it on her own initiative. She does it for love, out of loyalty, or because she has been downright forced to commit crime by a man.

Generally, if women enter textbooks of criminology it is merely to explain this gross under-representation of females in crime statistics. Some theorists find sex or gender differentials in criminality rates to be a true representation of reality. Biology and the disparity of gender roles may count for this, or maybe it is the difference in opportunity structure; but women really do commit far less crime than men. Other theorists find that crime figures reflect no more than police priorities and sentencing practices. They argue that as only a very small proportion of all offences become known to the police anyway; no inferences can be made for the complete law-breaking population. Under-representation of women in crime figures may be the outcome of "chivalrous" attitudes of individual law enforcement officials towards the weaker sex; or, to put it more bluntly, as the product "of a legal system that openly or latently supports or reinforces sexist ideology" (Box 1981:196). Criminal women are being relegated to "status offences" – this is a range of behaviours that violate parental authority such as running away from home, truancy, or behaving in an "incorrigible" way. Their deeds are being "medicalized" instead of criminalized.

Once there was "hope" that women would catch up with men. At the heyday of the second feminist wave in the 1970s, some criminologists predicted that "emancipation" or "liberalization" of women would bring them up to similar levels of delinquency as males, especially in violent crime. Thus, Freda Adler maintained: "Girls are involved in more drinking, stealing, gang activity, and fighting behaviour in keeping with their adoption of male roles...In departure from the safety of traditional female roles and the testing of uncertain alternative roles coincide with the turmoil of adolescence creating criminogenic risk factors which are bound to create this increase" (1975: 75). Girls in gangs could now be expected at any time, and when would the first female manager be convicted for white-collar crime? Adler writes, " For better or worse, they have lost many of the restraints which kept them within the law" (ibid.).

These "liberators" presented some statistical evidence to support their hypothesis. Although taken from later years, there is also some Dutch material in its favour. In 1987 there were 134 women in Dutch prisons. In 1996 their number had grown to 464 and at the end of the in 1990s (Frank, is this the correct year?) there were 700 women in Dutch prisons. But were they right? Was female offending really on the rise, and did this follow from liberation? Steffensmeier (1980) has shown that statistics had been used in a fragmentary and biased way, and he found that the rates of male imprisonment had also gone up. The sharp rise in the number of women in Dutch prisons reflects foremost an increase in expatriate offenders, such as Latinas smuggling drugs into the country. Other changes in female behaviour (related to the economic marginalisation of women) are likely to explain increases in female crime better than emancipation (Chesney-Lind 1997). Some criminologists may still be waiting for the first genuine girls gang, but so far they have not shown up. Female managers who have embezzled the company are still conspicuously scarce. The "liberation hypotheses" has been refuted.

How about organized crime? If women don't make it in simple violent and property crime, how would they fare in the underworld? Thus far, no theorist has explicitly predicted an advancement of women in the ranks of this crime sector that is the most male-dominated and patriarchal of all. Gangsters consider women as "different" and therefore untrustworthy and risky. Bas van Hout (2002), a Dutch crime reporter who knows the mindset and mentality of the Netherlands as well as anybody, finds women "worthless as criminals, and they will always be." Women should be excluded from all criminal projects because they would easily give away the secrets, even in a simple telephone conversation with a girlfriend. They are easily manipulated by the police and exploitable by the public prosecutor as crown witnesses. Mafia literature is full of examples. Men distrust women so fundamentally that they can never be accepted as members of the Mafia (Siebert 1996:55). "Never tell women anything about Cosa Nostra: it's one of the rules," said famous Mafia defector Tommaso Buscetta. "A Mafioso could be punished with death if he breathed a word about the organisation to his wife" (Longrigg 1998:xiii). Omerta, the code of silence in South Italian criminal organisations such as *Nadrangheta, Camorra, Sacra Corona,* or the *Mafia* itself, keep women out.

However, in the 1970s some leaders in organized crime began to break the code of silence themselves. The old Mafia *padrone* shared his life and times with an investigative reporter and a social science researcher. Especially in jail – where he has all the time in the world – he was willing to speak about his daring adventures, and the (American) public loves to read these stories. A long series of Mafia biographies are now among the best sources of knowledge on organized crime (although some of them are obviously self-aggrandizing and therefore flawed). They tend to corroborate the traditional role of women in the mob, being nothing much. Thus, Antonio Calderone, mid-level Mafia member of Eastern Sicily and famous pentito, tells the distinguished criminology professor Pino Arlacchi, "Women think in a certain way – all women, even those who have married Mafiosi or who come from Mafia themselves. When a woman's deepest feelings are hurt, she can't think anymore, there is no code of silence" (1992:165).

In the 1980s and 1990s the list of biographies was extended with the life histories of a daughter (Mafia princess) and a wife of famous American gangsters. Antionetta's father is Chicago Mafia's boss Sam Giancana (Renner 1984), and Rosalie had married into the Bonanno family (Bonanno and Donofrio 1990). Their stories showed that the men in question had created an absolute separation between their private and their underworld lives. The girls remained ignorant and innocent. The neighbourhood knew their fathers and husbands only as devout churchgoers and as the generous sponsors of community activities. The women were well taken care of, and if there were something about which they could complain it would simply be over-protection. If they experienced something of the gangster's life it would be by total accident. When little Antoinette opened the door of the hotel suite to answer the knock on the door from the waiter who brings breakfast, she finds her father in a rage. Only years later did she understand that this would have been a typical risky situation for a Mafia killing.

One of the first criminologists who understood that some women in organized crime families are not so innocent and ignorant as they want to convey has been historian Alan Block (1979). In his study of the rackets in Lower East Side New York in the early '20s, he stumbled over women who, on their own, operated as madams, loan sharks, thieves and fences, and who invested in landed property and the pleasure industry of the neighbourhood. He criticised the literature on deviant women in which they have been described only as victims of brutal men. "In this traditional litany of causes and concerns there is no room for female independence and equality in the world of adult crime. Women such as Rosie Hertz, Bessie Solomon [etc.]...make little sense" (Block 1979:193). As Block urged us to do "serious re-thinking" on female crime, he is, in fact, asking to test the emancipation hypothesis in retrospect. Other writers followed. Dubro and Rowland (1988) described how the bootleggers' imperium of Canada's crime boss Rocco Perri in the 1930s had, in fact, been run by women. Bessie Starkman was responsible for the financial side of Perri's enterprises and Annie Newman later took over when Rocco Perri went to jail. New Orleans local Mafia *don* Carlos Marcella would never appear in public without his cordon of forceful women (Calder 1995). Virginia Hill, "Bugsy" Siegel's glamorous red-haired mistress, who had become his partner and successor after Siegel was murdered, was now being recognised. She had become famous to the American public as the first Mafia moll who held her mouth shut when questioned by a Commission under Senator Kefauver in the 1950s. There seem to be godmothers after all!

Anti-Mafia organizations in Sicily and feminist criminology are now calling for a rethinking of the image of women in the Mafia ([Graziosi 2001). Are the mothers really so ignorant and innocent? Aren't they the ones who transmit Mafia culture onto their sons (Siebert 1996)? Are they not the ones who keep honour ideology alive, and who remind their men of their vendetta obligations? Some sisters and wives have been known to take over responsibility when their men were killed or had been taken off to jail. Rosetta Cutolo is probably one of the best-known women to take over a branch of the Naples' Camorra when her brother Raffaele got caught. There are traditional roles for women in criminal exploits, such as acting as the go-between in kidnapping cases or as carriers of money. Women may not show it to the outside world, but many of them exert considerable power within the confines of the "family." They make themselves known when their man or the organization is in public danger. When their men appear before the court they shout their moral indignation for the magistrates from the public benches.

Organized crime adapts itself to changing economic and legal environments. A further reason why women have now been recognized as active players in leading positions in the underworld has to do with new roles in the spectre of crimes. As women are considered beyond suspicion, they are able to fulfil certain functions more effectively than men. Women smuggle drugs across borders, they cash and stash money for the organization and open bank accounts in order to launder the proceeds of the organisation's criminal exploits. The Netherlands appears on the international crime scene with no less than three such famous women. Bettien Martens *(la bella Bettien)* was sent by members of Colombia's so-called Cali cartel to Europe with the purpose of establishing trading links for cocaine between the two continents. In 1992 she was arrested, together with her bosses in Rome, and subsequently decided to work with the police (Bovenkerk 1994). Thea Moear was one of a leading trio in the infamous drug smuggling organisation under of Klaas Bruinsma in the 1970s and 1980s. She told her story to reporter Bart Middelburg (2000) and appeared in Dutch television to tell about her criminal past. Shortly thereafter (and the age of over fifty) she was arrested in Panama for organising the smuggling of cocaine. Chinese-born Sister P. has become famous as an independent operating smuggler of human beings. It took the police a long time to find her responsible for organising the trip from the European mainland to England in which 58 Chinese died through suffocation in a neglected container on the back of a truck. The police would never have thought of a woman. In the world of Chinese organised crime the little lady (she would never go óut without her bodyguard of four) has gained a reputation as an especially tough negotiator (Meews 2002).

New criminological insights have made it possible to develop a more truthful and less stereotypical portrait of women's role in the world of organised crime. This has very direct consequences for the perceptions and the attitudes of the police and the judiciary. Women are increasingly being treated like men. In 1983, Mafia's drugs trafficking grandmother Nonna Eroina could successfully plead not guilty before the court as the very concept of Mafia excluded her from being part of that organisation (Kristensen and Smits 1996:50). Today's leading women in organized crime do not get away with that anymore. They also have to face the consequences within organized crime itself as women are no longer immune from getting killed. There are still many legal problems to solve (Graziosi 2001). Is a mother accountable for the deeds of her son? Ninetta Bagarella, the wife of Mr. Totò Riina, *capo di tutti capi* of Corleone, thinks not, since all she had done came out of motherly love. As long as women claim they have only been part of the family, they cannot be forced to testify against their husbands, brothers, and sons. However, "family" in organised crime circles does not necessarily mean relations of blood. It takes some time before the public prosecutor may convince the judge and the jury that the word "family" refers to quasi-kinship ties.

The increasing equality of women and men before the law has posed an interesting dilemma for feminist and multiculturalist legal scholars. Chesney-Lind (1997:161) summarises two opposing positions. *Position 1:* as women are now treated harder than before, they can only lose. Considering the fact that they have never been equal, women should now be treated not in the same manner as men because it is a male standard that equality is measured against. *Position 2:* the only way to eliminate the discriminatory treatment and oppression that women have experienced is to push forward continued equalisation under the law. The second position is now at the winning hand; the days of ignorance and leniency are over. The protagonists of women's emancipation have to look for new heroes.

Sure, there are enough! The recent change in dealing with the Mafia and organised crime in general has helped women to rebel. Widows and mothers of murdered Mafia victims have taken the witness stand. Their testimonies are often heart-rending. Courageous women have broken the oppressive silence of Mafia culture and have stepped forward to give secrets away (Kristensen and Smits 1996). *Donne contra la mafia* has become a powerful organisation that is supported by the Church and by left-wing political organisations. All Italians know the sorrowful story of Rita Atria, who came out of a Mafia family and decided to tell her story to magistrate Paolo Borsellino because she wanted to give her children a chance to grow up in a better world. When Borsellino was killed by a car bomb in 1992, she committed suicide. Three months later her mother went to the cemetery with a hammer to crush her headstone: "My Rita has been mistaken." The Mafia has spoken, but Rita became a new folk hero. Such women They constitute a fresh criminological object of study. The new heroines are defectors and activists: Mamma Carnevale, Serafina Battaglia, Rita Costa, Felicia Impastato, Guiseppina La Torre, and many, many more. Where are such women fighting the organized crime structures in the US, in the Netherlands, and in the rest of the world? Crime has become a female business!

Bibliography

Adler, F. 1975. *Sisters in crime.* New York: McGraw-Hill.

Arlacchi, P. 1993. *Leven in de mafia: Het verhaal van Antonio Calderone.* Amsterdam: Nijgh en Van Ditmar.

Block, A.A. 1979. Aw! Your mother's in the Mafia: Women criminals in progressive New York. In F. Adler and R.J. Simon, eds., *The criminology of deviant women.* Boston: Houghton Mufflin Cy.

Bonanno, R., and B. Donofrio. 1990. *Mafia marriage: my story.* New Tork: Morrow.

Bovenkerk, F. 1994. *La bella Bettien.* Amsterdam: Meulenhoff.

Box, S. 1981. *Deviance, reality and society.* London etc.: Holt, Rinehart and Winston.

Calder, J.D., 1995. Mafia women in non-fiction: What primary and secondary sources reveal. In J. Albanese, ed., *Contemporary Issues in organized crime.* Edited by. Monsey, N.Y.: Willow Tree Press.

Chesney-Lind, M. 1997. *Girls, women and crime.* Thousand Oaks etc.: Sage.

Dubro, J., and R. F. Rowland. 1988. *King of the mobs. Rocco Perri and the women who ran his racket.* Markham, Ontario: Penguin Books.

Graziosi, M. 2001. Women, the mafia and legal safeguards. *Forum on Crime and Society* 1:129-134.

Kristensen, S., and H. Smits. 1996. *Libere dalla mafia; Kerk, vrouwen en mafia op Sicilië: samenwerking en groeiend verzet.* Amsterdam: Vrije Univeriteit. (Thesis.)

Longrigg, C. 1998. *Mafia Women.* London: Vintage.

Meeus, T. 2002. Monopolist in mensensmokkel. *NRC Handelsblad* 23/24. (november).

Middelburg, B. 2000. *De godmother.* Amsterdam: L.J. Veen.

Renner, T.C. 1994. *Mafia princess.* New York: Avon Books.

Siebert, R. 1996. *Secrets of life and death, Women and the Mafia.* London and New York: Verso.

Steffensmeier, D.J. Sex differences in patterns of adult crime. 1965-1977. *Social Forces* 21:1080-1108.

van Hout, B. 2002. Vrouwen zijn waardeloze criminelen. *BLVD Moordnummer* 44.

Part III

Organizational Arenas

19

Meeting Cultures in Meetings
Impressions from an International Sports Arena

Walter E.A. van Beek

The arena

Arenas are the natural habitat of Arie de Ruijter: he lives in them, creates them and he uses them as a dominant metaphor of modern society (de Ruijter 2000). They are for him a way of life, as well as a way of studying life: arenas are both culture *and* the meeting place of different cultures. When he decided, long ago, to pursue a professional life of academic leadership, he mentioned in a conversation with me that part of his fieldwork would be done in meetings from now on. And so it was. For the most part my own fieldwork took on a different path, meeting cultures in other habitats – in fact, as exotic as I could find – but over the last years I have also increasingly been encountering cultures in office meetings as well. I speak here about sports, about draughts. International sports administration is an arena in itself, and often a hotly contested one at that. For instance, elections of IOC, FIFA, or UEFA presidents produce stories strongly reminiscent of national elections, with the politicking, networking, maneuvering, and bullying that are part and parcel of many the elections the world over. Many people, for a whole gamut of reasons covet high positions, among which the interest of sports is but one. People will go to great lengths to achieve their goal of being elected.

But besides being a regular arena in itself, these organizations are also a meeting place of various styles of leadership, of national expectations and priorities – in short, of cultures. The ways in which people strive for positions, exert power, and wield their personal influence over international organizations, are influenced by both their personalities and their cultures of origin. Different cultures, different notions of power, and different ways to run an organization – these all are revealed in the way meetings are conducted between the representatives of these various cultures. Thus, meetings are essentially intercultural arenas. It is one such an arena that I want to highlight here: the World Draughts Federation (FMJD, i.e. Fédération Mondiale du Jeu de Dames). I will closely analyze one specific case: an attempted coup against its president – namely, *me*. This is therefore an account of a personal experience of meeting cultures in meetings, with some theoretical reflections to highlight the main points of that intercultural encounter. The "other" culture in this particular case is the Russian organization culture, but the conclusions that arise from this essay roam wider than just to our Eastern European neighbors.

The date is March 2001, and the story begins in Moscow, at a hotel in the remote outskirts of the city.

The attempted coup

It was the only Assembly that I could not attend, due to the death of my father-in-law. So for the first time in the history of the Federation, a General Assembly (GA) was held without its president in charge. Also, for the first time, the meeting was in Moscow, as the World Championship was being played there, also for the first time. Strange as it may sound, during the now 64 years of Russian membership in the FMJD, the "Russians" had never ventured to organize a full-blown title tournament – not after the "change" in 1991, nor before, during the Soviet days. All the more remarkable as such a tournament would have been easy for them to organize. Matches, with two players vying for the title; yes, those had been played on Russian territory many times, along with minor championships for youth – but never a world championship. In retrospect it seems strange, and begs for an answer. Why? Perhaps we might be able to offer an answer later in this paper.

What was quite clear, however, was the reasons for holding the championship-*cum*-assembly in Moscow this time round. The president of the Russian Draughts Federation, a Moscovite of Oekraïnian extraction, who we shall call "K.," had offered to use Moscow as a venue at the last GA, held in Huissen in August 2000. The tournament, due for 2000, was in trouble. Riga, Latvia, the candidate of long standing had withdrawn at the last moment, and in fact announced its withdrawal during the Huissen Assembly. The GA made a courageous effort to rescue the Riga tournament – it was to be part of the Riga 2000 celebrations. The Latvian delegate, Mr. L., was also the

A scene from the 1998 Tallinn (Estonia) Assembly with the back of mr K. at the far left

organizer-to-be and received the full support of those assembled at the meeting. One argument for the withdrawal was curious, at least for me: there was to be no GA during the WC. Indeed, as the GA was to be financed from the tournament funds, and formed a serious budget item, the FMJD had tried to help the Latvians by financing the GA itself, in Huissen. This was a new argument for me – it had never surfaced before in the correspondence – and I proposed to have the present GA, and have the second half during the Riga tournament, should they be able to save the tournament.

In fact, the Executive Board had foreseen this eventuality, and I had contacted two other options, Italy and Brazil. Italy was not present at the meeting but had already indicated it had problems organizing at such a short notice. Brazil was present but had used its funds for the soon-to-be-held championships 64, and their budget did not allow for a second tournament. Then on came Mr K., promising that if the championship could not materialize in Riga, Moscow would host the tournament as well as the second part of the GA. The minutes state: "Mr K. announces that he will organize the GA and the WC in Moscow. He has the opportunity to find an emergency organization in Moscow and a prize money of $25,000 very easily." He harvested a loud and ringing applause, and really carried the day.

Personally, I was unconvinced, and with me many of my board members. Mr K. had quite a track record with the FMJD; had been part of the Executive Board, and had also been in the center of quite some controversies in the past. For instance, during the 1998 GA in Tallinn, Estonia, he had been severely reprimanded by the meeting for staging an unofficial championship on the small board ("64") without recognition by the FMJD. And even earlier, during the Assembly of 1990 in Groningen, he had been at the heart of a power struggle inside the Russian Draughts federation that spilled over into the General Assembly meeting.

In October 2000 it became clear that a major part of the Latvian Federation did not want to organize the WC after all, so the FMJD Board, meeting in November, began preparations for the Moscow event. We were worried waiting for the final OK by the Russian Sport Minister, about the prize money. "Russian promises" had become a standard expression in the FMJD. They are like election promises that never materialize.

The main Russian drive behind the tournament was clear: they wanted to organize the Assembly. Up for elections were two vice-presidencies: one for the 64-square board and the other for coordinator Asia. During the summer Olympic Games in London, the two main contenders for these posts had already indicated their intentions to me, and had tried to make a deal with the president: Mr K. for 64, and the Turkmen representative Mr D. for Asia. The sitting officials, respectively from Oekraine and Yakutsk (Sakha Republic, the far east of the Russian Federation), were also up for reelection, so we looked forward to an electoral battle. I was open for a change though I had my reservations about the Turkmen, who in a previous bout as Vice-president had done nothing. As far as I can remember, he did not attended even one board meeting. It was clear what was happening. Here was a tournament organized in order to win an election! And so, with some misgivings, after I had insisted that the Russians send all correspondence through the office – we still had heard nothing from the Sport Minister – and not my home, I went to Mali for a period of fieldwork in December.

Coming home a week later than expected due to a nasty fall in Bamako, while also recovering from a brain concussion, I found the letter of the Russian minister on my doormat. It had taken three weeks to arrive without a fax or copy to the office, and had been waiting over a week for me. In fact, the date on the letterhead was from before my departure to Mali. A fax would have cleared everything one month earlier.

So, here we were, in a hurry, with the tournament only two months away. In any case, Italy had become a chimera, so we decided to accept the Russian final offer: a tournament in hotel Kosmos, which I knew well. It was not a bad venue. The office sent out the invitations to the qualified players, and the complicated preparations to procure Russian visas for 20 players and numerous officials began. The delay of the Russian snail-mail had rendered the original dates obsolete, and negotiations started with Mr K about the final dates. I wanted a period at the end of March. He has a different window, and finally the dates were set for the period from 22 February right through to14 March. We communicate these, but later he proposed to postpone it a week in order to give him more time to find prize money. However, one can change dates only once for an event, and both the visas and the tickets had already been issued and booked.

The usual communications problems with Africa and Asia, and the perennial problem of the reserves were solved in time, though every decision took time and put the visa procedures under pressure. Visas are the Achilles heel of an international sport organization. The procedures vary according to country, and those of Russia are among the most complicated. For a tournament held in the Netherlands, the organization itself is in charge of issuing the invitations. Most embassies demand originals as e-mails and faxes are suspected of being forged. Russia is different. There, Mr. K. had to take a definitive list to the ministry of sport, which the ministry had to approve. The list would then be forwarded to the Ministry of Foreign Affairs. It is then their duty to fax the list to all relevant embassies, with specific code numbers, which they had to communicate to Mr K., and he with us, and we with the invitees. Only then, after this entire procedure was complete, was the invitation valid.

With a great effort on our part, we finally realized the presence of four Africans in Moscow (one well-known Senegalese grandmaster, three totally unknown players from Cameroon). Yet here, too, the communication was too slow. Their names and invitations came too late to be included for the championships in Moscow. In the end, the African players would arrive one day after the planned opening of events. I tried to convince Mr K. that he should start a day later, and compensate by deleting a rest day. But he refused. It later appeared that he had invested too much for the grand spectacle of the opening (TV and radio coverage, officials invited etc.), and an organizational failure – even a minor one – would not be welcomed. But the Dutch referee founds a solution, and the Africans were given a reasonable tournament start after all.

To compound the problems, the prize money was nowhere in sight. The $25,000 had become nothing more than a faint rumor. From the Netherlands we tried to find some interested parties, and kept insisting that the organization did its utmost to do the same elsewhere. I was not convinced of Mr K.'s efforts, and I was forced to grasp at a last straw. To aid Mr K. I decide to convert three special prizes (best win, best combination, best end game) from a cup into dollars, hoping to "shame" the Russian into also offering money prizes. But it didn't. In the end, there would be no prize money given, though the players only gradually become aware of this fact towards the end of the tournament.

Now, with the wisdom of hindsight and additional information from Russia, I think I misjudged Mr K., with some misunderstanding accruing from a difference in culture. Before the tournament I thought he gave the matter too little attention, and I wanted to spur him on (by our giving some prizes ourselves). Just after the attempted coup, I suspected him of deliberately having failed in coming up with prize money in order to heap more guilt upon the head of his scapegoat – me, the president. But it seems I was mistaken on both accounts. He did try to find prize money, but probably too little too late, and was not successful in the end. So our own gesture did not work. And also, although he did use the absence of prize money to discredit me during the coup, that was not planned as such. It simply happened. Russian complots, as we shall see, do exist but that does not mean they are always deliberate and planned long before their execution.

Then come the tournament, the GA, and – quite unexpectedly – the death of my father-in-law. This last, and quite unexpected, episode left me no choice but to hand over the gavel to my Polish VP, Mr P, and bid a distressed farewell to the Western delegates heading for Moscow. For their part, the players left with severe apprehensions – like entering into "the lion's den," as one of them put it.

Some of the things that eventually transpired were entirely expected. Mr K. did, indeed, use the GA as his personal day of triumph, as we all assumed he would. He had financed quite a few East European and Central Asian delegates from federations we hardly ever see represented in the West: Armenia, Azerbaijan, Georgia, Kazakhstan, Kirgistan, Turkmenistan, the Baltic Republics, Belarus, Mongolia, to mention but a few.

Mr K. was in full control and make the most of it. He took personal charge of arranging the lodgings in the hotel, translations, TV and radio coverage, and the flow of information. Moreover, tthe venue had been changed to a much cheaper hotel, deep in the Moscow woods, far from the end of the metro line.

The opening was a media spectacle that prominently featured Mr K., supplemented by the usual Russian folk dance group and the customary breaking of the large loaf of Russian bread – an ubiquitous ceremony in Eastern Europe. Interviews were held only with Mr K., and the FMJD board was kept in a continuous barrage of meetings, dealings, talks, and private conversations.

In far away Utrecht, I got wind that something more was afoot than just an election for two VP posts. Mr K.'s loyal Belarus partners has prepared a motion of distrust against the president, and at the start of the first day of the Assembly this motion was proposed and carried. Why, for what reason, was never indicated, other than a hint at the absence of prize money and even my own nonattendance. Some Africans telephoned me to ask if it was true that I was no longer interested in being president, as seemed to be implied by my absence. I had not expected this. Despite my reassurances, the motion was carried and I ceased to be president. I was not aware of these developments, besides which I had other things to occupy me, for at that very moment I was giving the eulogy at the funeral.

Interminable speeches during the Moscow coup: fatigue sets in with tournament director Ada Dorgelo, while the Polish Vice President still has to conduct the session.

But then, things started to go wrong for Mr K. The entire board, expertly led by the Polish VP, declared its solidarity in standing behind me and resigned as a bloc. This was not expected by the Russians and came as a shock. However, an even greater shock came when they wanted to proceed with the VP elections. Television and radio broadcasters were invited to witness the great event that was to be the moment of glory for Mr K. He was rightly confident that the East European delegates would approve anything he did, and his presumed mastery of the situation prevented him from expecting the blow that came. The non-Russophone delegations, headed by the Netherlands, France, the Africans, and Poland refused to have elections at all, arguing that now there was neither a functioning Board nor business on the agenda to appoint new officials to the Board. They not only opposed elections for president, they even threatened to boycott any other FMJD event in the near future.

This threat of future boycott by the non-Eastern European delegates was a serious one, especially since most of the financially well endowed tournaments are held in the Netherlands. Moreover, forcing an election now would mean harming the interests of the top players, who of course were present. The entire day was one of turmoil, of so many rapid, angry interchanges in all varieties of the Russian language that the translators could not keep up. What was to be Mr K.'s day of glory turned into a moment of utter defeat when the motion to carry on with the elections was defeated, for now most of the former Soviet satellites abstained from voting and the "West" carried the vote. Finally, the GA decided to ask the sitting Board (although all its members had, in practice, resigned) to prepare a new GA in the summer, and to prepare for new elections to sort out the impasse.

It was an emotional time when the Board members tried to sort out what had actually happened, and to decide whether they wanted to carry on in their functions or not. To fight or not to fight, that was the question – also for me. My absence at the meeting made it easier for me to carry on the duties I had undertaken nine years ago. After all, I was being voted against, but I did have the full support of all Board members. Bear in mind, I was also physically "out of the fray," and viewing the arena from afar. So I fought and we fought.[1]

This the Board did. We initiated a change in structure, thus transforming the FMJD from a monolithic federation into a federation with three semi-autonomous sections (100 squares, 64 squares, and Anglo-American). In the GA of Huissen in August 2001 the propositions were carried through without any problem, and most of the Executive Board, including the president, were reinstated. The coup was ended. The most ardent supporter of the change was Mr K. from Russia. The post of vice-president 64 was filled. It was neither Mr K. nor the sitting Board member from Russia who got the position, but an old friend of mine from the Ukraine. Only two delegates from Israel – who had not been to Moscow – and the delegate from Belarus tried to mount some opposition. Although they did manage to extract a compromise (a first term of the new structure of two years), their voices were largely drowned out in a general feeling of closeness and joint destiny.

Analysis of the attempted coup

What was "Russian" about the attempted Russian coup? In my view it was much more than a mere power struggle. Several cultural elements were at stake here. In fact, the power struggle was not very evident in so far as to this day it is still unclear what benefit my ousting would have brought to the coup makers: they had no alternative president ready. I had expected Mr K. himself to vie for the position, but he never nominated himself as a candidate. Ever since London 2000 did he frequently express that he had had enough of presidencies, and that he certainly did not hanker after that of the FMJD. At that time I did not believe him, but later conversations with him through a mutual friend cleared this up: he felt out of his depth outside Russia. The wider world beyond the vast confines of the Russian Federation, held no attraction to him. Not only was he a monolingual Russian speaker, he also had no interests or feelings for countries beyond greater Russia. The only thing he wanted was to have his hands free within his own territory, and that is how I now interpret the coup attempt. What stood in the way of his ambition, then, was the FMJD, which is a centrally led Federation with a clear and detailed system of rules and regulations. As vice-president 64, he would be bound by these, as well as be continually checked for compliance to these rules, as his predecessor was. Emptying the core, then, would have given him more leeway in his

Despite all politics, the Moscow 2001 World Championship produced a worthy champion: Alexei Tchizhov in interview.

own territory. It was also likely that he thought that a Dutch friend of his would be interested in the presidency, but that never materialized. On the other hand, it might not even have been so calculating after all. From the eternal tension between East and West in this sport, the option for one-upmanship was tempting in any case. A final possibility was that by this action, he could have diverted the widespread criticism directed at him by his own organization by finding the perfect scapegoat: Me, the FMJD president.

The attempted coup was full of cultural elements, and of ways to solve problems and handle relations between peers. The first cultural thing that sticks out was the Western view of an executive board in sports as a collegial organization of peers, with a division of portfolios that leaves each and every one secure in his own mandate, the president in general and representative functions, the tournament director in implementing the rules into proper tournaments, the treasurer for the money etc. For Eastern Europeans, however, presidents are always at the center of power, the "man who can decide anything." In their view a president should rule, not propose, and should dictate, not argue. Also, a president is someone who always has to win: his proposals, when turned down, are defeats.

In the Russian media coverage of draughts, great emphasis was paid to the fact that certain of my proposals were turned down at board meetings. This was portrayed by the Russian media as my defeat, as a president, and the victory of the Russian vice-president (who, in any case, is a good friend of mine) who had raised the perfectly valid arguments on which these proposals were turned down by the other members of the board. What, in other words, was being carefully crafted by the media was an image of me as an "unworthy" and "weak" president. This can be understood in the light of the fact that a meeting in Russian governance is an arena where one – particularly the president – has to win: to win not just one battle, not the battle that one picks, but all battles. For the Russians, their image of a champion is someone who always wins; and life is only bearable when one always wins (a definition formulated by a Russian gymnastic). The structure of a board is never between equals, but always a power arena where one has to score points, where getting what one wants is more important than the arguments.

Thus, when the motion against me was carried in the GA, the Eastern federations expected me to resign, after having been defeated. In fact, after the vote, they immediately thought that I was no longer president. However, Dutch organizational law operates differently (the FMJD is a corporate body under the Dutch law): the president can only be ousted if the motion specifies that it had the force of suspension *(schorsende werking)*. In this case, none of the attempted-coup takers had thought of that. For Easter Europeans, such a contentious vote brings a loss of face, which in their countries would normally bring early retirement to the official in question. The fact that the FMJD board nevertheless carried on its usual work, changed the statutes, and was reelected, was a possibility the Easterners never though possible.

Russians are used to having presidents who furnish the money for the organization, and have the work done by the vice-president. Though disappearing, this still is the ideal of many lower Russian officials and sportsmen. A corollary is that a president has to show this status as well: he has to display that he is financially well off, or even rich. In Russia it is a rich man who vies to become president; he foots the bills for tournaments and travel expenses. This is one reason why reelections of presidents hardly ever took place in the past, and why both instances of my reelection were highly contested after it became clear that my intended solution to problems was not to pour

All sports officials get full press attention: a press conference in Russia.

money into tournaments. Riches and power are thus powerful arguments in favor of a candidate. In all of their political reelections there had been rumors about powerful and rich Russians who vied for a presidential bid: the late general Lebed, then governor of Krasnoyarsk and one of the candidates for the Russian presidency, was said to have been interested. And recently, the name of Zhirinowski, leader of the ultra-nationalist party, was mentioned in the corridors of the Russian Sport Committee. Two years ago a Turkmen captain of industry was put forward as an official candidate, and I still wonder whether he knew anything about his candidacy.

The western ways are just as astonishing for the other side. For instance, it was entirely unexpected for the Russophiles when in the course of the coup attempt the entire board showed its solidarity behind the president. In Russian politics solidarity is not a dominant concept. As someone once said: "Anybody in Russian politics has two suitcases in his closet: one with the incriminating documents on his opponents, and one with his toothbrush and a change of clothes, if the first does not work out." A position on the board is more important than any personal solidarity, and old alliances are easily dissolved and new ones eagerly formed. Governance is the creation of continually changing networks of power, of alliances of interest, and of friendships for the day.

The second aspect to note is the intensity of the battle, in sport politics and in any arena. A conflict inside a board becomes a matter of life and death, shunning even the niceties of respecting one's right to mourn for a deceased relative. Votes are squeezed through pressure, and dissidents are threatened with such things as moving them out of the hotel.

Politics is a highly emotion business, also in sports. Why this intensity? In *Dealing with the New Russia* (Holden, Cooper and Carr 1997), the authors focus on examining emotions and intensity in Eastern business. Russian cultural governance carries a high voltage, and any work seems a combination of high intensity and emotion. Russians tend to work through bursts of creative energy, and little happens in the periods between. Russian politics shows the same alternation between outbursts of activity and mundane life. Intense but fleeting emotions also make for easy shifts in loyalties.

Characteristically, opinions, arguments and explications are never delivered while seated. If a Russian wants to say something, he stands up and makes an extended, ostentatious speech that last about five times longer than it would to say the actual content. Related to this is the notion of promise. I once said in an interview in 1996: "I could paper my walls with Russian promises." In the governance of the West, a promise is a commitment, whether oral or written down, and has to be kept. One has to be a responsible administrator, as good as one's word. For a Russian politician – and businessman – this is not so: a promise is a wish, something that one hopes to bring about. Even on paper! When I came back from Africa, I read the letter of the Russian sport minister the wrong way: I thought I had a guarantee for the tournament in that particular hotel, but in fact all I had in hand was a ministerial wish.

Promises are the essence of elections, of course. My main contender during my first bid for reelection in 1996 was the Minister of Finance of the Sakha Republic of the Russian Federation. He promised – or rather his campaign manager promised on his behalf, I never was totally sure – half a million dollar in prizes should he be elected. I was willing to step down and be his vice-president if this would be true, but I did not really believe it. Of course all the other players believed him. This resulted in a fierce election where I challenged him during the meeting to pay on the spot all arrears in the contributions due from the Russian Draughts Federation, of which he was the head. When he could not or would not do so, the promise of that huge prize fund was revealed to be nothing more than a fable. He then became vice-president and we have been working together on the best of terms ever since.

The third aspect is the importance of the managerial and governance positions themselves. Not only is the highly charged atmosphere of Russian decision-making the reason for the superior investments that Russians make to their sports officialdom, one's very position has a totally different bearing on situations than it does for their Western counterparts. One's position in an international organization – even a relatively small one like the FMJD – is, in and of itself, of supreme importance. It is much more than just a job, more than a title, and definitely much more than a task to perform. Being a sport official is an identity,[2] a crucial part of oneself, an official definition of one's existence that should never be relinquished. The aim is to become someone, and someone important, rather than serving an abstract cause (such as "the sport") or a higher value (like the Olympic ideals). Moreover, for Russians, a sport consists first and foremost of officials rather than just athletes, players, or sportsmen: athletes come and go, but officials remain. In mind, sports players also tend to stay a long time, but are still eclipsed by the staying power of officials. Mr. K is no stranger in this Jerusalem, as he has been around for two decades already in draughts. And despite his apparent loss after the attempted coup, was afterwards still is busy on his Russian turf. At our last meeting he produced as an aide Mr Koslov, a man who wall well eighty years of age. Koslov served as a claque for K, and he knew that I knew Mr Koslov well. By the time of my election in 1992, at which he was present, he had already been around for in the organization for 36 years. Koslov was in the delegation that brought Russia into the FMJD in 1954, and he accompanied Kuperman in his match against the Canadian Deslauriers in 1956, marking the definitive entry of Russian players at the draughts scene. Kuperman is still around, a living legend by now, but so is Koslov.

The corollary for the players is their huge insistence on titles, medals, cups, certificates and diplomas. This main symbolic capital of sports federations is judged quite differently in West and Eastern Europe, at least in the world of draught. Western European draught and chess players typically show some disdain towards these symbolic expressions of their exploits, and prefer to garner recognition directly through their actions – by winning the competition (and the prize money, of course). For Eastern players this symbolic capital is the life blood itself of sport, and sports titles and diplomas are mentioned and shown off in each social context and event. As a consequence, within the sports Executive Boards a continuous battle rages between scarcity-value and generous

In official pictures players form the entourage for the "core of sports", the officials

allotment: Western board players are afraid of title inflation, while Eastern players consider titles as easy coinage: the more the better.

So, officials never die, they just fade away, and return when most unexpected. One additional reason is that sport officialdom is not only about status and identity, but also provides a gateway to the West. In Soviet times both sports officials and sportsmen were among the very few who were permitted to leave the country, to compete abroad. The advantages were many and far reaching: experience of another world, a chance to buy Western commodities, and above all a means to make money by exchanging money. Officials were often in a unique position to buy foreign currency against cheap official prices and sell them at a profit.

Theoretical reflections

The governance culture of the East – and for that matter also of other areas of the world, such as Africa – shows some clear differences as compared with the notions of sports governance as they exist in the West. Sport governance in the West reflects, in fact, Weberian notions of bureaucracy and rationalism. In that notion the explicit goals of the organization and Weber's *"Zweckrationalität"* are absolutely dominant. The implementation of these principles constitute the following criteria for "good governance," in sports:

• the general goal dominates over personal aims

- the general good is not identical to state good
- the main loyalty is to the proper aim of the organization
- merit should prevail over favor
- performance should prevail over connections
- contracts should prevail over gifts

This model leads to a definite profile of a sports official, as someone who
- has no financial interest in his position
- has no economic interest in specific decisions
- has an identity independent of his post as an official
- combines personal distance with commitment in governance
- is loyal to rules and regulations, and the abstract notion of the "good of the sport"
- is not overly impressed by authority and hierarchy
- is oriented towards result rather than towards power
- is efficient rather than ebullient
- has a clear notion of time constraints
- leaves his post when his time is up

From the above it is clear that our nearest neighbors, Eastern Europe, do not share this model at all. The model described above is, in fact, the one for able volunteer amateurs – the official with many hats who, by virtue of his stature in other aspects of his life, can link external resources with the organization he serves. For the West this is the "heroism of distance," the glory of commitment to a higher goal. For the East, on the other hand, such a person is not to be trusted, for he is "un-captured," and his motives are hard to trace. Personal glory and private gain, the quest for power and status, are far easier to gauge in an opponent, than an "aficionado" who strives simply for the good of the sport. And in the East, the term "amateur" bears no positive connotations at all; one is either a professional or transient. The Russian model of the official is, I think, one for whom the following principles apply:
- personal good is never secondary
- main loyalties are towards oneself
- personal relations are more important abstract rules
- organizations are power arenas
- the ideals and goals of the organization are a discourse to be used in battles
- gifts, favors, and privileges accrue as a matter of fact and right to officialdom
- promises and contracts are merely expressions of hope and intent

This leads to a sport official who:
- is principally interested in power
- derives identity from his position
- does not shun the perks of his position
- is an apt window dresser

- sees his colleagues at least as sparring partners
- is careful with his dignity
- piously respects authority and is sensitive to hierarchy
- stays or comes back

This summing up reads like a difference between ideal and practice, rather than cultural differences between Western and East European sport. The Western official as sketched is an ideal type, who conforms to Weber's approach. In reality many (or most) sports officials do not measure up to all the standards mentioned. What is important however, that in the organizational-*cum*-meeting culture of the West, these ideals are engrained and incorporated. Checks and balances are created to rein in excesses and abuses against the Weberian model. Russian realism is based more on a Machiavellian approach, conditioned by particular circumstances. First, the economic realities of sportsmen from these two European regions are starkly different. For East Europeans, the notion of the "gentleman amateur" is absent, and sheer survival is still at stake. Second, the national political identity is, for East Europeans, not as self-evident as in the West, with its comfortable national identities, nicely bolstered but not dependent upon sports performances. But most importantly, the values of the West are not recognized as values in Eastern Europe: the gentleman model is not at all valued as an appropriate model for Eastern Europe by Eastern Europeans. It may use the same discourse, but it does not share its fundamental tenets.[3]

Throughout this essay I have used confrontations with Russian culture as the prime example of two styles of governance in the world of sport. But the differences are by no means restricted to East and West Europe. Examples from other culture areas can easily be added to show that the Weberian model, based a democratic division of power, on societal checks and balances, and on well-demarcated separation between private and public good, is in actual fact a rarity in the world, and in the world of sport. The model of the gentleman-official, like the original gentleman-athlete, is a model not shared by the majority of the world. Other cultures, such as those of Africa, Latin America, and Asia, exhibit their own variations in meeting cultures, their own complex blends of aims, goals and ideals in sports, which are all different from the Western European ideal. Some of those may result in amusing incidents, at least in Western eyes.

> When in the 1970s the great promoter of draughts in Mali, Grandmaster Mamina N'diaye, needed an airplane ticket or an "ordre de mission," he went to Mali's vice-president. With a draughts board under his arm, he easily got past the guards, as the vice-president was well known as a draughts aficionado. N'diaye then played with the vice-president, careful to win a few games, but to lose more (which in fact was not easy). Then the vice-president asked why he came, and N'diaye got his wish. In the course of this "thrashing" he was giving N'diaye, the vice-president got

the idea of participating in World Championship, to be held in Bamako in 1980. After all, he must be (at least in his own mind) one of the best in the world, for didn't he always win, even grandmasters like N'diaye? Mamina had quite a job dissuading him from that idea. "It would not suit your dignity," he argued. Eventually the vice-president agreed just to preside over the opening of the tournament.

The main point of this amusing anecdote is that this is that – simply an anecdote – for the West, yet it is a common problem in Mali, and something to be expected and dealt with through personal relations.

Towards an ethnography of intercultural meeting

In her book *The Meeting,* Helen Schwartzman (1989) describes in great detail the processes and contradictions, the coalitions and clashes of the arena called the meeting. Meetings may often be dull and uninspiring, boring and tiresome; but they are much more than simply a way to make rational decisions. As Schwartzman points out, "a communicative event such as a meeting may constitute a framework for verbal and non-verbal behavior with multiple functions for organizations and communities" (1989:39). This ethnography of meetings provides a privileged perspective on the production of meaning in social gatherings, thus yielding valuable insight into the construction of society, and into cultural differences in the use of meetings for socio-cultural ends. Still, the great majority of her material stems from mono-cultural situations (Schwartzman 1989:275, Smith and Peterson 1988:96), which as such can be compared, but they function fully within a single socio-cultural system.

Accounts of cultural clashes within meetings are rare. To some extent they are known from teaching situations, where the discussion of multicultural communication

Being a sports official is serious business!

has led to approaches which aim to create a "discursive interculture" (Koole and Ten Tije 1994:68, cf. Scollon 1995). In the tradition of the ethnography of communication, from which Schwartzman takes his lead, the focus is on differences in codes and on code switching of participants in multi-cultural settings. The contrast with the case of multiculturalism in the Netherlands is clear: in the setting of most multi-cultural debates in this country, a clear hierarchy between the host culture and the immigrants is compounded by the presence of their home communities, which produce these different codes. Code switching depends on community backing.

In international meetings, the setting is different. The home communities are absent; the format of the meeting, although standardized, is open to idiosyncratic cultural definitions, and so an arena is created for the display of individual prowess through cultural means. These gatherings do provide a subtle angle not only into understanding cultural differences, but also into the relationship between personality characteristics and socio-cultural setting (i.e. between agency and structure).

In the case of the attempted coup described here, personality was very important. Mr K. is undoubtedly a flamboyant figure, revered by his compatriots and follower, or dislike by his opponents. Western journalists found him an easy target for their most dangerous weapon – ridicule. Owing both to his personality and to our cultural differences, I found it very difficult to interpret his behavior. It was only thanks to the help of an emphatic "middleman," who was also a member of our Board and who also had lodged at Mr K.'s home, that I began to understand what had happened. In a long conversation I subsequently had with Mr K. in Moscow in April 2002, I found him amicable and cooperative. At our next meeting in the Ukraine in June 2002, I found him his usual ebullient and overconfident self. At our last meeting in August 2002, once again in Moscow, after political positions in Russia had changed once again, he was very business-like. Clearly, any problem between him and me was my own: I

Kuperman, seven times World Champion and a living draughts legend, is the epitome of staying power in mind sports

simply had to get used to the quick changes of a personal relationship that was constantly changing in relation to the vicissitudes of politics.

Russian culture, at least the political culture of contemporary Russians, throughout this tale, has been at the background of this small upheaval in the World Draughts Federation. The assessment between personality and background, between agency and culture, is difficult and the relation remains shifting and dynamic. Some features of Mr K.'s behavior are recognizably Russian (as compared with Dutch behavior): intensity of action, the small gap between dream and reality (cf. Tismaneanu 1995), and the supreme importance of (network) relations (see Leenders in this volume), documents, and formal insignia (cf. Billington 1998). But his way of transforming these cultural preferences into performance was uniquely his very own.

Russian political culture is in cange, as many studies have indicated (Shalin 1996, Lukin 2000, Tismaneanu 2000), and the actors in our little drama easily straddle the eras before and after 1991: sports politics in the East is still mostly made up of old "apparatchik," led by the remnants of the "nomenclatura." Occasionally, usually at the top levels, new elites who had formed elsewhere enter the arenas, but the bulk of officialdom is culturally still firmly rooted in the Soviet past.

All in all, international meetings offer an interesting window on the multicultural arena, and sport in particular provides a good example of the clash of cultures, and of the power of cultures to reinterpret formats, structures, and events. Sport is the most successful of all colonial exports in world history, together with the concept of the nation-state. As a concept inherited mainly from the British (van Beek 1997) sport has generated a huge general appeal, swept over the world, conquered all continents and been welcomed by all cultures. In so doing, it took a lot of extras in its slipstream: organizational structures, rules and regulations governing encounters, and a Western political culture. However, the host cultures, which eagerly adopted sports as a concept, adapted these extras to their own priorities, and so redefined formats, contents, and procedures of the organiational cadres of sport and the definition of sport officials, thus adding to the arena of sport proper another fascinating arena of cultural clashes.

Notes

1. We were adamant to prevent such an attempted takeover from ever happening again in the future, and especially to prevent the problems of the "64" version (the main bone of contention in our assessment of the attempted coup. The Board quickly got together to prepare a change in structure, and we transformed the FMJD from a monolithic federation into a federation with three semi-autonomous sections (100 squares, 64 squares and Anglo-American).

2. The farewell of Mr. B., my predecessor who had lingered on as vice-president 64, was a highly emotional affair. At the Board meeting after our anniversary reception, the members of the Board and some representatives from national federations said good-bye to him. There was ample reason to take leave of him, especially after the 1996 elections in Abidjan, but still all present took pity on him. He was in tears, shattered to say farewell to a job, to people, but first foremost, to an identity.

3. Characteristically, when speaking about draughts, the Eastern officials never speak about it as

a sport, but as the "draughts movement," a term evidently reminiscent of past times, but also one that denotes struggle, competition with other sports, without any connection to leisure, recreation, and general well being.

Bibliography

Ackroyd, S, and S. Fleetwood, eds. 2000. *Realist Perspectives on Management and Organizations.* London: Routledge.

Billington, J. 1998. *The Face of Russia: Anguish, Aspiration and Achievement in Russian Culture.* TV Books.

de Ruijter, A. 2000. *De Multiculturele Arena.* Catholic University of Tilburg. (Inaugural lecture.)

Holden, Cooper and Carr. 1997. *Dealing with the New Russia.* London: Wiley and Sons.

Koole, T., and J.D. ten Tije. 1994. *The Construction of Intercultural Discourse.* Amsterdam: Rodopi.

Lukin, A.A. 2000. *Political Culture of Russian "Democrats".* Oxford: Oxford University Press.

Shalin, D. 1996. *Russian Culture at the Crossroads: Paradoxes of Post-communist Consciousness,* Boulder, Colo.: Westview Press.

Smith, P. B., and M.F. Peterson. 1988. *Leadership, Organizations and Culture. An Event Management Model.* London: Sage.

Schwartzman, H.B. 1989. *The Meeting: Gatherings in Organizations and Communities.* New York: Plenum Press.

Schwartzman, H.B. 1993. *Ethnography in Organizations.* Newbury Park: Sage.

Scollon, R.T. 1995. *Intercultural Communication,* Oxford: Oxford University Press.

Tismaneanu, V. 1995. *Political Culture and Civil Society in Russia and the New States,* Princeton University Press.

Tismaneanu, V. 1997. *Fantasies of Salvation: Democracy, Nationalism and Myth in post-communist Europe,* Princeton, N.J.: Princeton University Press.

van Beek, W.E.A. 1997. Play, sport and culture. In W.E.A. van Beek and A. Dorgelo, eds. *The Fascinating World of Draughts,* pp. 7-15.

van Beek, W.E.A. 2002. Rondo, presto en andante. Ervaringen in sportbestuur, in E. van Hattem and P. Visser, eds. *Het WK 2001 in Moskou,* pp. 21-32. Universiteit van Twente.

Wilmott, R. 2000. Structure, culture and agency: rejecting the current orthodoxy of organization theory. In S. Ackroyd and S. Fleetwood, eds. *Realist Perspectives on Management and Organizations,* pp. 66-86. London: Routledge.

20

Trust and Distrust in Russian–Dutch Relations
An exploration[1]

Rieke Leenders

Introduction

Russian immigrants who start a new life in the Netherlands and want to become friends with Dutch people often confront a serious problem. Owing to their cultural and social background, their idea of friendship is often different[2] from that of Dutch people.[3] Consequently, instead of trust – a necessary element for friendship – this difference frequently provokes mutual distrust.[4]

In this era of globalization and multicultural cohabitation, Russian and Dutch people meet each other not only through friendships, but also in collegial teamwork. Sometimes, the result of these interactions is marriage. On the micro-level of social life, these kinds of social ties presuppose durability, emotional intensity, intimacy and reciprocity. As a first attempt to explore the problem, it is worthwhile to look more closely to the well-known anthropological concept of "reciprocity" (Mauss 1967). The "politics of emotions" implies that people weigh deliberately the pros and cons of "balanced," "generalized" and "negative" reciprocity, as Marshal Sahlins noted.[5] In intercultural meetings, this seems all the more imperative.

During Soviet times, an extremely elaborate system of reciprocity, called *blat*, operated in the U.S.S.R.. Everything that was rationed by the state was redistributed according to *blat*. In general, *blat* was embedded in horizontal, non-hierarchical, compassionate and warm social networks, and was generally perceived as morally acceptable. As the Russian sociologist Alena Ledeneva pointed out in her excellent study *Russia's Economy of Favors: Blat, Networking and Informal Exchange* (1998), *blat* had also many resemblances with notions of bribery, corruption, and other informal practices, like patron-client relationships.[6] However, *blat* was inextricably bound up with the Soviet system and far more elusive. It meant "the use of personal networks and informal contacts to obtain goods and services in short supply and to find a way around formal procedures" (Ledeneva 1998:180).[7] Due to the perennial shortage and to the state system of distribution, Russian people used friends to survive.

After *perestroika*, "using friends" simply as a means to survive became less common: "Post-Soviet conditions brought into being the rationalization of relationships even with the very closest" (ibid.:198). Mutual help decreased as the market economy expanded. Social networks were condensed to the family circle and personal networks broke up.[8] This raises the question of what of the phenomenon of friendship was subsequently left in post-Soviet Russia.

Eric Wolf describes "emotional friendship" as restricted to the two persons involved, with closure of the social circle and with a large and unspecified series of performances of mutual assistance and affect. Moreover, the charge of affect has to be seen as a device for keeping the relationship as one of open trust and open credit (Wolf 1973:12-13). Did old forms of friendship transform themselves in Russia into new ones, in a kind of "emotional friendship," as we understand it? Unfortunately, the analysis of Ledeneva stops here and other empirical and publicized data are not available yet.

Since the fall of the Berlin Wall in 1989, the Russian speaking community in the Netherlands has grown quickly. Today, I estimate its number to be approximately 30,000 legal and between 10,000 and 30,000 illegal persons. New evidence suggests that among them the number of Russian women married to Dutch men is grow exponentially.[9] What kind of relationship did all these Russians build up in their new homeland, after they emigrated to the West? Detailed empirical data are also lacking here.

Nevertheless, let us explore the topic more thoroughly. And let us look at Ledeneva's study and my own empirical data, gathered over five years of habitual visits to Russia and through regular contacts with Russians living in the Netherlands.[10] In addition, the comments of Russian friends on the first draft of this article are included. What is specific about notions of reciprocity of Russians today, and how could this help us to understand more of the problems of Dutch-Russian relations? Three themes seem to be important: 1) *blat* as a "feel for the game," (2) *blat* as emotion, and (3) *blat* as "concealment."

Blat as feel for the game

All friendship presupposes reciprocity. Everywhere "personal housekeeping books" motivate people's actions. As the Dutch sociologist Abram de Swaan (1996:91,93,94) pointed out so clearly, in this behavioral system all parties keep a kind of administration of debts and claims at the back of their heads.[11] Russians are no exceptions to this. "Instrumental friendship," as Wolf (1973:10-13) would characterize *blat*, exists in all societies where mutual, material interdependence and friendship run parallel with each other. What then could make it so difficult for them to create a relationship of trust with Dutch people?

During plan-socialism, Russians became masters in managing informal exchange networks. Bourdieu would call this their "social capital." *Blat* is a system of exchange in which people can show their "feel for the game." In "beating the system," they can be smart and efficient, clever and creative. They can bend the rules ad hoc and to their own will. "Beating the system" gives social esteem; "anti-systemic" behavior implies prestige.

In addition, Russians who have this "feel for the game" are able to show gratitude for help received without expecting gratitude in return. As Ledeneva points out, "It follows that one had to repay for *blat* favors on the one hand but not to expect repayment on the other." An informant once told her: "There are people … who try to clear up their obligations immediately but this is not appreciated in the *blat* relationship" (Ledeneva 1998:163). There is a folk saying in Russia, which expresses the need for keeping an eye to the future: *Ne plyui v kolodets, prigoditsya vody napit'sya* (Do not spit into a well, you still might need to drink from it) (ibid.:164-5).

Leon, 33 years old and living in Tomsk, is a real *blatmeister*. He is a perfect broker, whose tactics are smooth and cheerful.[12] He has a very good memory and knows most data about his *blat* contacts by heart. Working as an academically qualified employee at the research center of an oil company, for Leon to make *blat* contacts is not only something for which he has a natural talent, but is also hard work. *Blat* shapes his life style: he is very energetic. Leon wants to be known, and his contacts are his "social capital." He also likes to help others simply to feel useful to them, and he values people's gratitude, greetings, and smiles. He never says "no" immediately, but rather prefers the response "let me think what I can do for you." He may get nothing out of it at a particular moment, but the more people are obliged to him the easier his problems may be solved in the future.

To Leon, "beating the system" has become second nature, an unconscious passion to arrange things and problems. When something went wrong with his luggage at the airport, he immediately asked for the "book of complaints" and put in a lot of time and energy to make his point clear to the local manager. Due to a serious accident, he became paralyzed, unable to move any part of his body besides his arms. Nevertheless, with the help of his mobile telephone, even from his hospital bed he was able to involved all his friends and acquaintances in the process of his convalescence. With charm and politeness, he reprimanded, without any negative consequences, members of the medical staff who did not do what they had to do according to their function, or according to what they had promised him. Leon is not deceived by the illusion of warm and friendly relations, and has the practical sense always to feel the appropriate social distance correctly. Sometimes one can experience his power more explicitly when he keeps a person indebted by over-reciprocation; that is, deliberately going "over the top" with his generosity.[13]

When Russian people arrive in the Netherlands, they are initially inclined to use *blat* methods. Very soon, however, they realize that to "beat the system" and to show their "feel for the game" does not make much sense in daily life here. Common Dutch people are not impressed by their methods and do not go for *blat* exchanges. The Dutch-Russian anthropologist Helena Kopnina, who did research into Russian forms of self-organization in the Netherlands and Great Britain, also mentions this point in her dissertation: "Many Russians reported trying to approach English or Dutch officials 'informally' (by offering 'gifts') and being surprised by the 'lack of understanding' in the best cases and a 'call for authorities to intervene' in the worst. Most Russians gave up bribery having lived in the receiving country for a number of months" (Kopnina 2001:109).

Blat as emotion

For Russians, friendship means first and foremost helping each other. An informant once told Ledeneva, "Western people, in contrast to us, are very independent. They rely on themselves and do not fancy helping out or accepting help from others. Russians assume that they can always ask for help and will help themselves. I am sure that if I ask I will be helped. And the other way round. If I am asked, I drop everything and help the other person, because I can imagine myself in his place. Indifference or refusal is a psychological trauma. I try not to refuse, giving out everything I can" (Ledeneva 1998:163). Kopnina puts it even more strongly: "The Russian saying, *Drug poznayetsya v bede* (A friend reveals himself in times of trouble) implies that helping one out of trouble is the only way of assessing real friendship" (Kopnina 2001:118).

"Emotional friendship," according to Wolf (1973:10-13), can only exist in a context where a certain amount of material independence for the individual is the norm. Maybe Russia is also a kind of society where "interpersonal relationships...are not fully integrated into modern subjective individuality," as the American anthropologist L.A. Rebhun describes it rather abstractly for contemporary Brazil (Rebhun 1999:26). In Soviet times, *blat* tied into primary networks, like the family' and one's closest friends are the most morally acceptable. In this case it was part of the most basic moral rules, such as not cheating each another, not letting the other down, and keeping one's word. Ledeneva was told by an informant, "Between friends the requests can be unlimited, but at the same time, I will require from my friend to see why I can't help without taking offence. If I cannot, I cannot. He is supposed to believe that if I could I would do my best. It is mutual trust in each other. The relationship is based on the belief that we are friends and will do everything to maintain it" (Ledeneva 1998:147,150) Affective relations between those people create a kind of solidarity based on the private morality of the people involved (ibid.).

Olga, 51 years of age, is an art curator at the local art museum in Tomsk. She is by no means egoistic or calculative. Her best female friends are people of the same social status who help her without hesitation. She does not use the term of *blat* but conceives it in terms of mutual help. She values relationships in and of themselves, and does not think of them in terms of costs and benefits. However, she does take advantage of relationships when such possibilities arise. Potentially she is able to make use of her relatives and friends but she tries to do so only when moved by an urgent need. Her *blat* is full of warmth and humanity.[14]

When Russians decide to live in the Netherlands, they bring this notion of sharing with them. When 25-year-old Natalia arrived here a few years ago, she had many problems with her new Dutch schoolmates and friends. Her general opinion of them was that they did not share. In White Russia, where she came from, she used to prepare homework together with her schoolmates. Here she had to do it all by herself. She was also surprised that her schoolmates did not allow her to copy their answers during examinations.

Once, Natalia went with some Dutch friends to the beach. She asked one friend how many people would go with them and then she packed food and drinks in her backpack for everybody, as she was used to doing in Russia. To her great astonishment, everybody brought his or her own towel, and their own food and drink, which they consumed separately. Although she herself did not bring a towel because she expected someone else to have brought a big cloth for everybody to sit or lie on, nobody offered to share his or her towel with Natalia. Due to this lack of sharing, she felt uncomfortable on the beach. She thinks Dutch people are egoistic and individualistic and she feels more at ease with the family of her Turkish husband, whose ideas about sharing are more like her own.[15]

In Russia, hospitality is a crucial cultural form of reciprocity, and consequently is of great emotional value. Every time a Russian friend takes me to visit a Russian family, voluminous consumption is obligatory. When these people arrived in the Netherlands, they expect the same behavior in return and felt disappointed about the lack of hospitality here. For Dutch people, however, Russian hospitality provides them with a double problem. They are obliged to respond unconditionally to Russian hospitality, while simultaneously being aware of their own profound shortcoming in this respect.

Blat is a non-monetary way of doing things. During Soviet times, exchange of products and services replaced the exchange of money. As one of Ledeneva informants once told her, "One can't take money from a friend, we were just brought up like this." Another one said much the same thing: "No need to pay, it is a sign of friendship, no calculations between friends, I could be in the same situation myself..." (1998:41,148). Friendship is valued above money, as Leon commented to me after I sent a first draft of this article to him in Russia: *"Ne imei sto rublei a imei sto druzei"* (You do not need a hundred roubles but a hundred friends).

Eighty-year-old Katharina Mikhaelnovna, my landlady and the mother of a friend, did not want to accept money for my lodging in her house in the summer of 2002. Because of her low pension and low additional summer income from selling flowers on the local market she needed it badly, out of a sense of justice, I left money on the table before I left. When she found my money she was rather confused and angry about it and asked mutual friends for an explanation of my behavior.[16]

After *perestroika*, money began to play a larger role in Russian personal friendships. In a market economy with private property, good friends who try to start a private business together all too often experience that friendship and commercial business do not go well together. When "money-making" is involved, customary help provided for the sake of friendship, as in Soviet times, becomes tricky. An informant told Ledeneva: "[I]t has been so often the case that two friends running a business have turned into enemies and suspected each other of fraud" (1998:197).

Blat as concealment

Sharing problems was part of normal social behavior in Russia. Ledeneva writes about it: "It was taken for granted between friends in Soviet Russia that problems were shared and sharing became an invitation for help" (1998:169). However, sharing particular information was and still is quite a different topic. A good number of Russian people do not like to talk about the future, because talking about something unpredictable and therefore vulnerable could work as a self-destroying prophecy. Many women for instance do not tell anyone about their pregnancy until they can no longer hide it. In Russia, people have learned that life is unpredictable, and speculating about it makes no sense. Because of continuous financial uncertainties, a lot of Russian people also do not like to talk about what they will buy tomorrow, or where they will go for a holi-day next month, or what they will change in their house next year. Discussions about a planned common holiday stopped after I stopped talking.[17] This is in line with the empirical findings of the Polish sociologist Pjotr Sztompka (1996), who encountered in post-socialist Poland a considerable distrust regarding the future, and a general reluc-tance to plan.

Besides an aversion to shared plans, many Russian people also seem reluctant to call a spade a spade. In Russia, my close Russian friends often withheld crucial but sen-sible information that would have thoroughly influenced my plans and actions. With this behavior, they initially gave me the idea that they had a private strategy of their own; or even worse, that they conspired against me, both of which later proved to be not the case.[18] Ledeneva also encountered apparent concealment with regard to *blat*: "Many peo-ple were inhibited from identifying things they did or were forced to do by *blat*, for it could have disturbed their self-perception as honest and respectable people, damaged their self-esteem or presented their personal relations in the wrong light" (Ledeneva 1998:60).

Furthermore, Russians also make a distinction between their own actions and the actions of others. *Blat* was only *blat* when others performed it. "Perpetual switching of perspectives enables one to engage in *blat* practices and at the same time to distance one-self from them.... The most conspicuous feature of all the interviews was that the infor-mal deals were called '*blat*' when practiced by others but described in terms of friend-ship or mutual help in the case of personal involvement" (ibid.:6,68). For ideological reasons, *blat* could not be recognized even by the state as an attribute of the Soviet sys-tem. Ledeneva calls this denial of *blat* on both the societal and individual level the "mis-recognition game" (ibid.:68). These general circumstances imply a *niche* for other prac-tices exercised in "misrecognised" form.

Another example of this "misrecognition game" is the concealment of *blat* by way of what Ledeneva calls the "rhetoric of friendship" (ibid.:60). *Blat* communities suppress the use of "*blat*" and prefer the "we are friends" terminology. Since friendship is under-stood as the refusal to calculate debts, and as reinforcement to affective emotions, the rule of mutual obligations is concealed. For Ledeneva this "rhetoric of friendship" is essential for the functioning of *blat*: "[T]he sense of belonging and feelings of affection disguise *blat* relations and thus contribute to their efficiency" (ibid.:148). This "help dis-course" justifies the routine obtaining of services from friends.

One step further is just pretending. Wolf also recognizes the necessity of emotion in an instrumental relation: "Despite the instrumental character of such relations, a minimal element of affect remains an important ingredient in the relation" (Wolf 1973:13). He even concluded in this regard that "[i]f it is not present, it must be feigned" (ibid.).

As a professor of social sciences at an institute in Moscow, 60-year-old Varya arranges things without many problems. At first blush she behaves as though she likes a person and acts as a close friend. As it turns out, however, she is mainly interested in a person if she can use him or her to her own benefit. She does not hesitate to ask friends to help her and always goes to the right person when she needs something. Towards everybody, including officials, she behaves cordially. As soon as she gets what she wants, her behavior changes to a more businesslike attitude. She always manages to be at the right place at the right moment and then tries to look respectable, lively, and cheerful.

As a divorcée, Varya can be more involved with *blat* practices than married women. Her extra-familial status allows her to flirt regularly with men, which generates all kinds of help, from getting a new flat to obtaining help for repairs at home. Towards me, she is not too confiding about this main instrumental function of her lovers, although, according to the comments of my Russian friends, Russian culture approves of this kind of behavior. Her best female friends are people of lower social status who help her without hesitation because they know they will get something they need in return. For me as a Dutch person it was difficult to realize that I was only used for her personal aims.

The next step is simply to lie. V. Shlapentoch was struck by the "culture of lying" during Soviet times: "People were...forced to lie regularly in their professional work, faking reports on their production activity, pretending to fulfill orders, and participating each day in the various rituals" (Shlapentoch 1989:159). According to Ledeneva and in the terminology of Bourdieu (1990:234), the system of *blat* is particularly suitable for lying because it plays "a double game with truth." In this double game, the individual in a sense lies to himself, by constructing a "truth" whose sole function and meaning are to deny a truth known and recognized by all. "It is about a lie that would deceive no one, were not everyone determined to deceive himself " (Ledeneva 1998:72).

Russian people can go very far in preserving a relationship. Making up stories to maintain the bond is far more common in Russia than in the Netherlands. One of the skills of Valeri, a 38-year-old man living in Vladivostok and a "jack of all trades," is telling invented stories and anecdotes. Rather than giving a straight answer that could be perceived as unfriendly or uncooperative, he prefers to evade the question. He chooses to tell stories that, to most listeners, seem very credible. However, he is a bad communicator when it comes to information about his motives and plans. Honesty in providing more complex or sensitive information is not his natural way of doing things. He does not always speak frankly about matters that are neutral and self-evident for Dutch people, and will rather think up a story than say something that would harm his image as a rational or efficient man. As I discovered, maintaining his self-image and the relationship is more important to him than telling the truth.

Some concluding remarks

After scrutinizing the empirical data of Ledeneva, those of others, and of myself, I think the difficulties Russians have with building long-term personal relations of trust with Dutch people have to do, at least in the eyes of Dutch people, with the combination of three characteristics of "Russian behavior." This combination consists of (1) conspicuous skills at "beating the system," (2) ostentatious use of the "rhetoric of friendship," and (3) a desire to conceal what Dutch people like to share.

Could it be possible that the experienced differences between Russian and Dutch conceptions of friendship are more about scale than about content? Are we just discussing a spectrum of relations, with emotional friendship at the one end and *blat* at the other? Alternatively, are we chiefly talking about a difference in intensity of behavior, like "conspicuous" skills at beating the system and an "ostentatious" use of the rhetoric of friendship? Finally, is the "double game played with truth" specific to gift giving or *blat*, as Bourdieu and Ledeneva suggest? Is it not also a characteristic of all social relations? The more I think about the subject of friendship and the differences between Russian and Dutch conceptions of friendship, the more I become aware of my own tactics, etiquette, and practical skills of "misrecognition." My perpetual switching of perspectives (e.g. when the other person does it, it's wrong; when I do it, it's right), my frequently making an offer without saying it, my promising a return without mentioning it, my concealing of my expectations towards a friend-what is the essential difference between these and *blat* relations?

Has it perhaps to do with the fact that in the Netherlands friendship is more about emotional than material support? Material dependence determinates most instances of Russian reciprocity, even after *perestroika*, and the continuing practice of hospitality nationwide still sets a good example. However, like Russians, Dutch people exchange food and drinks with friends during celebrations, especially at major social stages of the life cycle, like the birth of a child, a marriage, or a funeral. Like the Russians, the Dutch help their friends when they have problems, are pregnant, or seriously ill. However, Dutch people do it in a different way.

In Russia, personal ties did not only break up in the last two decades, they were also transformed. My friends in Russia have commented that nowadays especially young people exchange friendship even without any material dependence. For them *blat* is no longer only about goods and services, but chiefly about information. In the market economy, one obtains new kinds of information normally by *blat*, above all about the quality of new products. This sort of information is an exceedingly scarce resource nowadays in Russia. From constructing good houses to finding tasty wines, one always needs friends.

Nevertheless, a difference in scale forms only part of the explanation. This exploration suggests at least two aspects concerning content. Firstly, by looking at the phenomenon of *blat* and some of its appearances, one may conclude that *blat* is commonly conceptualized as a generalized form of reciprocity. To expect that the receiver do or give something in return was and continues to be not done in most friendship relations in Russia. The rule that emerges is that to not expect some immediately return for one's favors is the best guarantee for a fruitful relationship, and constitutes a form of "social insurance" for obtaining needed help in the future. Given that in Soviet times this generalized form of reciprocity acted as the motor of the *blat* system, the notion must be deeply rooted in Russian mentality. For Dutch people however, this extreme long-term objective of a gift appears difficult to maintain, even for the most emotional types of friendship.

The second important difference that appears from the empirical data is about sharing information. The sociologists Selma Sevenhuijsen and Christien Brinkgreve argue that an important aspect of trusting somebody is letting the other care about something that one values.[19] Most Russian people whom I have met allowed me to share their moral support and experiences, but often refused to give me access to their more sensitive motives and plans. Within Dutch culture, trying to conceal motives or plans from friends is regarded as a sign of superficial friendship, and only approved in the realm of business.

Finally, it may be argued that what seems at stake here is the performance of reciprocity itself. Michael Jackson (2002:137) provides more insight to this problem when he focuses on the "inescapable ambiguity of exchange." How should one decide whether a gift has been returned, respects shown, honor satisfied, words heeded, or justice done? In the end, reciprocal behavior proves itself to be cultural behavior, which people mostly demonstrate rather routinely because their culture prescribes it. In intercultural relationships, however, it demands endless internal bargaining, calculations, and rationalization – in short, for a conscious politics of emotions. The Russian *habitus* of feigning warm relationships, faking stories, and concealing information, causes a lot of confusion for Dutch people about what is exactly being exchanged and why. At the same time, Dutch people have to decide incessantly and deliberately about the pros and cons of their own behavior. Jackson calls this the "intersubjective imaginary" of exchange. Further analysis of Dutch empirical data on friendship and anthropological research on post-Soviet forms of friendship in Russia and the Netherlands will help us to bring more clarity to this matter.[20]

Within a more specific context I want to define a "blatmeister" as a perfect broker with unconditional loyalty. In this sense Arie de Ruijter is the best "blatmeister" of Dutch cultural anthropology.

Notes

1 I thank Sergei Kirpotin, Judith Marquand, Tatjana Sherepanawa, Nicolai Protopopov, Henk Storm and Ton Zwaan for their help and comments on an earlier version of this article.
2 Pierre Bourdieu (1998) would call this a difference in *habitus*
3 See for a recent journal issue on 'Politics and Emotions in Post-socialist Communities' Svasek 2002. The development of friendship in these communities is not a prominent theme in this volume.
4 Kopnina concludes with regard to Russian immigrants in Great Britain: "It seemed that Russ-

ian people (...) are rejected by the British because of lack of common ground or understanding" (Kopnina 2000:116).

5   Sahlins (1972:193-6).

6   See for other publications about Russia's reciprocity system Alapuro and Lonkila 2000, Berliner 1957, Humphrey 2000, Lonkila 1997. See Abrahams 1999 for Finland.

7   Ledeneva gives also the following definition of *blat* which sounds more idealistic: A "complicated, culturally grounded, 'social alchemy' for tuning access to state property to one's own advantage but without stealing anything" (Ledeneva 1998:180).

8   Ledeneva links this to a more general process that is happening nowadays in Russia: "All personal networks in which mutual help was rendered underwent (...) processes of stratification" (Ledeneva 1998:199).

9   See Siegel (2001:111); Snel et al. (2000:35); NRC-Handelsblad (9-3-2002).

10 Leenders 2001 provides more detailed information about my background as a researcher in this field.

11 De Swaan (1996:92) gives the basic characteristics of this kind of reciprocity: 1) frequent and regularly contact; 2) during a long period of time; 3) with a growing willingness to cooperate and subsequently 4) a declining of distrust; 5) with rewarding behavior towards forms of cooperation and 6) punishing behavior towards negligence of cooperation.

12 Because of reasons of privacy all the names of my informants are changed.

13 Based on my own empirical data. See also Ledeneva (1998:167,171).

14 Author's own empirical data.

15 Author's own empirical data.

16 Author's own empirical data.

17 Pjotr Sztompka (1996) wrote an instructive article about trust and distrust in post-socialist Poland. See also the publication of the British sociologist from Polish origin Barbara Misztal (1996) for a discussion about the lack of trust in the same country.

18 When speaking about the draught sports arena in Russia, Walter van Beek's contribution in this volume gives rise to the idea of conspiring Russians because of their withholding information while managing a world-wide tournament.

19 Sevenhuijsen and Brinkgreve (2002:152,153).

20 Sandra Bell and Simon Coleman, the editors of *The Anthropology of Friendship* (1999), show that friendship can be a fruitful topic of anthropological research.

Bibliography

Abrahams, R., 1999, 'Friends and Networks as Survival Strategies in North-East Europe', in Bell and Coleman, *The Anthropology of Friendship* pp. 155-68. Oxford and New York: Berg.

Alapuro, R.and M.Lonkila, 2000, 'Networks, Identity, and (In)action,' *European Societies*, 2(1).

Bell, S. and S. Coleman, eds., 1999, *The Anthropology of Friendship*, Oxford and New York: Berg.

Berliner, J., 1957, *Factory and Manager in the USSR*, Cambridge, Mass.: Harvard University Press.

Bourdieu, P., 1998, *Practical Reason: On the Theory of Action*, Cambridge: Polity Press.

Humphrey, C., 2000, 'How is Barter done?: The Social Relations of Barter in Provincial Russia', in: Paul Seabright, ed. *The Disappearing Rouble: Barter Networks and Non-Monetary Transactions in Post-Soviet Societies* pp.259-97. Cambridge: Cambridge University Press,

Jackson, M., 2002, 'The Exterminating Angel: Reflections on Violence and Intersubjective Reason, *Focaal, European Journal of Anthropology*, 3:137-48.

Kopnina, H., 2001, *Invisible Communities: Russian Migration in the Nineteen Nineties in London and Amsterdam*. PhD Thesis, University of Cambridge.

Ledeneva, A., 1998, *Russia's Economy of Favours: Blat, Networking and Informal Exchange*. Cambridge: Cambridge University Press.

Leenders, R. 2001, *NWO Proposal 'Blat" or Binding Agent?: Russian Relationships of Reciprocity in the Netherlands,* Dossier number 261-98-907.

Lonkina, M., 1997, 'Informal Exchange Relations in Post-Soviet Russia: A Comparative Perspective', *Sociological Research Online* (Internet).

Mauss, M., 1967, *The Gift: Forms and Functions of Exchange in Archaic Societies,* London: Cohen and West.

Misztal, B.A.,1996, *Trust in Modern Societies: The Search for the Basis of Social Order,* Cambridge: Polity Press.

Rebhun, L.A., 1999, *The Heart is Unknown Country: Love in the Changing Economy of Northeast Brazil.* Stanford, Cal.: Stanford University Press.

Sahlins, M., 1972, *Stone Age Economics,* London: Tavistock.

Sevenhuijsen, S. and Chr. Brinkgreve, 2002, 'Trust, Familiarity, and Otherness: How to think about Trust using the Work of Norbert Elias', *Focaal, European Journal of Anthropology* 39:149-160.

Shlapentoch, V, 1989, *Public and Private Life of the Soviet People,* Oxford and New York: Oxford University Press.

Siegel, D., 2001, *Russian Biznes in the Netherlands* (Manuscript).

Snel, E., J. de Boom, J.Burgers and G. Engbersen, 2000, *Migratie, Integratie en Criminaliteit: Migranten uit voormalig Joegoslavië en de Voormalige Sovjet-Unie in Nederland,* Rotterdam: RISBO.

Svasek, Maruska, 2002, 'Politics and Emotions in Post-socialist Communities'. Special section *Focaal, European Journal of Anthropology* 39.

Swaan, Abram de, 1996, *De Mensenmaatschappij,* Amsterdam: Bert Bakker.

Sztompka, P., 1996, 'Trust and Emerging Democracy: Lessons from Poland', *International Sociology,* 11(1):37-62.

Wolf, Eric, 1973, 'Kinship, Friendship and Patron-Client Relations in Complex Societies', in: Michael Banton, ed. *The Social Anthropology of Complex Societies,* pp. 1-22. Londen/N.Y.: Tavistock.

21

Organizations: Culture, Power and Coordination

Jan Boessenkool

Introduction

It is an honor to be able to contribute to a book that has been edited especially for Arie de Ruijter. Not only was he my promoter, but over the past decade he has also been an inspiration for my own thoughts on organizations and organizational processes in general, and the concept of organizational culture in particular. As an anthropologist I believed in the dominance of the concept of culture in all our thinking and behavior, as well as in social relations in society and in organizations. From a theoretical point of view, this provided me with clarity and with a starting point. In the process of doing research, however, I slowly began to change my point of view. I began to focus on dispute within the process of denotation, and its consequences on conduct. I have seen how someone like Arie often strategically made use of – and sometimes, perhaps, also misuse of – the game of negotiation on definitions so that a (power) struggle will be decided in his favor. He did this in a very subtle way, and ultimately enjoying his victory. Arie sought to coordinate differences with but one goal – winning – thus illustrating that culture and cultural differences are compliant to power and not the other way around.

I was overjoyed when Arie gave a lecture in Tilburg, entitled "The Multicultural Arena" (de Ruijter 2000), at precisely the time when I myself had also embraced the metaphor of "arena" in talking about organizations. Interests and hierarchies of power is much more important for man's behavior than culture and cultural differences, as I thought Arie's oratory would confirm. In the final paragraph of my contribution I will return to this oratory. But first I wish to take Arie and the reader down memory lane towards the culture concept of organization, for it is a trip that is also representative of my own thinking towards this concept.

Organizations and culture

Many organizations, or rather those in who are in charge of organizations, are in a state of confusion, and are searching for (new) answers. This search began back in the early '80s, when economic stagnation meant that many company results were unsatisfactory. Japan's experiences put the West on the track of culture and cultural differences. The fact that the interpretation of these experiences is rather one-sided and distorted does not detract from the popularity of the Japanese success stories. Western managers found support in the consensus and harmony that (supposedly) existed in the Japanese business world (Ten Bos 2000). In hindsight, though, it has become clear that so-called lifetime employment must be taken with a pinch of salt (Bax 1991). Neverthe-less, the culture concept would appear to offer relief to many: culture in the sense of 'shared values,' of achieving goals by everyone pulling in the same direction? This per-spective has continued to dominate discussions up to this day, at first mainly in the business world, but later, in the '90s, within the non-profit sector as well. Everyone started to look for shared core values with which to redefine and share deadlocked identities. Managers and executives are continually impeded by differentiation and frag-mentation, which ought, preferably, to be erased. Various management courses have come up with the instruments and models with which to achieve this, by identifying conflict via a quick scan, and then to change this into a more desirable situation.

The extent to which cultural processes can be influenced always proves disap-pointing, which does not alter the fact that many still stubbornly persist. Many (failed) mergers bear witness to this, and it seems as if people either learn nothing, or refuse to learn anything from negative experiences. The exceptions are prepared to reflect more, and to sign up for university courses that focus on organizational culture and related concepts. He or she then learns from the academic gurus that cultural differ-ences and diversity are, in general (in our time), not only normal and a matter of course, but can also be valuable and productive, provided they are analyzed and used correctly. But what, then, can managers actually do with these splendid academic *tours de force* in their real-life situations? Why should these managers suddenly cease to value scarcity of differences and peace in their organizations? After all, difference still sows the seed of misunderstanding and conflict, something that no executive wants. Does the latter not then automatically mean that there is, and always will be, a need for uni-formity? Is not the search for core values and a common identity the expression of this?

In everyday life, we understand the culture concept to relate to such things as 'val-ues' and 'norms', or 'the way we do things here'. This sounds straightforward. Upon further analysis, however, values and norms prove to be very tricky concepts, just as the phrase "the way we do things here" is usually ambiguous. In organizational reali-ty, far too isolated and instrumental use is generally made of academic insights. This is the reproach quite frequently voiced by academics, probably because the organiza-tional culture concept refers to too many processes, and processes that are too com-plex. This indicates both the strength and the weakness of the concept. The wealth offered by the concept is undervalued. At the same time the theory is evidently unable to fit in optimally with organizational practice.

Enthusiastic pioneers

In his recently published book *Organizational Culture and Identity*, Martin Parker asks himself why *organizational culturalism* has become so popular, and what is wrong with much of the "management guru and textbook writing on this topic" (2000:2). He uses the term *'culturalism'* to identify the interest that managers have in cultural manip-ulation as opposed to the more academic approach, which has does not have (paid) intervention as its primary focus. Barley et al. (1988) refer to this difference at an early stage: the *practitioner's perspective* versus the *academic's perspective*. I will return to this distinction at a later point in this chapter. I have already hinted at the difference by pointing to the instrumental use of the culture concept.

Parker thoroughly analyses several works from the early eighties that have set a clear trend in the instrumental and functionalistic perspective, namely Peters and Waterman's *In Search of Excellence* (1982), Ouchi's *Theory Z* (1981), and Deal and Kennedy's *Corporate Cultures* (1982). This trend would appear to be extremely innovative with regard to writing on organizations, and organizational culture in particular. However, cultural and social aspects had already captured the attention of organizational researchers ever since the early twentieth century. Even so, this was particularly aimed towards increasing production (see the Hawthorne experiments), and humans were particularly regarded as production factors.

This does not alter the fact that the early '80s represent a breakthrough in the concept of organizational culture. In 1979, the first conference on organizational culture was held (Barley et al., 1988: 24; Pondy et al, 1983; Parker, 2000:9). In the same year, Andrew Pettigrew published an article in *Administrative Science Quarterly*, which is known as a forum for "highly quantitative and conservative management theory" (Parker 2000:9).

However, the publications mentioned above ensured an overwhelming interest in the concept from that point on. Incidentally, almost all of these publications can be placed within the practitioner's perspective. Interest amongst managers in the great quantity of "How To" books that followed was a result, to a great extent, of a combination of the poor economic situation and prospects in the Western world at the start of the '80s, and of the Japanese success story and the threat posed by this.

Success and failure are being linked to the leader's vision, to the unity and collectivity on the workfloor, and to the degree to which organizations are able to adapt to changing circumstances. Related to this, culture may be weak or strong, as indicated by Deal and Kennedy. For non-functionalistic anthropologists this is blasphemy in so far as, for them, culture (cultural analysis) is by definition a neutral affair. It is this normative claim in respect of the culture concept that repeatedly surfaces in the practitioner's perspective. The weakness of the concept lies in its instrumental use (prescription) of all the (new) insights that it generates. Its strength is the fact that it is always able to raise new questions about the state of affairs in modern organizations, and always from a different perspective.

For a long time, many anthropological colleagues regarded the growing interest in organizational processes with great suspicion and mistrust (and continue to even now). Traditionally, anthropologists are "supposed to" take the side of the *underdog* in the battle of the classes in society, even if there have been many exceptions to this position over the years. Anthropological research conducted in companies cannot mean anything other than betrayal: studies focusing on workfloor processes, from which management could profit. The innovators are repeatedly associated with ties and *Samsonites*. In the Netherlands, Koot, Verweel, and I have become embroiled in a long struggle to achieve recognition for the new discipline of "organizational anthropology," a struggle that has not yet been settled today.

Given the popularity enjoyed by academic courses focusing on the '(organizational) culture' concept, there is little danger that it will disappear any time soon. What, then, is its content? The content of the concept in respect of organizational culture is closely linked to the meaning given to the concept of culture itself. Various attempts have been made to distinguish, classify, and reduce the meanings to the underlying meta-theoretical and even paradigmatic principles. The concept of culture has an enormous wealth of meanings and derived functions. It was initially hoped that by discussing and recording these, uniformity would be achieved within the academic discussion, and, possibly, as a result, also within organizational practice.

The search for a meta theory: Martin

In the early nineties, the overwhelming number of publications focusing more or less explicitly on organizational culture caused several American authors to compare the many approaches, whether or not with the aim of arriving at a synthesis.

In 1985, the first textbook was published (Schein 1985), as were several review articles (by Ouchi and Wilkins, 1985, amongst others). In the same year, a critical reflection was published by Frost et al. (1985). Criticism focused particularly on the (alleged) functionalistic character of these approaches. This was followed by a phase in which the theory was defined in more detail, and a certain degree of disciplining and the formation of author networks occurs.

The books by Martin (1992) and of Trice and Beyer (1993) have a "state of the art" character. The authors explicitly state the necessity they felt in establishing order within the diverse approaches to (organizational) culture (Martin), and within the diverse description of reality (Trice and Beyer). To this end, Trice and Beyer have included as many as 1200, and Martin some 300 publications in their bibliographies. Trice and Beyer have used research material from various disciplines, and have attempted (in line with their implicit desire for unity) "the first synthesis of the growing literature in this developing field". An important motivator is the neglected central role played by culture in human behavior in organization studies.

Martin introduces three perspectives on culture, which she distills from the theoretical state of affairs current at the time. The "unity" approach regards culture as "the social glue that binds." Organizational practice portrays itself as a heaven of harmony and homogeneity. Martin is of the opinion that this is the (concept of) culture that managers want. As many other writers have done before them, they claim that a culture based on transparency, consistency, and consensus will result in a more effective organization, in which any form of ambiguity is considered deviant or even detrimental.

Apparently, competing perspectives exist in the differentiation approach. Theoretical and empirical attention is focused on the numerous contradictions that exist between groups and departments. There are (major) differences between informal behavior and the proclaimed culture of unity. This approach also pays attention to power processes.

In the fragmentation approach, ambiguity forms the essence of cultural description. It emerges from this perspective that culture is interpreted very differently by the organizational members. Unexpected similarities and differences exist right across all groups and departments (subcultures). Attention is paid to personal sense making. In this perspective, ambiguity and disagreements form the core of culture.

Although Martin generally takes a fragmentation perspective to the problem, she nevertheless rejects (for empirical and theoretical reasons) the claim that it is possible to choose between the three perspectives. Although, empirically, one of the perspectives may dominate for a time, this does not alter the fact that elements of the other two perspectives are also present at the same moment. From a theoretical point of view, none of the three perspectives is able to cover the complexity of organizational culture. Martin is of the opinion that most researchers have their own dominant perspective; the other two help the researcher to correct the dominant perspective's weaknesses.

By contributing the fragmentation perspective to the debate, which up to that point had been underexposed, Martin makes an interesting move in order to avoid the simplification of complex cultural processes. Frost et al. found Martin's – and Meyerson's (1988) – three perspectives so interesting and innovative that, in 1991, they dedicated an entire book to them, entitled *Reframing Organizational Culture*." However, they place perspectives next to each other, thus creating the impression that the corresponding cultural elements occur separately within the organization. Arguably, it would be more analytically fruitful to study the corresponding cultural forms and concepts in conjunction with each other. The pursuit of unity may, for example, actually cause unwanted conflicts to occur, while attention paid to differentiation may result in harmony.

The search for synthesis: Trice and Beyer

The title of the first chapter of Trice and Beyer's (1993) book – "How and Why Organizations are Cultures" – is an important indicator of where they fit within the various approaches to understanding culture. To them, organizations are cultures (cf. Smircich 1983, Frissen and Van Westerlaak 1990). Culture consists of *content* ("the substance of organizational cultures"), and the various forms in which content is communicated (symbols, language, practices, etc.). From their point of view, culture is the collective answer to the uncertainties and chaos inevitable in human experience – and in organizations. The authors refer to the content, or components, of these answers to uncertainties, fears and ambiguities as ideologies ("shared, emotionally charged belief systems").

Although reality is far too complex to include everything, the culture approach is far more comprehensive than, say, rational theories are. Cultures are collective, emotional, historical, symbolic, dynamic, fuzzy, etc. According to Trice and Beyer, it is precisely because of this that cultures, besides rational considerations, determine human behavior in general, and organizational behavior in particular. Although they take the position that organizations are cultures, for them the essence of culture is consensus (for Martin it is disagreement), as is evident when they state: "To avoid endless confusion, it seems sensible to reserve the term culture for situations in which there is some core of consensus" (Trice and Beyer 1993:15). This causes some surprise when compared with their definition of culture, in which "ambiguity and fuzziness" are essential components. Trice and Beyer intended their extensive work to form a bridge between theory and practice, a theoretical synthesis that can also be applied in organizational practice. The disadvantage of their more functionalistic and application-oriented approach is the insufficient amount of attention paid to the concept's orientation towards process. As such, their work belongs largely to the tradition of the "practitioner's perspective" (Barley et al. 1988). This perspective pays particular attention to the question of what culture is in practice, and how it can be used as a manager's tool. Trice and Beyer also pay a relatively great deal of attention to rational processes, and tend to look for simplification in the complex cultural issue, possibly to provide managers with instruments after all. As such, they overestimate, in my opinion, the rationality of organizational actions.

An overview

Trice and Beyer's volume contains a large number of approaches and shows the enormous versatility of the culture concept. At the same time, this is a weakness because there is barely any problematization, leaving you with the question of where to begin. The book by Martin is more appealing, particularly owing to her own shrewd observation that these phenomena may be regarded from different perspectives, thus facilitating different insights. What is more, her approach touches far more directly on the interests and positions of an organization's members, and, as such, the closely related power and identity processes.

Although he may be placed in the same academic tradition as Martin, Alvesson (1993) quickly voices his criticism to the "emphasis on ambiguity as a 'central feature of organizational culture'" (1993:110). He continues: "This interest in ambiguity can perhaps be seen as a reflection of the Zeitgeist" (ibid.). Alvesson recognizes that ambiguity is a central aspect of organizations, but is more inclined to regard it as a "modification of the 'differentiation view ...'" (ibid.:117). He does not view Martin's (and Meyerson's) three perspectives as competing and conflicting approaches, but places them next to each other: "The perspective I am proposing can be called a *multiple cultural configuration view*. (...) Organizational cultures are then understandable not as unitary wholes or as stable sets of subcultures but as mixtures of cultural manifestations of different levels and kinds (ibid.:118). Alvesson takes ambiguity seriously, without making it the center of his analysis. In doing so, he opens "the possibility of 'explaining' much uncertainty, confusion and contradiction" (ibid.: 118).

The approach that Parker takes is similar to that of Alvesson. From the early 1980s onward there was an explosion of enthusiasm for writing about and managing something called 'organizational culture'. The central assumption behind this rise of interest seemed to be that a hard 'scientific' management of institutions could and should be augmented with, or even displaced by, an approach that stressed a softer, more humane understanding of human values and culture. The time study engineer was to be replaced by the organizational anthropologist. ... there are important insights to be gained from applying the term 'culture' to organizations, but ... much of the writing ... has been most unreflexive about its core assumptions.'(Parker 2000:1)

From this excerpt, it would appear that Parker is trying to breath new life back into the academic and more reflexive approach to organizational culture. To this end, he first presents "the history of ideas about culture in organizations" and the reasons for the concept's popularity, and subsequently arrives at a "rather different way of thinking about organizations and culture" (Parker 2001:1). He goes on to write, "To put it simply, organizational cultures should be seen as 'fragmented unities' in which members identify themselves as collective at some times and divided at others" (ibid.: 1). Parker also argues for the elimination of the time-honored opposition between structures and actors – "in sum, organizational culture both as a constraint and as an everyday accomplishment". Following from this, he also regards organizations and identities (of employees) as two sides of the same coin, entirely in line with Giddens' concept of duality (1984): "If organizations shape the identities of their members, should managers seek to influence these identities in order to manage more effectively?" (Parker 2000:1).

An important basic assumption for Parker is "the idea of culture as an 'us' and 'them' claim, an identification" (Parker 2001:3), which he links to the relationship between 'structuralist and social constructionist accounts.' "In terms, of the structure/agency dualism," he writes, "I suggest that both culture and organization can be regarded as mediating terms between the determination of generalities and the agency of individuals" (ibid.:4). After analyzing several early seminal works (Peters and Waterman 1982, Deal and Kennedy 1982, and Ouchi 1981), Parker states that we should not take "managerial culturalist literature" too seriously because these are less about "what organizations are like than about what they should be like. It is prescriptive rather than descriptive" (Parker 2000:25). The problem of the functionalistic theory-based organizational literature is that it fixes rigidly on consensus by means of shared values, and barely leaves room for the differences in meaning – and, as such, different interpretations, conflicts, fuzziness and ambiguity – that always exist. In fact, (organizational) culture is usually reduced to shared values and norms. As such, Deal and Kennedy are able to speak of strong and weak cultures, which conflicts with the assumption that, as ongoing social constructions, organizations do not have any culture, but are cultures (Smircich 1983).

For Parker, too, this assumption results in three general principles: "Firstly, that terms like "organization" and "culture" should be understood as processes that, in some way, draw together history and everyday practice; or what sociologists call "structure" and "agency." Secondly, that these processes continually involve making shifting and temporary stabilizations of meaning with a wide variety of human and non-human resources. Finally, that these meanings are contested because there are always competing understandings of what people and organizations are and should be doing" (Parker 2000:81). The social construction process of meanings is continually concerned with unity and diversity, with what we have in common and in contrast; or in Martin's terms, that which integrates, differentiates and fragments (Martin 1992). What is concerned is the continuous construction of (cultural) boundaries, both within and between organizations. In other words, the core is formed by inclusion and exclusion mechanisms (according to de Ruijter 1996). Everyday practice teaches us that diametrically opposed to this core is the dominant approach that of 'everyone pulling in the same direction'. Rational steering is supplemented by a normative mission-driven approach. Steering very rarely occurs on the basis of an analysis of current content, but far more often on the basis of desired content.

Functions: from means of competition to increased reflexivity

Attention paid in the past to organizational culture was particularly inspired by the wish to influence human behavior in such a manner that production would increase. Essentially, the mainstream has never deviated from this. Until the 1960s and 1970s, the individual, as a production factor, played a subordinate role. For many years, market developments and technological improvements barely gave any cause to bring attention to the so-called "soft side" of life in organizations. Around 1980, however, this changed drastically, due primarily to intensified competition between Japan and the United States. Given technical possibilities (in the market) that were more or less equal, it was found that the individual and culture can be decisive. Almost self-evidently, cultural aspects are isolated from their context and from the wider culture concept (see the success factors described by Peters and Waterman (1982) for example). You would have to be crazy not to use these, and not to take time to calmly reflect upon whether the approach is scientifically sound. Parker speaks of "a practitioner-consultant model that regards culture as a normative glue that can be managed in order to ensure that organizations are more efficient" (2000:220).

People prefer to leave the latter to the academics, a great many of whom, as we have seen, started to concern themselves with organizational culture issue since the start of the 1980s. Broadly speaking, these academics may be categorized into two groups. Firstly, there are those who particularly wish to support managers by increasing the practicability of the difficult "culture" concept, and in so doing generate all sorts of useful and less useful handbooks. The second group consists of academics who (strongly) resist the instrumental character and the supposed flexibility of isolated aspects of culture. Parker refers to the first group of academics as "academic but functionalist," and the second group as anti-functionalist, with the starting point that organizations are cultures (2000: 221).

Whatever the case may be, the culture concept has preoccupied many in the last twenty years, offering direct support to management in their debate with colleagues at business schools and universities. However, the urge for controllability, flexibility and increased production continues to be just as prominent. It is striking that, particularly in management courses, real depth is still lacking in respect to the culture concept; in fact, most management courses are intended only to show how to increase the efficiency of production processes (including service). The instrumentality of such courses has hardly decreased. Evidently, they still meet a need, and participants believe that they will be able to optimize their own performance by "learning tricks." In practice, they can expect to be disappointed in this regard, as numerous conversations with course participants reveal. Sooner or later, they encounter something unanticipated by the tricks, something that requires unforeseen action to be taken.

More academic (reflection-focused) courses are intended to bring relief. But do they? On the surface of it, the answer is yes. The richness of the culture concept provides so many new insights and perspectives that participants continually indicate that they have learnt a lot, on the basis of which new initiatives start within their organizations. It is an interesting question whether or not these new insights are directly related to the culture concept, or whether the latter is simply a (very handy) means of better understanding organizational processes (in this case the actions of organizational members).

All in all, twenty years of organizational culture studies have proved very fruitful. It has particularly demonstrated that organizational processes may be viewed from many different perspectives. It makes it possible to ask numerous questions about organizational processes. The pitfall, however, is always that people are far too quickly inclined to believe that they have understood these processes, and suggest solutions that do not then appear to work.

Is this satisfactory? Has the concept given us what we hoped or expected? For many, probably not. The danger is that we will throw it on to the great pile of management and organizational concepts that come and go. And, as such, all of the enriching insights that the culture concept has produced in respect to organizational processes may hang in the balance. It is precisely these insights that must be maintained. Possibly, we will have to increase the functionality of these insights for those who should be able to profit from them on a day-to-day basis. The fact that this causes the culture concept itself to disappear into the background is a shame, but no more than that. This is probably the destiny of all concepts: their magic is always only temporary. This will also be the destiny shared by the successors of the culture concept.

Future

People act on the basis of interpretation and sense making. Sense and meaning are not fixed, but are always realized during a process of social construction. What is more, they are the subject of ongoing discussion and negotiation. To be able to understand meanings, we must gain insights into their creation, hence in the processes that precede them. Meanings and actions result from these processes. Organizations may be regarded as ongoing social and sense-making construction processes. If we wish to be able to influence these processes effectively in any way, then we must analyze them thoroughly. We talk of management or meaning. Is meaning not just another term for culture? On the one hand it is. After all, for many, culture is a system and process of patterns of sense making. On the other hand, it is a far more neutral term, which will not allow one to ignore the questions of "whose meaning is at issue?" and "how has this meaning been created?" Meaning offers the manager possibilities for control, provided he has sufficiently informed himself about the sense making of those concerned, and the "why" behind it.

Within the framework of management or meaning, Verweel (2000) calls upon the reader to focus on the issue of (renewed) binding, now that time-honored forms of identification have ceased for many. This search ought not to be accompanied by a one-sided integration approach. As such, he opposes the instrumentalization and mechanization of the social and the cultural. The concept of "binding" touches upon another important part of the culture concept, namely that of identity (compare, for example, Parker 2000 and Alvesson 1993). Verweel aims to approach the "binding" concept analytically, but it poses the risk, just as the culture concept does, that people will start to search for "the social glue that binds" the shared values and norms. This would, then, fit perfectly into the instrumental integrative perspective favored by managers, which is something that Verweel tries to resist by placing his emphasis on organizations as communities.

A second approach is that of de Ruijter's (2000), who points to the stratification of society and organizations, and uses the metaphor of the "arena." De Ruijter calls attention to the management of diversity, in the sense of multiculturalism. Multiculturalism is more than ethnic diversity. The concept aims to indicate the diversity of meanings. Rightly so, he concentrates on the power factor. As he points out, "the process of denotation is a dialogue as a social process (Bachtin 1981) and with that is captured in the hierarchy of power. The *'herschaftsfreie Dialog'* is a utopia as Habermas (1981) already stated" (de Ruijter 2000:8).

Furthermore, "models of and for reality are not compatible to cognitive categories. They are after all charged with emotions, affections and perspectives of behavior"(de Ruijter 2000:9). What for some is a representation of reality, is to other a construction of reality.

> Ordering implies the assigning of social positions – and also rights and obligations – to persons and groups. Power is intrinsically linked to ordering and thus to upper, middle and lower classifications. Setting boundaries and acquiring norms always involves creating legitimatising, regulating and institutionalizing of difference and inequality. Bourdieu (1991:221) has phrased this concisely: "What is at stake here is the power of imposing a vision of the symbolic world through principles of division. This division determines the ways in which identities are formed in the experience of daily life" (de Ruijter 2000:9).

Although de Ruijter uses the "arena" metaphor, in the end he also makes a plea for coordination, for the management of diversity, in the sense of multiculturalism. Multiculturalism is more than ethnic diversity, for the concept also refers to the diversity of meanings.

De Ruijter argues for the co-ordination of differences (in meanings). By doing so, he is suggesting that harmony becomes possible due to a better understanding of (each other's) differences. Armed with this better knowledge, conflicts can perhaps be avoided. This is at odds with the arena model, which states that sense making (and thus also any reconciliation) refers to positions and interests, and as such is related to power. If so, what is the chance that those with less power in the co-ordination process could play a significant role?

To pay attention to difference, and to plead for the coordination of differences, does not yet mean that everyone will be treated justly in society. Subservient groups will always have to strive for more equality through (hard) dispute, both in society as well as in organizations, if only to be (more) equal in the coordination process.

Would it not, from an academic perspective, be more accurate and more correct to concentrate on the analysis of current organizational processes without continually wishing to indicate how they could be different or better? Do we not fall back in the pitfall of functionalism and normativity by doing the latter? Is it not also our academic task to help those who want our help to increase their reflexive ability by teaching them to ask the right questions in their own organizational practice? Daily practice requires rapid decisions and changes. There is no time for reflection, or time is very rarely taken for this, in any event (Koot and Sabelis 2000). It is this divide between academic thinking and practical use that is evidently so difficult to span, or which translates itself into almost ridiculous solutions.

In the analysis of organizational processes, there should be a focus on the process of sense making (meaning), as this is the basis for (collective organizational) actions. The analysis of organizational processes will therefore (always) have to concentrate on retrieving the origin of these meanings. Meanings are formed by earlier experiences, and are continually (re)produced through interactions. At the same time, this is a process of negotiation. Thus, what is concerned is the analysis of these interactions, starting from the realization that it is a "struggle" in which participants come from different positions with differing interests. Many dislike the conflict and arena metaphors. I prefer them because they express the fact that a struggle is involved, thus breaking the illusion that organizational practice is focused on consensus and harmony. The basic principle is differences. It is not about resolving differences, but about the extent to which the struggle can be fought openly, and the extent to which the other is taken seriously. Elsewhere, the arena model is elaborated in more detail (see Anthonissen and Boessenkool 1998). The issue of identity is connected to this. The culture concept's promise has not been lost, but gains a deserved place in a context of organizations as political and cultural phenomena (Czarniawska-Joerges 1992).

Bibliography

Alvesson, M. 1993. *Cultural Perspectives on Organizations.* Cambridge: Cambridge University Press.

Alvesson, M. and H. Wilmott. 1996. *Making Sense of Management. A Critical Introduction.* London: Sage.

Anthonissen A. and J. Boessenkool. 1998. *Betekenissen van Besturen: Variaties in bestuurlijk handelen.* Utrecht: ISOR.

Barley, S., G. Meyer and D. Gash. 1988. 'Cultures of Culture: Academics, Practitioners and the Pragmatics of Normative Control', *Administrative Science Quarterly,* 33:24-60.

Bax, E.H. 1991. *Organisatiecultuur, technologie en management in een veranderende samenleving.* Utrecht: Het Spectrum.

Bos, R. ten. 2000. *Fashion and utopia in management thinking.*

Czarniawska-Joerges, B. 1992. *Exploring Complex Organizations: A Cultural Perspective.* Newbury Park, CA: Sage.

Deal T. and A. Kennedy. 1982. *Corporate Cultures.* Reading, MA: Addison-Wesley

Frissen, P. and J. van Westerlaak. 1990. *Organisatiecultuur.* Schoonhoven: Academic Service.

Frost, P., L. Moore, M. Louis, C. Lundberg and J. Martin eds. 1985. *Organizational Culture.* Beverly Hills, CA: Sage.

Frost, P., L. Moore, M. Louis, C. Lundberg and J. Martin eds. 1991. *Reframing Organizational Culture.* Newbury Park, CA: Sage.

Giddens, A. 1984. *The Constitution of Society.* Cambridge: Polity Press.

Martin, J. 1992. *Cultures in Organizations: Three Perspectives.* New Vork: Oxford University Press.

Martin, J. and D. Meyerson. 1988. 'Organizational Cultures and the Denial, Channeling and Acknowledgrnent of Ambiguity' in Pondy L., R. Boland and H. Thomas *Managing Ambiguity and Change.* pp. 93-125. Chichester: JohnWiley.

Ouchi, W.G. 1981. *Theory Z.* Reading, MA: Addison-Wes1ey.

Parker, M. 2000. *Organizational Culture and Identity.* London: Sage.

Peters, T. and M. Watennan. 1982. *In Search of Excellence.* New York: Harper and Row.

Pondy L., P. Frost, G. Morgan and T. Dandridge eds. 1983. *Organizational Symbolism.* Greenwich, CT: JAI Press.

Ruijter, A. de. 1996. 'Betekenisconstructie en sturing in een complexe wereld' in M. Gastelaars en G. Hagelstein eds., *Management of meaning: Besturen en organiseren als processen van betekenisgeving* pp. 9-24. Utrecht: ISOR/CBM. .

Ruijter, A. de. 2000. *De multiculturele arena.* Tilburg: KUB.

Schein, E. 1985. *Organizational Culture and Leadership.* San Francisco: Jossey Bass.

Smircich, L. 1983. 'Concepts of Culture and Organizational Analysis', *Administrative Science Quarterly,* 28:339-359.

Trice H. and J. Beyer. 1993. *The Cultures of Work Organizations.* Englewood Cliffs, NJ: Prentice Hall

Verweel, P. 2000. *Betekenisgeving in organisatiestudies: De mechanisering van het sociale.* Utrecht: ISOR.

Wilkins A. and W. Ouchi. 1983. 'Efficient Cultures', *Administrative Science Quarterly,* 28:468- 481.

22

Every Man to His Own Trade
An Anthropologist in the World of 'Wet and Dry'

Willem Koot

A strange encounter under Holland's *Groene Hart*

We descended quickly in a makeshift lift into the depths of a huge concrete pit that had been dug by the Ministry of Waterways and Public Works *(Rijkswaterstaat)*, to serve eventually as the entrance to the future HSL-Zuid (High Speed Train) Tunnel, under Holland's Groene Hart[1]. Estimated costs: over a billion euros.

It was ten in the morning on a bleak day. The cold March wind cut through everything, making me feel a bit tetchy out there in the polder. I had reported a few minutes earlier to the building hut to get kitted out in the special overalls and boots for this kind of activity, and to find a hardhat that fitted me. I had been invited by the manager of the HSL to visit the construction site of the tunnel. He wanted to show me – in his own words – "the new technology they're using here." The visit would also conclude in style a consultancy project I had carried out for Rijkswaterstaat (RWS). The aim of this project was to optimise the cooperation between headquarters and the project teams who were working on stretches of the route. I had been entrusted to an escort who would take me to the site where the gigantic driller was at work under the soft alluvial soil of the Groene Hart.

After descending into the 30-metre deep pit, I stepped out of the lift and was overwhelmed by feelings of reverence and admiration for the technological ingenuity that unfolded before me. How on earth had they managed to build such a deep pit with straight walls in this soft soil? I asked my guide, who told me that it was all down to highly revolutionary technology, which is applied hardly anywhere else. After some "Ohs" and "Ahs" from me, we walked slowly into the tunnel, which when it's finished will be the longest tunnel drilled through alluvial soil in the whole of Europe. After walking a mile or so we reached the driller. This rolling machine, about 200 metres long, was "drilling" away pieces of soft earth, and immediately placing concrete sheets on all sides of the hole to stop it from collapsing. It went a step farther than a technique that, only a few years ago, had been applied in Australia for the first time. This gargantuan machine was made in France and had been transported in parts and pieces to the Netherlands. The crew is international: Frenchmen, Italians, Germans, and (of course) Dutch technologists. The project, however, is headed entirely by RWS engineers.

The guided tour of the machine took about 20 minutes. My escort stayed behind to chat with some of the personnel and I decided to start walking back through the tunnel. As I strolled alone through that immense space I was struck by an even deeper sense of respect for this feat of engineering. The people who do this have a real profession, I told myself. Well, at least it delivers concrete results. And it takes plenty of brains and talent to do that. I became more and more absorbed in thought, and of course associations with my own field – anthropology – started to surface. I felt a slight sense of gloom as images of babbling figures echoing other peoples' ideas sprang to mind. Just as I was trying to suppress these feelings, I saw the vague shape of a man enter the tunnel (there wasn't a female in sight in that subterranean domain). He was walking straight towards me and, after a few moments, I recognized the director of the tunnel project. I decided, when he had got close enough to talk to, that I would tell him how impressed I was by this incredible piece of engineering. But he beat me to it. He said, "Mr Koot, I want to thank you for all you've done for us. By giving us more insight in the limitations of our own organizational and professional cultures, and by offering us behavioural alternatives, we were able to make a new start and to improve the team spirit and the mutual cooperation. If it wasn't for you we'd definitely have been well behind schedule and facing still more extra costs[2]. But that's not all. We're enjoying it again." I couldn't help grinning. He asked, "What's the joke?" So I told him what I had been thinking about. He added, "We engineers can learn a lot from anthropologists, I can assure you! We haven't learnt to put ourselves in someone else's position and to take the perspective of the other. This attitude is an real handicap in complex projects like the HSL where you must cooperate and communicate with people from different cultural and disciplinary backgrounds." He shook my hand and then made off in the direction of the driller. I turned again towards the exit, but couldn't stop thinking about the meeting. Images of clashing perspectives flooded my mind. I tried to identify the key differences and their causes and effects – also in terms of risks and opportunities for cooperation, innovation, sustainability, and coping with uncertainty. I then asked myself the question: what can the anthropologist mean exactly for the engineer and the organizations he works for?

My mind was made up by the time I reached the surface: I would unearth my earlier research and consultancy experience at Philips (see Koot, 1997 for cases) and relate them to my recent observations at RWS. Who knows? This analysis might lead to an "anthropology of the engineer," that could form part of a larger publication on the anthropology of professional cultures. So far, hardly anything had been written on this theme, even abroad.

This article, which I have dedicated to Arie de Ruijter, should be seen as a first step in this project. Arie de Ruijter has laid some important foundation stones for this project by ensuring that organizational anthropology could develop as an important sub-discipline in the Netherlands and play a pioneering role internationally. He achieved this by giving strong support to the early initiatives taken in the 1980s by Tennekes, Verweel, and me to identify a link between organizational science and anthropology. It was a brave move on his part, which did not go down well in all quarters (cf. Koot 1996). I am still deeply indebted to Arie for his encouragement and support.

But let us return to what this article is all about: the culture, identity, and group composition of the engineer, specifically those at RWS. Most of the RWS engineers come from the civil sector and specialize in either water or roads – "wet and dry" in the jargon. What is their vision of the world?

The engineer's vision of the world

In *Vita Activa* (1994), the well-known philosopher Hannah Arendt describes how the normative image of *homo faber* (man as a maker) has become established in the Western world, and how the interplay between thought, labour, and work, and their relationship with nature, have evolved. To the Greeks, says Arendt, nature had a truth and beauty that could never be matched by anything fashioned by human hands. Work and labour meant two different things. Work referred to thinking ("contemplation" based on observation); labour was something that was done by slaves. In fact, the *homo faber* was actually held in contempt by the Greeks. Indeed, this normative image only took root – but with a vengeance – with the invention of the telescope. This was when Western man realized for the first time that he could no longer rely on his own faculties to obtain knowledge, but had to make instruments and tools: "The road to new knowledge was not paved with contemplation, observation and speculation but with active intervention by *homo faber*, the process of manufacture and production"(ibid.:273). The guiding philosophy was that the human eye is misleading and everything one sees must be questioned. The only way to find the truth and unravel the mysteries of Nature was by building instruments. This search was seen as the quest of "modern" man. It was a challenge that "no man could meet alone; only the collective efforts of the best human minds could hope to be worthy of it...." (ibid.:277). The relationship between thinking and doing changed radically with all of this. Whereas the Greeks believed that true knowledge could only be gained by contemplation, the modern "enlightened" man, by contrast, believed that truth could only be approximated and that knowledge could only be gained by "doing," i.e. by making and building things. People had to *create* certainty before they could be certain of anything, and they had to do things in order gain knowledge. Thus, the engineer became the normative image for the actions of modern man.

But this led to a rationale that favoured models and schemes in which the consequences of actions could be estimated. As Arendt rightly points out, this did not only result in an emphasis on planning, programming, compartmentalization (cf. Latour, 1994) and neglect of the "unexpected," it also made it harder to cope with unknown phenomena. In a sense, it even engendered a fear of the world outside the rational scheme of things. Certainty could only be found within the safe confines of one's own mindset. The outside world became more and more unfathomable, partly because people were not being taught to broaden their horizons and confront the unknown. The result was a conservative, blinkered, introspective attitude, a fairly closed vision of the world and a one-sided response to formal, universal and non-personal knowledge.

The engineers gained more and more confidence in the centuries that followed,

spurred on by their technological successes and by interacting in a confined environment where they only met clones of themselves (Scott 1998). The engineer came to see
himself more and more as the main driver behind the renewal and improvement of
human existence. According to Scott, this led only to more tragedy and disappointment
because the planners and the engineers had so overestimated their ability and made
everyone subordinate to their planning that "the visionary intellectuals and planners ...
were guilty of hubris, of forgetting that they were mortals and acting as if they were
gods....their actions were animated by a genuine desire to improve the human condition – a desire with a fatal flaw" (ibid.:342), because "these schemes have failed their
intended beneficiaries" (ibid.:342-343).

The tendency to avoid uncertainty, the fear of the unknown, the overestimation
of the potential of technology for the well-being of Mankind, the partiality for formali-
ty, the need to compartmentalize, the lack of training in how to relate to other visions,
and the low levels of personal flexibility – all these eventually resulted in a permanent
psychological state, which we may refer to as a habitus (Bourdieu,1992). Because of
this, engineers have difficulty making the connection between processes and people,
playing the political game (because of their naivety, says Weggeman, 2002:406) and
cooperation, especially with people from another discipline. They lack the openness
that is needed to create a relationship of trust with the other party. In this respect Giddens remarked, "Trust on a personal level becomes a project, to be worked at by the
parties involved, and demands the opening out of the individual to the other. Where it
cannot be controlled by fixed normative codes, trust has to be won, and the means of
doing this is demonstrable warmth and openness... relationships are ties based on trust,
where trust is not pre-given but worked upon, and where the work means a mutual
process of self-disclosure" (1991:121).

Recently, Van Doorn and Spierings (2001) carried out an empirical study among
civil engineers in the Netherlands which examined, amongst other things, personal
characteristics (using the "Big Five Personality Test"). The results showed that engineers
have a strong affinity with their discipline, are very focused on the job, fairly stress-
resistant in their own (that's to say, "safe") working environment, are highly conscien-
tious and dedicated; but they lack openness and a readiness to accept change. The con-
tractors were no different in this respect from the managers of engineering bureaus or
departments. The same applied to the bosses and the specialists. The study empirically confirmed the image that can be built up by a historical-anthropological analysis of
the thought processes of the engineer.

So, what we have is a fairly homogeneous culture, which also makes basic
assumptions about elementary issues such as the relationship between Man and Nature,
the definition of truth, and how to view time and human activity. These are all fundamental questions that relate to a vast domain of notions about life and society. They
are approached in widely different ways in the world's main ideological, religious and
philosophical systems, such as Buddhism, Hinduism, Animism and the Philosophy of
Enlightenment (Kamsteeg and Koot, 2002). Hence, there exists a deeply rooted culture

in which answers are formulated for a huge range of diverse questions about life and society, which also have far-reaching consequences for the management and structure of companies.

I know from my own research and consultancy activities at RWS (particularly from some complex large-scale projects like HSL-Zuid) that cooperation, change, transference, and sustainability are the least developed aspects of the company. People try to bring about change by planning projects, but with no thought paid to the normal primary process or to the relevant criteria. The result is a lot of commotion around these projects in terms of people, money, and PR, but next to no embedment of the desired interactions. So, cooperation in a project like the HSL or the Betuweroute proves a huge challenge. After all, it involves contacts with all sorts of people and "outside" organizations (local and regional authorities, action groups etc.), and no one has the knowledge or experience for this. There are complaints in all sorts of internal reports and memos about stagnation and overrunning budgets as a result of this lack of cooperativeness. Transference is already seriously underdeveloped in companies, which should be very careful in what they do with their knowledge. It seems then that scarcely any lessons have been learned from earlier projects, such as the Delta Works, and that people virtually start from scratch when organizing and managing a project like the HSL. In this project almost no transference took place during the changeover phases (e.g. decision-making > development > implementation).

A casual observer who wanders through this department and casts his eye over some PR brochures might get the impression that RWS is fairly innovative. The office walls are covered in cartoons and drawings that send up the traditional, rigid technocrat and bureaucrat, and in the corridors hang sport posters that depict the RWS as a learning organization. The implications are self-evident: this is a modern and alert department that is reflective and deeply critical of itself.

If the observer were to look more closely, however, he would quite quickly reject this conclusion, or at least, radically revise it. The average RWS-er turns out to have only a superficial knowledge of the jargon of the outside world. Closer scrutiny reveals that this knowledge has no connections with the deeper layers of the departmental culture, or with the representations organized around it. Traditionalism and renewal are two totally different representations that take place separately from each other. Only on very rare occasions do they brush shoulders, only to jump apart again to keep an appropriate distance. The prospect of renewal only seems to provide a reason for not making any real changes ("We do so much already"), and for sticking to the time-honoured RWS routine. Take, for example, knowledge management. This is a topic that is supposedly high on the departmental agenda. Discussions are taking place all the time about knowledge banks and knowledge circles, but very little has been done about embedding new knowledge in the company. It should also be noted that here the word "knowledge" is open to different interpretations (cf. Berends and Weggeman 2002). Sometimes it refers to beliefs or ideas of the truth, but far more often it is about rules, image, and cultural questions. In other words, people constantly have to ask themselves which kind of knowledge plays a role in which representation.

Do RWS engineers form a "professional community"? If so, does this further reinforce their culture? Before tackling this question let us try to build up a picture of a
"professional community."

A professional community?

So far, relatively few studies on corporate culture have paid any attention to professional cultures. Those that do usually focus on the role of professional cultures in the
formation of corporate sub-cultures (see, for example, Trice and Beyer 1993). After all,
companies often consist of various professional groups that may be differentiated
according to, say, ideology, values, rituals, and symbols. But sometimes, as in the case
of RWS, one specific culture is dominant and almost the entire organization can be seen
as a "community of professionals" (cf. Van Maanen and Barley 1984).

According to the latest publications, professional communities are identified by a
number of characteristics. *The members feel a collective identity* (obviously, this differs
in strength depending on the community). In other words, they feel a communal fate,
they identify with each other, and they often experience situations in terms of "us" and
"them." In a sense, the world outside is hostile and contacts with it are almost always
perceived from this viewpoint – a viewpoint of distrust and suspicion, which after time
leads to ethnocentrism (we know best). External contacts are also kept to a minimum
(cf. Becker 1951, who describes this so aptly in reference to the music community).

Membership in the community also creates a sense of personal pride and is a key
factor in building up a positive self-image, for, the commitment to the professional
community is "lifelong" and, as such, is one of the most important determiners of identity (after gender and ethnicity). All these elements figure strongly among RWS engineers. They feel totally united with their profession and are intensely proud of their
achievements as individuals and as a group. To illustrate this, let me mention that I have
regularly seen an RWS engineer point from my window and say that "all that lovely
stuff out there" (usually a viaduct or bridge) was due to him. They can also go into rap-
tures when confronted with a wonderful feat of engineering. At RWS this is often
accompanied and underscored by the suggestion that "despite everything they have
ensured that the Netherlands stays dry." This reflects a strongly romanticized, heroic
idea of the role played by civil engineers in the Netherlands, a role that is heavily
stressed in brochures and PR films.

Another characteristic of professional communities is that *the members share an
ideology, often a system of symbols and cognitive schemas, and use each other as a standard of good behaviour.* Usually, distinct processes of culturization have also formed,
along with the associated *"rites de passage"* (often accompanied by a qualification, or
membership in a formal or informal professional club, or promotion/degradation rites).
Such a shared system of values, norms, and symbols is unquestionably present at RWS
and organized around the aforementioned thought processes of engineers and their
training. A degree from Delft University of Technology is seen as a passport to the com-

munity, evidence that you belong to "our world," and come from the right stock. Incidentally, the time you took to get your degree does not appear to matter very much. I have met plenty of engineers in the higher echelons of the ministry who took over 7 years to qualify.

Another characteristic is that *through their profession, the members are confronted with the same emotions and doubts and have developed a collective system for dealing with them* (cf. doctors, who have tacitly agreed with each other not to get over-involved with patients as it could emotionally destroy them). The emotions of the engineer lie mainly in the technical sphere. Try observing a group of engineers at a floodgate system if you want to see where their feelings lie. Like kids who have just built a crane out of Meccano, they look lovingly at the technological construction. I have been involved many times in training sessions and courses for engineers. These gatherings often called for highly divergent activities and working methods. The participants only became really enthusiastic when they got the chance to build something. Their anxieties arise from possible calculation errors for a construction job, or the risks inherent in a building or a dyke. Other risks from cooperation and suchlike get far less attention than building projects.

Another characteristic is that *contact with the community members is often continued outside work; free time is also spent together* (as in the case of the computer freaks of Silicon Valley or the residents of an army base). The RWS engineers scored a bit lower on this count than, say, the computer freaks of Silicon Valley, army base residents, or medical specialists in the Netherlands. The members of these groups spend their social life almost entirely within their own professional circle. The engineers are a bit less fastidious and introvert, but they still tend to choose their friends from the domain of science.

The result of all this is a blinkered approach, a certain autism and ethnocentrism in relation to "others" (whereby an ideal typology is often constructed of "the other"). To the engineer, the epitome of "the other" is the arts graduate, who is interested in the soft things in life, such as relationships, personality traits, and culture. Or in other words, like an anthropologist.

It should be clear by now that the thought processes of engineers are deeply embedded in RWS, and that engineers form a fairly close-knit community. Both these factors mean that in this department, cooperation is often an effort, and change is very difficult to realize. The problems become particularly evident in complex projects such as HSL-Zuid, where the engineers had to work together with countless "others" (other specialists, the Dutch Railway, action groups local authorities etc.) and were faced with many uncertainties (responses of others, but also new drilling techniques). What can the (organizational) anthropologist offer the RWS engineer, and how can he, as one of the "others," get through to him and bring about a change in his habits, and thus the company?

The contribution of the (organizational) anthropologist

It is extremely difficult to change a company, especially if the corporate culture is underpinned by an ideology and is firmly rooted in practices pertaining to recruitment, selection, rewards, discipline etc (Koot and Van Marrewijk 1996). Often, there is forceful resistance in such cases. This arises not only because people are afraid of change, but also because they can scarcely imagine a different approach to cooperation, management, and customers, and are simply unaware that they have fallen into all sorts of habits and routines.

The notorious "Baron van Münchhausen syndrome" crops up every time a change is introduced: how to get out of the mire! It is only natural for companies to express their culture in the way they organize their change processes. The "new values" presented by an organizational consultant, or through conferences or publications, are often verbally endorsed but are not applied in practice – sometimes on purpose, but mostly unintentionally.

For years serious efforts have been underway at RWS to change the company. This is why the project model was chosen which can be roughly described as follows. Someone in the company reads or hears about an interesting societal trend and decides to send his boss a memo about it. If he thinks that he can use this to steal a march on his colleagues (this is the case if the trend can be interpreted as contemporary), he orders a study. When the study is ready it is sent to a group of colleagues who, after a positive assessment, decide to set up a project group with its own budget and its own working space. After this definition, design, and preparation phase, the project group undergoes the final two phases of the "standard" RWS project cycle: realization and after-care. After-care usually amounts to the ritualistic completion of the project with the presentation of the report and some drinks and snacks.

The project-based approach fits in well with the departmental and engineering culture at RWS, which is geared towards control, planning, and compartmentalization. There is no connection with everyday affairs either in terms of content or hierarchy. The director(s) who are committed to the project usually do not draw conclusions for their own management style or assessment methods. So, in the end, all the promising ideas of the project group are "left in the air."

There are two ways of realizing real changes in this culture: firstly, through self-reflection and then through consistent steering with all the appropriate instruments, and secondly, by adapting and structuring recruitment and selection criteria, and changing the management styles. But often there is no consistency in the steering (e.g. the structure may change but not the management style or assessment and selection criteria.) and no self-reflection. If anyone has looked at the existing culture then this is usually in general terms (e.g. "we are a regulated, job-oriented, bureaucratic organization that wants a more commercial approach"), and very little serious attention is paid to the factors underlying the culture.

But how can self-reflection be realized in a large organization like RWS? It seems to me that it has to start with the formal and informal leaders. This is also how I approached the organization of HSL-Zuid. After all, they held the power and were responsible for the management, so they can also ensure that the steering instruments are adapted. And they can "pass on the baton" and push others into self-reflection.

An anthropologist can prove extremely valuable in the process of self-reflection. As I have said before (Koot 1995), he is an expert in organizing fundamental doubts about individual cultures thanks to his intensive experience with "the other." Lemaire (1990:25) even coined an expression for this: "the anthropological doubt," which he sees as a logical extension of the Cartesian doubt. With this in mind I started a session with the HSL engineers by asking what they understood by the term "Mozambican management." At first they associated it with chaos and mismanagement (due to a lack of planning and organization). Later we identified assumptions that lie at the heart of the Enlightenment ideals and their paradoxical consequences (such as that radical planning leads to chaos and time shortages). Needless to say, we then returned to Mozambican management, and the question arose of what we could learn from it. But there was also a deeper awareness of the implications of change and cooperation for their own engineering culture. This eventually led not only to interventions in the company, but also marked the start of better cooperation and cohesion in the upper echelons of the HSL. This process of improvement is still continuing and some project managers have applied voluntarily for a course in organizational anthropology.

Even so, self-reflection is, of course, only effective if the advisor manages to persuade people to take responsibility for what has happened in their company, and for the changes that need to be implemented. This is a difficult and laborious process that involves a lot of confrontation, but which must not exceed the limits of personal safety and of what is proper. What this boils down to is a fine balance between rejection and endorsement, and criticism and support. If this happens in the right way, it will deliver many positive results. This is what I learned from my encounter in the tunnel under the Groene Hart.

Notes

1   A relatively calm countryside situated in the area between the Dutch major cities Amsterdam, Rotterdam and Utrecht.
2   There was already an enormous overrunning of the budget of one billion euro's.

Bibliography

Arendt, H. 1994. *Vita Activa*, Meppel: Boom.
Baalen, P, M. Weggeman, and A. Witteveen. 2002. *Kennis en management*, Schiedam: Scriptum.
Berends, H, and M. Weggeman. 2002. Kennis, kennisdefinities en kennismanagement. In Baalen i.a., *Kennis en Management*. Schiedam: Scriptum.
Becker, H. 1951. The professional dance musician and his audience. *American Journal of Sociology* 57:136-144.
Bourdieu, P. 1992. *Opstellen over smaak, habitus en het veldbegrip*. Amsterdam: Van Gennep.
Giddens, A. 1991. *The Consequences of Modernity*. London: Sage.

Kamsteeg, F., and W. Koot. 2002. De weerbarstigheid van het beheersingsdenken. In T. Jaspers et al, eds, *De bindende werking van concepten. Reflecties over participatie, binding en betrokkenheid in opvoeding en onderwijs, arbeid en zorg.* NWO series, part 2. Amsterdam: Aksant.

Koot, W. 1995. *De complexiteit van het alledaagse.* Muiderberg: Coutinho.

Koot, W, and A van Marrewijk. 1996. Cultuurverandering bij politieorganisaties. In D. Hilarides, ed. *Handboek voor politiemanagement,3*, pp. 1-20. Alphen aan de Rijn: Samsom.

Koot, W. 1996. Antropologie als studie van het bedrijfsleven: uitverkoop, overleven of een juweel van een kans? *Etnofoor* 9(2):51-65.

Koot, W. 1997. The Strategic Utilization of Ethnicity in Organizations. In S. Sackmann, ed., *Cultural Complexity in Organizations.* London: Sage.

Latour, B. 1994. *Wij zijn nooit modern geweest,* Rotterdam: Van Gennep.

Lemaire, T. 1990. *Twijfel aan Europa: zijn de intellectuelen de vijanden van de Europese cultuur?* Baarn: Ambo.

Scott, J. 1998. *Seeing like a State.* New Haven: Yale University Press.

Trice, H., and J. Beyer. 1993. *The Cultures of Work Organizations.* Englewood Cliffs: Prentice Hall.

van Doorn, B., and P. Spierings. 2001. *Kwaliteitsborging en samenwerken in de civiele bouw.* Tilburg: IVA-publikaties.

van Maanen, J., and S. Barley. 1984. Occupational communities, culture and control in organizations. *Research in Organizational Behaviour* 6:287-365.

23

Commitment and Community in Organizations

Paul Verweel and Peter Leisink

Introduction

Arie de Ruijter's research is characterized by a sound basis in theoretical anthropology combined with a preference for a multidisciplinary approach, of which philosophy, linguistics, social geography, and sociology are among the most important elements. His managerial preferences lie in creating an organizational context in which researchers from different disciplines can meet in multidisciplinary teams. Our contribution aims to demonstrate a similar approach in the field of organizational studies. We should like to relate general problems of organizational theory with organizational sociology and anthropological insights into topical themes of bonding and identity in organizations.

After an introduction of the themes, a theoretical exploration, and an anthropological plea for the recognition of the rationality of community relations alongside mechanical task-centered rationality in organizations will be presented.

> Large glass and concrete buildings, which may or may not have been of architectural value, have been replaced by small, cheerful ones with open areas, work cubicles, and a few offices for top management. Staff come and go. Nobody any longer has a workplace of his or her own. People make calls, surf the net and e-mail from their study at home, from their car, the garden, the restaurant, or the golf course. Their territory is everywhere and they only visit the central office building for social reasons, to have a bit of a chat.
>
> Middle management has disappeared. That carefully selected layer, built up over the period of mergers, has been shown to be superfluous because there is nobody around for them to manage any more. Top executives are, in fact, the only full-time inhabitants. They have been unable to adapt to more virtual forms of organizational community and they still have rooms filled with works of art and personal knick-knacks intended to make the place pleasant, cozy. They continue to arrange theme sessions so as to collect staff around them; but for them, too, the most important means of communication has become the Net. Meetings have, after all, been done away with because nobody wants to waste their time any more taking part in exhausting marathons with low productivity. Not many people even show up for the Friday afternoon get-together with drinks. The gatherings that the staff organizes for themselves in commu-

nities that they themselves choose are indeed well attended, but management is not usually invited to them (after Munster et al. 1999:5-7).

As this impression of the "new times" illustrates, people's relationships with and within organizations are subject to change. It is true that this version of a virtual organization is not yet widely prevalent, a fact which is, for example, also borne out by the small portion of the labor force doing telework. However, as organizations change through the flattening of hierarchies, outsourcing of competencies, empowerment of work teams, and other changes which can be understood in relation to social processes of individualization, informatization, and globalization, social and organizational traditions and certainties will disappear, and the power of organizations to contribute to creating an identity or to becoming the object of identification will diminish (Albert et al. 2000).

At the level of organizations, some managers are unconvinced that the effects of such changes will be fully beneficial. As the resistance of managers towards teleworking demonstrates, the management of organizational processes is believed to be predicated upon physical presence and surveillance of employees, as well as upon direct interpersonal interactions that are the basis for organizational commitment. Such beliefs can be judged as flowing from instrumental concerns about organizational performance. In fact, management's interest in organizational commitment, which has gone along with a large amount of research from the 1980s onwards, seems to spring from a belief that committed employees are prepared to work hard and to continue their relationship with their employing organization (Arnold et al. 1998:209). Notwithstanding this apparent instrumental interest in organizational commitment, an increasing number of organizations have attracted public interest by the emphasis they put on the notion of their organization as a "community" that accepts social responsibility. This latter notion, summarized by the organization accepting responsibility for people, planet, and profit, involves the claim that companies do not exist just for the financial interests of their shareholders; they have a broader social function, of which the well-being of their employees is but one. This idea has been welcomed by governments and politicians who worry about the impact of social transformations, such as individualization, informatization, and globalization, on their societies. Their worry that these social transformations will cause the erosion of social bonds and values could be met by civil society and private sector organizations taking up an active role in generating social cohesion.

Evidently, social transformations have an impact on work organizations themselves. For instance, the dismantling of the bureaucratic organization and the rise of virtual organizations, which are associated with the emergence of the network society, have an impact on managers, employees, and organizational relationships (Cooper and Rousseau 1999). Yet, such concepts as *empowerment* and *organizational culture* can be regarded as good reasons to examine what opportunities employment organizations provide for community and social bonds. Of course, this need for community and social bonds, which people as "social beings" are supposed to have, can be met in forms other than through work organizations – through clubs and social movements, for instance. But this chapter will concentrate on work organizations because these occupy a central place in many people's lives, even when they become more virtual in nature.

The question that this chapter will attempt to answer is twofold. First, does the recent interest of work organizations in organizational commitment and community go along with a new meaning of commitment and organizational relationships? Second, what could be the theoretical outline of a concept of an organizational community that could offer employees an opportunity to identify with, and enable work organizations to play an important role in, creating social cohesion in the networking age?

We will first clarify our theoretical approach to organizational commitment. After introducing the central concepts, we will distinguish between various types of commitment and organizational relationships, and deal with human resource policies which organizations use (or have the potential to use) in order to promote organizational commitment. We will then survey some case evidence, which suggests that organizations have not given a new meaning to commitment and organizational relationships. We will end by discussing the issue of the organization as a working and living community, and the opportunities for creating work organizations which are communities not only for working, but also for living. It is in such communities that human and social rationality can give organizational commitment and social bonds an entirely different meaning.

Organizational commitment: a double-edged sword

Organizational commitment is an issue both for the management of organizations and for employees. New organizational concepts reflect the desire of the management of organizations to bring about greater loyalty on the part of staff, as well as on the part of customers (an aspect of organizational strategies on which we will touch occasionally). Employees have their own commitments and needs for social bonds, which are to a greater or lesser extent focused on their work organization. These two perspectives will be elaborated upon.

Organizational commitment and management

The assertion that commitment is an issue for organizations may appear to contradict common experience. Indeed, ever since the 1970s, work organizations in the market sector of advanced economies have responded to technological and economic developments with a variety of different strategies, including the reduction of labor costs, increased quality of production and of services, flatter organizational structures, greater flexibility of work and organizations, outsourcing, and so on. Somewhat later, public sector organizations went through similar processes involving privatization, liberalization, budgeting, the introduction of market mechanisms, and new public management. Parallel to these organizational changes, a whole range of "new" management concepts has been promulgated, such as total quality management, human resource management, knowledge management, and cultural management. These provide managers with a range of strategies from which they can choose in order to cope with the uncertainties that confront them (Grint 1997; Karsten and van Veen 1998).

Despite management interest in benchmarking and best practices, organizations pursue different strategies. This differentiation needs to be understood partly in relation to a variety of external situations, for example the extent that the market in which an organization operates is confronted by economic globalization and changes in the organization's central technology. However, organizations are also capable of making strategic choices of their own accord, even if these are not unrestricted but rather are based on the organization's definition of the situation, its earlier choices, and the constraints and opportunities these present (cf. Ghemawat 1991; Mintzberg et al. 1999; Pascale 1990). Thus, organizational strategies in general, and those relating to human resources in particular, are in part based on and express a certain management view regarding the members of the organization. This view of the employee has undergone a dynamic development characterized by variation and selection (Verweel 2000). In the '80s and '90s, the dominant discourse focused on the rigidity of the labor market and the need for flexibility, whereas in the course of the '90s there came to be an increasing focus on the "new employee" (de Korte and Bolweg 1994), a concept which referred to a high-skilled emancipated employee who was supposed to regard employment as a business partnership. In the present discourse of the knowledge-based and networking society, interest focuses on the recruitment of specific groups on the labor market (high-skilled employees as well as ethnic minorities and asylum seekers) and on organizational commitment. Management has come to realize that employees differ in all sorts of ways (age, gender, education etc.) and that they bring with them a range of motives and types of commitment to their work – meaning that organizations have to deal with the question of how this diversity can be managed.

Given the strategies that organizations have pursued (reduction of labor costs and so on), recent management interest in issues of organizational commitment and trust (see for instance, Tyler and Kramer 1996) may raise suspicion. The creation of a contingent workforce and the implementation of such concepts as "employability" (which at least in the Anglo-Saxon context are associated with a shift of responsibility for providing the worker with a job), have served to discourage employee loyalty to work organizations. However, rather than rejecting management interest in organizational commitment and generally dismissing the idea of "trust" as mere rhetoric, this interest can also be understood as a recognition on the part of management that changes in organizational practices are bound to have an impact on employee behavior. The real question is, "what kind of interest management is driven in concrete human resource practices?" Does human resource management practice express an essentially calculative conception of organizational commitment, in which an effort to boost trusting relationships is undertaken because a decline in trust would entail costs? Recognizing such interest in organizational commitment, and recognizing trust as representing a rational choice approach, both help in our ability to critically examine human resource practices and distinguish the calculative conception of trust from what Tyler and Kramer call a "social conception of trust" (1996: 5), in which trust has social meaning beyond rational calculations. According to this social conception of trust, people may help others or their group because they feel it is the morally appropriate action to do, or because they identify with the group.

Of course, management discourse may refer to this social conception of trust for instrumental reasons, and it can attempt to allude to group or organizational identification as a means to hone employee exertion. However, it is unlikely that management can achieve such aims without any consistent action on its own part. From the management point of view this illustrates the double edge of organizational commitment: the organization cannot do without, but its pursuit will entail obligations and may be dangerous when viewed from a calculative rational choice approach.

Employees and organizational commitment
An interesting question is whether the image of the staff contained within the organizational discourse fits in with the meaning which employees themselves give to their work, their career, and organization. And how does that sense making develop in relation to organizational strategy and practice as well as in relation to personal circumstances (life cycle) and extra-work interests? Framing the issue in these terms demonstrates an interest on the part of employees in a dynamic and context-sensitive approach to sense making. This suggests that the meaning which employees give to their work, career, and organization can evolve in relation to contexts which have little or nothing to do with the organization, such as becoming a parent or being successful in sport, as well as in relation to the time dimension of their occupational and life career. Thus, employee commitments to work, profession, and organization, and the way in which they construct their individual identity and identify with their colleagues or professional group, must be understood contextually (cf. Casey 1995).

The importance of this "contextuality" can be illustrated by various studies relevant to the topic of organizational commitment. Hochschild (1997), for example, attracted attention by showing that American workers were working increasingly long hours so as not to have to be at home. Organizations have become more attractive as a result of new styles of management, and of care and appreciation for staff, whereas the home situation has become less free because of agreements as to the distribution of childcare tasks and the associated conflicts caused by both partners having a paid job. In contrast, the central thesis of Sennett's study (1998), with its emphasis on flexibility and transience, is that the new capitalism forces career-oriented employees to hop from one job to another, and to constantly move house. This means that they no longer feel at home anywhere, are unable to enter into any lasting forms of relationships, and can no longer even develop any kind of coherent life story. The point here is not whether Hochschild or Sennett is closer to the truth as regards the views of employees. Within a "perspectivist" view of science (Fay 1996), it is more interesting to assume two different perspectives on organizational realities. The important point is that the authors come up with differing significances which employees are believed to attach to work, and to organization in interaction within the relevant contexts of organizations/work/capitalism and home/care/society. This underlines the conclusion of Tyler and Kramer's survey of research of trust in organizations: future research should explore the situational dimensions that contribute to shaping trust (Tyler and Kramer 1996:12), or organizational commitment and community for that matter.

As in the case of management, organizational commitment is a double-edged sword for employees. On the one hand employees can have professional or work commitments and can identify with the group of colleagues with whom they collaborate, and such commitments and identifications need not necessarily go along with organizational commitment. On the other hand, management can relate to such employee commitments and identifications, and make them instrumental for organizational purposes.

Central concepts
Commitments
The concept of organizational commitment refers to a person's attachment to the employing organization (Arnold et al. 1998:203). This means that organizational commitment entails an affective commitment or emotional attachment to the organization. In addition to this component, Allen and Meyer (1990) distinguish between "normative commitment," which refers to a person's felt moral obligation and responsibility to the organization, and "continuance commitment," referring to a person's perception of the costs and risks associated with leaving the organization. This latter component is closely related to one of the supposed behavioral outcomes of organizational commitment, namely staying with or leaving the current organization. However, this behavioral outcome is, as Arnold et al. observe, also dependent on labor market constraints (1998:211). Another behavioral outcome attributed to organizational commitment is the willingness to exert effort on behalf of the organization.

Both affective and normative commitments refer to the employee's commitment to the "organization," but we concur with the critique of the organization as a single entity with a united goal (ibid.). It is adequate to differentiate between a person's commitment to his colleagues or work group, to his supervisor, and to "the organization," meaning top management. Having observed this differentiation, a person's commitment to his work group may still be judged by management on the basis of whether one remains with the organization. It would be wrong, however, to interpret this as identification with the values and goals of the organization, just as one's leaving an organization could follow from causes other than a lack of organizational commitment.

Arnold et al. (1998: 211-212) distinguish between the behavioral approach and a kind of social exchange approach. They maintain that giving them positive experiences can foster people's commitments. Such positive experiences could be derived, for instance, from appreciation by managers, or from intrinsic job characteristics (such as job autonomy), or extrinsic factors (including pay and other employment conditions). They report that intrinsic job characteristics are particularly important in fostering affective commitment. However, other authors see such intrinsic job characteristics as a major component of another type of commitment, which is not mentioned by Arnold et al., and which could be regarded as a potential competitor of organizational commitment. This type of commitment is called "professional commitment" by some authors (see Schomaker 1999), or "career commitment" by others (Mueller et al. 1992). Career commitment relates to the employee's identification with and involvement in his job or career. This type of commitment is primarily associated with professionals. Professionals are traditionally regarded as being primarily oriented towards their profession, and therefore are assumed to have strong professional commitment and low organizational commitment. However, the growth of interest in the emergence of "new" professionals has led to the hypothesis that the relationship between professional and organizational commitment is contingent, depending on such factors as the type of professional and the type of organization (Schomaker 1999). Although research in this field is still fresh, one important conclusion that can be drawn is that organizational commitment should not be studied in isolation from other commitments and social contexts.

Types of organizational relationships

Viewing commitments as social exchanges, we assume that people develop commitments through interaction with others. At the level of the organization the relationships which are produced as a result of these interactions have certain characteristics that can be more or less attuned to particular types of commitments, as shown by examining different types of relationships. Van Heerikhuizen and Wilterdink (1993) distinguish between economic, political, affective, and cognitive relationships. These different types of relationships express the ways in which people in all sorts of communities depend on one another. Economic relationships originate from dependencies associated with the production and distribution of scarce goods. Political relationships refer to those based on the compulsion that individuals can exert over others. Affective relationships relate to processes of identity and belonging, with all the positive and negative feelings people have for one another. And cognitive relationships involve dependencies resulting from processes of acquiring and transferring knowledge. This categorization, needless to say, is an ideal one in the sense that in actuality, combinations of the different types often occur, and social relationships therefore can comprise several different types of relationships simultaneously.

Economic relationships

For employers and employees, employment contracts regulate economic exchange relationships. The employer purchases labor potential and pays for it; the employee makes his or her labor available for a certain period, and receives payment in return. In this view, it is in the employer's interest to make use of the employee and of the various approaches to management which have succeeded one another in the course of time, from scientific management to human resource management, for these can be viewed as different attempts to achieve the maximum or optimum use of this human capital. The main concern is the effective and efficient utilization of the time that the organization has purchased. Conversely, the economic view (not uncommon among some trade unions) considers the employment contract as reflecting an unequal exchange relationship whereby the employee is exploited because he or she produces more value than that what he or she is paid for.

The relationship between the organization and the employee entails an economic exchange between two parties. From this perspective, the relationship will continue as long as the employee is convinced that it offers the best possible return (in terms of the pay and career opportunities which he receives) on his "investment," and as long as the employee perceives no attractive alternatives in the labor market. Allen and Meyer subsume this type of calculation under the term "continuance commitment," which refers to a person's perception of the costs and risks of leaving the organization. The implication of Allen and Meyer's distinction between three components of organizational commitment seems to be that the other two components – affective and normative commitment – do not contribute to the intention to stay or leave the organization. In this respect Arnold et al. (1998:211) offer another model of organizational commitment in which the decision to stay is the outcome of all three components, in addition to labor market constraints. Adopting their model, the act of leaving the organization can be understood as the outcome of a process in which economic calculation is but one consideration of reflexive monitoring.

From the perspective of management, the interest in the economic relationship is grounded in the possibilities it offers for sustaining company performance and for employee retention. Thus, for instance, offering employees stock options is based on motives to recruit valued and often highly skilled workers, to retain them, to motivate them to contribute significantly to the firm, and to build a sense of community thereby enhancing worker identification with the firm (Shperling and Rousseau 2001). However, as Shperling and Rousseau (2001: 26-27) point out, economic means will not necessarily enhance affective commitment without other practices being in place which promote worker attachment to the firm; and their use runs the risk of rewarding the disloyalty of mobile workers and eroding the goodwill of workers who do not threaten to quit.

Political relationships

Organizational relationships are political relationships in the sense that they are based on the compulsion which some people can exert over others. A trend that appears to be spreading is that control through overt coercion by organizational hierarchy is being replaced (or supplemented) by control through self-managed observance of organizational policies, as for instance through various forms of direct employee participation (cf. EPOC Research Group 1997). The motives of the majority of managers – at least in the Netherlands (Huijgen and Benders 1998) – for introducing direct participation is their belief that direct participation has positive effects on both company performance and quality of work, and that employees have a right to participate.

Traditionally, direct participation, which comes with responsible autonomy, has been more prevalent among high-skilled employees, but this does not mean that political relationships and compulsion are not features of what would now be called knowl-edge-intensive organizations. In fact, one interesting explicit demonstration of compul-sion exists in IT-firms where employers have used the legal construct of the competi-tion clause to retain employees. The phenomenon of the competition clause has existed in the Netherlands since 1907, and was originally meant to prevent an employee with specific knowledge and customer-relationships leaving the current firm and taking a job with the competition. Lately, the tight labor market has occasioned IT-firms to make use of the competition clause with a view to retaining their scarce IT-professionals. This, in turn, has motivated the government to restrict the use of the competition clause to specific situations and for a maximum of one year, with financial compensation to be paid to the employee.

Affective relationships
Interest in the importance of organizational commitment and identification arose in the early 1980s from the analysis of organizational excellence and of Japanese styles of management. The employee's identification with the organization was believed to make the employee more committed and more willing to contribute to organizational per-formance since the employee feels part of the larger collective with which he identi-fies, particularly when that organization is intent on generating a sense of "we" by focusing on the differences with competing organizations (Shperling and Rousseau 2001:33). In this way organizations can become more than work organizations. A large number of historical examples have been reported on of the close-knit community within and around the organization. "Modern manors," as Jacoby (1997) calls them, which offer not only employment but also welfare, including company housing and recreational facilities. The community which grew up around such companies as Kodak, Sears, and Thompson in the United States, and Philips and Shell in the Nether-lands, may today appear to be total institutions. But from the historical point of view, these companies were at home in the glory days of Fordism. Nevertheless, there are examples today of companies which are more than merely a place where people work. For example the companies that provide their staff with all kinds of facilities ranging from breakfast in the "living room" to dry-cleaning and shopping service. The increased interest in organizational cultures has made clear the significance of such affective rela-tionships, and their influence on life within organizations.

Affective relationships do not merely involve identification with *the organization*, however. The expansion of one's sense of self to include larger sets of social entities can involve the identification of the employees not with the work organization per se, but with *their colleagues* and with their *own class*. Various types of identification can also occur simultaneously and in conflict with one another (Guest 1987). Identification is therefore not exclusively a matter of managerial strategy.

Cognitive relationships
Since the 1990s there has been increasing interest in such matters as learning organi-

zations and knowledge management; and with this has come an interest in another source of organizational commitment – cognitive commitment. Cognitive relationships within organizations can be recognized in situations in which there is, for example, a policy with respect to the training and development of employees or groups of employees. Highly skilled and professional employees are believed to be particularly interested in opportunities for lifelong learning and development. Management skepticism that organizational policies of offering such opportunities would not generate return on investment in human capital because those employees would leave the organization, is unfounded, according to some research (e.g. Gasperz and Ott 1996). The reason is that high-skilled employees would favor working at organizations which offer such development and career opportunities. Other research, however, has shown that high-skilled employees who have benefited from such human resource development policies have a high degree of organizational commitment, but still decide to leave the organization for different reasons, such as the professional "challenge" of working at another organization (Schomaker 1999).

Commitments, identification and the duration of relationships

Identification, in the sense of the individual expanding his sense of self to include a group of people or an organization, is associated with the idea of the individual cooperating with others and contributing to the group. One effect of group identification is, as Tyler and Kramer (1996:6-7) observe, that expectations increase that others will reciprocate. Another effect is also known, namely that people who trust others feel some sort of moral duty or commitment towards them. They are found to continue to cooperate, irrespective of the behavior of others in the group, and not to leave groups even when, from an instrumental point of view, it is in their interest to do so. While the first effect is consistent with a rational choice explanation, according to which the individual will stay with the organization as long as the organization satisfies the type of needs which drive him, the second effect would result in a long duration of organizational relationships without permanent efforts on the part of the organization to reciprocate the contributions of its employees. This explains why organizations have been interested in bringing about affective and normative commitments, with "cultural management" as a means to accomplish this.

Interest in organizational culture as an agent of identification grew with the study of organizational excellence by Peters and Waterman (1982). They argue that one of the factors producing excellence is the extent to which organizations succeed in creating shared meaning. They refer to this as a strong, shared culture in which the members possess the same values and norms that constitute a set of basic principles for thinking and acting. This set of principles functions as a point of reference for identification on the part of employees. A strong culture endows the organization and its members with the fighting spirit with which to distinguish themselves from other organizations and their members, thus creating an "us group" versus a "them group." Culture thus has an integrating effect for the individual and the organization. Cultural management therefore focuses on providing a culture, and socializing people into it.

Other authors such as Martin (1992) question this approach to organizational culture because it does not take account of the diversity of people's needs and of cultural differences. This diversity of needs has been made clearer by research into customer
loyalty. In service organizations, the relationship between the organization and the customer, the contact with the customer, and the supporting system for implementing that
contact (including evaluating it by means of quality systems), has become the central
focus of management. In a virtual economy, customers who used to be imprisoned in
a supply-oriented local economy have potentially global and demand-driven options
available to them. This "increased" customer freedom has led management to place
greater emphasis on opportunities for binding customers from within the company. Van
der Loo and Mante-Meyer show that the issue that arises here is one of customer relationship management appealing to a diversity of customers. They find that the influence of socio-cultural turbulence within society has made people's needs more diverse.
Therefore, they propose four socio-cultural models for customer loyalty: (1) the predictable customer, who can be turned into a "regular" customer by following the familiar rules, (2) the "flighty" customer, who is always searching for new short-term kicks,
(3) the intimate or relational customer, who constantly wishes to have the communality and permanence of the relationship confirmed, and (4) the powerless customer who
is constantly suspicious, believing that only lucky breaks show that an organization,
product, or service provider can be trusted. Each of these customer groups is in search
of a different significance with which to give substance to the type of relationship they
desire, and each of them requires a different type of discourse with the organization. It
is important to note that there is no direct association between the type of customer
and the duration of the relationships between organization and customer. Identification
with the organization in categories of customers with few contacts with the organization can go along with greater continuity in the sense of returning as a customer over
time, in contrast to groups with large numbers of contacts.

The recognition of the importance of cultural differences is also relevant for the
issue of employee retention. This constitutes the basis of the second approach of cultural management. These differences may derive from functional (different departments), socio-cultural (related with ethnicity, gender or age), or political (groups within organizations) origins. This approach does not aim at the socialization of all members
within a shared meaning, but at coordinating the cultural differences through dialogue
between the different parts of the organization, between groups within the organization, and between individuals. In the course of the dialogue, the differences are not
eliminated but are used in the task-oriented and social sense to serve one's own purposes and those of the organization. According to this approach, identification with the
organization arises when the aim of the organization makes possible the aims of the
various departments, groups, and individuals. Identification is offered by the organization, but it is also actively given substance by its members without the differences
between the members being eliminated. Identification is created within and through

discussion, and not by socializing people into a common culture defined in advance. In other words, identification involves shared experience and not shared meaning. In the United States, this "management of diversity" approach has become familiar primarily as an approach to organizing different ethnic groups, but it has also been more broadly applied to organizational cultures (Martin 1992).

A new meaning of commitment and organizational relationships?

Having outlined the various types of employee commitments and organizational relationships, we can now address the question whether we are living in a period in which the interest of work organizations in organizational commitment and identification goes along with a new meaning of commitment and organizational relationships.

The interest of management magazines in the issues of organizational commitment and identification does suggest that these have taken a new meaning for organizations in the 1990s. Survey research, for instance, of firms in the various sectors of the information and communication industry confirms that almost all firms regard identification and the binding of their employees as very important (Leisink et al. 2000). This industry includes such organizations as computer hardware and software companies, IT and management consultancies, advertising agencies, multimedia and Internet companies, audio-visual producers and graphic designers. The way in which these firms attempt to recruit and retain employees demonstrates a great variety of human resource policies in which the appeal to various types of commitment can be discovered (cf. Computable/ FNV Bondgenoten 2000; Leisink et al. 2000; Van Wijk 2000).

It is striking that some organizations focus mainly on the economic possibilities for organizational commitment, such as in the form of stock options, bonuses, lease cars, WAP telephones etc. Other organizations, by contrast, emphasize the fact that they do not wish to bind their employees by "golden chains," but focus instead on being a community and providing a "living space," thereby promoting social bonds and emotional attachment to the organization. Finally, there are a large number of knowledge-intensive companies which attach a great deal of importance to knowledge management and to associated HRM policies aimed at employability, and at career-development elements which appeal to employees for whom career commitment is significant.

For management of organizational commitment to be effective, it is obviously essential that there to be a fit between the subjective commitments of the staff and the organizational policies. It is questionable, however, to what extent organizations are genuinely interested in their employees' commitments. Organizations in the ICT sector were concerned mainly with the phenomenon of job-hopping and losing staff, particularly when the labor market was tight. Furthermore, human resource policies in this sector expressed a primarily instrumental attitude to organizational commitment. This became very evident from 2000 onwards, when the Internet hype was over and the economic situation became less buoyant. An example may be taken from Pricewater-houseCoopers Consulting. That company made use of various economic means and career programs to bind their employees when it was confronted with thirty percent employee mobility on an annual basis. In early 2002, however, it decided to offer financial incentives to ten percent of its consultants in the Netherlands so as to induce their voluntary resignation. While this example of economic means to bind employees (or to un-bind them) can be considered consistent human resource policy from an economic rational point of view, this view on organizational relationships would be less expected in the case of companies that emphasize they are community. However, one multimedia firm, "Lost Boys," which represented the success of the new economy and grew to employ over 600 employees in nine countries (serving international customers like Volkswagen and Nokia), had for a long time based its image on being a community with an informal culture. But in 2001, it announced the immediate redundancy of 65 of its Amsterdam-based employees. From one day to the next these employees saw their XS-cards and email accounts blocked, and they were told that the firm would not offer redundancy pay because it was not legally obliged to do so.

It appears that the significance which organizations attach to employee loyalty is contingent on economic factors, and that company turnover and profits are assessed from a shareholder rather than a stakeholder perspective. At the same time that Lost Boys was laying off its employees, its founder-owner sold the company and then subsequently bought its very buyer, Icon Medialab, in order to become a global industry leader. The same shareholder perspective dominates in the case of ABN-AMRO, one leading international bank, whose retail bank in the Netherlands still makes a sizeable profit, although less than in the past. The bank employees are known for their loyalty, with a cashier serving nineteen years of employment on average. But now the bank management reframes this loyalty as problematic. The board of the retail bank has decided that it wants to "take leave" of about twenty percent of its employees before 2004, and has sent three quarters of all employees a letter telling them that they "are dispensable" and that no guarantee can be given concerning their job in the organization. All this has caused much distress and loss of motivation among its employees.

Surveying this evidence of the way in which management makes sense of organizational commitment, a new meaning to organizational commitment and relationships cannot be discovered. What about the employees? Those who believe that new types of identification have arisen refer to the development of organizational strategies, such as flexibilization and employability, which are supposed to have undermined the traditional basis of employee identification with the work organization. Employees are supposed to have replaced their identification with their work organization with new forms of identification; with virtual communities, which may include a virtual community of colleagues in addition to other communities (for example, Munster et al, 1999). There are examples that indicate that traditional employee loyalty, symbolized by the gold watch as a reward for forty years of faithful service, is no longer generally appreciated. On the other hand, there is not much empirical evidence to support the supposition that informatization and individualization result in increasing numbers of flexiworkers and a trend towards virtual organizations, the consequence being that

organizations are no longer living entities to which individuals bind themselves for
lengthy periods. The proportion of flexi-workers in the Netherlands is about ten percent, and it is even possible to identify a slight downward trend because the tight labor
market allows employees to demand a permanent contract instead of a flexi-contract.
This, in turn, is associated with the fact that various studies have shown that the so-
called "new employee" (de Korte and Bolweg 1994), who is supposed to prefer flexi-
contracts and job hopping, constitutes a minority of employees with a flexible contract.
The majority prefers a stable employment relationship. The attitudes of Dutch employees towards aspects of organizational relationships do not appear to reflect a shift
towards a positive evaluation of virtual communities. A recent survey showed that a
majority of Dutch employees expect that competition at work will increase, that fellowship will decrease and that employee loyalty will decrease in the next two decades,
but the majority also regard these developments as undesirable (Ester, Vinken 2001).
This evidence does not indicate a new meaning in regard to organizational commitment
and relationships. However, the fact that a majority of employees regard future developments as undesirable suggests that the germ of an alternative concept of organizational relationships is forming. Thus, it appears that the reason for the interest in organizational commitment and identification is the result not so much of a new meaning
of organizational commitment and relationships, as it is of changes in management discourse in which the rhetorical pendulum has swung back from "lean and mean" to
"identification and involvement."

The emancipation of the organizational community

There is a fundamental reason, in our view, to deal with the need for a new meaning
of organizational relationships. We consider that up to now the management approach
to organizational commitment has been of a highly instrumental nature. The question of
identification is viewed from the perspective of how the human contribution can be opti-
mized or even maximized in order to improve the quality and quantity of production.
Identification of people with one another and with the organization is predominantly at
the service of the task-oriented aims of the organization. Where methods of structural
reorganization (mergers, networking, business process redesign etc.) reach their limits
as a means of increasing production, the interest shifts to methods of social and human
re-engineering, HRM, organizational culture, self-management etc. However, a mechanical approach to social and human matters is ultimately dominant. This mechanization
is the result of the instrumental rationalization of social life, which appears to be the
dominant perspective in theoretical studies as well. In fact, Barley (1988) has shown by
means of a statistical analysis of almost 200 articles that the instrumental approach to
culture has superseded the interpretative approach. In particular, the economic value of
manipulating organizational cultures, and the attention paid to the rational control of
diversity by steering towards a unified culture, is dominant (Barley 1988:51). We concur
with this view. Our study (van Hees and Verweel, forthcoming) of the life cycle of organizational images has shown that this development actually applies to a large number

of other popular images. In the initial phase of their development, various concepts – like "self-management" and the "learning organization" – display both instrumental and social variants. In the following phase, however, the focus shifts towards the instrumental aspects of the concept, which are directed towards organizational aims (such as increased profits and continuity) and organizational control.

Following Bahlmann and Meesters (1998) and Ritzer (1993), we think that rationalization has been at the cost of the intellectual and social life in organizations. The instrumental mechanistic approach enables us to tackle what is "tangible and manifest" (organizational structures, decision-making and information systems, and so on). It is embedded in the enlightenment thinking, from which, according to Bahlmann and Meesters, "the original enlightened, humanist and social ideas have increasingly disappeared from the picture" (1998:28). They argue that successive approaches have taken too little account of the fact that it is not the organization that needs to be the ultimate criterion, but the individual. They conclude that the point is not merely what is tangible, but specifically what is intangible – human relationships, cultural aspects, and the transcendent (1998:190).

If we wish to restrict the influence of the mechanization principle, then we need to choose a different starting point than has been usual up till now. We need to resituate the organization within the development of man and society with a view to the human and social needs which organizations can serve. Viewed in this light, the essence of an organization cannot merely be contained in a business-science definition, in which the effectiveness and efficiency of material production becomes the aim of the organization. Even a sociological approach in which the organization contributes (simultaneously with material production) to producing and reproducing social relationships, fails to do justice to the social element, if the social element is only considered as a socialization mechanism and as a means of improving productivity and effectiveness. For as such, the organization is no longer a means for serving people's needs but a goal in itself to which people and human functioning have been subordinated.

The analysis by the anthropologist Bailey (1977) provides an inspiring example of re-conceptualizing the essence of organization. Bailey adopts the position that an organization is the mixed product of the rationality of production (with its mechanistic leanings) and the rationality of the social (with its human slant), for the organization is simultaneously a community for working and for living. The working community is concerned with production and with organizing that production. These concerns are designed and evaluated according to the rationality of effectiveness and efficiency within an instrumental "aim-means-output" relationship. It is the prevailing economic laws of the operation of the market which dictate these processes. The living community, on the other hand, is driven by a different rationality, the essence of which can be defined as "people treated as ends in themselves." There is no need to make any reference to the rationality of production in order to emphasize the importance of the social and human aspects. The human aspect is, and must be allowed to be, an end goal in itself. It may or may not promote productivity. The value of the organization is therefore to be found not only in increasing profits or the service provided as the highest goal, but also in the experience and sense making of the individual. The organization therefore becomes the means, and the individual the measure of things.

Thus, relationships within organizations are shaped by two types of rationality, which often operate simultaneously in human action. Here, the issue of rationality posed by Weber, Tönnies, and Durkheim can be seen returning in full measure in a variant of its own. *Wertrationalität* and *Zweckrationalität*, and the development of *Gemeinschaft* and *Gesellschaft* (or of mechanical and organic solidarity), here enter into an entirely new relationship within organizations. Even in the digital world of e-commerce, such community features as trust, loyalty, and identity are indispensable organizational principles (Rheingold 1993). Old issues turn out to be relevant once more, and they lead to new views of contemporary developments. In analyzing how people work and live within an organization, the point is to gear the rationality of production to the rationality of the social. The point is not to reduce the social to the productive, or, to put it differently, the human to the material, but to do justice to both autonomous rationalities. Organizing involves both the production of the material and of the human (Benjamin in Visser 1998:328). If we do not insist on this, we cannot avoid objectifying the subjective, and in so doing help to instrumentalize the life goals of mankind (Visser 1998:340).

In Western society, the production of material goods has reached such a high level that any further instrumentalization (i.e. appealing to the need to provide for people's material needs) becomes almost ridiculous, at least as long as the distribution of goods to the Third World and Third World areas of the West is not an issue (Castells 1996). This may open up the opportunities for advancing the rationality of the social. Another relevant phenomenon is the shift in the labor market. The demand for labor, primarily in the service sector, has increased rapidly, and prospects are that this demand will increase even further over the course of the next decade, despite the economic dip in 2001-2002. This means that organizations will have to persuade staff to join the organization by holding out attractive prospects to them. The need to induce staff loyalty by means of something more than just an economic relationship is making itself felt. Organizational identification by means of non-material conditions is becoming more important.

An interesting implication of interest in organizational identification inspired by social rationality concerns the issue of social cohesion. Whereas social cohesion was, up to now, seen as the primary concern of public social policy, in the future civil society and the private sector could come to play a more important role, as identification with clubs and work organizations acquires increasing significance.

In short, within the actual practice of organizations in the Western world, conditions are being created (cf. De Geus 1997) or can be created which place the social relationships within organizations at the center of attention, and which create opportunities to tackle the instrumentalization of the social. In the networking age, management will be faced by the new challenge of enacting the concept of organization with the meaning of community of working and living.

Conclusion

We began this chapter with a picture of the organization in the networking age which is assumed to correspond with new forms for existing types of organizational commitment. In that picture physical proximity, an office of one's own, and middle management were no longer a part of things. In our view, however, that picture – whether or not it is a realistic one – will not constitute a major break with the past. The question of what new meaning organizational commitment and relationships will acquire needs to be answered at a much more fundamental level than that at which organizations presently frame the question. This involves the question of how they can assure themselves of the loyalty of their personnel in order to hone organizational performance and to retain their employees as long as they wish. The fundamental issue is whether in the late modern era it will be possible for organizational actors to enact a new meaning to organizational relationships by merging organizational commitment based on the mechanistic rationality of the organization of production, with the individual and social need for identification with the living community and its social and human rationality. It may be that not all organizational actors make sense of organizational community in this way, but at least many employees value community, fellowship, and loyalty. If such a social rationality is not possible, then the form but not the meaning of organizational commitment and relationships may be able to renew itself. The current state of development of theoretical concepts and the material circumstances in Western societies suggest that such a reflexive modernization of organizational relationships is viable, but also that such a development depends on the reflexive actions of the various organizational actors, including managers and employees, as well as shareholders, financiers, suppliers, and customers.

Bibliography

Albert, S., B.F. Ashforth, and J.E. Dutton. 2000. Organisational identity and identification: charting new waters and building new bridges. *Academy of Management Review* 25 (1):13-17.

Allen, N.J., and J.P.Meyer. 1990. The measurement and antecedents of affactive, continuance and normative commitmentto the organization. *Journal of Occupational Psychology* 63:11-18.

Arnold, John, Cary L. Cooper, and Ivan T. Robertson, eds. 1998. *Work Psychology. Understanding Human Behaviour in the Workplace*. Harlow: Pearson Education Ltd. (Third Edition.)

Bahlmann, J.P., and B. Meesters. 1998. *De organisatie die nooit bestond*. Schoonhoven: Academic Service.

Bailey, F.G. 1977. *Morality and expediency. The folklore of academic politics*. Oxford: Blackwell.

Barley, S.R. 1988. Cultures of culture: academics, practitioners and the pragmatics of normative control. *Administrative Science Quarterly* 33.

Casey, C. 1995. *Work, Self and Society*. London: Routledge.

Computable/FNV Bondgenoten. 2000. *Werken in de ICT-sector: onder welke voorwaarden?* Amsterdam: FNV Pers.

de Geus, A. 1997. *The Living Company; Habits for Survival in a Turbulent Environment*. Longview Publishing.

de Korte, A., and J. Bolweg. 1994. *De nieuwe werknemer*. Assen: Van Gorcum.

EPOC Research Group. 1997. *New forms of work organisation. Can Europe realise its potential?*

Luxembourg: Office for official publications of the European Communities.

Ester, P., and H. Vinken. 2001. *Een dubbel vooruitzicht. Doembeelden en droombeelden van arbeid, zorg en vrije tijd in de 21e eeuw.* Bussum: Coutinho.

Fay, B. 1996. *Contemporary Philosophy of Social Science. A Multicultural Approach.* Oxford: Blackwell.

Gasperz, J., and M. Ott. 1996. *Management van employability.* Assen: Van Gorcum.

Ghemawat, P. 1991. *Commitment: The Dynamic of Strategy.* New York: The Free Press.

Grint, K. 1997. *Fuzzy Management.* Oxford: Oxford University Press.

Guest, David. 1987. Human Resource Management and Industrial Relations. *Journal of Management Studies* 24(2):503-521.

Hochchild, A. 1997. *The Time Bind. When Work Becomes Home and Home Becomes Work.* Owl Books.

Huijgen, F., and J. Benders. 1998. Het vallende kwartje; directe participatie in Nederland en Europa. *Tijdschrift voor Arbeidsvraagstukken* 14(2):113-127.

Karsten, L., and K. van Veen. 1998. *Managementconcepten in beweging: tussen feit en vluchtigheid.* Assen: Van Gorcum.

Koot, W., and I. Sabilis. 2000. *Over-leven aan de top.* Utrecht: Lemma

Leisink, P., J. Teunen, and J. Boumans. 2000. *Multimedia: de pioniersfase voorbij. Organisatiestrategie en personeelsbeleid rond multimedia in de media- en informatie-industrie.* Veenendaal: GOC.

Martin, J. 1992. *Cultures in organizations. Three perspectives.* New York/Oxford: Oxford University Press.

Mintzberg, H., B. Ahlstrand, and J. Lampel. 1999. *Op strategie-safari; een rondleiding door de wildernis van strategisch management.* Schiedam: Scriptum Management.

Mueller, C., J. Wallace, and J. Price. 1992. Employee commitment; resolving some issues. *Work and Occupations* 19(3):211-236.

Peters, T.J., and R.H.Waterman. 1982. *In Search of Excellence: Lessons from America's Best Run Companies.* New York: Harper and Row.

Rheingold, H. 1993. *The virtual community.* New York.

Ritzer, G. 1993. *The McDonaldization of Society.* Thousand Oaks: Sage.

Schomaker, P. A. 1999. *Wie bindt, die wint.* Nijmegen: Nijmegen School of Management. (Thesis)

Sennett, R. 1998. *The Corrosion of Character.* New York/London: Norton and Company.

Shperling, Z., and D.M. Rousseau. 2001. When Employers Share Ownership with Workers. In C.L. Cooper and D.M. Rousseau, eds., *Trends in Organisational Behavior* pp. 19-44. Chicester: John Wiley and Sons.

Siebers, Hans, Paul Verweel, and Arie de Ruijter. 2002. *Management van diversiteit in arbeidsorganisaties.* Utrecht: Lemma.

Tyler, Tom R., and Roderick M. Kramer. 1996. Whither Trust? In Roderick M. Kramer and Tom R. Tyler, eds., *Trust in Organizations: Frontiers of Theory and Research* pp. 1-15. Thousand Oaks, London, New Delhi: Sage.

van Heerikhuizen, B., and N. Wilterdink. 1993. Het terrein van de sociologie. In N. Wilterdink and B. van Heerikhuizen, ed. *Samenlevingen.* Groningen: Wolters-Noordhoff.

van Munster, O., C. Gehrels, M. Merckx, and P. Adriaanse. 1999. *De tekens van de nieuwe tijd.* 's-Gravenhage: Berenschot Fundatie/Elsevier Bedrijfsinformatie.

van Wijk, E. 2000. *Arbeidsbeleving bij communicatie-adviesbureaus 2000.* Amstelveen: VEA.

Verweel, P. 2000. *Betekenisgeving in organisatiewetenschap.* Utrecht: Universiteit Utrecht.

Visser, G. 1998. *De druk van de beleving.* Nijmegen: SUN.

Weick, K. 1995. *Sensemaking in Organizations.* Thousand Oaks/London/New Delhi: Sage.

24

Proximities and Distances
The Impact of Networking in and around Four
Asylum Seekers' Residences in the Netherlands

Marja Gastelaars

This essay examines the impact of COA's local networking efforts on the space need-ed by individual asylum seekers in the Netherlands, to achieve "self-reliance" in their everyday lives. COA, the Central Body providing Residence to Asylum Seekers, works for the Dutch Justice Department and is assigned to keep the asylum-seekers that enter our country available for their juridical procedures. Accordingly, it is expected to per-form permanent surveillance and to provide the asylum seekers with a residence and some basic provisions. In recent years, however, the Dutch Justice Department express-ly wished to enhance the efficiency and effectiveness of its work.

Accordingly, COA's employees on location are expected to adapt to a new regime. As a part of this they are expected to explicitly encourage the so-called *self-reliance* of the asylum seekers. COA's workers were expected to perform a change in their reper-toires, accordingly, from "helper" to "guide" (COA 2001). This new repertoire was aimed at encouraging asylum seekers to take some responsibility of their own, as a part of their juridical procedures. They were also expected to take care of their everyday activities in and around the houses themselves, instead of being cared for by COA. They had to find ways of their own into local sports clubs, churches, and mosques, and other informal local networks on and around their locations. And they were expected to participate, on their own behalf, in the highly institutionalised Dutch local networks performing education, health care, and social work. I am interested here not so much in the actual change of routine and repertoire for COA's local employees (I have dis-cussed this elsewhere, see Gastelaars, in press) but rather in the symbolical impact of the local networking efforts that COA performs in terms of the structural spaces pro-vided to individual asylum seekers to perform self-reliance.

In fact, and in tune with Yanow's interpretative approach of processes of policy implementation, it is not a straightforward implementation process that is to be pre-sented here. The various parties performing on location, asylum seekers included, are certainly not regarded as the passive recipients of COA's policy intentions. On the con-trary, they are regarded as the active local "producers" of relevant meanings (Yanow 1996:26). Moreover, and in the words of Czarniawska, such local producers may be expected to participate in specific local *action nets,* in which "it is the actions rather than the actors that are connected" (Czarniawska 2000:9), in spite of the heterogeneous and even contradictory meanings that may be locally produced. The local networking performed by the various parties on and around COA's locations can be seen as a potential *materialisation* of such action nets, in which all parties, the asylum seekers included, play their parts.

The fieldwork: four asylum seekers' residences compared[1]

The fieldwork on which this contribution is based was undertaken at four COA locations between October 2000 and March 2001. The four asylum seekers residences are compared in terms of the spaces they provide towards asylum seekers' ability to perform self-reliance. Many parties on and around these residences were interviewed, including a small but representative sample of asylum seekers (see Gastelaars et al. 2002:264-270, for an extensive methodological account). For the latter, we availed ourselves of the services of interpreters, except in those instances when the respondents had sufficient command of the Dutch language.

I will rely, firstly, on empirical data gathered at *The Convent*, a traditional Asylum Seekers' Centre (AZC) with 230 residents. It is established in a former Roman Catholic convent in a fairly remote village in the south of the Netherlands. On this location, most activities were conducted indoors. Our assumption was that such a traditional asylum seekers' centre, particularly a geographically isolated "COA-fortress" like this one, cannot be expected to relate extensively to the outside world. Nor does it provide sufficient personal space for individual asylum seekers to perform any self-reliance in their everyday negotiations (see also Geuijen 1998). Conversely, COA locations that are socially more embedded appear to be more promising in this respect. Our simple assumption was that when most activities other than housekeeping were to be conducted outdoors, this would physically but also symbolically encourage asylum seekers to find ways of their own (Gastelaars et al. 2002:17-19).

The Convent is compared, first, with *The Hotel*, a so-called "Additional Residence" *(Aanvullende Opvang,* AVO) with 68 residents in a large suburban villa. This villa, a former residential home for the handicapped, is situated in a fairly decent neighbourhood, in a village nearby a somewhat larger town in the north of Holland. It contains a large number of residents in one location. Yet it can be expected to promote the asylum seekers' self-reliance because many of their activities are performed outdoors. But in particularly the COA-locations providing private houses in regular neighbourhoods are expected to provide sufficient space. Accordingly, we have investigated two "Central Arrangements for Private Housing" *(Centrale Opvang Woningen,* COW) in the east of the country. There, COA provides private houses in regular neighbourhoods.

Moreover, in both cases COA's offices and those of its juridical chain partners are removed to rather distant locations. Here, the asylum seekers are not only encouraged to make use of the available local networks, but also to find their ways to both the informal and the formal provisions that are locally available. One of these residences, *The Village,* has 93 residents living in 14 houses, scattered throughout a predominantly agrarian community. The other, *The City,* with its 203 residents in 60 houses, can be found in various neighbourhoods of a small Hansa-city, with the exception of one that is locally known as Little Istanbul, because of the many Turkish immigrants living there. All four of these COA locations are rather small in comparison with the average size of COA's locations, as their numbers of inhabitants do not exceed 250.

In the remainder of this essay I shall pay attention to those networking efforts on location that may be considered relevant to the production of the asylum seekers' self-reliance. First of all, I shall pay attention to COA's attempts at network control as part of the context in which the local networking is performed. Next, I shall report on the effects of COA's local networking efforts as they directly relate to *the asylum procedure.* Thirdly, I shall describe the local networking that is performed around the asylum seekers' everyday activities in and around the residences provided by COA. Fourthly, I shall also describe the activities that are officially labelled as "social and cultural" or as "day-structuring" by COA on location, but that when seen from the asylum seekers' point of view involve finding one's way about in the various local social networks provided outside. Fifthly, I shall discuss some aspects of the asylum seekers' participation in the *highly institutionalised local networks* that provide education, health care, and social work. And finally, I shall end with some comments on the individual networking the asylum seekers themselves appear to be performing.

My aim is, first, to analyse the *physical proximities and distances* that are performed in the networking on and around COA's locations, producing a *physical* organisation of activities both of the employees of the various organisations and of the asylum seekers that are locally involved. In this context I shall also pay attention to the input of "material actors," such as computer systems, buildings, and mobile phones (see Yanow 1996, 156ff.). The second purpose of this analysis is to demonstrate how this physical networking may also re-focus mutual expectations, and thereby reframe the mutual relationships between the various parties. The physical networking efforts on and around COA's locations may reinforce the *symbolical proximities and distances* that are locally performed. Accordingly, they may ultimately encourage the asylum seekers' self-reliance on location because the roles of all parties are also symbolically re-defined.

Local networking: beyond managerial control

The networking efforts I discuss here move beyond the networking that has become part and parcel of current public governance (see Kickert et al.1997). Such *complex networking* is established through managerial efforts. It is expected to create stable relationships between organisations and institutions around a specific issue (Kickert et al. 1997:30-31). When seen from this managerial point of view, this networking usually promises a certain open-ness and flexibility of such relationships. It also creates new power-dependencies and, consequently, some loss of managerial control.

To be sure, such "managed" local alliances with other parties have always been a part of COA's involvement in the local communities where it provides residences to asylum seekers. For instance, COA has always participated in the local "juridical chain" that performs the asylum procedures. And, similarly, it has always been associated with local public administration and with other local service providers. The local networking efforts I am discussing here, however, include informal networking efforts in particular. They do not only involve the institutional parties that may be considered relevant, but also many individuals and even "material" actors, such as bicycles and mobile phones.

Consequently, and not unlike many other managers in a similar predicament, COA's central managers and policy makers are intensely pre-occupied with what could be called the network's *"remote control."* Such remote control is usually performed by IT-supported infrastructures, aimed at routing individual clients and at performing an almost panoptical monitoring at the same time. In a similar vein, COA has introduced individual *case-management* as part of its new regime: individual counselling designed to facilitate either the incorporation of individual asylum seekers into the Netherlands, or their return to their countries of origin, depending on the outcome of their procedures. COA also reinforced its computerised client-following system in order to keep an eye on what is going on locally.

In this contribution, both the local counselling efforts and the computerised client following system will be treated as a part of the local negotiations. It is assumed here, following Yanow, that the actual local outcomes of the processes *cannot* be predetermined and controlled.

Enduring COA's regime

Apart from the circumstances that forced them to leave their countries of origin, I will assume that asylum seekers apply for admittance to the Netherlands of their own accord. Once they have applied for an asylum procedure in our country, however, they are delivered to the COA. Accordingly, there are many arrangements on location that may physically remind them of COA's surveillance and control.

For instance, the physical transfer of individual asylum seekers from one location to another. COA-central has developed a set of rules designed to "objectively" establish an individual's entitlement to a transfer, known as the "First In First Out" (FIFO) principle. The longer an asylum seeker stays in a "concentrated" residence like The Convent, the greater the chance that he or she will be allowed to move to a residence like The Hotel, or even to a private house like the ones provided in The Village or The City.

But before a decision is taken concerning an individual case, COA's medical officers related to the location where the applicant currently resides are expected to look over the available dossiers, and so, too, the local Aliens' Services representatives. The decision-making appears to an extent to be left up to their discretion. Moreover, it appears to be treated very much as a part of the local rewarding system performed by COA's personnel. The latter may not spare particularly those asylum seekers who think that they can speed up their transfers by "acting out." "When such an individual has quoted a preference for Amsterdam, we try our best to get him or her transferred to Groningen [in the far North] or to Limburg [in the far South] instead," one COA official once told me.

This state of affairs certainly frustrated COA's personnel at the receiving end of the transfer insofar as they expected – particularly with a private house on offer – that their prospective residents' capacities would be appropriately screened. Some of these personnel even suggested that their local considerations did not appear to affect the decision-making process at all. "It sometimes even looks as if they simply dumped the family to our residence." To the asylum seekers themselves, this way of dealing with their transfers simply confirms their dependency on fairly impenetrable machinations. One of them even confessed to being surprised by the offer of his current private house: "One of the COA people told me, 'I am going to give you a present'. Because I worked very hard from the beginning to learn Dutch". And another, "Maybe I've won the Bingo."

COA's surveillance

But many other activities on location can be physically related to COA's surveillance, too. For instance, COA and its partners are very keen on the prevention, or containment, of any incidents in which asylum seekers may be involved, although its physical surveillance was often performed, not by COA itself but by others on location. When one enters The Convent, for instance, the first thing one sees are the uniformed Security Guards, seated behind a glass wall, 24 hours a day, 7 days a week. In the Hotel, the local owner-manager and his personal staff performed the 7x24 hour's surveillance. But also on the locations with private housing, the asylum seekers not only had to submit to a specific set of house rules – e.g., no long-term visitors allowed, no pets – but also to weekly visits by the maintenance men. Accordingly, even there most asylum seekers reported "being permanently watched."

A more direct version of COA's surveillance, however, is provided by the so-called "stamping." As part of the juridical procedure, asylum seekers staying with COA are expected to demonstrate their availability for the procedure by regularly reporting to the Aliens Service. In the past, asylum seekers were expected to stamp on a weekly basis, but in the course of our research project the frequency of the reporting was reduced to once a month, mainly because of the considerable physical distances between the private houses and the offices of the Aliens' Service. The cynical argument provided was that the asylum seekers – and certainly the ones with private houses – had "too much to lose" by not showing up, which was the risk of the more frequent stamping requirement.

In The Convent and The Hotel the stamping frequency was also changed but the physical arrangements remained the same. Yet, on the two locations with private houses, The Village and The City, COA decided for various reasons – among them the local access to its IT-supported client surveillance system – to move its offices to another location, some distance away from the asylum seekers' homes. In both cases the new offices were relocated to the quite grim-looking site of a COA Reception Centre for asylum seekers newly arrived in the Netherlands. So, in this instance, while "distancing" itself, physically, from its asylum seekers, COA moved physically closer to the juridical chain. These physical changes also performed some symbolical changes for the asylum seekers involved. Most asylum seekers we interviewed appeared to appreciate this "new distance." It provided sufficient physical space for their relationships with COA's personnel to become more "businesslike."

The procedure moving front stage

The procedure itself is physically present, on location, in the form of the so-called "procedural meeting." In this meeting the Immigration and Naturalisation Service (IND) produces its data on the "state of affairs" concerning individual juridical cases, as does the representative of the Aliens' Service that is responsible for the material implementation of the procedure. COA's local representatives also report on the behaviour of individual asylum seekers. In the residences with private housing this meeting was performed somewhere "outside," but in The Convent and in The Hotel, most of the juridical chain partners had an office within the buildings themselves. Yet even there the procedural meeting remained "back stage."

Currently, however, ever since the Justice Department's insistence on a stricter application of the Aliens' Law, COA was not only expected to co-operate more closely with its juridical chain-partners, but also to make the procedure more transparent and tangible to the asylum seekers themselves. From now on COA was held physically responsible for some of the follow-up of the various procedural steps. Thus, COA's new case managers were expected to "counsel" the unfortunate asylum seekers whose applications in the so-called "first instance" had been rejected. Eventually, in the case of a final rejection, the COA would have to evict the asylum seekers from their homes. This move from "soft" to "hard" (to use COA's terms) applied to all residences we investigated.

A representative of a local Aliens Service summarised the symbolical advantages of this new counselling provided by COA's representatives. "When people have been visited by the COA-employee one week in advance, and it has been explained to them what the police was intending to do, then they at least can work through their emotions." Yet, although many of them discussed their procedures at length, the asylum seekers themselves did not recount such actions. COA's own employees had some trouble taking on their new role, too. They even appeared to regard a proper physical distance as a prerequisite for its adequate performance. In particular, COA's employees in The Convent and The Hotel wanted to move their offices to a more distant location. They tried to keep their distance from their clients by employing strict office hours but did not always succeed in avoiding chance meetings. More physical distance would help them avoid physical confrontations in the aftermath of the juridical decisions. At present, some of them even sounded quite worried: "You literally see them turn mad."

Performing activities in and around the house

Providing residence means providing locations where people can perform their everyday activities in and around the house, 7 days a week. These activities involve housekeeping, maintenance of the house, cooking, eating, sleeping, raising children, shopping, etc. In fact, this area of life provides an action net in which most people – women in particular – know exactly what to do, provided there is sufficient room available for them to do it. And, with all their cultural differences, asylum seekers are no exception to this rule. The physical qualities of the housing arrangements are very important in this area of life

(No) personal space

In this respect, The Convent and The Hotel in particular stood out in a negative sense. These locations cannot provide a "home", i.e., sufficient private space to perform most housekeeping activities. For instance, in the new wing of The Convent there were two floors with rather small rooms on either side of long corridors, each of which had a bathroom of its own. But, according to one of COA's employees, "those tiny family rooms are actually much too small…. We put refrigerators and TVs into them, but there is still the same number of people in the same number of square meters. They used to be called bedrooms but now they have been turned into complete flats." The asylum seekers all agree that the private space is cramped.

This situation was particularly aggravated by the "collectivisation" of the kitchens and of other provisions on these locations. For instance, in The Convent there were two kitchens with a large number of cooking stoves. The residents would take their cooking utensils and prepared their food in the kitchen, and then they returned to their rooms with their meal. One asylum seeker told us, "Our kitchen is on the ground floor. We live one floor up. That is always dangerous, walking up with hot pans, with children running up and down. I can drop it on their heads. That is always risky." The Hotel elicited similar comments. Moreover, the new COA-policy of self-reliance "allows" the asylum seekers to clean these provisions themselves – for less than one Euro an hour. Accordingly, the local state of hygiene became a common complaint among asylum seekers. The "publicness" of their private lives accentuated the crowdedness of these locations.

As could be expected, the asylum seekers' predicament in this area of life was quite different in The Village and The City, as locations with private houses. These houses might not be perfect, but the asylum seekers did at least have some private space. As one of them told us, "You get your own mail, your own phone…you can manage on your own, be independent." Moreover, this physical arrangement also provided sufficient room for COA's local personnel to manage their move from "we'll take care of it" to "help yourself," as required by the new regime. It allowed them to remain responsible for all financial arrangements and for the application of COA's house rules, but to minimize their face-to-face contacts with individual asylum seekers. The asylum seekers did not appear to mind.

Upon arrival they were visited not by COA's case-managers, but by the local maintenance men that also kept an eye on things. "After a couple of days I drop in to see whether everything is there," one of them told us. "Then I start explaining right away how to use the washing machine and other things, when to put the garbage out, and when the empty bottles are collected. Where the shops are in the neighbourhood, the sport facilities, the elementary school." In such practical matters the asylum seekers were left very much to their own devices. Yet many of them told us how they found their ways, and were helped, not only by the maintenance men but also by other informal local brokers (cf. Boissevain 1974). Some even reported being befriended by their neighbours. Generally speaking, though, it would be quite exaggerated to expect asylum seekers and their neighbours to share a "community feeling." They did appear to accommodate each other, and to gain a *distant trust* over time, *like the familiar strangers* that are characteristic of so many modern neighbourhoods (see Anderiesen and Reijndorp 1990).

The case of The Convent suggests that this may also be due to the local physical arrangements. There, the residents only needed to leave the building to do their supermarket shopping or to visit friends and relatives, and most of this was performed outside the village. The local social consequence was quite predictable: a never-ending performance of mutual distrust. At all locations, however, the asylum seekers did report confrontations on the basis of racial connotations. For instance, when they went shopping in the local supermarket: "Yesterday I had to open my bags. And when I am looking around for a present, they ask: 'Can I help you?' And when I say that I am just looking they ask again. They're just controlling you." A local owner of a supermarket near The Convent confirms that asylum seekers – with very little money and plenty of time on their hands – are very likely to browse a lot, like many other people in similar situations. But unlike those others, and "because my hair is black," they appeared not to go unnoticed. Another local supermarket manager near The Hotel confirmed the latter, providing his own reasons. According to him, asylum seekers perpetrated nine out of ten shopliftings. The new local proximity of the asylum seekers encourages local distancing as well.

Finding ways of one's own

A very important issue that also affects their self-reliance is that asylum seekers are not allowed to work in the Netherlands. This means that they have to find ways to spend their days in another way. This is why in most asylum seekers' residences the activities that are called "social and cultural" in Dutch policy language, or "day structuration" by the COA, are considered very important. In concentrated residences such as The Convent and The Hotel, many of these activities are organised indoors. Yet in The Hotel it was noted that the asylum seekers appeared to spend much of their time outside because of its well-situated location. Accordingly, and as most social geographers would be able to tell us, it is not so much the physical qualities of the location itself as its *spatial embeddedness in the local environment* that appears to be important. So are some of the material provisions: not only money, but also bicycles, mobile phones, and other means of communication and transport.

Although COA furnishes its residences and pays the rent, and, to an extent, gas and electricity, the asylum seekers' weekly allowances remain very low: 39 Euro a week per adult, 16 Euro per child. Moreover, most asylum seekers are not allowed to drive a car because it is very difficult for them to obtain a valid driving license in the Netherlands. So asylum seekers are quite dependent on local public transport, walking, and on the bicycle of course. COA often provides a small amount of extra money to buy the latter and most locations offer cycle lessons and bicycle repair courses. We were confronted with many stories about the inability to cycle, and about broken bicycles and the impossibility to repair them, or about the costs associated with bicycles and bicycle repair. For these asylum seekers, the bicycle appears to symbolise getting nowhere in the Netherlands.

Depending on the local circumstances, the distances from the asylum seekers' residences to, for instance, sport halls and cheap supermarkets in a nearby town, may turn out to be quite overwhelming. This was the case in The Convent, but also, and more surprisingly, in some of the hamlets around The Village. "Good" locations, as far as the local distances are concerned, were provided by The Hotel and, with the exception of the distant hamlets around The Village, by the two locations with private houses. In these places asylum seekers did seem to meet quite regularly in local community centres. They went to Christian churches or to a nearby mosque, or participated in local sport clubs. They were even involved in voluntary activities, for instance at their children's elementary schools.

Yet, as social geography teaches us once more, differences between individuals according to the age and life situation, and the actual physical mobility of the asylum seekers may rate such physical distances differently. We found evidence on all locations that asylum seekers are like everyone else in this respect. Young people are more mobile than older ones; men more than women; and women without children, or with partners and children, more that single mothers. Moreover, we found that traumatised people, of any age and circumstance, may not be inclined to move at all.

But there are also symbolical distances to be bridged. Sometimes it proved quite difficult for the asylum seekers to find access at all. In some cases, COA's employees or other people in the direct environment had to perform as informal local brokers. For instance, in The Village, where a local COA-employee was also the president of the local soccer club, and introduced some of "his" asylum seekers to his club: "The asylum seekers know I am the club's president, so they know where to find me." A woman we interviewed in one of the hamlets around The Village illustrated the possible effect of the absence of such local mediation. In spite of the "advice" given to her by COA she had a hard time finding out exactly where to go and whom to approach in order to join a women's club she wanted to take part in. So she eventually decided not to go.

Stuck between integration and return
A standard provision for asylum seekers in the Netherlands is the compulsory language courses in Dutch. They are financed by COA and taught by local volunteers associated with the local Refugee Council or with other local organisations. Sometimes the quali-

ty of these courses is very good, and, although both style and quality of performance can be locally very different, all locations provide them. With COA's new regime, however, asylum seekers that have been given their "first negative" are not allowed to take these courses any more.

Accordingly, the courses became symbolic for the "integration into Dutch culture," as opposed to "the return to one's country of origin." At The Hotel, for instance, where the language course provided by COA itself nearly lost all its pupils, most local volunteers moved to another location where they continued teaching, supported by the local government of a nearby town. Quite a few of the asylum seekers we interviewed followed them there, in spite of the longer distance they had to overcome. In The City and the Village, however, where the community's own regional practical colleges provided the courses in Dutch, the local preferences took a quite different turn in the face of the new procedure. Some of the local representatives of the colleges even questioned the relevance of providing Dutch courses at all to people who, in any case, were not expected to be permitted to remain in the country. They were also willing to provide other courses, and in English, too! Most asylum seekers we interviewed on these locations, however, appeared to be not too keen to make use of this generous offer, perhaps because they did not like its possible implications: their return to their countries of origin. "Why should I choose?"

Negotiating institutional boundaries

We have already seen how individual local brokers may facilitate individual asylum seekers' access to local churches and football clubs. In the case of more formal institutions, such as education and health care, however, the situation appears to be more complicated. Institutional providers in education and health care usually perform intake procedures and diagnostic repertoires of their own aimed at the "proper" selection and classification of their (prospective) participants. So, in spite of the fact that such provisions are often locally available by definition, and their access is relatively free, they may provide some institutional boundary patrol. The need to negotiate these institutional boundaries may even prevail over the institution's physical proximity.

Indeed, the asylum seekers' access to primary health care illustrates that institutional participation may not always turn out as simple as it appears. All asylum seekers in the Netherlands are entitled to some degree of primary health care and to all other health care provisions as well. Moreover, most of these provisions are offered at locations not too far from the asylum seekers' residences; if not, the means to get to them is provided by the COA. However, a local officer of the so-called Medical Service for Asylum seekers (MOA) suggests that there may be some learning processes involved with the access to Dutch health care institutions. According to her, many asylum seekers appear to expect too much from Western medicine, anyway, and have to get used to the "non-invasive" Dutch traditions. Moreover, according to this officer, asylum seekers are not always acquainted with such apparently simple things like an "appointment." On the contrary, they appear to "consider it quite ridiculous not to be able to just shamble into the doctor's office at a self-appointed time. Or they are accustomed to just sit down in the waiting room and wait for three hours or more." These symbolical aspects involved in the asylum seekers' access to the health care system appear to confront them and their health care providers with some cultural confrontations.

However, the local elementary schools are often quoted as the ultimate example, where the impact of such cultural confrontations appears to be very limited indeed. With the exception of the traditional asylum seekers' residences, of which The Convent is an apt illustration, all asylum seekers' children of "school age" are to be admitted, nowadays, into regular local elementary schools. In the Netherlands most of these schools are located a walking distance away. Particularly in the locations with independent houses and at The Hotel, all asylum seekers' children were "guided" directly by COA to local elementary schools.

However, there are some specific Dutch traditions in providing access to elementary schools. For instance, there is the strict Dutch adage of (denominationally) free school choice, according to which parents that insist upon another school have the right to choose. Some of our professional respondents in The Village and The City even suggested that Islamic parents might prefer Christian schools for their children, but we found very few asylum seeker parents who did.

As a matter of fact, the asylum seekers' children from The Hotel were all attending a single non-denominational school. The City and Village children attended neighbourhood schools from a variety of denominations, and their physical proximity appeared to overrule all other considerations. A representative of the school in the case of The Hotel even argued that attendance at a nearby elementary school would facilitate the integration of both the children and their parents into Dutch society in a physical manner. "It grows on them as a natural thing, parents taking their children to school, everyday, and their children find playmates, playing at other children's homes."

Yet there were also teachers who suggested that the children's parents might also have to pay a symbolical price for this integration. "I think our pupils here are taught to be independent, open-minded, and so on. And these parents are not used to that, in their own cultures...." Some of the parents mentioned how their children were particularly confronted with the affluence of their Dutch peers. Most of the parents, however, appeared to be particularly keen on improving the futures of their children. They were mainly interested in their academic achievements, and even appeared to dislike it when the school compared their children with other immigrant children whose achievements seemed inferior. And, indeed, according to their teachers, many of the asylum seekers children learned very fast, and appeared also to settle quite easily – almost too easily, according to some teachers – to their new Dutch environments. The symbolical boundaries may still be there to be negotiated, but, in spite of quite a few cultural confrontations, the negotiations appeared to be both meaningful and manageable to all parties involved. Moreover, they appeared to be quite independent of the physical distances that were to be performed.

Three networking patterns: mutual physical avoidance, individual involvement, and institutional boundary patrol

That COA's physical networking may also symbolically provide spaces for the asylum seekers on location to perform self-reliance in their everyday negotiations may now be sufficiently clear. It may also be evident that COA's performance in this respect differs, if we compare its traditional concentrated locations, such as The Convent, with its locations providing private housing. Yet, I also think that I have demonstrated that the impact of this local networking may also differ, depending especially on the area of life, or even on the action net under consideration. It is along these lines that I would like to point out some specific patterns with special reference to the COA-locations with private houses.

Firstly, there is the pattern of *physical avoidance* coupled with *remote control*. It is mainly produced by COA itself and by its juridical chain partners in and around the action net that performs the asylum procedure. This pattern appears to have helped COA itself to effectively change its role, and to perform the new, much stricter regime of the Justice Department. In particular, the locations with private housing (The City and The Village) provided COA's personnel with sufficient space to effectively move its repertoire from "soft" to "hard" through its new involvement with the juridical procedure. The asylum seekers themselves, however, appeared also to appreciate this new distance, although they, too, acknowledge that this certainly would not change the nature of COA's regime. In the end, it does not affect the asylum seekers' ultimate dependency on the juridical procedure, nor the very limited juridical self-reliance they are granted in this respect.

Secondly, more self-reliance has been created in the pattern that is produced by the asylum seekers' own local activities in and around the residence. I would like to label this pattern the asylum seekers' *individual involvement in local social networks*, both in a physical and in a symbolical sense. Here, also, the locations with private housing helped COA's own employees to manage their retreat from a policy of "we'll take care of it" to one of "help yourself," although COA's local maintenance men still continued to perform their weekly surveillance. However, this pattern is centred much more around the initiatives of the asylum seekers. Many of them did find sufficient room to perform initiatives of their own, particularly in the local action nets performing sports and religious matters, although in some cases they had to be helped by local brokers. But even if the asylum seekers were left to their own devices in this respect, they did not appear to mind.

Thirdly, the institutionalised regimes on and around the locations we investigated appeared to perform a different pattern altogether. I would call this a pattern of *institutional boundary patrol,* in which the asylum seekers are expected to negotiate the symbolic boundaries the institutions provide. Here, the physical distances do count but appear to be much less relevant to the asylum seekers' own negotiations. Moreover, here COA and its regime appear to move into the background while the professional representatives of the institutions appear to take its place. Most importantly, however, the asylum seekers themselves are explicitly expected to try to "fit in" or "integrate" into these local action nets. Yet in spite of the general physical availability of institutions of this kind, particularly where the latter is concerned, some questions remain. For instance, how do the local institutions perform their gate-keeping efforts, and how do they deal with asylum seekers in this respect? How do they deal with them on an everyday basis while their professional treatments are performed? Do they also practice some *reverse integration.*[2]

Self-reliance?

However, in spite of this apparent improvement in the spaces allowed to individual asylum seekers to perform self-reliance, there still may be some doubt as to the degree in which COA provides its asylum seekers with any self-reliance at all. After all, the individual networking efforts as performed by the asylum seekers themselves provides an indispensable resource for performing self-reliance. For instance, like other migrants they are often embedded in trans-national networks with their compatriots and relevant others. And although, as we have seen, some of this networking may even be encouraged, to an extent, on and around COA's locations, most of it is actually being performed on a world wide basis, and quite independently of COA or even of the Netherlands.

Such individual networking is, in fact, considered to be quite decisive for any individual migrant's future, and the asylum seekers are no exception to this rule. Even in our research project we found some evidence confirming the argument of the American anthropologist Portes (Portes 1998; see also Engbersen et al. 1999), that the local embeddedness of the asylum seekers' movements does improve their individual "social capital" accordingly. Portes suggests that in particular "individual social networking" reinforces the capacity of individuals to command scarce resources by virtue of their membership in these networks. The individual asylum seekers' access to the Dutch system of education may prove to be a case in point. Yet, we should also be reminded, here, of the fact that in the Netherlands asylum seekers are not allowed to work. Accordingly, we also found plenty of evidence that most asylum seekers were quite eager to maintain relationships with their countrymen or with other migrants by using all available means, including the Internet and mobile phones. This specific networking capital often helps them, both within and outside our country, to provide access to the countries – and to the provisions – of their preference.

But, of course, we should not forget that asylum seekers are migrants of a very specific kind. They present themselves to COA and to the other juridical chain partners to have their claims assessed, and to be granted a "proper" status as a refugee in the Netherlands, not as a migrant per se. Accordingly, asylum seekers are often quite dependent on the relationships and involvements they develop in and around their residences, and on the resources COA has to offer. Moreover, we must realise that the specific *liminality* (Turner 1969) of their situation – "in between" being allowed to live in the Netherlands and being accepted as a "proper" inhabitant – may encourage them to think quite instrumentally about their efforts to integrate into Dutch society, regarding them simply as a possible "way into" our country. Thus, it may be considered a shame or simply a matter of course, but, due to the fact that its work is so closely related to the asylum seekers' juridical procedures, COA provides very little "real" networking capital to the migrants committed to its care.

Notes

1   The material presented here has been reported in Dutch in Marja Gastelaars et al., 2002. I wish to thank Janneke van der Horst and Marlous van Leeuwen for their extensive fieldwork, and Karin Geuijen for developing the initial design of the project and supervising it. I am responsible for the theoretical framework presented in the final report. I wish to thank Arie de Ruijter for his encouragements that I take on this task. I also wish to thank COA, Jos van der Werff in particular, for their extensive material and immaterial support of the fieldwork. I also wish to thank my colleague Marie-Jeanne Schiffelers for her comments on an earlier version of this essay.
2   A phrase coined by Anderiesen and Reijndorp (Lammers and Reijndorp 2000:6).

Bibliography

Anderiesen, Gerard, and Arnold Reijndorp. 1990. *Eigenlijk een geniale wijk. Dagelijks leven in de Indische buurt.* Amsterdam: Het Spinhuis.

Boissevain, Jeremy. 1974. *Friends of Friends. Networks, Manipulators and Coalitions.* Oxford: Blackwell.

COA. 2001. *Inrichtingsplan Opvang.* Rijswijk. COA.

Czarniawska, Barbara. 2000. *A City Reframed. Managing Warsaw in the 1990s.* Amsterdam: Harwood Academic Publishers.

Engbersen, Godfried, Joanne van der Leun, Richard Staring, and Jude Kehla. 1999. *Inbedding en uitsluiting van illegale vreemdelingen.* Amsterdam: Boom.

Gastelaars, Marja. (in press.) Performing the clients' self-reliance in the public sector. The case of the asylum seekers' residences in the Netherlands. Paper submitted to *Social Work and Social Sciences Review.*

Gastelaars, Marja, Karin Geuijen, Marlous van Leeuwen, and Janneke van der Horst. 2002. *Tussen arena en netwerk. Leefbaarheid en draagvlak bij de lokale opvang van asielzoekers.* Amsterdam: SWP.

Geuijen, Karin. 1998. *Asielzoekers aan het woord. Cliëntwaardering in Asielzoekerscentrum Rosmalen.* Utrecht: CBM.

Kickert, Walter J.M., Erik-Hans Klijn, and Joop F.M. Koppenjan. 1997. *Managing Complex Networks. Strategies for the Public Sector.* London, Thousand Oaks, New Delhi: Sage.

Lammers, Bart, and Arnold Reijndorp. 2000. *Buitengewoon. Nieuwe vormen van wonen, zorg en service in IJburg.* Rotterdam: Nai.

Portes, Alejandro. 1998. Social capital: its origins and applications on modern sociology. *Annual Review of Sociology* 22:1-24.

Turner, Victor. 1969. *The Ritual Process.* Ithaca, New York: Cornell University Press.

Yanow, Dvora. 1996. *How does a policy mean? Interpreting policy and organizational actions.* Washington D.C.: Georgetown University Press.

25

Constraints and Constructions of Meaning in an Asylum Seekers' Residence Centre

Karin Geuijen

From my fieldwork journal

The former monastery next to a busy road about four kilometres away from the town centre, in which the asylum seekers' residence centre is located, is old. Behind the big wooden door of the entrance, placed in the middle of the symmetrical façade, two uniformed men in the porter's lodge ask for my identity papers. I have to fill out my name on a form, stating the time of entrance, and the reason of my coming here. Several people stand in front of the glass wall of the porter's lodge to have a look at the list of names of people who received post today, and they want to collect their letters. Others ask for aspirin. Still others want to know on which telephone their incoming telephone call can be answered. Passing through the swinging doors leads me to the tiled entrance hall. People speak on the public telephones in many different languages to enquire about the loved ones left behind in their own countries, or about their asylum procedure, while noisy children run around. Climbing up the wide stone stairs brings me to the long corridors left and right, with many doors on each side. Behind each of these doors there is a packed room with at least two single beds, one table with some chairs, two or more small cupboards, a small refrigerator and a television set. In each room lives a family or at least two single persons. Each corridor has a door of the common kitchen which contains about eight gas cookers, some sinks, and many small locked cupboards. The aroma of food from every part of the world is mixed with the smell of damp and dirt. A bit further down the corridor one finds the common showers and toilets. They are built from cheap materials, some doors are broken, some washbasins are clogged. About thirty women, men, and children of all ages, nationalities, religions, have to use them. On the first floor there is the recreation room in which two men play ping-pong. Other men sit at some tables talking to each other or just staring. There are no women around. Some staff members walk around the corridors I am walking through, carrying walky-talkies so they can contact each other at any moment. Bundles of keys hang from their belts. All those keys fit locked doors. One of them is for the separate toilets for staff members. Others are for their own office and their colleagues' offices. Each one also has a passkey that fits the locks of the doors to asylum seeker's rooms. In a corner of the building is the locked door to the director's room.

Asylum seekers' residence centres (*asielzoekerscentra*, AZC) are constantly in the news in the Netherlands. Much is written and said about reception and accommodation of asylum seekers, usually in connection with the high inflow, the shortage of accommodations, the long waits, or the resistance on the part of surrounding residents. Few consider the views of asylum seekers and staff at the centre concerning the accommodations. This article addresses the significance that accommodations at AZCs have for asylum seekers, as well as for the staff and the management.[1] I will demonstrate how these various groups of actors interact with one another and try to deal with the very narrowly circumscribed conditions set by the social and political context of life at the AZCs. To interpret this situation I will use Martin Parker's ideas on organizational culture, which he defines as the "contested local organization of generalities" (2000:214-215). This definition implies three aspects. First, widely generalized assumptions always inform the terrain on which local organizational understandings emerge. Second, the existence of divisions within organizations in regard to responses to change is central in the constitution of local cultures. To Parker, these divisions are common possible classifications of difference and similarity, of "us" and "them." Third, Parker points out that all organizations make different local mediations of general assumptions.

In this article I will show some of the classifications that are made at the AZCs in which I did my research. First I will introduce the three actors. It turns out that the three general groups one would be inclined to see at first glance – asylum seekers, staff, and managers – are more ambiguous than one would expect them to be, and form alliances with one other in ways one would not expect them to. "Us" and "them" turn out not to be so straightforwardly defined. It demonstrates that classifying is about making multiple claims about membership categories (Parker 2000:87). Second, I will show how the power imbalance between these groups affects their definitions of the situation. I will point out some generalised assumptions on which understandings emerge in the AZCs discussed here, and show how some classifications get to be successful by using those generalised assumptions in specific ways. Third, I will describe how these groups try to cope with the situation they can alter only marginally. Finally, the external conditions of the AZCs will be discussed in further detail, making clear that the political, institutional, and societal context is crucial for what can and cannot be said and done within AZCs.

Three groups

The AZC comprises three general groups with divergent interests: residents, staff, and management. However, they are not as unambiguous as might be thought at first sight. I will analyse this with the help of Parker's idea of the "process of making multiple claims about membership categories" (2000:87). The thousands of people living in AZCs classify themselves and others not only in terms of nationality, education, age, gender, or previous position in the country of origin, but also with respect to legal status and other aspects. Many "us" and "them" classifications are made depending on the context. They overlap and are contested in a dynamic process. The differences are valued accordingly.

The A-status which one receives after being acknowledged as a "real refugee" is not a neutral fact but a means of escape and a token of acknowledgement by the surroundings in general: "we" the real refugees and "them" who still have to prove they are. Nationality is another important criterion for distinction. Asylum seekers from countries such as Iraq and Iran are likely to look down on their counterparts from African nations: "we" the white people, who have serious asylum claims, and "them" the black people, who just laugh all day and therefore cannot have any asylum claims that should be taken seriously.

Living with a family or alone is anther possible classification. These classifications are, of course, not arbitrary. They can be made because of more or less common assumptions within and outside of the organisation: legal categories in the Refugee Convention, racial images, images of family values and care etc. These categories overlap: a person can be an asylum seeker whose first application was rejected, and be an Iranian and a woman who lives on her own, all at the same time. Depending on the context at a certain moment, one or the other category will be dominant for this person, and as a consequence one or the other membership. It is not difficult to imagine that these multiple identifications might lead to problems in every day life at an AZC.

The staff is not homogeneous either. Differences exist in terms of background and education, and in the kind of work they do in different areas of the AZC, such as in the medical facility or the technical services. Here, too, differences in status are obvious. Each AZC has only one director.[2] There are large differences between the various directors of the AZCs. When a number of new AZCs were established within a short period of time, some AZC social workers were promoted to directors without any specific training or experience. Others had been working for years as directors in other business sectors before becoming the director of an AZC. Among themselves, directors discuss these and other differences. Employees at the head office of the Central Asylum Seekers' Reception Services (COA) in Rijswijk also spend time discussing these differences. All the groups involved label these distinctions in terms of their management capacities, and/or in terms of their commitment.

Asylum seekers as involuntary clients

Asylum seekers are involuntary clients at an AZC. Lipsky (1980) has shown that being an involuntary client means putting up with a virtually limitless amount of indifference, humiliation, or discomfort. The situation also affects people's self-perception and makes them feel dependent, powerless, or angry.

Asylum seekers experience an added dimension at an AZC: they are non-citizens who have submitted a request to another state. This position complicates the relationship considerably: what claim do they have? Asylum seekers are often keenly aware of this situation, as apparent from the following statement by an Iranian women who has been waiting at an AZC for nearly three years without receiving a definitive decision regarding her asylum application:

> I understand the Dutch government's problems with accommodating asy-
> lum seekers. I am not the only one. I should not expect too much from

the government. Sometimes I feel I am a burden to the people here. We
have to accept the rules as they are here. This is not our native country....As asylum seekers we should be grateful to this society.

During this transaction with the organization, people are subjected to clear limits. They
forfeit part of their identity. They are prohibited from practising their profession or
studying, and receive an allowance that is insufficient for them to engage in outside
activities. Residents of a care facility are very dependent. In the course of the transaction the client's encapsulation can become so great that they end up being hospitalised.
Some of the symptoms consist of a lack of self-esteem, the doldrums, and apathy.
Sometimes the client's personal input consists of nothing more than maintaining a
recognisable personality. Since asylum seekers are not allowed to study or to work to
earn a living, it is as though there is no real "outside" world for them, no world for
them outside of the centre.

Experiences of asylum seekers at AZCs
The asylum seekers I interviewed in reference to the accommodations often raised
issues they considered important. Everybody mentioned the unfathomable legal procedure, insecurity about the outcome, and about how long they would still have to wait.
They also mentioned their fear of deportation, and total dependence on an institution
they were powerless to influence. "Iraqis do not have to prove anything, whereas I
have to present written evidence of everything for them to believe me." "Treating us
this way is inhuman." "First they make us sick, then they award us C-status. If I get sick,
I don't even need the C-status to stay. Is this democracy? What kind of system is it?"
    The asylum procedure gives rise to rampant speculation in the extensive network
of rumours within and among the AZCs. This grapevine of rumours exists primarily
because most people find the asylum procedure obtuse and have no idea why everything
takes so long. They do not understand why the first decision is negative for nearly everybody, or why some people do and others do not ultimately receive a residence permit.
    A second issue concerns *the long wait* at the AZC, the sense of being in limbo, of
being superfluous, useless, and the lack any purpose in this way of life. "All we do is
eat and sleep, we live like animals." "Each day is the same, every day I know what will
happen; it's killing me." No means are available for making independent choices, to
run one's life as one sees fit: "My life is slipping by. For years I have done nothing but
wait. I used to work very hard. Now the time just passes. I could do a lot for this country. Why won't they let me work?" This feeling relates to a lack of self-esteem and identity. "I feel worthless, like a disposable object." "The psychological effects or traumatic
experiences from the homeland are less serious than the ones here. We are stuck here
for three or four years without any prospects." "I used to fear dying; now I fear going
insane." The long wait in limbo has other consequences as well: "People rarely have
much to occupy their time at an AZC. Boredom leads them to gossip. People need to
chat. There is far too much gossip here."

Many people are terribly *lonely*. They are afraid or unable to contact those they have left behind. They hardly know anybody in the Netherlands and are sometimes suspicious of the others at the AZC. They find little support and understanding among fellow asylum seekers. "We talk about only about football and life at the AZC, not about anything else." Apparently, they receive little support from staff members in taking decisions or in dealing with emotions and tensions. "They say they understand, but they don't. You have no idea what life is like here."

Privacy was also mentioned often in the interviews. Nearly all single individuals share a room, and families living in one or two rooms find the situation virtually unbearable, especially for extended periods: "We share a room with our two children. The eldest is being treated at a regional institute for mental healthcare. We simply cannot get an additional room. We have separated the children's bunk beds with a curtain." "We do everything in one room: sleeping, eating, studying, and watching television. The situation is difficult." Nor is there any privacy between the rooms: "Everybody hears and sees everything here."

In about half of the interviews, AZC residents mentioned feelings of *insecurity*. Women and girls, in particular, mentioned feeling unsafe at times: "I do not feel safe. What kinds of people live here? Especially because I am a woman. I do not feel this way when I am with other women. I have a son and a daughter. I worry more about my daughter. A Somali girl was nearly raped here." Another woman said: "The showers and lavatories are not really safe. Sometimes men open the door. I never go to the recreation area. Men smoke and drink there and follow me around asking about things that are none of their business." A man said: "I do not feel safe. There are a lot of strange people here. I am one of the dangerous people because I cannot control myself. I am a danger to myself and perhaps to others as well. The court feels the same way." Parents *worry about their children*. A Somali father explained:

> "My daughter is nearly three. She was born here. As a parent, I feel very sad when she asks when we will move into a house....Children bear the brunt of this situation. They do not speak their native language and do not know Dutch. At the AZC they see people with all different backgrounds, cultures and languages. Children see a lot of bad things: people who are drunk, or aggressive, or traumatized, or drug abusers. These people resort to these pursuits to avoid feeling how time passes. They have no other option. But if a child grows up this way, what will happen later? The child will know no better than to follow the same course."

Some associate the AZC with a prison, in part because of the uniformed guards at the entrance, but also because they can never really get away; they lack the means to run their own lives, and the wait is endless. "The situation is worse than being in prison. At least there you know when you will be released." During their stay at an AZC, asylum seekers have to get a stamp from the Aliens Police every week. "Every week for five years. It feels inhuman. I had to do the same in Algeria, so you can imagine how I feel about it."

Staff as street-level bureaucrats

The work of AZC staff is generally divided into two main tasks. Some staff members work on the "material" tasks (the equipment, buildings, communal facilities, and rooms). They plan who is to live in which room, they check the safety and hygiene, they are responsible for the cleaning of the building etc. Others do the "immaterial" tasks (the so called "socials"): they monitor clients, they organise several activities (sports, language courses etc.), they inform clients about the organisation's rules, they inform the public about the AZC etc.

AZC staff are street-level bureaucrats. Lipsky defines street-level bureaucrats as public service workers who interact directly with clients and have substantial discretion in the execution of their work (1980:3). Generally, they take *ad hoc* decisions that target individuals. Typical street-level bureaucrats include teachers, policemen, social workers and healthcare workers. These people's main attraction to their work is usually the opportunity to help people, in addition to job security and good fringe benefits (Lipsky, 1980:185). In the process they encounter several problems inherent in this type of organization: the organization's general objective is obvious, but agency goals are vague and sometimes contradictory. This problem is related to "society's" contradictory impulses (Lipsky, 1980: p. 165). The same holds true for the accommodations for asylum seekers. The facilities should be basic but also humane. These concepts can be confusing. On the one hand, asylum seekers should not be an excessive expense and should not integrate. On the other hand, they are not supposed to earn a living and must be able to acculturate as quickly as possible once they leave the AZC. Therefore, they should not become hospitalized.

Another problem for staff in these types of organizations is that their work is evaluated according to very vague criteria. Supervisors have difficulty perceiving how staff perform their individual tasks: they do not observe the direct contact between staff and residents and often have only reports from the staff to go by. Many asylum seekers are unaware that a complaint procedure exists. When they learn about it, they believe that filing a complaint will be of little use.

Directors as middle managers

The administration of an AZC is a typical case of middle management. The director is in charge of the "division," which he runs fairly autonomously. He also mediates between the needs and requirements of the staff and the central COA in Rijswijk. On the one hand, managers are concerned with performance and costs, and those aspects of process which expose them to critical scrutiny. Staff members seek to maintain their autonomy but at the same time have to comply with their superior's directives. This may cause them to perceive their interests as separate from management's interests, especially when they consider the management policy objectives to be illegitimate (Lipsky 1980). On the other hand, the director perceives himself as part of the AZC and its staff, while at the same time being in conflict with the Rijswijk's interests.

Many AZC managers hardly have any contact with the asylum seekers living in "their" AZC. This sometimes leads to conflicts with staff members who are in continuous interaction with clients. AZCs are part of a modern bureaucracy which owes its legitimacy to its commitment to standards of fairness and equity. Lipsky rightly points out that street-level bureaucrats are constantly confronted with the apparent injustice of treating people alike.

Power imbalance in the struggle to define problems and solutions

Being unwilling clients affects both asylum seekers and the organization. The organization does not need to take complaints very seriously. It has little to lose from disgruntled clients. The organization considers the respective interests differently of those of clients, those of the "government," or those of "society" (powerful and less powerful parties). The organization's mission is central: managing the presence of asylum seekers in the Netherlands and ensuring that these people remain available for the asylum procedure.

All service organizations use control methods to maintain order. The AZC also has many such "order makers": reporting to the reception, the administration's fixed hours of business, the information desk, the infirmary, getting a stamp from the Aliens Police on Wednesday afternoon. These rules curtail the freedom of movement for clients. At the AZC, like elsewhere, the arrangement of time and space often caters more to the organization's needs than to those of the residents. In many cases asylum seekers are unaware of the reasons behind these rules.

An ongoing power imbalance exists between the agents in the AZC. One example of this power imbalance concerns the use of space at the AZC. As I noted earlier, staff members close their office doors behind them. They also use separate lavatories that are not open to asylum seekers. They carry around large bunches of keys, often chained to their belts.

The power imbalances in the "definition of the situation" surface in various ways, within both the AZC and the broader environment. Aside from the main office of the Central Asylum Seekers' Reception Services (COA), management and staff of individual centres have adopted several fashionable terms, such as "self-sufficiency," "individual responsibility for the residential conditions," "co-determination," "representation," the "enterprising client" etc. Whereas management and staff adopted these terms, the asylum seekers do not always interpret them in the same way as the management and the staff do. The differences in interpretation lead to disagreement about cleaning and other issues. Staff and management often believe the residents should share the cleaning responsibilities between each other, being "responsible for the residential situation." Many asylum seekers feel that the upper levels of the bureaucracy – the director, for instance – should arrange for cleaning because they themselves foresee a lot of trouble with their neighbours if they have to negotiate with them on this subject. If things will not work out, which is not unlikely because people do not choose to enter these relationships, they will still be forced to be neighbours.

These discrepant definitions of the situation can be applied to volunteer work as well. The COA views volunteer work as a way to involve asylum seekers in activities. Asylum seekers are rarely interested. A lot of them know little of the substance or potential opportunities that such employment might have in the Netherlands. The volunteers whom the asylum seekers come into contact with in the Netherlands are usually only AZC volunteers, like Dutch teachers. Many asylum seekers assume that these people are unprofessional and just cannot find a regular job. In their countries of origin, most volunteer work is for charity. Moreover, they prefer to be paid for their labour rather than "work for nothing." Some of them have, however, expressed an interest in practical training at a company to demonstrate their skills. Such arrangements are prohibited in the Netherlands for asylum seekers because it is thought this would lead to too much integration into society.

In interpreting these cases, what may be helpful is Parker's suggestion (2000:214) that groups in organisations use some generalised assumptions on which understandings emerge in specific ways. Local staff and management use phrases like "individual responsibility for the residential environment" to motivate asylum seekers to clean the AZC. They also try to motivate asylum seekers to do volunteer work. These kinds of actions and beliefs have their roots in theories on individualisation. The claim that is expressed about taking responsibility has persuasive power to staff and management because its roots are taken for granted. Individualization is generally perceived as good and important, but it has another side to it that is not mentioned in this context. It is not only about taking responsibility, but also about having a say and having control. Staff and management express only one of these sides. Even though they are – at least to some extent – interacting with asylum seekers on an every day basis, they may not be constantly aware of the limitations asylum seekers face in their every day lives. Limitations that range from not being allowed to choose another place to live, not being allowed to be able to sleep in a separate room from one's children, not being allowed to work and earn ones own money, and not being allowed to learn to speak the language well. These limitations for asylum seekers are not always completely balanced by the claims to take responsibility by asylum seekers.

Asylum seekers on the other hand do not voice their opposition in a similar vein, using generally accepted assumptions. They express their problems with this situation as personal problems. Their opposition can thus be dismissed as being non-cooperative. As Parker writes "...organisations are populated and influenced by people who occupy different power positions depending on their access to wider common assumptions that effectively legitimate certain actions and beliefs but not others" (2000:226). Being able to present a certain definition of the situation as real, by high status or well off people or groups, makes it real in its consequences. In the AZC this leads to poignant examples in which neither staff nor asylum seekers are able to handle the situation. I will return to this below.

On some occasions the various parties adopt each other's definitions. Structurally weaker parties take over definitions from their more powerful counterparts. So some asylum seekers said, "The staff members try but are limited by the rules imposed from above." In some cases staff members also represent the interests of the management. "He is resisting the demands recently imposed from above but can do little more than he already is." Sometimes parties explicitly appeal to each other for understanding. "I am merely doing my job." The above differences between the interest groups indicate that the triad – management, staff, and residents – is overly simplistic. At various moments members of one or more of the three groups enter coalitions with those of another group.

This struggle is also affected by the absence of direct advocates for the issues within a certain AZC. The representatives of VluchtelingenWerk (Dutch Refugee Council) at the AZCs do not always view this role as their responsibility. They mainly provide legal advice. Many residents do not consider the residents' committee – if one exists – to be their representative and advocate. Moreover, resident turnover is high, whereas the staff and management remain the same. These last parties protect their interests, either independently or jointly, via the works council. Finally, many asylum seekers have no prospects for influencing decisions about their situation and are even afraid to speak up, for who knows how such action might affect the asylum procedure.

Each of these heterogeneous groups – asylum seekers, staff, and management – also relates to a different external environment. For asylum seekers the way their asylum procedure proceeds is of supreme importance. Their feelings about (almost every other aspect of) their life depend on it. For staff, the legal procedure has only very limited importance. It makes hardly any difference for their daily work which decision the IND has made about a client's request. Staff members often know nothing about why individual asylum seekers felt forced to leave their country. Some staff members say they do not want to be informed about these reasons or about the proceedings of the asylum procedure of individual clients because it makes it more difficult for them to do their job in – what they deem – a professional manner. So staff and clients who interact on a daily basis interpret completely other contexts as relevant. For the management, still another context is of the utmost importance. For them The Hague – i.e. parliament and the Department of Justice – is crucial. At that place the limits and opportunities which COA gets or can create for itself are determined. For individual asylum seekers this is just of marginal importance. Different parties refer to their relevant context during interactions with other parties. Sometimes, the other, less powerful party adopts these relevant contexts. At other times it just leads to miscommunication.

In general, Parker's ideas on classification may be helpful to interpret the different groups and their relations within and between. As he states, not only are the resources which people can use to classify others almost unlimited, but different people may orient themselves differently at different times (2000:89). He suggests that multiple membership is not only possible, but also highly likely. In the AZCs we have found many overlapping, contested classifications, depending on the context. Parker thinks that accounts of these differences are not random or un-patterned because the recourses that people use to classify and identify are widely used. Based on his own research he identifies three classifications in particular: spatial, generational, and occupational/professional. In these AZCs we can find not only spatial and occupational classifications, but also legal and cultural ones. Sometimes spatial classifications between "we" the staff and management, and "they" asylum seekers, are central, particularly in instances such as when members of the staff lock the doors behind them and spend their time in their offices. Sometimes other spatial classifications are central, between "us" at this AZC-location, and "them" at the COA head office, who know little about what is going on here. Sometimes occupational classifications are central: "we" the social workers and "they" the security service, and of course "we" the staff and "they" the asylum seekers who have no jobs here. Legal classifications at other times are central: "we" the citizens of this country, and "they" who are aliens. Also cultural ones, gender classifications and many more exist. In whatever way people most often classify themselves and are classified by others as either asylum seekers, staff, or management, this seems less unambiguous than might be expected.

Coping with the situation at an AZC
Coping strategies of asylum seekers at an AZC
Asylum seekers devise various coping strategies for dealing with their situation.[3] These strategies comprise three categories. Firstly, some asylum seekers engage in all kinds of activities (work, education, and sports) and establish social contacts: "Working at the restaurant is nice. Doing something besides eating and sleeping makes you feel like a person again." A Kurdish man from Iraq, who misses the wife and children he left behind, relates, "I take Dutch lessons and work at the centre every day. I am quite satisfied. Being active gets me tired and helps me worry less. I feel a sense of satisfaction and am happy to be of service to this country. Three times a week I do exercises. Often I think about my children back in Kurdistan and wonder how they are doing. I try to get them off my mind by keeping busy. As soon as I return to my room, it starts all over again."

Second, other asylum seekers become apathetic or are hospitalized, especially after an extended stay at an AZC with no prospect of definitive approval of their asylum application. Asylum seekers are largely excluded from the decision-making process, both in the asylum procedure and at the AZC. "Hospitalization" may be interpreted as a coping strategy due to extended involvement in an organization where one lacks any actual influence is taxing. Turning one's back on the organization and retreating in apathy can be the result. Staff members complain, "Residents show too little initiative in undertaking activities or becoming self-sufficient. Often they fail to attend Dutch lessons."

Finally, some asylum seekers become "difficult." Just because asylum seekers are involuntary clients does not mean they have no power whatsoever over the course of events. After all, staff members depend to some extent on the attitude of the asylum seekers. Lipsky lists means available to involuntary clients: making trouble, procrastinating, expressing anger, demanding their rights – basically, complicating the work of the staff in ways the staff want to avoid (1980:57). One asylum seeker said, "Clearly, the rules are not enforced consistently here. If I make a fuss, things change. If I behave myself, I get nowhere."

Coping strategies among AZC staff

AZC staff members work under severe psychological pressure. They are deeply committed and want to provide humane accommodations to people in need. This is typical of such care facilities. If staff members are unable to remedy the causes of problems (as they perceive them) they use certain coping strategies to handle the psychological pressure associated with their work. Walkup (1997) has identified four phases that are not necessarily consecutive and may even coincide. At each stage, staff members will leave the organization.

First, because they understand that the situation is very difficult for the asylum seekers, and that mountains of work wait for them, new staff members tend to keep working harder. "The COA keeps sending more people. We have no influence whatsoever on the COA's policy. They do not view the situation from a psycho-social or a humanitarian perspective. They make us crowd the people together. We are always the bad guys. I disagreed with the policy of putting three people in one room, but I had no choice. Nobody can keep up with the workload forever." Another relates, "I often feel uncomfortable here. I am forced to do things I feel ashamed of."

To avoid facing their own inability to remedy the situation staff members keep their distance from the clients. Sometimes this effort involves complex and cumbersome procedures to curtail questions from clients. At other times staff members retreat as much as possible within their own group. "At some other AZCs asylum seekers are not even allowed to enter the corridor where the staff offices are. The residents used to drive me mad with their constant interruptions. The present arrangement is a major improvement. Nobody comes to the new offices of the reception staff." Staff members view the practice of answering the questions asked by asylum seekers while remaining reserved as a sign of professionalism.

A third coping strategy among staff, if keeping distance is no longer sufficient or becomes impossible, is shifting the blame on to others – the MPs, the administrators and the bureaucrats are all responsible for the sorry state of affairs. They claim they have no way of changing the system and use this excuse to avoid taking any action. Sometimes they blame the clients for the difficult situation by treating them with suspicion. "Residents try things with new staff members that never would have worked with the others. Imagine their delight when they succeed. You may think you're on to everything and won't fall for any of their tricks, but you'd be surprised at what they pull."

Fourth, in some cases the situation is made bearable by maintaining an illusion of success to retain a sense of dignity and expertise. Client needs are subconsciously redefined so that they are indeed accommodated by the organization's actions. Doing so resets the balance between supply and demand. "Previously, when volunteers taught Dutch classes, the results were mediocre. The courses currently taught by teacher trainees are a vast improvement."

Coping strategies of management

Directors rarely discuss the needs and requirements of asylum seekers. They have virtually no direct contact with them and several admit they know virtually nothing about their affairs. Many have stopped keeping office hours: "I know what is coming, but I can do nothing about it." Directors have also devised several ways of dealing with their situation. Most seek a compromise between the interests of their staff and the demands of the COA main office. Some go along with these demands and are perceived by staff as hiding behind the rules. Others foster an internal "we-ness" by blaming the centre's problems on the COA main office. Occasionally a director may openly resist these demands from the COA main office and will receive official orders.

As has been noted earlier, management insists on defining asylum seekers and their situation in terms of self-sufficiency and the enterprising client. Moreover, fashionable business-world jargon, such as "client friendliness" and "client orientation," is also introduced. These terms are generally employed to improve an organisation's effectiveness and output, but these terms can also be utilized to accommodate the divergent wishes among clients, like for customized care (Gastelaars 1997). Nevertheless, "customer" may not be an appropriate label for the users of an asylum seekers' residence centre. Using this kind of fashionable terms and management instruments may reflect managerial attempts to re-define asylum seekers in a more businesslike manner, but may also be expressions of coping strategies of COA's management itself when trying to deal with an awkward situation.

The different coping strategies of the various parties influence each other, sometimes to their disadvantage. "Resistance" or "trouble-making" on the part of the asylum seekers can reinforce the tendency among the staff to blame the asylum seekers for everything that goes wrong. On the other hand, the staff's reserve can give the asylum seekers a sense of powerlessness and make them revert to inactivity. Meanwhile, the efforts of management to turn a complicated situation into a more business-like enterprise may inadvertently reinforce the sense of failure the other parties experience.

The accommodation of asylum seekers in a broader context

Parker has pointed out that the organisational context deeply influences the course of events within organisations. "[S]ome claims of actors within organisations do in practice have more persuasive power than others largely because they are put forward by high status or well resourced members or groups within the organization and/or because they echo claims being made by high status or well resourced individuals or groups 'outsided' the organization, in other localities that have the capacity for control at a distance" (Parker 2000:225). For actors in AZCs two basic policy frameworks play a crucial role in this respect: the policy on asylum procedures, and the policy regarding asylum seeker's accommodations. In the Netherlands the Ministry of Justice is responsible for both, admission and accommodation. The Ministry had assigned the Immigration and Naturalisation Service (IND), to process asylum requests. The Central Asylum Seekers's Reception Services (COA) provide the actual accommodations, and it is also commissioned by the Ministry of Justice. Just as hospital patients base their appreciation of their treatment rather on its curative aspects (convalescence and medical quality) than on its care component (such as staff attentiveness), in a similar manner the appreciation of asylum seekers is contingent to a great extent on the speed and quality of the asylum procedure.

The accommodations of asylum seekers reflect current government policies. But they also reflect the more general public support system for the admission and accommodation policy for asylum seekers, which maintains a close vigil over the AZCs. The people running the system answer to these parties. Support within and outside the government is presumed to be limited to the most basic needs of asylum seekers until they acquire resident status.

In addition to deeply affecting the quality of life at the reception centres, the context has coloured the impressions of asylum seekers of their functioning in Dutch society. One young asylum seeker explained,

> I could make friends at school, but I choose not to. People have a problem with asylum seekers. I don't want them to know [that I am one], so I cannot make friends. If I did, I would have to tell them: 'I am an asylum seeker,' since they would obviously want to stop by to visit me. I save my money for decent clothes to avoid looking like an asylum seeker. People think: 'They have no money, they're uncivilized.' So I try to dress well, but it's expensive. I had a girlfriend for a while. I didn't tell her I was an asylum seeker at first. When her mother found out, she made her break up with me. I wasn't surprised. She was trying to protect her daughter. Perhaps I'm infectious....

Conclusion

The situation at AZCs is complicated, to say the least. At this one location the various actors are involved in processes of making multiple claims about membership categories. They each have different definitions of the situation. Between them there is a structural power imbalance. The power positions of staff and management depend on their access to wider common assumptions that effectively legitimate certain actions and beliefs to the detriment of others. Coping strategies not only differ but often also influence each other to their disadvantage. Following Parker's theory on context and classification, combining social constructions of individualisation theory and interpretations of the political, institutional, and societal context with the recognition of multiple divisions within the organisation, seems to provide an understanding of why life in AZCs leads to dissatisfaction and frustration felt by (almost) all actors, though not in the same way for each of them. This is a tragic situation because whatever the actors may choose to do, and however hard they try, it can never work out well. There are no good guys and bad guys. For the structural reasons I have mentioned above, a solution *within* this situation may be very hard to find.

Notes

i   This article is based on a study at two asylum seekers' residence centres and interviews with 86 asylum seekers, 21 staff members, 8 directors and 6 volunteers. Some of the interviews with asylum seekers were conducted by a staff member at an asylum seekers' residence centre. The study was commissioned by the Central Asylum Seekers' Reception Services *(Centraal Orgaan Opvang Asielzoekers,* COA), which was interested in the opinions of its clients and staff regarding the central reception facilities with a view toward appropriate modifications in its quality standards.

2   At the time this research was carried out the local manager was in charge of a more or less autonomous organisation, which is what each AZC was despite the fact that AZCs were in fact divisions of the national Central Asylum Seekers' Reception Services (COA). Since then the organisational structure has changed. At this moment the local manager's autonomy has been severely restricted by the senior regional manager, who manages several AZCs at the same time, and is responsible for budgets.

3   The term "coping strategies" suggests intent and the use of corresponding means to this end. While such is not the case here, I use this term for lack of a better one.

Bibliography

Gastelaars, M. 1997. *'Human Service' in veelvoud: Een typologie van dienstverlenende organisaties.* Utrecht: SWP.

Geuijen, K. 1997. Tijdelijke bescherming, terugkeer en integratie van vluchtelingen: een onmogelijke combinatie? *Beleid en Maatschappij* 24(5):209-220.

Geuijen, K. 1998. Refugees, Nation-States, and the European Union in a World with Blurred Borders. In Marja Gastelaars and Arie de Ruijter, eds., *A United Europe: The Quest for a Multifaceted Identity,* pp. 127-150. Maastricht: Shaker Publishing.

Goffman, E. 1984. *Asylums: Essays on the social situations of Mental Patients and Other Inmates.* Suffolk: The Chaucer Press. (Originally published in 1961.)

Hasenfeld, Y. 1983. *Human Service Organizations.* New Jersey: Prentice Hall.

Lipsky, M. 1980. *Street-level Bureaucracy: Dilemmas of the Individual in Public Services.* New York: Russell Sage Foundation.

Parker, M. 2000. *Organizational Culture and Identity: Unity and Division at Work.* London: Sage Publications.

Walkup, M. 1997. Policy Dysfunction in Humanitarian Organizations: The Role of Coping Strategies, Institutions and Organizational Culture. *Journal of Refugee Studies* 10(1):37-60.

26

Culture and Education
Curriculum Adaptation in Five Community
Technical Institutes in Honduras

Jan Ooijens

Introduction

In addition to my numerous conversations with Arie de Ruijter about the relationship between culture, education and development, I have also repeatedly exchanged thoughts with him on this subject, within more official settings. The importance of adapting the curriculum of basic education to the socio-economic and cultural situation of the students or education participants was the central item in these discussions. In writing my dissertation, which had as its central theme the functionality of adult education, de Ruijter played an inspiring role as one of my two supervisors. What also comes to mind is the discussion with him that ensued from my paper "Basic Education and Culture," which I presented in June 1994 at the international conference on Cultural Dynamics in Development Processes, in Zeist. The conference was sponsored by the Netherlands National Committee for UNESCO and the inter-university research school CERES in order to help elaborate a perspective and methodology for the integration of socio-cultural factors in development processes and projects. This conference was co-ordinated by de Ruijter.

In the introduction of the UNESCO publication that was generated by the Zeist conference, de Ruijter et al. state:

> Local knowledge, local beliefs systems, local practices, in short local cultures play an important role in guiding human action and in holding together the fabric of society. Instead of a hindrance to progress which should be eliminated, culture nowadays emerges as the fountainhead of unexpected local expertise and local wisdom which can profitably be used in the battle for a better life. Although there is a vast number of (kinds) definitions of culture in circulation, for the time being a general definition will suffice of culture as the conventional way of understanding reality, defining and solving problems, and selecting and articulating emotions in society. These routinized patterns of action and emotion are connected with the elementary problems and issues with which people are faced: the provision of food, protection against the climate, the relation between the sexes, care for children, the ill and the weak, the pro-

tection of one's own group and territory, as well as more philosophical questions such as the meaning of life and death, or the place of the human being in the cosmos (de Ruijter et al. 1995:5).

At this conference I discussed three projects of formal education in Central America, which had been realised in the course of the 1990s with the financial aid of the Netherlands in order to attain a more functional primary education. With the technical support of UNESCO, the Guatemalan, Costa Rican, and Nicaraguan Ministries of Education had in their respective countries realised projects (SIMAC, SIMED and SIMEN) to raise the quality of formal primary education. Attention was directed to the decentralization of education, and the delegation of responsibilities to the local level. The project activities were directed at the adaptation of *primary education* curricula to national, regional, and local developments, with special attention paid to the characteristics, needs, interest, expectations, and perceptions of the lives of the pupils and parents. The basic elements for adopting a curriculum that aims at a more functional education for children, can be summarised as follows:

(1) The adaptation of curricula is regarded as an integral, participatory, flexible, creative and innovative process;

(2) The implementation of syllabuses is democratic in nature and contains elements of co-partnership in decision-making and self-administration;

(3) The recipient of education, regarded as carrier of an inherited culture, is the principal subject of curriculum.

In this article, I will briefly discuss a recent experience in the field of high school education in five Institutes of Secondary Education in the southern Department of Lempira, Honduras, along the border with El Salvador. This Honduran programme was a collective effort made by the Secretary of Education, the Departmental Director of Education of Lempira, the Rural Development Project of the South of Lempira (PROLESUR), the directors and teachers of the five institutes, parents, students and the community as a whole. All of these actors have, since 1995, tried to structure and contextualise curricula that, in the framework of community participation, aim to improve the availability of institutional education that has been adapted to the socio-economic and cultural situation of the region. In addition, this project in Lempira, which received technical support from the FAO, was in several ways geared towards finding a better conjunction between existing development projects and the local socio-economic and cultural conditions and needs of the region.

As a consequence of the efforts, the five Institutions of Secondary Education with only the 'Common Cycle' (the first three years of secondary education) were converted into a Community Technical Institute (CTI), whose common cycle is oriented towards agricultural-forest production and towards bachelor's degrees (bachilleratos) in Agricultural Sciences and Forest Sciences. These institutes are: Jacobo Orellana, in the municipality of San Francisco; José María Medina, in the municipality of Candelaria; La

Virtud, in the municipality of La Virtud; Juan Manuel Gálvez, in the municipality of Tomalá, and David Hércules Navarro, in the municipality of Guarita.

The results presented in this article are based on interviews with functionaries who were involved in the programme (during two field visits in June and October of 2002 I had the opportunity to obtain a general overview of the technical and organisational functioning of the Curriculum Adaptation Programme of the five CTIs[1]), as well as on various documents put together by the personnel of the programme. After a brief description of the context of experience in South Lempira, sections 3 and 4 will deal with the transition from Institutions of Secondary Education to CTIs, and will give a general idea of the fundamental aspects of the curriculum adaptation. In the preceding sections, I will describe the revision of the curriculum and some implications for the CTIs, after which section 6 will show some of the programme's achievements. In section 7, efforts at adapting the curriculum to the regional culture are treated. Some problems and difficulties are mentioned in sections 8 and 9, and final comments are made.

South Lempira: context[2]

The southern region of the Department of Lempira consists of a corridor through southeast Honduras, the majority of which borders on El Salvador. It constitutes an area of 2,177.9 km^2 representing 50.8% of the total area of this Department, and has 125,000 inhabitants distributed among 18 municipalities. The region is located in the centre of the "triangle of northern Central America," (Honduras, El Salvador and Guatemala) in the mid-upper region of the Lempa river basin shared by Honduras and El Salvador. The basin's water and energy producing capacities make it strategically important to El Salvador.

Due to its biophysical characteristics, the southern region of Lempira is an ecological network of arid tropical forest with predominantly mountainous, forest topsoil. The current conditions and characteristics of the region's agricultural, forest and livestock production have generated, among others, cyclical food shortages, diminishing supplies of trees for firewood and building, deforestation, and poor management of the forest resources, soil and water, leading to the general deterioration of cultivation. The shallow, mountainous ground and depleted soil tend to cause soil erosion. Traditional agriculture, livestock, and forest production are practised.

According to a 1995 diagnosis, the region's condition was hardly encouraging, occupying the highest ranking on the country's poverty chart. The road infrastructure was deficient (all roads were dirt and difficult to access, and could only be travelled by four-wheel drive vehicles). There was a lack of communication media (only Salvadoran TV and radio stations could be received) and of government services such as education, healthcare and infrastructure. The population in general received very little attention. In this very isolated region, 85% of the population lived below the poverty line. They face a high risk of food insecurity. Statistics revealed that over 60% of the population suffered from an inadequate diet, and malnutrition (64% of infants suffer malnutrition) was endemic. The absence of piped water and latrines were aggravating factors. The socio-economic indicators showed that there was only one doctor for every 25,000 inhabitants. There was no potable water or waste management, and the infant mortality rate was 70/1,000.

The numbers in the area of education were just as discouraging: illiteracy of 55% and in some communities as high as 80%, high levels of school drop-out, and a lack of teachers and every type of didactic material. Students who had completed secondary school (generally speaking, they only reached the third year) had to migrate to other villages and cities in the country to continue their study. Few of them returned to their communities after completing their education, with the exception of some primary and secondary school teachers. The majority of these students could not contribute to the local or regional development because their skills and abilities were not co-ordinated to meet the needs of the municipalities. To reverse the process of migration at the local and regional level, the need has been identified to invest in secondary education in order to form the leadership for change over the medium and long term.

With funds donated by the government of the Netherlands in conjunction with the technical support of the FAO, the Secretary of Natural Resources launched the PRO-LESUR in 1995. The objective of this project was to respond to the marginalisation of the production systems, the deterioration of the environment, and food insecurity. The strategies adopted by PROLESUR, which has a long relationship with the CTIs, included promoting the adoption of new technologies, initiating processes of capitalisation, in-service training, and the training of peasant leaders (to be transferred from peasant to peasant). The project promoted a serie of activities at the family, community, and municipality levels. The priorities at the family level were to improve the household, adopt a package of technologies at the farm level, manage watersheds, control fire, etc. At the community level, the priority was the creation of CODECOS (Comitees of Communal Development), the entrepreneurial organisation of co-operative banks in particular, adult education and the incorporation of women in all levels of decision making. At the municipal level, the priority was the formation of an association of municipalities of South Lempira (now brought together in co-operative groups) and the promotion of the creation of savings, credits and other types of co-operatives.

Factors that were influential in reforming the CTIs and the selection of careers were (1) the poor economic state of the communities, (2) poor use of natural resources, (3) an agricultural production that was only at subsistence level, (3) a high migration rate, (4) the lack of trained personnel and educational opportunities in the region, (5) an education not well adapted to the local context, and (5) the need for courses of study tied to food security and natural resource management.

Transition from institutions of secondary education to Community Technical Institutes with a bachelor in agricultural and forest science

Until 1997, these five Institutes of Secondary Education were small educational institutions that generally offered preparatory training for continuing studies at a higher level. Every institute was founded in the 1980s with the aim of creating opportunities for the youths who completed primary education and would continue their formal education. In these new schools, students could discover their vocation and decide if they would continue their education up to a middle or bachelor's level, thus preparing them for a university education.

These secondary education institutes offered only the common cycle (*Ciclo Común*), not a final level of education. Students who stopped their studies for economic reasons were unable to develop skills and abilities to realise productive activities. And when they joined in the productive activities of the communities, they did so in the same traditional manner as those who had only secondary school education. The common cycle curriculum that the schools offered lasted three years, during which students studied 10 subjects in the first and second years, and nine in the third year. The schedule load per week was 32 class periods of 45 minutes each.

The lack of evolution in the institutions meant that only a few young people finished a career at the middle or university level, and the impact that education had on improving the communities was reduced to having little or no effect on the improvement of the natural resource management, or on the economic or social development of the communities. The parents as well as the students and teachers recognised that, after finishing three years of study, the education offered by the institutions was not adequate to enable the students to participate in a productive activity within their communities, or in the national labour market, or in the socio-cultural organisation of their communities.

The process of educational curriculum adaptation at the five CTIs in South Lempira began in 1995 when a group of community members from the area involved in the PROLESUR started working to increase the educational opportunities at the schools in their communities. And so the five directors of the CTIs in Guarita, Tómala, La Virtud, Candelaria, and San Francisco made a formal agreement with the functionaries of PROLESUR to create a curriculum that would contain professional training, and offer solutions to the problems of low production and productivity, the undiscriminated exploitation of natural resources, the high rate of illiteracy and the lack of organisation.

Since October 1995, the PROLESUR and the teachers of the five CTIs have co-operated with the Secretary of Education and the technical personnel of the General Directory of Educational Planning to conduct investigations, workshops, and seminars to elaborate an adapted curriculum. One of the actions of PROLESUR and the Secretary of Education was to create the programme of curriculum adaptation in the five CTIs of South Lempira by incorporating the "Management and Conservation of Natural Resources" in the curriculum of every school, and by offering the secondary school students a curriculum that is more in line with the interests, expectations, and the physical, ecological, and social characteristics of their communities.

After several meetings and workshops with parents and CTI-teachers where it was discussed how to socialise an eventual program, the Ministry of Education proposed to adapt the curriculum in the five schools that, in addition to academic training, would offer technical training and teaching of the specific skills of management and conservation of the natural resources of the communities. This reform would set the groundwork needed for sustainable development and training of human resources through an education model, for developing and managing family farms of agricultural-forest production, and by involving the teachers, students, parents and community leaders.

Considering the academic and physical structure, the teaching and support staff, didactic materials, equipment, tools, laboratories, and the academic achievement of the students, a structure was revealed when the five CTIs were analysed upon which a programme of improvement of education could be built. During a necessary period of transition to adjust to the changes, the institutions had to transform progressively into places that will attend to the region's badly needed human development. In 1997, PROLESUR and the Secretary of Public Education signed a five-years agreement (1997 – 2002) through which the Secretary incorporated in its annual budget the financial support required for teaching and for paying for a support staff, maintenance, and the materials needed to carry out the curriculum adaptation. It was also agreed that PROLESUR would search for the support of external financial donors necessary for realizing the different aspects of the programme.

In its State General Budget of Income and Expenditures for the fiscal year of 1997, the National Congress approved the allocation of 2,431,403 Lempiras ($ 150,000 U.S.) to finance the costs of converting the five secondary schools of South Lempira into CTIs. This conversion was to begin by improving the "common cycle" educational programme by orienting the curriclum towards agro-forest production and management in family farms. In addition, a bachelor's program in agricultural sciences was created in Guarita, La Virtud, Candelaria, and San Francisco, and a bachelor's degree in forest sciences in Tomalá. The Secretary of Education continued to pay the teachers the normal rate and a large portion of the additional funds were appropriated for the salaries of three agricultural engineers at every institute. These professionals had to attend to the technical aspects of the new curriculum plans.

The external financial aid for four years – amounting to a total of $ 452,894 (U.S.) would come from the Netherlands, adding to the funds of PROLESUR. This contribution was utilized for logistics, the training of the teaching staff in variuos courses and workshops for currículum adaptation, and for different aspects of technical assistance. The funds covered all the costs of mobilizing national personnel to assist at the ITCs' workshops and activities, the cost of the Unity of Coordination (composed by the directors of the ITC), and the necessary costs of reproducing the didactic materials and of staging pilot and innovative activities.

Curriculum adaptation at the CTIs: some general aspects

The name "Community Technical Institute" was chosen for several reasons. The institutes are "technical" because they teach agricultural and forest techniques in addition to training professional farmers, and agricultural, forest, and pastoral production technicians. At the same time they are "community" institutes because they focus on the family farm unit, and enable the community to participate in the training of students, whereby endogenous knowledge is also valued and studied. As a norm, these institutes do not teach techniques that ordinarily would never be applied in the communities. They use practical demonstrations to teach, by way of examples, the most suitable techniques. Besides, the institutes are community related because their goal is to promote community development through community extension, and to offer non-formal educational services to persons excluded of the educational system.

The main goals of curriculum adaptation include:

(1) reforming the curriculum of the Comun Cycle, augmenting the practice activities with community development, rural extension and rural development, and training the students to plan, develop, and manage agricultural and forest family farms;

(2) increasing education possibilities by converting the existing schools into CTIs that will offer a three-year-long bachelor's programme in agriculture and forest management, and by creating a middle-level education programme consisting of six years of studies;

(3) training the directors in the management of the CTIs, and in explaining the materials and contents of the teaching methods to the teaching staff;

(4) training the teaching and administrative staff of every school in the philosophy of a development programme like that of the PROLESUR;

(5) producing and putting into use new teaching materials;

(6) creating a reference library at every CTI according to the region, with resources on forestry, techniques, and management of agricultural products and on other subjects supporting the content of the bachelor programme's or the Diversified Cycle's courses.

The new curriculum can be characterised as follows. The CTIs' study plan emphasises the human activity aspect of agriculture and forest production. It prepares students for practical work in the community as well as for going on to higher studies. The study plan combines studying with practical fieldwork, which is conducted as much as possible on the land of the students' parents and at the school plot. The new curriculum also includes community extension activities, and aims at integrating the work of the technicians and the teachers of the CTIs. Finally, the techniques taught and applied in the practices have been tested in the region's development projects.

The curriculum adaptation programme proposes to offer education that pertains to the socio-cultural characteristics of the target group and validates their cultural identity. It aims to focus the curriculum proposed at the national level on the interests, motivations, and expectations of the various target population groups. The programme proposes to centre the curricular process on the student as a "being in a situation." In addition, it regards the specific culture of the groups as significant material for the learning and teaching process.

The nucleus of the CTIs' curriculum adaptation activities is the development and management of family farms. In addition to experimental demonstration plots on CTIs' own properties, at least three family farms in every community will develop allotments for "practice activities" with the students, in relation to agricultural and forest production. With the active and direct participation of the owner of the plot, the students will plan, develop and manage a farm at the family production level. The farm owners agreed with the schools to permit the students to management the farms for six to eight years. Afterwards, the farmland will be returned to the control of the owners. According to the curriculum, it is fundamental that the students put what they've learned in the classroom into practice on every farm they work, that they incorporate new techniques adapted to the region that boost the area's production while conserving the environment and rationally utilizing the natural resources. Working in the family farms resulted in new "practice activities," including activities oriented towards community development and rural extension. The programme of developing family farms also considers the incorporation of the farms of leading producers. The institutes associated with them would be given the opportunity to teach the experiences of some special technologies developed on these successful farms.

Curriculum revision and some implications

The curriculum adaptation in plans and programmes was developed, in cooperation with the technicians and teachers of the institutes, and in consultation with the students, parents, producers cooperating with PROLESUR, and with other members of the communities, in order to respond to the regional needs, and so as to know their point of view on the possible distibution of academic and practical teaching.

The study plan of the common cicle

The CTIs of South Lempira were converted from institutes offering only the common cycle to institutes with a common cycle oriented towards agricultural and forest production. The number of subjects of the common "curriculum of general culture" increased, and the subjects involving "practice activities" changed as a result. Now practical activities are related to agricultural and forest production, community development, rural extension, and rural development activities in accordance with the social, economic, and cultural situation of the region. By implementing the "practice activities," the agricultural and forest techniques for production systems in mountainous soils, as developed by the PROLESUR, were validated and diffused.

Each theme of the subject "practice activities" was attended by three persons – an instructor of practice activities, an agronomist, and a forestry specialist – all of whom are supported in their fieldwork by the other teachers of the institute acting as coordinators. These changes have brought the number of class hours per week from 32 up to 45.

As consequence of these changes, students will be prepared to follow studies in any of the diversified curricula. If they cannot continue their study, they will receive basic training in order to carry out productive activities in their communities and in preparation for becoming the future leaders of their communities.

Adaptation of the diversified cycle
Beginning in February 1997, the diversified curriculum was elevated to the level of a three-year-long bachelor's course (a bachelor normally last two years) in agricultural sciences, and a bachelor's degree in forest sciences. At this curriculum level, all of the schools offered an extended academic career related to agriculture, forestry, management of small livestock operations, and efficient processing of agricultural and livestock products, while teaching the importance of maintaining quality and hygiene standards in handling and processing. Such an extended academic career covered all of the registration prerequisites demanded by the National Autonomous University of Honduras in order to follow university courses.

The diversified curriculum for these bachelor's courses was based on the first 13 subjects of the current study plan for the "bachelor's course in arts and sciences," and on the regular "bachelor of agricultural and forest sciences" for the technical training. However, the courses on the management and production within agricultural, forest, and pastoral systems had been specially adapted to mountainous terrain of South Lempira. The study plans included subjects for training students in community development, rural extension, integral natural resource management, and for generating knowledge in order to promote sustainable production. The number of class hours increased to 55 per week.

Some implications
The curriculum adaptation has had serious implications for the CTIs. These are summarised below:
(1) thirteen more hours of work per week than the normal programme of the common cycle curriculum, and 15 more hours of work than the regular diversified curriculum (for practical and technical work, and community extension and development);
(2) the practical work was carried out on family-owned and family-operated farms; all the teachers (not only the technicians) had to be trained and involved in the work on the farms and in the communities;
(3) the model of learning applied at the CTIs was oriented towards the active participation of the students, and an education methodology was created based on the study/work axis – a non-traditional method that motivates students, and has a significant impact on them;
(4) there was a direct correlation between theory and practice; maintaining a proportion of 60% practice and 40% theory in the learning/teaching process improved and increased the students' knowledge;
(5) the level of awareness of the need to protect the natural resources was raised;
(6) in the didactic field, there were improvements in the process of planning the contents, objectives, and teaching methods of the courses. Improvements were also noted with regard to the learning of new concepts, and to the adopting of new techniques by the teachers (supported with didactic materials, equipment, books and tools).

Some of the programme's accomplishments
The quality of education
After realizing a pilot experience of four years, the institutes have been able to train more personnel for the continuity and sustainability of the curriculum adaptation programme. There are now more of the necessary teaching materials for the different subjects of education, and the CTIs receive the minimum infrastructure, materials, and equipment necessary for developing their activities.

According to a 2001 impact evaluation, 100% of the teachers thought that the process of curriculum adaptation in the CTIs had substantially improved the quality of teaching and learning. The graduates from the CTIs had a good knowledge base. The teachers (as well as the students) acknowledged that developing the family farms as a teaching/learning model enabled them to carry out curriculum adaptation with the participation of all of the teachers at the institutes. They were able to elaborate and revise the plans, contents and objectives of the courses, field practices, and a system of evaluation. This allowed them to adjust the process of learning/teaching to concrete realities, with the primary intention of improving the education offered.

The students involved with the methodology of teaching/learning acquired sufficient knowledge, abilities, and skills to continue studying or to efficiently enter the productive labour market of the region. The students also acquire an attitude of promoting, within the context of the communities, actions oriented at the conservation, improvement, and management of natural resources and the technical and social development of the communities.

Increase in registration
The educational model has been fairly well accepted by the communities, as reflected by the increase in the student body in the last three years in each of the CTIs (see Table 1).

Table 1. Levels of registration at CTIs, according to gender and year

Year	Female	Male	Total
1997	266	239	505
1998	270	275	545
1999	273	302	575
2000	336	302	638
2001	412	458	870

The CTIs have improved the opportunities for young men and women of the region to continue studying – something that previously was nearly impossible due to the economic costs, and the distance from house to school. Parents consequently feel satisfied that their children (the girls in particular now have the opportunity to study a profession without having to leave their community. The students appreciate learning the new techniques, their working experience on the family farms, and giving assistance to the primary schools.

Community extension activities
In the course of working on the family farms, the CTIs have been able to cooperate with communities in the training of parents and community members by carrying out productive projects utilising various soil and forest conservation techniques (the 'Quez-tungual System,' the use of mulch, 'live' and 'dead' barriers, etc.). In addition, local organisation activities, promoting the CODEM (Municipality Development Committees), have been realised.

Something that deserves special attention is the assistance that students of the CTIs have provided to 25 primary schools that sought o cooperate with the programme. In consultation with the technical staff of the institutes, these primary schools developed extension sessions in which teacher and students participated. The sessions dealt with the management of school vegetable gardens and soil; water and forest management were also practised. With the children they discussed the situation in their communi-ties and realised discussion groups around the themes of environmental conservation, organised demonstrations, and assistance in planting and managing school vegetable gardens. In these discussion groups various techniques of managing agricultural prod-ucts (corn, beans, yucca, jicama, chilli's, etc.) on mountainous terrain (as living barri-ers, minimal ploughing, etc.) were also explained.

Before 1996, the CTIs rarely if ever participated at all in the communities. The rela-tions between the CTIs and the communities have greatly improved. Moreover, the par-ents who participated with their children and the CTIs in the process of introducing the new curriculum appreciate that their children provide a service to their community, and that they are learning about the socio-cultural situation of the region. According to the programme documents, throughout the year 2001 the five CTIs have worked with 700 families in 17 communities.

Efforts at adapting the curriculum to the culture of the region
Preparatory phase
In 1995 technicians from the General Direction of Educational Planning of the Secre-tary of Public Education gathered at each of the schools information about the interests and expectations of the communities in regard to the revisions of the curriculum. The students and parents showed interest in studying agriculture, or learning a trade that would enable them to work as agricultural producers or to get a salaried job.

The technicians also held meetings with students, parents and teachers to deter-mine the ecological characteristics of the region, the local agricultural production, live-stock production, and/or forest, soil and water management, and the situation of the communities in general. PROLESUR also arranged meetings with the communities, in which various teachers of the CTIs participated in order to identify, analyse, and prioritise in a participatory way the participants' needs. In 1996 all this gathered information was presented in a cultural report, which is now part of the material for the "community development course" in the study programme.

Training the Staff
In 1999, the PROLESUR project signed an agreement of mutual support with the Catholic University to offer to professionals and teachers in the region a three-year schooling as "technicians of rural development." Most of the instructors of these courses were from the same region as the participants. Twenty-one professionals were registered, five of whom probably will graduate in March 2003. They are expected to become CTI teachers.

Much attention was given to the "training on location" of the teachers. This was considered better than sending a selected few to be trained in other parts of the country on scholarships. This method is cheaper and allows more teachers to be trained. Moreover, in this way the curriculum adaptation and the training can correspond better to real conditions of the region.

The teachers training programme was made to adhere to the objectives of PROLESUR as closely as possible. Various training sessions and workshops were offered for the teachers and technicians of the CTIs. Independently of the training courses on technical aspects, on social aspects, and on didactic items, much attention was given to methods for extending the CTIs into the communities. For this reason, the teachers and technicians received different hours of training on rural extension and participatory research, the development of local capacities, and on methodological aspects of participatory planning and situational analysis.

A new culture among the teaching staff
The entire teaching staff (and not only the technicians) had to support the realization of the planned field activities. For this reason, during the periodical meetings between teachers and technicians, the planning and programming of the academic and field activities were done together. By integrating the personnel of the ITC in this way, one tried to avoid automatically classifying the teachers at the technical institutes either as "technicians" or as "teachers," for this gives the impression that the "technician" is not involved with the teaching, and visa versa.

The role of the (academic) teacher in the new modality of the CTI had to change radically. In addition to being the teacher of the subject, they also had to coordinate and supervise groups of students in the tasks of planning, development, and management of the farms – in this way acting as a direct support for the technicians in carrying out the practice activities planned for the communities.

Different teachers of "academic subjects" worked on the farms and realised activities in the communities. This increased their interaction with members of the community. However, for many of them, participation is still limited, and in some institutes there exist a certain resistance among these teachers.

Production of educational materials

In Central America there are very few educational materials for the training of farmers in agricultural, forest, and pasture management in mountainous terrain found in dry tropical forest zones. Fortunately, PROLESUR had already documented and systematised quite a lot of this sort of information. In the context of the programme, a library of basic texts was donated to every institute. It is important to note that the teachers learned to create their own didactic materials suited to the context of South Lempira, either by designing them or adapting existing material available in Honduras and elsewhere in Central America.

In their fieldwork on the farms, the students established, under the supervision of the technicians, demonstration and teaching plots, production plots and plots to test new techniques and plant types. The students had to write detailed field reports about their practice sessions, and these reports will later serve as testing and consulting material for themselves and other students.

Community extension

The teachers as well as the students confirmed that by developing the family farms as a teaching/learning model, the development of community extension activities and of rural and community development projects were promoted. This reinforces the connection of the CTIs with the communities.

Every CTI has established family production farms in the communities, whose goal it is to have the students analyse and understand the new technologies promoted by PROLESUR and the endogenous knowledge of the communities in regard to traditional farming methods. Many parents who are farmers come to these farms to teach the students the techniques they apply on their own parcels. In that way, the CTI creates a situation whereby communities participate in training the students through the family farm, and the local farmers will benefit from the knowledge of new technologies brought by the students, and the local endogenous knowledge will be appreciated and preserved.

Problems and difficulties

Socio-economic problems

An important obstacle for improving the teaching system is the poverty level of the families. Many of the students' families do not own enough land, which makes it more difficult to apply the new techniques on their own land in the future.

Organisational problems

The government, through the Secretary of Education, is in charge of the teaching, of administrating and managing the staff, and annually contracts 22 professional agricultural and forest specialists, trained at university level, to serve in technical and teaching functions at the five CTIs. At the end of 2002 the government decided to continue this national contribution to the programme. However, the main problems of the technicians are the delayed salary payment, the status of temporary employment, and the instability of their position. There is a degree of indifference at the national level, and no concern for the administrative efficiency of the programme. Moreover there are insufficient resources available to incorporate the CTI technicians into the ranks of teachers with formal contracts.

Technical problems
The most notable technical problem for an adequate functioning of the CTIs is the lack of availability of fertilisers, and of materials and equipment for the practice activities and for the handling and processing of the agricultural and livestock products. These should be provided by the Secretary of Education. Also needed is to fortify the libraries of the CTIs and promote the custom among the teachers of lecturing to the students.

Final comments: much needs to be done
Dubbeldam states, "Formal education is often of very limited relevance to the pupils concerned, given the situation in which they live. The national curricula of formal education in general prescribe a uniform syllabus for all schools, irrespective of the conditions and needs of the pupils and their communities. The low level of adjustments between the cultural situation in the homes and the so-called dominant culture is a major problem. The home situation has been forgotten too often." (Dubbeldam 1993; see also Thompson 1981). In most cases the opportunities for teachers to adapt education to the local situation are very limited. Rural education in particular bears only a very limited relation to children's everyday experience, and provides them with knowledge that can only be used in cities (Ooijens in de Ruijter 1995: 173).

During my visits to the Lempira-project, I observed that participatory techniques in the execution phase of an education programme and working with indigenous teachers seem to be excellent instruments for integrating local culture. The teachers (preferably natives of the region) and students learn how simple social research is conducted in order to adapt programmes to the development objectives and needs of the population. In turn, one should try to incorporate the local knowledge and participation of the population in the educational processes. In general, I agree with Chambers (1980), who states, "Development workers and educators need to change their paternalistic attitude towards small farmers 'with the old-fashioned ideas and techniques that should be replaced as soon as possible.' They must respect the identity of the people and initiate a process of authentic development. Not modernism but usefulness should be the criterion in the selection of ideas and techniques. One often finds a parallel system of knowledge which is complementary, usually valid, and in some respects superior to scientific knowledge....Local people have much detailed knowledge of soils, of plant indicators, of fertility, and weather patterns, and the like."

The project described here tries to promote the participation of the students in the planning, preliminary research, programming, and execution phases of the programme. However, following Freire's ideas, still more emphasis could be placed on abolishing "banking education": the transmission of information by an inaccessible and authoritarian source to a passive receiver without stimulating the latter to develop independently and in accordance with her or his ideas and needs. The new approach assumes to regard students not as objects of the programme, but as active subjects and participants.

The project has given special attention to the training of the teachers in order to promote working in a participatory manner, and to change the attitudes and practices of educational personnel. Regarding the extension activities of the students, the importance of a previous study of the community has been emphasized. However the realisation of the participatory study of the world of the student is still is failing and has to be made more extensive in order to collect more useful information for programming the pedagogical process, and for intensifying the relations between the groups concerned with the educational community. Such a study should stimulate a more participatory and democratic attitude of teachers and directors of the schools with respect to alternative study and programming techniques. In this way teachers may become more aware of the situation in the community and in the educational institution. More training in participatory techniques are therefore necessary.

The different actors involved have different expectations of the objectives of curriculum revision. Many parents still see formal academic education as the best way to a better future for their children. They think that practical activities in the curriculum limit the children's opportunities and hinder them from attaining higher academic levels.

The problem of the teachers is their unfamiliarity with the philosophy of the new curriculum. Many feel they are confronted with the difficult task of adapting syllabi to the world of the pupils. The experience of the teachers is limited and many of them are deeply rooted in the old system.

In summary, I would like to state that the Lempira project strives for real functionality in formal education. Functionality in education means being aware of the basic points, which are the environment and needs of the student, his family, and his community. To achieve this functionality it is necessary to promote the integration of family, school, and community to search for a better connection between the school and the community. It is also necessary to make adequate use of community resources in the learning process. It is also necessary to complete the national curriculum with the contribution from the world of the student and the social environment of the school, in addition to promoting curricular innovations by introducing new and diverse forms of learning. Finally, it is necessary to strive for an integration of learning experiences, learning contents, and techniques in accordance with existing curricular policies (Ooijens in de Ruijter 1995:183).

Notes

1   See Ooijens, 'Informe de la visita de monitoreo al Proyecto de Adecuación Curricular', August 2002, and Ooijens, et al, 'El Proyecto de Adecuación Curricular'. October 2002. Other important sources for this article are various internal documents from the project. I frequently referred to these sources of information. Some texts I have utilized without citing them.
2   Taken from the document 'Lempira Sur 1994-1998: Informe sobre la experiencia del Proyecto' (1998) and from the document 'Documento del proyecto de Adecuación Curricular' (1998).

Bibliography

Chambers, R. (1980) *Rural Poverty Unperceived. Problem and Remedies.* World Development Report Background Paper. Washington, D.C.: The World Bank.

De Ruijter A. and Lieteke van Vucht Tijssen (eds.) (1995) *Cultural Dynamics in Development Processes.* The Hague: Netherlands Commission for UNESCO.

Dubbeldam, L. (1990) "Education and Productive Life in Developing Countries." In Boeren, A.J.J.M. and K.P. Epskamp eds., *Education, Culture and Productive Life 25-35.* The Hague: CESO paperback No. 13.

Espinoza Vergara M. et al (2000) *Education for Work in poor rural areas: A viable strategy of non-formal education.* Turin: International Training centre of the ILO.

Ministry of Development Cooperation (1990) *Nieuwe kaders voor ontwikkelingssamenwerking:Een Wereld van Verschil* The Hague

Ooijens. J. (1986) *Functionele Alfabetisering in Santa Fe de la Laguna.* The Hague: CESO.

Ooijens. J. (1995) 'Basic Education and Culture' In de Ruijter A. and Lieteke van Vucht Tijssen eds., *Cultural Dynamics in Development Processes* The Hague: UNESCO Publishing/Netherlands Commission for UNESCO.

Thompson, A.R. (1981) *Education and development in Africa.* London: The Macmillan Press Ltd.